STEPHENS' VISUAL BASIC PROGRA[M] 24-HOUR TRAINER

D0470485

Continues

Stephens' Visual Basic® Programming

24-HOUR TRAINER

Stephens' Visual Basic® Programming

24-HOUR TRAINER

Rod Stephens

WILEY

Wiley Publishing, Inc.

Stephens' Visual Basic® Programming 24-Hour Trainer

Published by
Wiley Publishing, Inc.
10475 Crosspoint Boulevard
Indianapolis, IN 46256
www.wiley.com

Copyright © 2011 by Wiley Publishing, Inc., Indianapolis, Indiana

Published simultaneously in Canada

ISBN: 978-0-470-94335-9

Manufactured in the United States of America

10 9 8 7 6 5 4 3 2 1

For general information on our other products and services please contact our Customer Care Department within the United States at (877) 762-2974, outside the United States at (317) 572-3993 or fax (317) 572-4002.

Wiley also publishes its books in a variety of electronic formats. Some content that appears in print may not be available in electronic books.

Library of Congress Control Number: 2010942177

For Benoît Mandelbrot (November 20, 1924–October 14, 2010) who showed that even small things can contain infinite possibilities.

ABOUT THE AUTHOR

 **ROD STEPHENS** started out as a mathematician, but while studying at MIT, discovered how much fun programming is and has been programming professionally ever since. During his career, he has worked on an eclectic assortment of applications in such fields as telephone switching, billing, repair dispatching, tax processing, wastewater treatment, concert ticket sales, cartography, and training for professional football players.

Rod is a Microsoft Visual Basic Most Valuable Professional (MVP) and has taught introductory programming at ITT Technical Institute. He has written more than 20 books that have been translated into languages from all over the world, and more than 250 magazine articles covering C#, Visual Basic, Visual Basic for Applications, Delphi, and Java. He is currently a regular contributor to DevX (www.DevX.com).

Rod's popular *VB Helper* web site (www.vb-helper.com) receives several million hits per month and contains tips, tricks, and example programs for Visual Basic programmers. His C# *Helper* web site (www.csharphelper.com) contains similar material for C# programmers.

You can contact Rod at RodStephens@vb-helper.com or RodStephens@csharphelper.com.

ABOUT THE TECHNICAL EDITOR

JEFF CERTAIN is a software architect at Colorado CustomWare, where he mentors more than 30 developers. He is heavily involved in the technical community and has been a Microsoft MVP for VB.NET since 2007. He has written articles for *CoDe Magazine* and *Visual Studio Magazine* and has performed technical editing for other VB programming books. In addition, he presents to user groups frequently and has taught several weeks of a graduate-level course in software methodologies for Colorado State University.

CREDITS

EXECUTIVE EDITOR
Robert Elliott

SENIOR PROJECT EDITOR
Kevin Kent

TECHNICAL EDITOR
Jeff Certain

PRODUCTION EDITOR
Rebecca Anderson

COPY EDITOR
Luann Rouff

EDITORIAL DIRECTOR
Robyn B. Siesky

EDITORIAL MANAGER
Mary Beth Wakefield

FREELANCER EDITORIAL MANAGER
Rosemarie Graham

MARKETING MANAGER
Ashley Zurcher

PRODUCTION MANAGER
Tim Tate

VICE PRESIDENT AND EXECUTIVE GROUP PUBLISHER
Richard Swadley

VICE PRESIDENT AND EXECUTIVE PUBLISHER
Barry Pruett

ASSOCIATE PUBLISHER
Jim Minatel

PROJECT COORDINATOR, COVER
Katie Crocker

COMPOSITOR
JoAnn Kolonick,
Happenstance Type-O-Rama

PROOFREADER
Jen Larsen, Word One New York

INDEXER
Johnna VanHoose Dinse

COVER DESIGNER
Michael E. Trent

COVER IMAGE
©fajean/istockphoto.com

ACKNOWLEDGMENTS

THANKS TO ROBERT ELLIOTT, Kevin Kent, Luann Rouff, Mary Beth Wakefield, Ashley Zurcher, Tim Tate, Jim Minatel, and everyone else who worked so hard to make this book possible. Thanks also to Jeff Certain for keeping me from putting my foot too deeply in my mouth.

CONTENTS

INTRODUCTION

SO YOU WANT TO LEARN VISUAL BASIC PROGRAMMING? Excellent choice!

Visual Basic is a powerful, all-purpose programming language that enables you to build robust applications that run on the desktop or over the Web. Visual Basic provides all the tools that you need to build a huge variety of applications:

➤ Database applications

➤ Point of sales systems

➤ Web applications

➤ Two- and three-dimensional graphics programs

➤ Image processing and photo manipulation systems

➤ Computer-aided design (CAD) systems

➤ Document layout and printing systems

➤ Hardware control systems

➤ High-performance games

➤ Much, much more

 This book refers to Visual Basic using its full name only, but Visual Basic programmers often refer to the language as VB. You'll also often see it referred to as VB in discussions on the Internet.

Of course, there are some problems that you won't be able to solve even with Visual Basic. If you want a program that picks the winning number on a roulette wheel or that can predict stock prices, you may have better luck using tarot cards (or a degree in economics), but for tractable problems Visual Basic is a great choice.

This book is a self-paced guide to Visual Basic programming in the Visual Studio environment. It uses short, easy-to-follow lessons, reinforced by step-by-step instructions, screencasts, and supplemental exercises to help you master Visual Basic programming quickly and painlessly. It explains how to write Visual Basic programs that interact with the user to read inputs, calculate results, and display outputs. It shows how to read and write files, make printouts, and use databases.

This book won't make you an expert, but it will give you a solid understanding of how to write Visual Basic programs. When you've finished reading this book and working through the Try It sections, you'll be able to write nontrivial programs of your own. You may not be able to accurately pick winning lottery numbers (if you do, please let me know!), but you will be able to build some useful programs. And you'll be ready to learn more about specialized topics such as database programming, file processing, and graphics.

WHO THIS BOOK IS FOR

This book is for anyone who wants to learn how to write programs using Visual Basic. Whether you want to move into a lucrative career as a software developer, add a few new skills to your resume, or pick up a fascinating new hobby, this book can get you started.

This book does *not* assume you have any previous programming experience. It assumes you can turn your computer on and surf the Web, but that's about it for previous qualifications. It is suitable as a first programming book for high school or college students, but its self-paced, hands-on approach also makes it ideal if you're trying to learn to program on your own.

I say all this because I don't want to receive a bunch of flaming e-mails complaining that the material in this book is too basic. So I'm warning you right now: If you've been programming in C++ or C# for 16 years, don't blame me if a lot of this material seems pretty simple to you. Don't waste your time complaining; go find a more advanced book.

WHAT THIS BOOK COVERS (AND WHAT IT DOESN'T)

This book explains Visual Basic programming. It explains how to write, debug, and run desktop applications that interact with the user and the computer. It shows how to understand object-oriented concepts, perform calculations, manipulate files and strings, produce printouts, and interact with simple databases.

Programming in any language is an enormous topic, however, so this book doesn't cover everything. It doesn't explain how to design databases, build cryptographically secure web applications, create multithreaded programs that run on multiple cores or computers, or build massive networked games like *World of Warcraft*. All of those tasks are possible using Visual Basic, however, and after you finish this book you'll be ready to move on to more advanced books that cover those topics.

To make everything fit into a single book, I had to make some tough choices about what to include and what to omit. This book focuses on desktop applications because if you want to learn Visual Basic programming, then you probably have a computer that can run applications. It doesn't cover ASP.NET programming using Visual Basic — not because it's a bad thing to learn but because it's a less self-contained learning environment. Visual Studio will enable you to build ASP.NET web applications, but unless you have a web server that supports ASP.NET you won't be able to exercise the full power of ASP.NET.

Similarly, there are many ways to approach database programming. In this book, I've tried to give you a taste of database programming without being completely overwhelming. The book's lessons explain how to use objects to manipulate data in a database and how to use the Entity Framework to perform simple database queries. Database programming is an enormous topic, however, and no general programming book can hope to cover it in its entirety.

Still, while no introductory book can cover every programming topic, the topics this book does cover give you a good foundation of fundamental programming skills that you can use as a base for further study.

THE WROX *24-HOUR TRAINER* APPROACH

Educators have known for many years that different people use different learning styles most effectively. Personally, I learn best by watching and doing. However, different students may learn best by:

➤ Reading a textbook

➤ Looking at nonwritten material such as pictures and graphs

➤ Listening to an instructor lecture

➤ Watching someone demonstrate techniques

➤ Doing exercises and examples

Good instructors try to incorporate material that helps students with all of these learning styles. Combining text, lecture, demonstration, discussion, and exercises enables every student to pick up as much as possible using whichever methods work best.

Like a good instructor, this book uses materials that address each learning style. It uses text and figures to help visual learners, screencasts that provide visual demonstrations and auditory instruction, step-by-step instruction to help you do it yourself, and exercises for independent study.

The book is divided into small, bite-size lessons that begin with a discussion of a particular concept or technique, complete with figures, notes, tips, and other standard fare for instructional books. The lessons are short and tightly focused on a single task so you can finish each one in a single sitting. You shouldn't need to stop in the middle of a lesson and leave concepts half-learned (that is, if you turn off your phone).

After describing the main concept, the lesson includes a Try It section that invites you to perform a programming exercise to solidify the lesson's ideas.

The Try It begins with a high-level overview. It then contains several subsections:

➤ **Lesson Requirements** describes the exercise so you know what should happen.

➤ **Hints** provides pointers about how to solve the trickier parts of the problem.

➤ **Step-by-Step** provides a numbered series of steps that show exactly how to solve the problem.

A screencast on the accompanying DVD shows me (the author) working through the Try It problem. Additional commentary at the end of the screencast highlights extensions of the lesson's main concepts.

After the Try It's Step-by-Step section, the lesson concludes with extra exercises that you can solve for further practice and to expand the lesson's main ideas. I recommend that you at least skim the exercises and ask yourself if you think you could do them. Solutions to all of the exercises are available for download on the book's web site.

WEB SITES

Actually, the book has two web sites: Wrox's version and my version. Both sites contain the book's source code.

To find the Wrox web page, go to www.wrox.com and search for the book by title or ISBN. Once you've found the book, click the Download Code link on the book's detail page to obtain all the source code for the book. Once you download the code, just decompress it with your favorite compression tool. Alternatively, you can go to the main Wrox code download page at www.wrox.com/dynamic/books/download.aspx to see the code available for this book and all other Wrox books.

To find my web page for the book, go to www.vb-helper.com/24hourvb.html.

The one thing that a good classroom experience offers that this book doesn't is direct interaction. You can't shout questions at the instructor, work as a team with fellow students, or discuss exercises with other students.

Nonetheless, there are at least three things you can do to get this kind of interaction. First, join the Wrox P2P (peer-to-peer) discussion forum for this book. As the section "p2p.wrox.com" later in this introduction indicates, you can join the discussion forum to post questions, provide answers, see what other readers are doing with the book's material, and generally keep tabs on book-related topics. I highly recommend that you join the discussion right away so you don't forget. (You can join other Visual Basic discussion groups on the Web, too, but this one is dedicated to this book and you know I'll be watching it closely.)

Second, you can browse or subscribe to my newsletters at www.vb-helper.com/newsletter.html to receive occasional newsletters describing new example programs, articles, and commentary. Many of the entries describe tips, tricks, and short example programs that demonstrate techniques you may find useful for your Visual Basic programs.

Finally, if you get stuck on an exercise or some other program you're working on, e-mail me at RodStephens@vb-helper.com. I won't solve the exercises for you, but I'll try to clarify problems or give you any hints you need so you can solve them yourself.

GETTING THE MOST OUT OF THE BOOK

This book provides a lot of tools that you can use to best match your learning style, but you have to use them. If you learn best by reading text, spend more time on the text. If you like step-by-step instructions, focus on the Try It's step-by-step exercise. If you learn best by watching and listening, focus on the screencasts.

Then, after you've finished a lesson, use the exercises to verify that you've mastered the material. And don't be afraid to invent programs of your own. Just because an idea isn't in the book doesn't mean it wouldn't make good practice.

HOW THIS BOOK IS STRUCTURED

This book is divided into six sections, each containing a series of short lessons. The lessons are generally arranged in order, with later lessons depending on earlier ones, so you should study the lessons more or less in order, at least until sections V and VI. The lessons in sections V and VI cover slightly more specialized topics and their order is less critical.

PERSISTENT PROGRAMS

A number of the lessons work with the SimpleEdit example program. This program starts as a simple form containing a few controls in Lesson 3 and grows into a serviceable word-processing application before all is done.

Each time a lesson asks you to add to this program, it tells you to copy the previous version. If you skip a step, you may not have the necessary version available. In that case, you can download the version you need from the book's web site.

For example, the instructions for Lesson 6's Exercise 1 say to copy the version you built for Lesson 5, Exercise 5. If you skipped that exercise, you can download the Lesson 5 material from the book's web site and use the version of SimpleEdit that it contains.

The following sections describe the book's contents in detail.

Section I: The Visual Studio IDE and Controls

The lessons in this section explain how to use the Visual Studio integrated development environment (IDE) and how to use the controls that make up a user interface. These form the foundation on which you build everything else in a Visual Basic program.

Lesson 1, "Getting Started with the Visual Studio IDE," explains Visual Studio. It describes some of the IDE's useful features and demonstrates how to build a simple program and run it. From the very first lesson, you'll be able to build a program!

Lesson 2, "**Creating Controls**," explains what controls are, what they are for, and how to use them. It shows how to add controls to a form to make a user interface. In Visual Basic programs, controls are critical for getting the job done.

Lesson 3, "**Making Controls Arrange Themselves**," explains how to use control properties to make controls automatically rearrange themselves at run time to take full advantage of the available space. When the user resizes a form, the controls can automatically move and resize as needed.

Lesson 4, "**Handling Events**," explains what events are. It shows how to catch events to respond to user actions so the user can interact with the program.

Lesson 5, "**Making Menus**," explains how to add main menus and context menus to an application, and how to respond when the user selects a menu item. By responding to menu events, the program gives the user an easy and well-understood way to control the application.

Lesson 6, "**Making Tool Strips and Status Strips**," explains how to build tool strips and status strips, and how to handle their events. Tool strips provide a faster method for the user to control the application than menus, while status strips provide useful feedback to let the user know what the program is doing.

Lesson 7, "**Using RichTextBoxes**," explains the `RichTextBox` control and shows how to manipulate it with code. The `RichTextBox` enables the user to enter text and, if the program provides the right tools, lets the user format the text with different fonts, colors, bullets, and other text decorations.

Lesson 8, "**Using Standard Dialogs**," explains how to use standard dialogs to display messages and questions, change fonts and colors, browse for folders, and let the user select files for opening and saving.

Lesson 9, "**Creating and Displaying New Forms**," explains how a program can display new instances of forms and interact with the controls on those forms. This is important for more complicated programs that cannot do everything they need to on a single form.

Lesson 10, "**Building Custom Dialogs**," explains how to use new forms as custom dialogs. It shows how to display a custom dialog and determine which button the user pressed to close it.

Section II: Variables and Calculations

The lessons in this section deal with variables and calculations. They explain how variables hold values and how a program can use them to calculate results. Whereas the lessons in Section I explain how to make controls that enable the user to enter information, the lessons in this section explain how to do something with that information.

Lesson 11, "**Using Variables and Performing Calculations**," explains how to declare and use variables and constants, and how to perform simple calculations. It also shows how to convert information from one data type to another. For example, it demonstrates how to take an age entered by the user and convert it from a textual value (for example, "47") into a numeric value (47). (It's a small distinction to a person but a huge one to a program.)

Lesson 12, "Debugging Code," explains techniques for finding and fixing bugs. It shows how to determine which line of code the program is executing, examine and modify variable values, and use watches to keep track of variable values. Almost every nontrivial program starts with a bug or two. This lesson shows how to find those bugs.

Lesson 13, "Understanding Scope," explains how scope restricts a variable's accessibility to certain pieces of code. It also explains why a programmer should restrict scope as much as possible.

Lesson 14, "Working with Strings," explains how to combine, manipulate, and format strings. It explains the `String` class's `ToString` and `Format` methods, which enable you to build nicely formatted strings to show the user.

Lesson 15, "Working with Dates and Times," explains how to use date and time values. It explains the `Date` and `TimeSpan` classes, and shows how to use and format them.

Lesson 16, "Using Arrays and Collections," explains single- and multi-dimensional arrays and collection classes such as `List` and `Stack`. It explains how to declare and initialize arrays and collections.

Lesson 17, "Using Enumerations and Structures," explains how to define and use customized data types such as structures and enumerations. These help make the code easier to understand, debug, and maintain.

Section III: Program Statements

The lessons in the previous sections explain how to write code that flows through a series of steps, one at a time in a predefined order. The lessons in this section explain how to make code follow more complex paths. They explain how code can choose between one path and another and repeat operations. While controls and message boxes are more visible pieces of an application, these statements let the program do most of its work.

Lesson 18, "Making Choices," explains how programmers can control the flow of code with `If`, `Select Case`, nested `If`, and cascading `If` statements. These statements let the program take different actions depending on the situation.

Lesson 19, "Repeating Program Steps," explains looping code that uses statements such as `For`, `For Each`, `Do`, and `While`. It explains how to use these statements to iterate through a series of integer values, arrays, and lists, and how to break out of loops.

Lesson 20, "Reusing Code with Procedures," explains how a programmer can write procedures and why procedures are important. It explains the syntax of declaring subroutines and functions, defining return values, and using parameters passed by value or by reference.

Lesson 21, "Handling Errors," explains how to use `Try` blocks to handle unexpected errors. It also explains how to raise errors to tell other parts of the program that something has gone wrong.

Lesson 22, "Preventing Bugs," explains bug proofing techniques that make it easier to detect and correct bugs. It explains how to use `Assert` statements to validate inputs and results so you can catch bugs quickly, rather than let them remain hidden in the code.

Section IV: Classes

Structures, enumerations, and procedures are all programming abstractions that let you think about pieces of the program at a higher level. For example, when you call the `CalculateInterest` procedure, you don't need to know how it works, just that it does.

The ultimate programming abstraction is the class. A class lets you think about data and functions packaged as a single unit. For example, a `Customer` class might include data (name, employee ID, office number) together with functions (`ScheduleWork`, `PrintPaycheck`).

The lessons in this section deal with classes. They explain how to create and use classes and how to use more advanced class features such as generics and operator overloading.

Lesson 23, "Defining Classes and Their Properties," explains how to define classes. It explains the main benefits of classes and how to build simple properties to hold data for classes.

Lesson 24, "Defining Class Methods and Events," explains how to add methods and events to a class. Methods enable the program to make an object perform some action, and events enable an object to tell the program that something interesting has happened.

Lesson 25, "Using Inheritance and Polymorphism," explains two of the most important and confusing aspects of classes: inheritance and polymorphism. It explains how you can make one class inherit from another to reuse code and how you can make an object of one class behave as if it were from another class.

Lesson 26, "Initializing Objects," explains constructors, destructors, and initializers, and shows how to use them to make creating objects easier.

Lesson 27, "Fine-Tuning Classes," explains how you can overload and override class methods. These techniques enable you to make classes more flexible and easier to use.

Lesson 28, "Overloading Operators," explains operator overloading. This technique enables you to define the behavior of operators such as +, *, and % for objects other than numbers.

Lesson 29, "Using Interfaces," explains what a class interface is and how to build one. Just as a program's user interface defines features that a program shows to the user, a class interface defines features that a class shows to the program's code.

Lesson 30, "Making Generic Classes," explains how to build new generic classes. Lesson 16 shows how to use generic collection classes such as `List` to work with specific kinds of data. This lesson explains how you can build your own generic classes and methods.

Section V: System Interactions

Earlier lessons explain how to enable a program to interact with the user. The lessons in this section explain methods a program can use to interact with the operating system and other programs.

Lesson 31, "Reading and Writing Files," explains how a program can read and write files. It explains how to use streams to manipulate the text in a file all at once or in pieces — for example, one line at a time.

Lesson 32, "Using File System Classes," explains ways in which a program can use classes to find, examine, and manipulate directories and files. It describes file-handling classes such as `DriveInfo`, `DirectoryInfo`, `Directory`, and `FileInfo`.

Lesson 33, "Printing," explains how to create printouts and print previews. It describes how to draw simple shapes and text on one or more pages sent to the printer.

Lesson 34, "Using the Clipboard," explains how to move text, images, and other data in and out of the clipboard. Using the clipboard in this way is somewhat crude, but it's simple and flexible, enabling your program to interact with many others without understanding anything about how those other applications work.

Lesson 35, "Providing Drag and Drop," explains how a program can use drag-and-drop to interact with other programs. It explains how to start a drag, provide "drag over" feedback, and handle a drop. Like the clipboard, drag and drop enables your program to interact with others without knowing how the other programs work.

Section VI: Specialized Topics

The lessons presented in the earlier sections cover topics that are generally useful for a large variety of programs. Whether you are writing a sales tax calculator, an invoice tracking system, or a word guessing game, techniques such as handling events, debugging code, using `If` statements, and printing will be useful to you.

This section introduces topics that are more specialized, so you might not need them in every program you write. For example, localizing your application for different locales is important for some applications but not for every program you write.

Each of the lessons in this section provides a sense of what its topic is about, and offers enough detail to get started, but a lesson cannot cover its topic in complete detail due to the topic's length and complexity.

Lesson 36, "Using the My Namespace," explains the `My` namespace, which makes using certain .NET features easier. This namespace provides shortcuts for performing common tasks such as reading and writing entire files; saving and restoring program settings; and checking the network's status.

Lesson 37, "Localizing Programs," explains how to make programs that can run in multiple cultures. It shows how to use different text and images for different locales and discusses some of the other issues an international application must address.

Lesson 38, "Manipulating Data with LINQ to Objects," explains how you can use Language-Integrated Query (LINQ) to filter and extract values from collections and other enumerable lists into new ones. This enables you to perform database-like queries on data stored in program objects instead of in an actual database.

Lesson 39, "Manipulating Databases with the Entity Framework," explains how you can use the Entity Framework (EF) to manipulate database entities as if they were objects inside the program. It enables your program to treat records in tables as if they were instances of classes and enables your program to fetch, modify, and save records while treating them as objects.

Appendices

This book's appendices summarize useful information for handy reference.

Appendix A, "Glossary," explains common programming terms that you may encounter while studying Visual Basic programming.

Appendix B, "Control Summary," summarizes each of the standard controls provided by Visual Basic. You can use it to help select the right control for your needs.

Appendix C, "What's on the DVD?," goes into more detail about using the DVD that comes with the book.

WHAT YOU NEED TO USE THIS BOOK

To get the most out of this book, you need to install Visual Studio 2010 and Visual Basic.

You don't need any fancy version of Visual Studio or Visual Basic Professional Edition. In fact, the Professional Edition, Team System Development Edition, and Team System Team Suite versions don't really add all that much that you're likely to want when you're just getting started. Mostly they add support for performing unit tests, managing test cases, profiling code, building code libraries, and performing other tasks that are more useful for programming teams than they are for individuals, particularly beginners. In short, to work through this book, the Express Editions (which are free) are good enough.

The following list describes some links that you may find useful for learning about and installing different Visual Studio products:

- ➤ **Visual Basic Developer Center** (msdn.microsoft.com/vbasic): This page contains links to Visual Basic information such as downloads, "getting started" articles, and other resources.

- ➤ **Visual Studio Developer Center** (msdn.microsoft.com/vstudio): This page contains links to Visual Studio information such as downloads, "How Do I" videos, and other resources.

- ➤ **Visual Studio Express Edition home page** (www.microsoft.com/express/Windows): This page contains information about Express Editions of Visual Studio products such as Visual Basic, Visual C#, Visual C++, and Visual Web Developer.

Sometimes Microsoft moves their links around, so the URLs listed here may not work by the time you read this. In that case, just go to Microsoft's web site msdn.microsoft.com and search for the location you want, such as "Visual Studio Express Edition home page."

At a minimum, visit the Visual Studio Express Edition home page (www.microsoft.com/express/ Windows) and download and install Visual Basic Express Edition. You should also occasionally check the Visual Basic home page for service packs and extra tools that may be available.

Running any version of Visual Studio will require that you have a reasonably fast, modern computer with a large hard disk and lots of memory. For example, I'm fairly happy running my Intel Core 2 system at 1.83 GHz with 2GB of memory and a huge 500GB hard drive. That's a lot more disk space than necessary but disk space is relatively cheap, so why not buy a lot?

You can run Visual Studio on much less powerful systems but using an underpowered computer can be extremely slow and frustrating. Visual Studio has a big memory footprint, so if you're having performance problems, installing more memory may help.

Of course, buying a superfast, quad-core desktop system with 6GB of RAM and 1TB of disk space will give you outstanding performance, but it will add dramatically to the $0 you're spending on Visual Basic Express Edition.

CONVENTIONS

To help you get the most from the text and keep track of what's happening, several conventions are used throughout the book.

> **SPLENDID SIDEBARS**
>
> Sidebars such as this one contain additional information and side topics.

 Boxes with a warning icon like this one hold important, not-to-be forgotten information that is directly relevant to the surrounding text.

 The pencil icon indicates notes, tips, hints, tricks, and asides to the current discussion. They are offset and placed in italics like this.

 References such as this one tell you when to look at the DVD for screencasts related to the discussion.

As for styles in the text:

➤ New terms and important words are *italicized* when they are introduced. You can also find many of them in the glossary in Appendix A.

➤ Keyboard strokes look like this: [Ctrl]+A. This one means to hold down the [Ctrl] key and then press the A key.

➤ URLs, code, and e-mail addresses within the text are shown in monofont type, such as `www.vb-helper.com`, `x = 10`, and `RodStephens@vb-helper.com`.

```
I use a monofont type with no highlighting for most code examples.
```

```
I use bold to emphasize code that's particularly important in the present context.
```

The Code Editor in Visual Studio provides a rich color scheme to indicate various parts of code syntax such as variables, comments, and Visual Basic keywords. That's an excellent tool to help you learn language features in the editor and to help prevent mistakes as you code. However, the colors don't show up in the code in this book.

SOURCE CODE

As you work through the examples in this book, you may choose either to type in all the code manually or to use the source code files that accompany the book. (I like to type in code when I work through a book because it helps me focus on it line by line so I get a better understanding.)

Many of the examples in the book show only the code that is relevant to the current topic and may be missing some of the extra details that you need to make the example work properly. To fill in the missing pieces, you may need to write your own code or download the book's code.

All of the source code used in this book is available for download on the book's web sites. As I indicated earlier in this introduction, either go to the Wrox web site (`www.wrox.com`) and search for the book or visit my web page for the book at `www.vb-helper.com/24hourvb.html`. Any updates to the code will be posted in both of these places.

At the Wrox web site, because many books have similar titles, you may find it easiest to search by ISBN. This book's ISBN is 978-0-470-94335-9.

ERRATA

The Wrox editors and I make every effort to ensure that there are no errors in the text or in the code. However, no one is perfect, and mistakes do occur. If you find an error in one of our books, such as a spelling mistake or a faulty piece of code, we would be very grateful for your feedback. By sending in errata you may save another reader hours of frustration, and at the same time you will be helping us provide even higher quality information.

To find the errata page for this book, go to www.wrox.com and locate the title using the Search box or one of the title lists. Then, on the book details page, click the Book Errata link. On this page you can view all errata that have been submitted for this book and posted by Wrox editors. A complete book list, including links to each book's errata, is also available at www.wrox.com/misc-pages/ booklist.shtml.

If you don't spot "your" error on the Book Errata page, go to www.wrox.com/contact/techsup-port.shtml and complete the form there to send us the error you have found. We'll check the information and, if appropriate, post a message to the book's errata page and fix the problem in subsequent editions of the book.

P2P.WROX.COM

For author and peer discussion, join the P2P forums at p2p.wrox.com. The forums are a Web-based system for you to post messages relating to Wrox books and related technologies, and to interact with other readers and technology users. The forums offer a subscription feature to e-mail you topics of interest of your choosing when new posts are made to the forums. Wrox authors, editors, other industry experts, and your fellow readers are present on these forums.

At p2p.wrox.com you will find a number of different forums that will help you not only as you read this book, but also as you develop your own applications. To join the forums, just follow these steps:

1. Go to p2p.wrox.com and click the Register link.
2. Read the terms of use and click Agree.
3. Complete the required information to join as well as any optional information you wish to provide and click Submit.
4. You will receive an e-mail with information describing how to verify your account and complete the joining process.

 You can read messages in the forums without joining P2P but in order to post your own messages, you must join.

Once you join, you can post new messages and respond to messages other users post. You can read messages at any time on the Web. If you would like to have new messages from a particular forum e-mailed to you, click the Subscribe to This Forum icon by the forum name in the forum listing.

For more information about how to use the Wrox P2P, be sure to read the P2P FAQs for answers to questions about how the forum software works as well as many common questions specific to P2P and Wrox books. To read the FAQs, click the FAQ link on any P2P page.

E-MAIL ME

If you have questions, comments, or suggestions, please feel free to e-mail me at `RodStephens@vb-helper.com`.

SECTION I
The Visual Studio IDE and Controls

The lessons in this section of the book explain how to use the Visual Studio (VS) integrated development environment (IDE). They explain how to use the IDE to create forms, place controls on the forms, and set control properties. These lessons describe some of Visual Basic's most useful controls and give you practice using them.

You can do practically all of this in the IDE without writing a single line of code! That makes Visual Studio a great environment for rapid prototyping. You can build a form, add controls, and run the program to see what it looks like without ever creating a variable, declaring a procedure, or getting stuck in an infinite loop.

The lessons in this section explain how to get that far. A few of these lessons show how to add a line or two of code to a form to make it a bit more responsive, but for now the focus is on using the IDE to build forms and controls. Writing code (and fixing the inevitable bugs) comes later.

▶ **LESSON 1:** Getting Started with the Visual Studio IDE

▶ **LESSON 2:** Creating Controls

▶ **LESSON 3:** Making Controls Arrange Themselves

▶ **LESSON 4:** Handling Events

▶ **LESSON 5:** Making Menus

▶ **LESSON 6:** Making Tool Strips and Status Strips

▶ **LESSON 7:** Using RichTextBoxes

▶ **LESSON 8:** Using Standard Dialogs

▶ **LESSON 9:** Creating and Displaying New Forms

▶ **LESSON 10:** Building Custom Dialogs

1

Getting Started with the Visual Studio IDE

The Visual Studio integrated development environment (IDE) plays a central role in Visual Basic development. In this lesson you explore the IDE. You learn how to configure it for Visual Basic development, and you learn about some of the most useful IDE windows and what they do. When you finish this lesson, you'll know how to create a new project. It may not do much, but it will run and you'll be ready for the lessons that follow.

> *Visual Studio is a development environment that you can use with several programming languages, including C#, Visual Basic, Visual C++, and F#. Visual Basic is a high-level programming language that can read inputs, calculate results, display outputs to the user, and perform other operations typical of high-level programming languages.*
>
> *The .NET Framework also plays an important role in Visual Basic programs. It includes classes that make performing certain tasks easier, runtime tools that make it possible to execute Visual Basic programs, and other plumbing necessary to build and run Visual Basic programs.*
>
> *Normally you don't need to worry about whether a feature is provided by Visual Studio, the Visual Basic language, or the .NET Framework. They all go together in this book, so for the purposes of this book at least you can ignore the difference.*

INSTALLING VISUAL BASIC

Before you can use Visual Basic to write the next blockbuster first-person game, you need to install it, so if you haven't done so already, install Visual Basic.

You can install the Express Edition from www.microsoft.com/express/Windows. If you think you need some other version (for example, you're working on a big project and you need test management, source code control, and other team programming tools), go to Microsoft's Download Center at www.microsoft.com/downloads and install the version that's right for you.

It's a big installation, so downloading it could take a while.

TALKIN' 'BOUT MY GENERATION

Developers talk about different generations of programming languages ranging from the very primitive to quite advanced. In a nutshell, the different generations of languages are as follows:

➤ **1GL** — Machine language. This is a series of 0s and 1s that the machine can understand directly.

➤ **2GL** — Assembly language. This is a translation of machine language into terse mnemonics that can be easily translated into machine language. It provides no structure.

➤ **3GL** — A higher-level language such as FORTAN or BASIC. These provide additional structure (such as looping and subroutines) that makes building complex programs easier.

➤ **4GL** — An even higher-level language or development environment that helps build programs, typically in a specific problem domain.

➤ **5GL** — A language for which you specify goals and constraints, and the language figures out how to satisfy them. For example, the database Structured Query Language (SQL) enables you to use statements like SELECT FirstName FROM Employees. You don't need to tell the database how to get the names; it figures that out for you.

Visual Studio provides code snippets that let you insert standard chunks of code into your program, IntelliSense that helps you select and use functions and other pieces of code, and more. That makes Visual Basic a 4GL (or perhaps a 3.5GL depending on how high your standards are).

CONFIGURING THE IDE

When you first run Visual Studio, it asks how you want to configure the IDE. You can pick settings for general development, Visual Basic, Visual C#, and so forth. Because you're going to be focusing on Visual Basic development, select that option.

These settings determine such things as what keystrokes activate certain development features. You can certainly write Visual Basic programs with the Visual C++ settings but we may as well be on the same page, so when I say, "Press F5," the IDE starts your program instead of displaying a code window or whatever Visual C++ thinks F5 means.

Microsoft has a series of PDF files that summarize key bindings for different settings available at www.microsoft.com/downloads/details.aspx?FamilyID=92CED922-D505-457A-8C9C-84036160639F.

If you ever want to switch to different settings (for example, if you got carried away during installation and selected the general settings and now want the Visual Basic settings), you can always change them later.

To change the settings later, open the Tools menu and select Import and Export Settings to display the Import and Export Settings Wizard. You can use this tool to save your current settings, reload previously saved settings, or reset settings to default values.

To reset settings for Visual Basic, select the Reset All Settings option on the wizard's first page and click Next.

On the next page, indicate whether you want to save your current settings. When you've made your choice, click Next to display the page shown in Figure 1-1. Select the Visual Basic Development Settings option and click Finish. (Then sit back and wait. Or, better still, go get a coffee because this could take a while. Visual Studio has a *lot* of settings to reset, and it could take several minutes depending on how fast and busy your computer is.)

FIGURE 1-1

BUILDING YOUR FIRST PROGRAM

Now that you've installed Visual Basic, you're ready to get started. Launch Visual Studio by double-clicking its desktop icon or by selecting it from the system's Start menu.

To create a new project, press [Ctrl]+N to display the New Project dialog box shown in Figure 1-2. Alternatively, you can open the File menu and select New Project.

FIGURE 1-2

 The screen shots of Visual Studio in this book may not look exactly like what you see on your screen. Visual Studio is extremely customizable so you can show or hide tools, resize windows, and move things around until two systems may look very different. You will also see different features depending on the version of Visual Basic you install. For example, if you install the Express Edition, you won't see some of the more exotic project types shown in Figure 1-2.

Expand the Visual Basic project type folder on the left and select the template for the type of project that you want to build on the right. For most of this book, that will be a Visual Basic Windows Forms Application.

Below the list of project types, you need to enter the name that you want to give the application. It's not completely trivial to change the name later so take a moment to pick a good one.

Initially Visual Studio creates the new project in a temporary directory. If you press [Ctrl]+[Shift]+S or select the File menu's Save All command, the Save Project dialog shown in Figure 1-3 appears.

Save Project			? ❌
Name:	WindowsApplication1		
Location:	C:\Users\Developer\documents\visual studio 2010\Projects	▾	Browse...
Solution Name:	WindowsApplication1	☑ Create directory for solution	
		☐ Add to source control	
		Save	Cancel

FIGURE 1-3

On this dialog you need to enter three key pieces of information:

➤ **Name** — This is the application's name. Visual Studio creates a folder with this name to hold the program's files. This name also gets built into the program in several places so later it can be hard to change every occurrence correctly. This is pretty advanced so I won't cover them here. Fortunately, the difference is seldom a problem, but it's usually better to just pick a good name when you start and stick with it.

➤ **Location** — This is where you want Visual Studio to put the project's folder.

➤ **Solution Name** — If the Create Directory for Solution box is checked (which it is by default), Visual Studio creates a folder with this name at the Location you entered. It then places the application's folder inside the solution's folder.

Therefore, if the Create Directory for Solution box is checked, you get a filesystem layout that looks like this:

```
SolutionFolder
    SolutionFiles
    ApplicationFolder
        ApplicationFiles
```

If the Create Directory for Solution box is not checked, you get a filesystem layout that looks like this:

```
ApplicationFolder
    ApplicationFiles
```

 An application contains a single program. A solution can contain several applications. A solution is useful when you want to build applications that go closely together. It's particularly useful if you're building a library of routines plus an executable program to test the library.

All of the applications you build in this book are single programs so they don't really need to be inside a separate solution folder. Most of the time, I uncheck the Create Directory for Solution box to keep my filesystem simpler.

By default, Visual Studio places new projects in your Projects folder at some obscure location such as C:\Users\Developer\My Documents\visual studio 2010\Projects. The exact location on your system may vary. Later it can be hard finding these projects in Windows Explorer (for example, to make a copy).

To make finding projects easier, set the location to something more intuitive such as the desktop or a folder named VB Projects on the desktop. The next time you create a new project, Visual Studio will initialize the location textbox to this same location, making it easy to find your projects.

After you create a new project, the result should look like Figure 1-4.

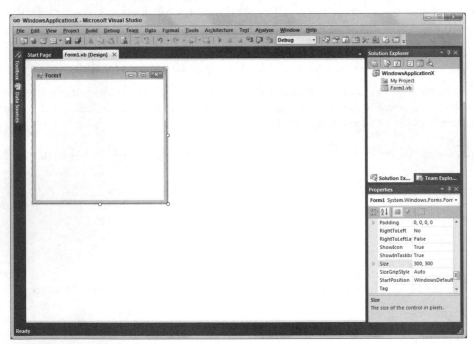

FIGURE 1-4

If you have previously edited a project, you can quickly reload it from the File menu's Recent Projects and Solutions submenu. You can also load a solution into the IDE by double-clicking the solution's .sln file.

The rest of this lesson deals with the features available in Visual Studio, some of which are displayed in Figure 1-4. Before you launch into an inventory of useful features, however, press F5 or open the Debug menu and select Start Debugging to run your new program. Figure 1-5 shows the result. Admittedly, this first program isn't very fancy, but by the same token you didn't need to do much to build it.

This first program may not seem terribly impressive but there's a lot going on behind the scenes. Visual Basic has built a form with a bunch of useful features, including the following:

➤ A resizable border and draggable title bar.

➤ Minimize, maximize, and close buttons in the upper-right corner.

➤ A system menu in the upper-left corner that contains the commands Restore, Move, Size, Minimize, Maximize, and Close.

➤ An icon in the system taskbar.

➤ The capability to use [Alt]+[Tab] and Flip3D ([Win]+[Tab]) to move between the application and others.

FIGURE 1-5

➤ Other standard window behaviors. For example, if you double-click the form's title bar, it maximizes (or restores if it is already maximized); and if you press [Alt]+F4, the form closes.

➤ Different appearances depending on the operating system and the theme you're using.

Unless you're an absolute beginner to Windows, you probably take all of these features for granted, but providing them is actually a lot of work. Not too long ago you would have had to write around 100 lines of code to handle these sorts of issues. Now Visual Studio automatically builds a form that handles most of these details for you.

You can still get in and change the way things work if you want to (for example, you can set a form's minimum and maximum sizes), but usually you can ignore all these issues and concentrate on your particular application, not the Windows decorations.

A SUITABLE EXECUTABLE

Whenever you run a program in the IDE, Visual Studio builds an executable program with an .exe extension, normally in the project's bin\Debug subdirectory. You can run the executable by simply double-clicking it — for example, in Windows Explorer.

That doesn't mean the executable is suitable to run on any old computer. If you copy that file to another computer, it won't run unless the .NET Framework runtime libraries have been installed there. If that computer has Visual Studio installed, you're all set, but if it doesn't you'll need to install the redistributable yourself.

To install these libraries, go to Microsoft's download web page www.microsoft.com/downloads and search for ".NET Framework redistributable." Pick the version that matches the one you're using (version 4.0 if you're using Visual Basic 2010) and install it on the target computer.

Then you can copy Visual Basic executables onto the system and run them.

COPYING PROJECTS

Sometimes you may want to copy a project. For example, you might want to save the current version and then make a new one to try things out. Or you may want to give a copy of the project to a friend or your programming instructor.

To make a copy, you might look in the File menu and see the Save As commands. Don't be tempted! Those commands copy single files, not the entire project. Later when you try to open one of those files, you'll discover that Visual Studio cannot find all of the other project pieces that it needs and you'll be left with nothing usable.

To correctly copy a project, find the solution or application folder in Windows Explorer and copy the project's *entire* directory hierarchy. Alternatively, you can compress the project directory into a zipped file and then copy that. Just be sure that whatever copying method you use brings along *all* of the project's files.

Note that you can delete the `bin` and `obj` subdirectories if you'd like to save space. Visual Studio will recreate them whenever it needs them later.

 Compressing a project into an archive is very useful because it keeps all of the project's files together in a package. In particular, if you ever need to e-mail a project to someone (e.g., if you e-mail me at `RodStephens@vb-helper.com` *for help), you can remove the bin and obj directories, compress the project folder, and e-mail the package as a single file. (If you're sending the project to your instructor as part of an assignment, rename the compressed file so it contains your name and the name of the assignment — for example,* `RodStephens6-1.zip`.)

EXPLORING THE IDE

The Visual Studio IDE contains a huge number of menus, toolbars, windows, wizards, editors, and other components to help you build applications. Some of these, such as the Solution Explorer and the Properties window, you will use every time you work on a program. Others, such as the Breakpoints window and the Connect to Device dialog box, are so specialized that it may be years before you need them.

Figure 1-6 shows the IDE with a simple project loaded and some of the IDE's most important pieces marked. The following list describes these pieces:

1. **Menus** — The menus provide all sorts of useful commands. Exactly which commands are available, which are enabled, and even which menus are visible depends on what kind of editor is open in the editing area (#4). Some particularly useful menus include File (opening old projects and creating new ones), View (finding windows), Project (adding new forms and other items to a project), Debug (build, run, and debug the project), and Format (arrange controls on a form).

2. **Toolbars** — The toolbars provide shortcuts for executing commands similar to those in the menus. Use the Tools menu's Customize command to determine which toolbars are visible.

FIGURE 1-6

3. **Solution Explorer** — The Solution Explorer lists the files in the project. One of the most important is Form1.vb, which defines the controls and code for the form named Form1. If you double-click a file in the Solution Explorer, the IDE opens it in the editing area.

4. **Editing area** — The editing area displays files in appropriate editors. Most often you will use this area to design a form (place controls on it and set their properties) and write code for the form, but you can also use this area to edit other files such as text files, bitmaps, and icons.

5. **Toolbox** — The Toolbox contains controls and components that you can place on a form. Select a tool and then click and drag to put a copy of the tool on the form. Notice that the Toolbox groups controls in tabs (All Windows Forms, Common Controls, Containers, Menus & Toolbars, and so on) to make finding the controls you need easier.

6. **Properties window** — The Properties window lets you set control properties. Click a control on the Form Designer (shown in the editing area in Figure 1-6) to select it, or click and drag to select multiple controls. Then use the Properties window to set the control(s) properties. Notice that the top of the Properties window shows the name (Label1) and type (System .Windows.Forms.Label) of the currently selected control. The currently selected property in Figure 1-6 is Text, and it has the value First Name:.

7. **Property description** — The property description gives you a reminder about the current property's purpose. In Figure 1-6, it says that the Text property provides the text associated with the control. (Duh!)

8. **Other windows** — This area typically contains other useful windows. The tabs at the bottom enable you to quickly switch between different windows.

Figure 1-6 shows a fairly typical arrangement of windows but Visual Studio is extremely flexible, so you can rearrange the windows if you like. You can hide or show windows; make windows floating or docked to various parts of the IDE; make windows part of a tab group; and make windows automatically hide themselves if you don't need them constantly.

If you look closely at the right side of the title bar above one of the windows in Figure 1-6, for example, the Properties window, you'll see three icons: a drop-down arrow, a thumbtack, and an X.

If you click the drop-down arrow (or right-click the window's title bar), a menu appears with the following options:

➤ **Float** — The window breaks free of wherever it's docked and floats above the IDE. You can drag it around and it will not redock. To make it dockable again, open the menu again and select Dock.

➤ **Dock** — The window can dock to various parts of the IDE. I'll say more about this shortly.

➤ **Dock as Tabbed Document** — The window becomes a tab in a tabbed area similar to #8 in Figure 1-6. Unfortunately, it's not always obvious which area will end up holding the window. To make the window a tab in a specific tabbed area, make it dockable and drag it onto a tab (described shortly).

➤ **Auto Hide** — The window shrinks itself to a small label stuck to one of the IDE's edges and its thumbtack icon turns sideways to indicate that the window is auto-hiding. If you float the mouse over the label, the window reappears. As long as the mouse remains over the expanded window, it stays put, but if you move the mouse off the window, it auto-hides itself again. To turn off auto-hiding, select Auto Hide again or click the sideways thumbtack. Auto-hiding gets windows out of the way so you can work in a bigger editing area.

➤ **Hide** — The window disappears completely. To get the window back, you'll need to find it in the menus. You can find many of the most useful windows in the View menu, the View menu's Other Windows submenu, and the Debug menu's Windows submenu.

The thumbtack in a window's title bar works just like the drop-down menu's Auto Hide command does. Click the thumbtack to turn on auto-hiding. Expand the window and click the sideways thumbtack to turn off auto-hiding. (Turning auto-hiding off is sometimes called *pinning* the window.)

The X symbol in the window's title bar hides the window just like the drop-down menu's Hide command does.

In addition to using a window's title bar menu and icons, you can drag windows into new positions. As long as a window is dockable or part of a tabbed window, you can grab its title bar and drag it to a new position.

As you drag the window, the IDE displays little drop targets to let you dock the window in various positions. If you move the window so the mouse is over a drop target, the IDE displays a translucent blue area to show where the window will land if you drop it. If you drop when the mouse is not over a drop target, the window becomes floating.

Figure 1-7 shows the Properties window being dragged in the IDE. The mouse is over the right drop target above the editing area; therefore, as the translucent blue area shows, dropping it there would dock the window to the right side of the editing area.

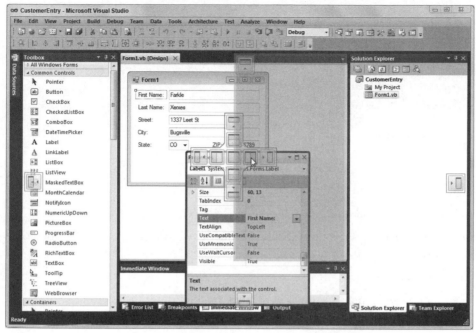

FIGURE 1-7

The drop area just to the left of the mouse represents a tabbed area. If you drop on this kind of target, the window becomes a tab in that area.

CUSTOMIZATION MODERATION

Visual Studio lets you move, dock, float, hide, auto-hide, and tabify windows. It's so flexible that it can present as many different faces as a politician during an election year.

Feel free to customize the IDE to suit your needs; but if you do, keep in mind that your version of Visual Studio may look nothing like the pictures in this book. To minimize confusion, you may want to keep the IDE looking more or less like Figure 1-6, at least until you get a better sense of which tools will be most useful to you.

TRY IT

In this Try It, you prepare for later work throughout the book. You locate web resources that you can use when you have questions or run into trouble. You create and run a program, explore the project's folder hierarchy, and make a copy of the project. You also get a chance to experiment a bit with the IDE, displaying new toolbars, moving windows around, and generally taking the IDE for a test drive and kicking the tires.

Note that the solutions for this lesson's Try It and exercises are not all available on the book's web site. The Try It and some of the exercises ask you to experiment with the IDE, rather than produce a finished program, so there's really nothing to download. In later lessons, example solutions to the Try It and exercises are available on the book's web sites.

Lesson Requirements

In this lesson:

➤ Find and bookmark useful web resources.

➤ Launch Visual Studio and start a new Visual Basic project.

➤ Experiment with the IDE's layout by displaying the Debug toolbar, pinning the Toolbox, and displaying the Output window.

➤ Run the program.

➤ Find the program's executable, copy it to the desktop, and run it there.

➤ Copy the project folder to a new location and make changes to the copy.

➤ Compress the project folder to make a backup.

Hints

➤ When you create a new project, be sure to give it a descriptive name.

➤ When you save the project, put it in an obvious location so you can find it later.

➤ Before you compress the project, remove the `bin` and `obj` directories to save space.

Step-by-Step

➤ Find and bookmark useful web resources.

1. Open your favorite web browser.

2. Create a new bookmark folder named Visual Basic. (See the browser's documentation if you don't know how to make a bookmark folder.)

3. Go to the following web sites and bookmark the ones you like (feel free to search for others, too):

➤ My VB Helper web site (`www.vb-helper.com`)

➤ This book's web page (`www.vb-helper.com/24hourvb.html`)

➤ This book's Wrox web page (go to www.wrox.com and search for ISBN 978-0-470-94335-9)

➤ Visual Basic Express Edition MSDN forum (social.msdn.microsoft.com/Forums/en-US/Vsexpressvb/threads)

➤ Visual Basic IDE MSDN forum (social.msdn.microsoft.com/Forums/en-US/vbide/threads)

➤ Visual Basic Language MSDN forum (social.msdn.microsoft.com/Forums/en-US/vblanguage/threads)

➤ Visual Basic General MSDN forum (social.msdn.microsoft.com/Forums/en-US/vbgeneral/threads)

➤ The Visual Basic Developer Center (msdn.microsoft.com/vbasic)

➤ Launch Visual Studio and start a new Visual Basic project.

1. If you don't have a desktop icon for Visual Studio, create one.

    a. Open the Windows Start menu and find Visual Studio. Either browse for it (it's probably in a folder named Visual Studio 2010 and the program is called Visual Studio 2010) or use the menu's search textbox to find it.

    b. Right-click the program, open the Send To submenu, and select Desktop (Create Shortcut).

2. Launch Visual Studio. Double-click the desktop icon or open the system's Start menu and select the Visual Studio 2010 program.

3. Create a new project.

    a. Press [Ctrl]+N or open the IDE's File menu and select New Project.

    b. Expand the Visual Basic project types folder and select the Windows Forms Application template.

    c. Enter a good project name and click OK.

➤ Experiment with the IDE's layout by displaying the Debug toolbar, pinning the Toolbox, and displaying the Output window.

1. Open the Tools menu and select Customize. On the Customize dialog box, select the Toolbars tab and check the box next to the Debug toolbar. Experiment with the other toolbars if you like. Close the dialog box when you're done.

2. If the Toolbox is auto-hiding (it should be after you first install Visual Studio), float the mouse over it until it expands. Click the thumbtack to pin it.

3. To display the Output window, open the View menu, expand its Other Windows submenu, and select Output. Grab the Output window's title bar and drag it around. Move it over some drop targets to see where it lands. When you're finished, drop it at the bottom of the IDE as shown in Figure 1-6.

➤ Run the program.

   1. Press F5 or open the Debug menu and select Start Debugging.

   2. Try out the form's minimize, maximize, and close buttons, and the commands in the form's system menu. Move the form around and resize it. Marvel at the fact that you didn't need to write any code!

   3. Press [Ctrl]+[Shift]+S or use the File menu's Save All Files command to save the project. Be sure to put it in an easy-to-find location.

➤ Find the program's executable, copy it to the desktop, and run it there.

   1. Start Windows Explorer and navigate to the location that you specified when you saved the project.

   2. Find the folder named after the project. Open that folder and examine the files inside. Notice the .sln file that you can double-click to reopen the solution in Visual Studio. Notice also the bin and obj directories.

   3. Enter the bin directory and move into its Debug subdirectory. It contains several files, including the executable named after the program but with the .exe extension. Right-click the executable and select Copy.

   4. Right-click the desktop and select Paste to copy the executable to the desktop.

   5. Double-click the copy of the executable on the desktop.

➤ Copy the project folder to a new location and make changes to the copy.

   1. In Windows Explorer, return to the location where you created the project and you can see the project's folder.

   2. Right-click the project's folder and select Copy.

   3. Right-click the desktop and select Paste to copy the project folder.

   4. Open the copied project folder and double-click the .sln file to open the copied project in Visual Studio.

➤ Compress the project folder to make a backup.

   1. In Windows Explorer, return to the project's folder. Find and delete the bin and obj directories.

   2. Move up one level so you are in the location you specified when you created the project and you can see the project's folder. Right-click the folder, expand the Send To sub-menu, and select Compressed (Zipped) Folder.

   3. E-mail copies of your first project to all your friends and relatives!

 Please select Lesson 1 on the DVD to view the video that accompanies this lesson.

EXERCISES

1. Build a solution that contains two projects. (Create a project named Project1. Save it, checking the Create Directory for Solution box, and name the solution Ex1-1. Then open the File menu, expand the Add submenu, and select New Project to add a new project named Project2.)

2. This lesson explains only a tiny fraction of the ways you can customize Visual Studio. Try another one by making your own toolbar. Select the Tools menu's Customize command. On the Toolbars tab, click the New button and name the new toolbar MyTools. Then on the Commands tab, click the Toolbar radio button and select your toolbar. Now use the Add Command button to add tools to the toolbar. Search the command categories for useful tools. The Debug and Format categories contain some useful commands.

3. This lesson also describes only a few of the windows Visual Studio offers. Use the menus to find and display the Output, Immediate, Error List, and Task List windows. Put them all in tabs at the bottom of Visual Studio (#8 in Figure 1-6).

4. Some tools are only available when Visual Studio is in a certain state. Look in the Debug menu's Windows submenu. Then start the program and look there again. Most of those windows are useful only when the program is running and you are debugging it. (I talk about some of them in later lessons.)

5. Later lessons spend a lot of time describing the form and code editors, but Visual Studio includes a lot of other editors, too. To try out the Icon Editor, open the Project Menu, select Add Existing Item, browse to an icon file, and click Add. (If you have a version of Visual Studio other than the Express Edition, you can also create a new icon file by using the Project menu's Add New Item command.) Now you can double-click the icon file in the Solution Explorer to reopen the icon in the editor.

6. Use steps similar to those that you used in Exercise 5 to open or make a cursor file that looks similar to the icon you built in Exercise 5. After you create the file, right-click below the list of cursor types (initially just "32" 32, 1 bit, BMP") and select New Image Type to give the cursor the types "16" 16, 24 bit, BMP" and "32" 32, 24 bit, BMP." You can copy and paste the images from the icon into the appropriate cursor types. Set each cursor type's hotspot.

You can find solutions to Exercises 1, 5, and 6 in the Lesson01 folder inside the download available on the book's web site at www.wrox.com or www.vb-helper .com/24hourvb.html.

2

Creating Controls

Way back in the computer stone ages, when programmers worked by candlelight on treadle-powered computers and hand-carved wooden monitors, input and output were very simple. The computer wrote text in toxic green on the bottom of a monitor and the text scrolled up as the monitor became full. The user typed on a keyboard to enter text at a single input prompt, and that was about it. Multiple windows performing useful work simultaneously, forms displaying labels and textboxes, buttons, scrollbars, full-color images, and even mice, existed only in the fevered dreams of science-fiction writers.

Today these things are so commonplace that we take them completely for granted. They appear in desktop software, web pages, laptops, handheld computers, and even cell phones. Building these sorts of objects in the old days would have been extremely difficult, but today it's practically trivial to add them to your application.

You already saw in Lesson 1 how easy it is to make an application (albeit a trivial one) that displays a form that runs independently of the others on the computer. It's almost as easy to use labels, textboxes, buttons, scrollbars, images, menus, popups, and everything else that makes up a modern application.

Visual Basic makes all of these objects and more available as controls.

In this lesson, you learn how to add controls to a form. You learn how to size, position, and arrange controls. You also learn how to use a control's properties to change its appearance and behavior at design time and at run time. When you're done with this lesson, you'll be able to build a professional-looking form.

UNDERSTANDING CONTROLS

A *control* is a programming entity that combines a visible appearance on the screen and code to manage it. The code defines the control's appearance and behavior.

For example, a `TextBox` control displays a blank area on the screen where the user can type information. The code that is part of the control determines how the control draws itself and provides normal textbox features such as multi-line or single-line behavior; scrolling and scrollbars displayed as needed; copy, cut, and paste; a context menu displayed when you right-click the control; the capability to navigate when the user presses the [Tab] key; and much more.

WHAT'S IN A NAME?

By convention, the names of control types use *Pascal casing* where multiple words are strung together with the first letter of each word capitalized — for example, `TextBox`, `ProgressBar`, `Button`, and `PictureBox`.

In addition to controls, Visual Basic provides components. A *component* is similar to a control except it has no visible piece on the form. For example, the `Timer` component acts as a clock to enable the program to do something at regular intervals. The `Timer` interacts with the program, but it doesn't display anything visible to the user. (Some components such as `ErrorProvider` and `ToolTip` may produce visible effects on the screen, but the components themselves are not visible on the form.)

The features of controls (and components) fall into three categories: properties, methods, and events.

Properties

A *property* determines the appearance and state of a control. If a `Car` were a control, its properties would be things like `Color`, `NumberOfCupHolders`, `CurrentSpeed`, and `TransmissionType`. Your program could set a `Car` control's `Color` to `HotPink` (to attract the attention of other drivers) or set its `CurrentSpeed` to `110` (to attract the attention of the police).

For a programming example, the `TextBox` control has a `Font` property that determines the font it uses and a `ForeColor` property that determines the color of its text.

Methods

A *method* is an action that the control can perform. Your code can *call* a method to make the control do something. For example, the `Car` control might have methods such as `Start`, `Stop`, `EjectPassenger`, and `MakeOilSlick`. Your program could call the `MakeOilSlick` method to make the car spray oil out the back so you can escape from spies.

For a programming example, the `TextBox` has a `Clear` method that removes the control's text and an `AppendText` method that adds text to the end of whatever the control is currently displaying.

Events

An *event* occurs when something interesting happens to the control. The control *raises* or *fires* the event to tell the program that something happened. For example, a `Car` might have `RanOutOfGas` and `Crashed` events. The `Car` control would raise the `Crashed` event to tell the program that the user had driven it into a tree. The program could then take action such as calling an ambulance and a tree surgeon.

For a programming example, the `TextBox` has a `TextChanged` event that tells the program that its text has changed. When the event occurs, the program could examine the text to see if the user entered a valid input. For example, if the `TextBox` should hold a number and the user entered "One," the program could beep and change the `TextBox` control's `BackColor` property to `Yellow` to indicate an error.

Later lessons discuss events and the code that handles them in greater detail. This lesson focuses on adding controls to a form, arranging them, and setting their properties.

CREATING CONTROLS

Adding controls to a form is easy. In fact, it's so easy and there are so many different ways to add controls to a form that it takes a while to describe them all.

Start by creating a new project as described in Lesson 1. Open the form in the Form Designer. (If the form isn't already open, double-click it in Solution Explorer.)

The following list describes some of the ways you can put controls on the form:

➤ Click a tool in the Toolbox to select it. Then click and drag on the form to place a copy of the control on the form.

➤ Click a tool in the Toolbox to select it. Then hold down the [Ctrl] key while you click and drag on the form to place a copy of the control on the form. When you release the mouse, Visual Studio creates the control and keeps the control's tool selected in the Toolbox so you can make another control of that type.

➤ Double-click a tool in the Toolbox to select it to create an instance of the control on the form at a default size and position.

➤ Select one or more controls that are already on the form. Press [Ctrl]+C to copy them and then press [Ctrl]+V to paste them onto the form.

➤ Select one or more controls on the form. While holding down the [Ctrl] key, drag the controls to a new location. Visual Studio makes a copy of the controls, leaving the originals in place.

There are several ways to select controls on the Form Designer. Click on a control to select only it. Click and drag to select multiple controls.

Hold down the [Shift] or [Ctrl] key while clicking or clicking and dragging to toggle whether controls are in the current selection.

If you want to deselect all controls, simply click on the form's surface or press [Esc].

The first method (selecting a tool and then clicking and dragging to create a control) is probably used most often, but some of the other methods are particularly useful for creating a lot of very similar groups of controls.

For example, the top of the form in Figure 2-1 holds four rows, each of which holds a `Label` and a `TextBox`. You could easily build all of these controls individually, but you can build them even faster if you make the first row and then copy and paste it three times. You'll still need to change the `Labels`' text but the basic arrangement can be done without going back and forth to the Toolbox.

FIGURE 2-1

SETTING CONTROL PROPERTIES

After you've added controls to a form, you can use the Properties window to view and change their property values. If you have more than one control selected, the Properties window shows only the properties that the controls have in common.

For example, if you select a `TextBox` and a `Label`, the Properties window shows the `Text` property because both `TextBox` and `Label` controls have a `Text` property. However, it won't display the `Multiline` property because the `TextBox` control has that property but the `Label` control does not.

The Properties window provides special support for many control properties. For example, Figure 2-2 shows the Properties window when a `TextBox` is selected.

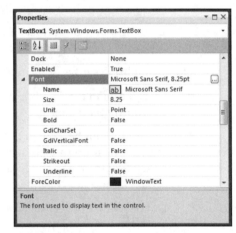

FIGURE 2-2

Notice that the `Font` property contains its own sub-properties — `Name`, `Size`, `Unit`, `Bold`, and so forth. Click the triangle next to a property to expand or collapse it and show or hide its subproperties.

Also notice in Figure 2-2 the ellipsis to the right of the `Font` property. If you click that ellipsis, the dialog box shown in Figure 2-3 appears. You can use this dialog box to edit the font subproperties and see a sample of the font.

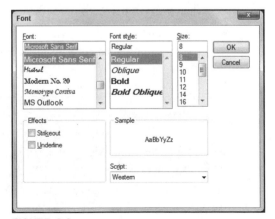

FIGURE 2-3

The Properties window provides appropriate support for other properties when it can. Many properties can hold only certain values. For example, the Font control's Italic, Bold, Strikeout, and Underline subproperties can take only the values True or False. The Font control's Unit subproperty can take only the values World, Pixel, Point, Inch, Document, and Millimeter. In these cases, the Properties window provides a drop-down listing the allowed choices.

Control Names

Whenever you create a control, Visual Studio gives it a rather nondescript name such as Label2, TextBox5, or PictureBox1. Although these names tell you what kind of object the control is, they don't tell you what it is for, which is much more important when you later need to use the control in your code.

To make using controls easier, most Visual Basic developers use a *control prefix naming convention*. In this convention, a control's name begins with a short prefix indicating its type, followed by text describing the control's purpose. For example, a textbox in which the user should enter a first name would be called txtFirstName.

Table 2-1 lists prefixes for the most common controls.

TABLE 2-1

CONTROL TYPE	PREFIX
CheckBox	chk
ComboBox	cbo
Form	frm
GroupBox	grp
Label	lbl
ListBox	lst
PictureBox	pic
RadioButton	rad
TextBox	txt

You can find a more complete list of prefixes at msdn.microsoft.com/library/aa263493%28v=VS.60%29.aspx. This list is somewhat dated (it's been around for at least 10 years), but it will give you a good start.

CONVENTION DISSENSION

This is not the only naming convention people use. Becoming increasingly popular is a *user interface prefix convention* where all controls use the same prefix "ux." The idea is that it shouldn't matter whether the user selects a value from a ListBox or a ComboBox; the names should be the same (for example, uxNumItems).

Microsoft recommends that C# programmers use full control name suffixes, as in firstNameTextBox. I haven't found the corresponding recommendation for Visual Basic programmers, but I suspect it would be the same.

All of these conventions have their advantages, the most important of which is consistency. Pick a convention and stick with it. That will make your code easier to read and understand.

Note that you don't need to assign descriptive names to every control, just the ones that you will need to use in the code. You often don't need to name Labels, GroupBoxes, and other purely decorative controls.

You can learn more about Microsoft's naming conventions at msdn.microsoft.com/library/0b283bse.aspx and support.microsoft.com/kb/110264.

Popular Properties

You'll learn about key control properties as you go along, and you can see a summary of key properties for specific controls in Appendix B, but for now Table 2-2 summarizes some of the most useful properties. Note that not all controls have every property. For example, a Button cannot display a border so it has no BorderStyle property.

TABLE 2-2

PROPERTY	PURPOSE
Anchor	Determines how the control sizes itself to use the available space. Lesson 3 describes this property further.
AutoSize	Determines whether the control automatically resizes itself to fit its contents.
BackColor	Determines the control's background color.
BackgroundImage	Determines the image that the control displays.
BorderStyle	Determines whether the control displays a border. This can be None, FixedSingle, or Fixed3D.
Dock	Determines how the control sizes itself to use the available space. Lesson 3 describes this property further.

PROPERTY	PURPOSE
Enabled	Determines whether the control will interact with the user.
Font	Determines the font that the control uses.
ForeColor	Determines the control's foreground color. For controls that display text, this is usually the text's color.
Image	Determines the image that the control displays. (Some controls have Image, others have BackgroundImage, a few have both, and some cannot display any image. No one said this was completely consistent!)
Items	For controls such as ListBox and ComboBox, this is the list of items that the user can select.
Location	Gives the control's location in pixels from the upper-left corner of whatever it is in (for now, assume it's in the form). Location includes X and Y subproperties. For example, the value (10, 20) means the control is 10 pixels from the form's left edge and 20 pixels from its top edge.
Name	Gives the control a name that your code can use. You should always give a descriptive name to any control that you will refer to in code.
Size	Gives the control's width and height in pixels. For example, the value (75, 30) means the control is 75 pixels wide and 30 pixels tall.
Tag	This property can hold any value that you want. For example, you might put text or a number in several Buttons' Tag properties so the code can easily tell the Buttons apart.
Text	Many controls have a Text property that determines what the control displays. For Labels and TextBoxes, Text determines the text they show (pretty obvious). For controls such as ComboBoxes and ListBoxes, Text determines the control's current selection. For a Form, which in some sense is really just another kind of control, Text determines what's displayed in the title bar.
TextAlign	Determines how text is aligned within the control.
Visible	Determines whether the control is visible.

Some property values may propagate to the controls they contain. For example, if you set a Form's Font property, any Labels on the Form will use the same Font. This does not always work for all controls and properties, however. For example, if you change a Form's ForeColor property, Labels on the Form use that color but GroupBoxes do not.

If you want some practice with these properties, create a new project and give them a try. Create a Button and set its Text property. Also, click the form and set *its* Text property. Change the form's Font property and see what happens. You can experiment with some of the other properties such as Image and ForeColor if you like.

Modifying Properties in Code

This lesson doesn't really go into handling control events very much (Lesson 4 does that), but I do want to explain how to set properties in code. Besides, it's easy, sort of fun, and it'll enable you to make a program that does something more than just sit there looking pretty.

First, to make a simple event handler, double-click the control in the Form Designer. That opens the Code Editor and creates an empty *event handler* for the control's default event. For Button controls, that's the Click event. Whenever the user clicks a Button at run time, it raises its Click event and this code executes.

To change a property in code, type the control's name, a dot (or period), the name of the property, an equals sign, and finally the value that you want to give the property. For example, the following statement sets the Left property of the label named lblGreeting to 100. That moves the label so it is 100 pixels from the left edge of its container.

```
lblGreeting.Left = 100
```

The following code shows a complete event handler:

```
' Change the Label's properties.
Private Sub btnMoveLabel_Click(ByVal sender As System.Object,
 ByVal e As System.EventArgs) Handles btnMoveLabel.Click
    lblGreeting.Left = 100
End Sub
```

In this code, I typed the first line that starts with an apostrophe. That line is a *comment*, a piece of text that is contained in the code but that is not executed by the program. Any text that comes after the apostrophe is ignored until the end of the current line. You can (and should) use comments to make your code easier to understand.

I also typed the line that sets the Label's Left property.

Visual Studio typed the rest when I double-clicked the btnMoveLabel control. You don't need to worry about the details of this code right now, but the sender parameter is the object that raised the event (the Button in this example) and the e parameter provides extra information about the event. The extra information can be useful for some events (for example, in the MouseClick event it tells where the mouse was clicked), but it's not very interesting for a Button's Click event. The Handles clause at the end indicates which event this code handles.

Simple numeric property values such as the 100 used in this example are easy to set in code, but some properties aren't numbers. In that case, you must set them to values that have the proper data type.

For example, a Label's Text property is a string so you must assign it a string value. The following code sets the lblGreeting control's Text property to the string Hello:

```
lblGreeting.Text = "Hello"
```

Notice that you must include the string "Hello" in double quotes to tell Visual Basic that this is a literal string and not some sort of Visual Basic command. If you leave the quotes off, Visual Basic gets confused and gives you the cryptic error "'Hello' is not declared. It may be inaccessible due to its protection level."

Over time, you'll get used to messages like this and they'll make some sense. In this case, the message just means, "I don't know what the word 'Hello' means."

There are two more syntactic points I want to mention now with this piece of code as an example: line continuation and relaxed delegates.

Line Continuation

Visual Basic is a line-oriented language. That means every command must fit on a single line of code. Sometimes, however, a line of code may be too long to fit reasonably on your computer screen, so Visual Basic allows you to break a "single" line of code across multiple lines on the screen.

One way to do that is to use a *line continuation character* consisting of a space and underscore. If you end a line with a space and underscore, then Visual Basic joins it with the following line.

For example, the following code shows another way to write the preceding code. Notice the line continuation character at the end of the line of code after the comment. Visual Basic considers everything from `Private Sub` to `btnMoveLabel.Click` to be part of the same line of code.

```
' Change the Label's properties.
Private Sub btnMoveLabel_Click(ByVal sender As System.Object, _
 ByVal e As System.EventArgs) Handles btnMoveLabel.Click
    lblGreeting.Left = 100
End Sub
```

Visual Basic also supports *implicit line continuation*, which allows it to guess when a line has been continued without a line continuation character. If you break a line of code at a point where Visual Basic can determine that the line is incomplete, it will merge that line with the following line. This is why the original version of the preceding code works.

Exactly where Visual Basic can figure out that you broke a line is a bit hard to understand. Usually you can break a line after an equals sign, operator such as +, or comma and Visual Basic will figure it out. If you can't break a line nicely so Visual Basic can use implicit line continuation, you can always use a line continuation character.

Relaxed Delegates

Visual Basic also supports *relaxed delegates*, which let you simplify an event handler's parameter list. If the event handler won't use its parameters, you can simply omit them. The following code shows a relaxed version of the preceding code.

```
' Change the Label's properties.
Private Sub btnMoveLabel_Click() Handles btnMoveLabel.Click
    lblGreeting.Left = 100
End Sub
```

When Visual Basic creates an empty event handler for you, it always includes the parameters but you can remove them if you don't need them. From now on, the examples shown in this book will omit parameters to make the code easier to read, unless the code needs to use them.

Other Property Types

The preceding example uses the simple numeric property `Left` but other property values have more exotic data types such as `Date`, `AnchorStyles`, and `Point`. When you set these properties, you must make sure that the values you give them have the correct data types. I'm going to ignore most of these for now, but one data type that is relatively simple and useful is `Color`.

A control's `ForeColor` and `BackColor` properties have the data type `Color` so you cannot simply set them to strings such as `Red` or `Blue`. Instead, you must set them equal to something that also has the type `Color`. The easiest way to do that is to use the colors predefined by the `Color` class. This may seem a bit confusing but in practice it's actually quite easy.

For example, the following two statements set a `Label` control's `ForeColor` and `BackColor` properties to `HotPink` and `Blue`, respectively:

```
lblGreeting.BackColor = Color.HotPink
lblGreeting.ForeColor = Color.Blue
```

The following code shows how the MoveLabel example program, which is available as part of this lesson's code download on the book's web site, changes several `Label` properties when you click a `Button`:

```
' Change the Label's properties.
Private Sub btnMoveLabel_Click() Handles btnMoveLabel.Click
    lblGreeting.Left = 100
    lblGreeting.Text = "Hello"
    lblGreeting.BackColor = Color.HotPink
    lblGreeting.ForeColor = Color.Blue
End Sub
```

ARRANGING CONTROLS

The Form Designer provides several tools to help you arrange controls at design time. The following sections describe some of the most useful: snap lines, arrow keys, the Format menu, and the Layout toolbar.

Snap Lines

When you drag a control around on the form, the Form Designer displays *snap lines* that show how the control lines up with the form and other controls. Figure 2-4 shows the Form Designer displaying snap lines indicating that the `Button` control is located a standard distance (12 pixels) from the form's top and left edges. On your screen the snap lines appear in light blue.

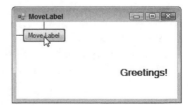

FIGURE 2-4

You can drag the control away from this position; if you do so, the snap lines disappear. When you drag the control close to one of the form's edges, the control jumps to the standard distance and the Form Designer displays the snap lines again.

The Form Designer also displays snap lines to show how controls align. In Figure 2-5, I dragged a second button below the first. Different snap lines show that:

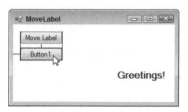

FIGURE 2-5

➤ The second button is the standard distance from the form's left edge.

➤ The second button's left and right edges line up with the first button's edges.

➤ The second button is a standard distance (6 pixels) below the first button.

FIGURE 2-6

Other snap lines show how the control contents line up. In Figure 2-6 snap lines show that the Label is the standard distance from the second Button, and that the Label's text baseline lines up with the baseline of the second Button.

Arrow Keys

In addition to dragging controls with the mouse, you can move controls by pressing the arrow keys. Select one or more controls and then use the left, right, up, and down arrow keys to move the control(s) one pixel at a time. This method is slower than using the mouse but gives you finer control.

When you move a control with the arrow keys, the Form Designer doesn't display snap lines so you may want to keep an eye on the control's Location property in the Properties window to see where it is.

The Format Menu and Layout Toolbar

The Format menu contains many commands that arrange one or more controls. Table 2-3 summarizes the Format menu's submenus.

TABLE 2-3

SUBMENU	COMMANDS
Align	Aligns groups of controls. Options include left, middle, right, top, bottom, and center.
Make Same Size	Makes controls have the same width, height, or both.
Horizontal Spacing	Adjusts the horizontal spacing between controls. It can make the space between controls equal, smaller, larger, or zero.

continues

TABLE 2-3 *(continued)*

SUBMENU	COMMANDS
Vertical Spacing	Works like the Horizontal Spacing submenu except it adjusts the vertical spacing between controls.
Center in Form	Centers the controls vertically or horizontally in their container. If the controls are inside a container like a `Panel` or `GroupBox`, these commands center the controls within the container, not the form.
Order	These commands send a control to the front or back of the stacking order. This is useful if you have controls that overlap so some are behind others.

The Layout toolbar contains the same commands as the Format menu but in a handy toolbar so they're easier to use. The buttons display little pictures that show how they align controls.

 How these tools arrange controls depends on how you select the controls. One of the selected controls, normally the first one you select, is the group's dominant control. The dominant control is marked with white boxes, whereas the other controls are marked with black boxes.

When you use an arranging tool, the dominant control determines how the others are arranged. For example, if you select the Format ⇨ Align ⇨ Lefts command, the other controls are moved so their left edges line up with the dominant control's left edge.

To change the dominant control in a selected group, click on the one you want to be dominant (without holding down the [Ctrl] or [Shift] keys).

 TRY IT

In this Try It, you get some practice building a user interface. You place controls on a form and arrange them so they line up nicely. You also get some practice setting control properties at design time and changing them at run time.

 You can download the code and resources for this Try It from the book's web page at www.wrox.com or www.vb-helper.com/24hour.html. You can find them in the Lesson02 folder in the download.

Lesson Requirements

In this lesson:

➤ Add controls to a form and arrange them as shown in Figure 2-7. (Note the form's title and the fact that it uses a fixed tool window style border instead of a normal, thicker resizable border.)

➤ Give the key controls names.

➤ Set properties at design time on the result label (at the bottom in Figure 2-7) to make the label:

    ➤ Display its text centered.

    ➤ Show a border.

    ➤ Use a 16-point Comic Sans MS font.

    ➤ Remain invisible until the user clicks the OK button.

➤ Make the OK button the form's default button so it fires when the user presses [Enter]. Make the Cancel button the form's cancel button so it fires when the user presses [Esc].

FIGURE 2-7

➤ Add code behind the OK button to display the result label shown in Figure 2-7, giving it a green background.

➤ Add code behind the Cancel button to display the result label with a hot pink background and the text "Operation Canceled."

Hints

➤ Create the First Name label and textbox first and arrange them. Then copy and paste them to make more labels and textboxes.

➤ Use the Format menu or Layout toolbar to center the buttons and the result label.

Step-by-Step

➤ Add controls to a form and arrange them as shown in Figure 2-7. (Note the form's title and the fact that it uses a fixed tool window style instead of a normal, thicker resizable border.)

1. Start a new project named NewCustomer. Remember to put it somewhere easy to find.

2. Use the Properties window to set the form's `Text` property to "`New Customer`."

3. Use the Properties window to set the form's `FormBorderStyle` property to `FixedToolWindow`.

4. Create the First Name `TextBox`.

    a. Click the Toolbox's `TextBox` tool and then click and drag to place a `TextBox` on the form.

    b. Drag the `TextBox` into the form's upper-right corner.

5. Create the First Name `Label`.

    a. Click the Toolbox's `Label` tool and then click and drag to create the `Label`.

    b. Drag the `Label` to the form's upper-left corner so the snap lines show that the `Label` is a standard distance from the form's left edge and that its baseline aligns with the `TextBox`'s baseline.

    c. Use the Properties window to set the `Label`'s Text property to "`First Name:`".

    d. Click the `TextBox`. Drag the left drag handle until it is a standard distance from the `Label`.

6. Make copies of the `Label` and `TextBox`.

    a. Click and drag to select both the `Label` and `TextBox`.

    b. Press [Ctrl]+C to copy the controls. Press [Ctrl]+V to paste new copies of the controls.

    c. Drag the new controls into position.

    d. Use the Properties window to set the `Label` Text properties.

    e. Repeat as needed.

7. Make the ZIP `Label`.

    a. Set the bottom `TextBox`'s Text property to `12345-6789` and size it appropriately.

    b. Create a `Label` for the ZIP code and align it with the `TextBox`.

8. Make the State `ComboBox`.

    a. Use the Toolbox to make a `ComboBox` (see Figure 2-7). Set its Text property to `WW` and resize the box so the text fits reasonably well.

    b. Align the `ComboBox` to the ZIP code `TextBox`.

    c. With the `ComboBox` selected, look in the Properties window and click the `Items` property. Then click the ellipsis (…) button on the right to open the String Collection Editor. Enter `CO`, `AZ`, `WY`, `UT`, and any other state abbreviations that you want to use and click OK.

    d. Use the Properties window to set the `DropDownStyle` property to `DropDownList`.

The `DropDownStyle` *value* `Simple` *displays a* `TextBox` *where the user can type and a list below it.*

The value `DropDown` *displays a* `TextBox` *where the user can type and a drop-down arrow that makes a drop-down list appear.*

The value `DropDownList` *is similar to* `DropDown` *except the user can select only from the drop-down list and cannot type new values.* `DropDownList` *is often the best choice because it prevents the user from typing garbage.*

9. Make the `Buttons`.

    a. Double-click the Toolbox's `Button` tool twice to make two `Buttons`.

    b. Drag one `Button` so it is a nice distance below the `TextBoxes`. Drag the other `Button` so it's aligned horizontally with the first.

    c. Click and drag to select both `Buttons`. Select Format ⇨ Center in Form ⇨ Horizontally.

    d. Use the Properties window to give the `Buttons` the `Text` values OK and Cancel.

10. Use the Toolbox to make the result `Label`. (Don't worry about its size and position right now.)

➤ Give the key controls names.

    1. Give the key controls the names shown in Table 2-4. You don't need to name the other controls because the program won't need to refer to them. (Actually, this example doesn't refer to the `TextBoxes` or `ComboBox` either, but a real program certainly would. A form wouldn't contain `TextBoxes` and `ComboBoxes` that it won't use.)

TABLE 2-4

CONTROL	NAME
First Name `TextBox`	`txtFirstName`
Last Name `TextBox`	`txtLastName`
Street `TextBox`	`txtStreet`
City `TextBox`	`txtCity`
State `ComboBox`	`cboState`
ZIP `TextBox`	`txtZip`
OK `Button`	`btnOk`
Cancel `Button`	`btnCancel`
Result `Label`	`lblResult`

➤ Set properties at design time on the result label (at the bottom in Figure 2-7) to make the label:

    ➤ Display its text centered.

        1. Set the `Label`'s `TextAlign` property to `MiddleCenter`.

        2. Set the `Label`'s `AutoSize` property to `False`.

        3. Set the `Label`'s `Size` property to `260, 43`.

        4. Use the Format menu or Layout toolbar to center the `Label` on the form.

➤ Show a border.

1. Set the Label's BorderStyle property to Fixed3D.

➤ Use a 16-point Comic Sans MS font.

1. Expand the Property window's Font entry. Set the Name subproperty to "Comic Sans MS." Set the Size subproperty to 16.

➤ Remain invisible until the user clicks the OK button.

1. Set the Label's Visible property to False.

➤ Make the OK button the form's default button so it fires when the user presses [Enter]. Make the Cancel button the form's cancel button so it fires when the user presses [Esc].

1. Click the form and use the Properties window to set the form's AcceptButton property to okButton.

2. Similarly, set the form's CancelButton property to cancelButton.

➤ Add code behind the OK button to display the result label shown in Figure 2-7, giving it a green background.

1. Double-click the OK button to create an event handler for its Click event.

2. Type the bold text in the following code so the event handler looks like this:

```
' Display the success message.
Private Sub btnOk_Click() Handles btnOk.Click
    lblResult.Text = "New User Created"
    lblResult.BackColor = Color.LightGreen
    lblResult.Visible = True
End Sub
```

➤ Add code behind the Cancel button to display the result label with a hot-pink background and the text "Operation Canceled."

1. Double-click the Cancel button to create an event handler for its Click event.

2. Type the bold text in the following code so the event handler looks like this:

```
' Display the canceled message.
Private Sub btnCancel_Click() Handles btnCancel.Click
    lblResult.Text = "Operation Canceled"
    lblResult.BackColor = Color.HotPink
    lblResult.Visible = True
End Sub
```

Now run the code and experiment with the program. Notice what happens when you press the [Enter] and [Esc] keys while focus is in a TextBox. See what happens when focus is on one of the buttons.

 Please select Lesson 2 on the DVD to view the video that accompanies this lesson.

EXERCISES

1. Make a tic-tac-toe (or naughts-and-crosses) board similar to the one shown in Figure 2-8. (Hints: Make three labels for each square, named after the rows and columns. For the upper-left square, name the labels `lblX00` for the little X label, `lblO00` for the little O label, and `lblTaken00` for the big label. The "00" part of the name means row 0, column 0. Give the smaller labels `Click` event handlers that set the `Text` property of the corresponding big label appropriately. Don't worry about the rules such as not allowing someone to claim a square that is already claimed.)

FIGURE 2-8

2. Modify the tic-tac-toe program from Exercise 1 so that instead of displaying X or O in each square, it displays a picture. Use your favorite football team logos, a cat and a dog, your picture and your boss's, or whatever. (Hints: Use `PictureBox`es instead of the large `Label`s. Add two hidden `PictureBox`es to the form. To set their `Image` properties, click the ellipsis next to the `Image` property in the Properties window, click the Import button, and browse for the image files. Finally, instead of setting a `Label`'s `Text` property, the `Click` event handlers should set the appropriate `PictureBox`'s `Image` property equal to one of the hidden `PictureBox`'s `Image` properties. Set the `SizeMode` property of each `PictureBox` to `Zoom`.)

3. Make a program with a `Label` that says "Move Me" and four `Button`s with text (0, 0), (200, 200), (200, 0), and (0, 200). Make each `Button` move the `Label` to the corresponding position by setting its `Left` and `Top` properties.

4. The solution to Exercise 3 moves its `Label` in two steps by setting its `Left` and `Top` properties. Modify the program so it sets the `Label`'s `Location` property in a single step using code similar to this:

```
lblMoveMe.Location = New Point(0, 200)
```

5. Build a menu selection form similar to the one shown in Figure 2-9. (Hint: Set the `PictureBox`'s `SizeMode` property to `AutoSize`.)

FIGURE 2-9

 You can find solutions to this lesson's exercises in the Lesson02 folder inside the download available on the book's web site at www.wrox.com *or* www.vb-helper.com/24hourvb.html.

3

Making Controls Arrange Themselves

Lesson 2 explained how to add controls to a form and arrange them nicely. Using those techniques, you can create forms like the one shown in Figure 3-1.

FIGURE 3-1

That form looks okay in Figure 3-1, but what if the user enlarges the form as shown in Figure 3-2? Pretty lame, huh? Although the form is bigger, the areas that contain data are not.

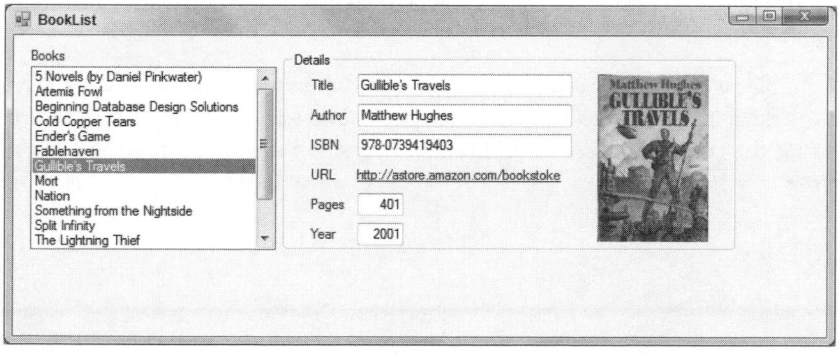

FIGURE 3-2

The URL for the book selected in Figure 3-2 is too long to fit within the `GroupBox`, so it is truncated even though the form has extra wasted space on the right. The `ListBox` isn't big enough to display all of its items even though there's wasted space at the bottom. It would be nice if the controls rearranged themselves to use the available space and display the entire URL and more list items.

Figure 3-3 shows another problem with this form. If the user shrinks the form, the `TextBoxes` and URL `LinkLabel` are chopped off, the Year `Label` and `TextBox` are chopped in half vertically, the `ListBox` doesn't fit, and the cover picture is completely missing.

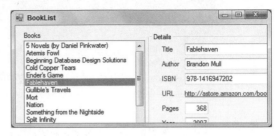

FIGURE 3-3

The program would look nicer if the controls were shrunk so you could at least see their edges. Some of the values still wouldn't fit but at least the form wouldn't look so amateurish. You could even prevent the form from shrinking so it's too short to display the Year controls.

This lesson explains some simple ways you can make controls rearrange themselves to take advantage of whatever space is available, and how to give the form minimum and maximum sizes so the user can't make it completely useless.

RESTRICTING FORM SIZE

Forms (and in fact all controls) have `MinimumSize` and `MaximumSize` properties that you can use to restrict the form's size. Simply set these properties to a width and height (or set their `Width` and `Height` subproperties) and the form does the rest.

For example, to prevent the user from making the form shown in Figure 3-3 too small, you can set the form's `MinimumSize` property to `515, 233`.

USING ANCHOR PROPERTIES

The `MinimumSize` property prevents the user from making a form too small but it doesn't solve all of the problems shown in Figures 3-2 and 3-3. When the user resizes a form, it would be nice if the controls changed their sizes to match.

The `Anchor` property enables a control to resize and move itself when its container resizes. This property can take one or more of the values `Top`, `Bottom`, `Left`, and `Right`, in any combination. These values indicate that the control's edges should remain the same distance from the corresponding edges of its container.

If an Anchor's *values don't include either* Left/Right *or* Top/Bottom, *the control moves to keep itself the same distance from the middle of the form. For example, if a* Button's Anchor *property is simply* Bottom, *it moves so it remains the same distance from the middle of the form horizontally.*

This fact enables you to keep one or more controls centered. For example, place several Buttons *near the bottom of a form and use the Format menu to center them horizontally. Now if you set their* Anchor *properties to* Bottom, *the group of* Buttons *remains centered when the form resizes.*

For example, initially a control's Anchor property is set to Top, Left so it remains the same distance from its container's top and left edges. If you resize the form, the control doesn't move.

For a more interesting example, suppose you place a TextBox on a form, set its Multiline property to True, arrange it so its edges are 12 pixels from the edges of the form, and set its Anchor property to Top, Bottom, Left, Right. When you resize the form, the TextBox resizes itself so its edges remain 12 pixels from the form's edges.

 The Anchor *property cannot resize a control such as a* Label *or* LinkLabel *if that control has* AutoSize *set to* True. *In that case, the control has its own ideas about how big it should be.*

To set the Anchor property at design time, you can type a value like Top, Left, Right into the Properties window or you can use the Properties window's Anchor editor.

To use the editor, click the Anchor property in the Properties window. Then click the drop-down arrow to the right to make the editor shown in Figure 3-4 appear. Click the skinny rectangles to select or deselect the anchors that you want to use. (In Figure 3-4 the top and right anchors are selected.) When you're finished, press [Enter] to accept your changes or [Esc] to cancel them.

Using the Anchor property, you can solve the problems shown in Figures 3-2 and 3-3. Table 3-1 shows the Anchor property values used by the controls, enabling them to take advantage of the form's available space.

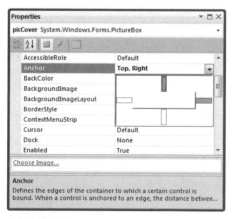

FIGURE 3-4

TABLE 3-1

CONTROL	Anchor **PROPERTY**
Books ListBox	Top, Bottom, Left
Details GroupBox	Top, Bottom, Left, Right
Title TextBox	Top, Left, Right
Author TextBox	Top, Left, Right
ISBN TextBox	Top, Left, Right
URL LinkLabel	Top, Left, Right
Cover PictureBox	Top, Right

Now when the form resizes:

➤ The ListBox stretches vertically to match the form's height.

➤ The GroupBox stretches vertically and horizontally to use as much of the form's width and height as possible.

➤ The TextBoxes and LinkLabel stretch horizontally to be as wide as possible while still fitting inside the GroupBox.

➤ The PictureBox moves with the GroupBox's right edges so it leaves as much room as possible to the left for the TextBoxes and LinkLabel.

Figure 3-5 shows the result. Now the ListBox is big enough to show all of its items and the LinkLabel is big enough to show the entire URL.

FIGURE 3-5

Note that the TextBoxes and LinkLabel do *not* stretch horizontally when the form resizes; they stretch when the GroupBox that contains them resizes. In this example, when the form stretches, the GroupBox stretches; and when the GroupBox stretches, the TextBoxes and LinkLabel stretch.

USING DOCK PROPERTIES

The Anchor property can handle most of your arranging needs but some combinations of Anchor values are so common that Visual Basic provides another property to let you handle these situations more easily: Dock. The Dock property lets you tell a control to attach itself to one of the edges of its container.

For example, a menu typically attaches to the top of a form and resizes horizontally to fill the form when the form resizes. You could provide that behavior by setting the menu's Anchor property to Top, Left, Right, but setting Dock to Top is even easier.

The Dock property can take one of six values. Left, Right, Top, and Bottom attach the control to the corresponding edge of its container. Fill makes the control take up any space left over after any other controls' Dock properties have had their way, and None detaches the control so its Anchor property can take over.

 The Dock *property cannot resize a control such as a* Label *or* LinkLabel *if that control has* AutoSize *set to* True.

The Dock property processes positioning requests in a first-come-first-served order based on the controls' stacking order on the form. In other words, it positions the first control that it draws first; the second next, in whatever space is still available; and so forth.

Normally the stacking order is determined by the order in which you add controls to the form, but you can change the order by right-clicking a control and selecting Bring to Front or Send to Back. If you're working with a complicated set of Dock properties and the stacking order is messed up, it's often easier to delete all of the controls and start over from scratch.

Figure 3-6 shows a form holding five docked Labels (with AutoSize = False). The numbers in the controls' Text properties indicate the order in which they were created, which is also their stacking order. The following list explains how the form's space was divvied up among the Labels:

1. The first Label has Dock = Top, so it took the top part of the form.

2. The second Label has Dock = Left, so it took the left edge of the remaining area (after the first Label was positioned).

3. The third Label has Dock = Right, so it took the right edge of the remaining area.

4. The fourth Label has Dock = Bottom, so it took the bottom edge of the remaining area.

5. The final Label has Dock = Fill, so it fills all of the remaining area.

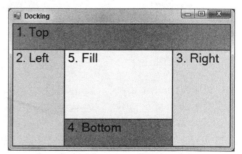

FIGURE 3-6

DOCKED MENUS

In one typical docking scenario, a form contains a `MenuStrip` with `Dock = Top` and a container such as a `Panel` with `Dock = Fill` so it takes up the rest of the form. All the other controls are placed inside the `Panel`.

You can also add `ToolStrips`, `ToolStripContainers`, and `StatusBars` with the appropriate `Dock`

FIGURE 3-7

properties to put those controls in their correct places. Figure 3-7 shows a form holding a `MenuStrip` (`Dock = Top`), a `ToolStripContainer` (`Dock = Top`) containing two `ToolStrips`, a `Panel` (`Dock = Fill`), and a `StatusStrip` (`Dock = Bottom`).

TRY IT

In this Try It, you have a chance to practice using the `Anchor` and `Dock` properties to build the application shown in Figure 3-8.

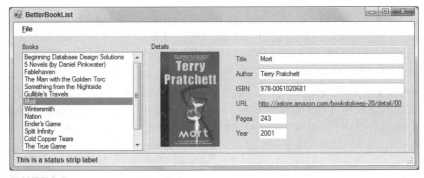

FIGURE 3-8

When the form resizes, the `TextBoxes` and `LinkLabel` stretch horizontally. The `PictureBox` also stretches vertically. Notice in Figure 3-8 that the cover image is rather tall and thin. When the `PictureBox` grows taller, it can display a larger version of the cover image. The control displays the image as large as possible without distorting it.

Note that the program you build won't actually do anything except sit there looking pretty and resize controls when the form resizes. The techniques you need to make it respond to list selections are covered in later lessons. (The solution available for download uses those techniques, but don't worry too much about them for now.)

You can download the code and resources for this Try It from the book's web page at www.wrox.com or www.vb-helper.com/24hourvb.html. *You can find them in the Lesson03 folder in the download.*

Lesson Requirements

In this lesson:

➤ Create the program's three main controls: a MenuStrip, a Panel, and a StatusStrip. Use Dock properties to make these three controls stay in their proper positions.

➤ Add controls to the Panel.

➤ Use the Anchor property to make the ListBox stretch vertically when the form resizes.

➤ Use Anchor properties to make the TextBoxes and LinkLabel stretch horizontally when the form resizes.

➤ Use the Anchor property to make the PictureBox resize vertically when the form resizes.

Hints

➤ Remember that the TextBoxes and LinkLabel stretch with the GroupBox that contains them, not the form itself.

➤ To make the File menu, add a MenuStrip to the form, click it, click the Type Here box that appears, and type **&File**. (The ampersand gives the "F" the underline.) Making the menu do something useful is covered in Lesson 5, so don't worry about it now.

➤ To make the status strip label, add a StatusStrip to the form and click it. Click the little drop-down arrow on the StatusStrip and select StatusLabel. Click the new StatusLabel and use the Properties window to set its Text to "This is a StatusStrip."

➤ Add some items to the ListBox and add a picture to the PictureBox, but don't worry about making the program take any actions.

Step-by-Step

➤ Create the program's three main controls: a MenuStrip, a Panel, and a StatusStrip. Use Dock properties to make these three controls stay in their proper positions.

1. Start a new project. Set the form's Size and MinimumSize properties to 726, 286.

2. Add a MenuStrip to the form. (Notice that by default the MenuStrip has Dock = Top.) See the "Hints" section to create the empty File menu.

3. Add a Panel to the form. Set its Dock property to Fill. Set its BackColor property to light green.

4. Add a StatusStrip to the form. (Notice that by default the StatusStrip has Dock = Bottom.) See the "Hints" section to create the "This is a StatusStrip" label.

➤ Add controls to the `Panel`.

   1. Add controls to the form in roughly the positions shown in Figure 3-8.

   2. Set the `LinkLabel`'s `AutoSize` property to `False` and make it the same size as the `TextBoxes`.

   3. Enter some `Text` values in the `TextBoxes` and `LinkLabel` so you have something to look at. Enter enough items in the `ListBox` so they won't all fit when the form is its initial size.

   4. Set the `PictureBox`'s `SizeMode` property to `Zoom`. Place a relatively tall, thin image in its `Image` property.

➤ Use the `Anchor` property to make the `ListBox` stretch vertically when the form resizes.

   1. Set the `ListBox`'s `Anchor` property to `Top, Bottom, Left`.

➤ Use `Anchor` properties to make the `TextBoxes` and `LinkLabel` stretch horizontally when the form resizes.

   1. Set the `GroupBox`'s `Anchor` property to `Top, Bottom, Left, Right`.

   2. Set the `TextBoxes`' and the `LinkLabel`'s `Anchor` properties to `Top, Left, Right`.

➤ Use `Anchor` properties to make the `PictureBox` resize vertically when the form resizes.

   1. Set the `PictureBox`'s `Anchor` property to `Top, Bottom, Left`.

Run the program and see what happens when you resize the form.

 Please select Lesson 3 on the DVD to view the video that accompanies this lesson.

EXERCISES

1. (SimpleEdit) Create a new project named SimpleEdit, putting it somewhere you can easily find so you can add enhancements in later lessons. Give it a `MenuStrip` and `StatusStrip` with appropriate (default) `Dock` values. Add a `RichTextBox` control and set its `Dock` property to `Fill`. (That's all for now. In later lessons you add features to this program.)

2. Make a New Customer dialog box similar to the one shown in Figure 3-9. Make the First Name, Last Name, Street, City, and Email `TextBoxes` resize horizontally when the form resizes. Use the OK and Cancel buttons as the form's accept and cancel buttons, and attach them to the form's lower-right corner.

FIGURE 3-9

3. The `SplitContainer` control displays two areas separated by a splitter. The user can drag the splitter to divide the available space between the two areas. Make a program similar to the one shown in Figure 3-10. Feel free to use a different picture and information. Make the `PictureBox` display its image as large as possible without distortion. Set the bottom `TextBox`'s `MultiLine` property to `True` and make it stretch vertically and horizontally as the form resizes. Make the other `TextBoxes` stretch horizontally. Set the `SplitContainer`'s `Panel1MinSize` and `Panel2MinSize` properties to `100`.

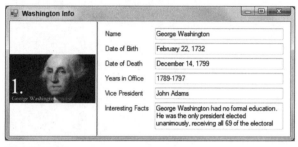

FIGURE 3-10

You can find solutions to this lesson's exercises in the Lesson03 folder inside the download available on the book's web site at www.wrox.com *or* www.vb-helper.com/24hourvb.html.

Handling Events

An *event* is something that a control raises to tell the program that something significant has happened. Events are extremely important because they are the main way the user controls the program. When the user clicks buttons, drags sliders, and selects menu items, events tell the program that something has happened so it can take action.

As Lesson 2 briefly explained, when the user clicks a `Button`, the `Button` raises a `Click` event. An *event handler* can *catch* or *handle* that event and take appropriate action such as displaying a message, performing a calculation, or downloading the latest *Dilbert* comic from the Web.

`Click` is a very useful event, but it's only one of hundreds (if not thousands) of events that your programs can catch.

This lesson explains how you can catch events other than `Click`. It describes some of the most useful events provided by common controls and, as a bonus, explains how you can display messages to the user when events occur.

MAKING EVENT HANDLERS

The easiest way to build an event handler is to double-click a control in the Form Designer. This creates an empty event handler for the control's default event and opens the event handler in the Code Editor. You then insert the code needed to take whatever action is appropriate.

The following code shows the empty `Click` event handler created for a `Button`. (Visual Studio puts the first two lines on a single line in the Code Editor. I split them so they would fit the book's dimensions.)

```
Private Sub btnCrashSystem_Click(ByVal sender As System.Object,
 ByVal e As System.EventArgs) Handles btnCrashSystem.Click

End Sub
```

Notice the `Handles btnCrashSystem.Click` clause at the end of the event handler's declaration. That indicates that this code handles the `btnCrashSystem` control's `Click` event.

> *Also remember that relaxed delegates let you remove the event handler's parameters if you don't want to use them.*

Probably the most commonly used events are the `Click` events raised by `Buttons`, `ToolStripMenuItems` (which represent menu items), and `ToolStripButtons` (which represent toolbar buttons). For these controls and many others, you almost always want to use the default event handler, so double-clicking them is the easiest way to go.

> *If you're not ready to write the real event handler code, you can write a placeholder event handler. One easy way to do that is to use `MessageBox.Show` to display a message. For example, the following code displays a placeholder message for the File menu's Save command:*
>
> ```
> Private Sub mnuFileSave_Click(ByVal sender As System.Object,
>   ByVal e As System.EventArgs) Handles mnuFileSave.Click
>     MessageBox.Show("File > Save not yet implemented")
> End Sub
> ```

Most controls provide dozens of other events that you can catch. To create an event handler for one of these nondefault events, select the control in the Form Designer. Then click the lightning bolt icon near the top of the Properties window to make the window list the control's events. Figure 4-1 shows the Properties window displaying some of the events that a `Button` can raise.

To create an empty event handler for an event, simply double-click the event's name in the Properties window's event list.

You can also type the name that you want to give the event handler. When you press [Enter], Visual Studio creates the event handler and opens it in the Code Editor.

If your code already contains event handlers that could handle the event, you can click the event and then click the drop-down arrow to the right to select one of those event handlers.

The Code Editor gives you another way to create event handlers. Select the control that you want to give an event handler in the left drop-down at the top of the editor. If you select an event from the right drop-down, shown in Figure 4-2, Visual Studio creates a new event handler for that event.

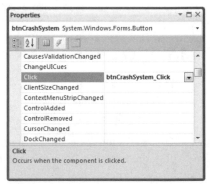

FIGURE 4-1

Finally, you can type in the code for an event handler. This can be difficult if you want the event handler to use parameters, but if you use relaxed delegates to omit them, typing in an event handler from scratch isn't too hard.

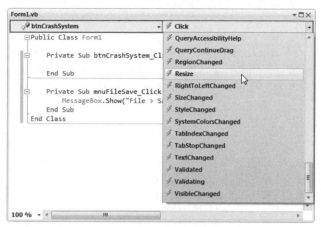

FIGURE 4-2

USING EVENT PARAMETERS

All event handlers include parameters that provide additional information about the event. Later lessons say more about parameters and how you can use them, but for now you should just know that sometimes they are useful.

For example, the following code shows a `Button`'s `Click` event handler. The parameters `sender` and `e` provide extra information about the event.

```
Private Sub btnCrashSystem_Click(ByVal sender As System.Object,
  ByVal e As System.EventArgs) Handles btnCrashSystem.Click

End Sub
```

In a `Click` event, the `sender` parameter tells you what control raised the event. In this example, that's the `Button` that the user clicked.

The `e` parameter has the `EventArgs` data type, which doesn't give you a lot of additional information. Fortunately you usually don't need any additional information for a `Button`. Just knowing it was clicked is enough.

Some event handlers provide really useful information in their parameters. For example, the `e` parameter provided by the mouse events `MouseClick`, `MouseMove`, `MouseDown`, and `MouseUp` include the X and Y coordinates of the mouse over the control raising the event. Those values are crucial if you're trying to build a drawing application or need to track the mouse's position for some other reason.

The FollowMouse example program shown in Figure 4-3 (and available as part of this lesson's code download) uses a `MouseMove` event handler to make two scrollbars follow the

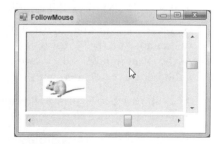

FIGURE 4-3

mouse's position. When you click on the area in the center of the form, the program moves the picture of the mouse to that position.

The program's form contains a green `Panel` control that holds a `PictureBox` that displays the mouse image. The form also contains `VScrollBar` and `HScrollBar` controls. The scrollbars' `Maximum` properties are set to the width and height of the `Panel` so they can hold the coordinates of any point in the `Panel`.

Tracking Mouse Movement

The program's first event handler, which is shown in the following code, catches the `Panel`'s `MouseMove` event whenever the mouse moves across the `Panel`. Note that the `Panel` raises the event only when the mouse is over the `Panel` itself, not when it is over the `PictureBox` inside the `Panel`.

```
' Move the scrollbars to track the mouse.
Private Sub panField_MouseMove(ByVal sender As System.Object,
 ByVal e As System.Windows.Forms.MouseEventArgs) Handles panField.MouseMove
    hscrMouse.Value = e.X
    vscrMouse.Value = e.Y
End Sub
```

The code sets the scrollbars' `Value` properties to the mouse's X and Y coordinates so the scrollbars' thumbs follow the mouse.

Detecting Mouse Clicks

The second event handler, shown in the following code, catches the `Panel`'s `MouseClick` event and moves the `picMouse` control to the mouse's current position:

```
' Move the mouse picture here.
Private Sub panField_MouseClick(ByVal sender As System.Object,
 ByVal e As System.Windows.Forms.MouseEventArgs) _
 Handles panField.MouseClick
    picMouse.Left = e.X
    picMouse.Top = e.Y
End Sub
```

REMOVING EVENT HANDLERS

To remove an event handler, simply delete its code.

If you want to disable an event handler without deleting the code — for example, if you might want to reenable it later — just remove (or, even better, comment out) the `Handles` clause from the end of the event handler's declaration. Without the `Handles` clause, Visual Basic thinks the code is still valid but not associated with the event.

The following code shows the previous `MouseClick` event handler with the `Handles` clause commented out (notice the apostrophe):

```
' Move the mouse picture here.
Private Sub panField_MouseClick(ByVal sender As System.Object,
 ByVal e As System.Windows.Forms.MouseEventArgs) _
```

```
' Handles panField.MouseClick
    picMouse.Left = e.X
    picMouse.Top = e.Y
End Sub
```

 If you delete a control from a form, Visual Studio removes any `Handles` *clauses that involved the control. If you later add another control with the same name, the event handlers are not automatically attached to the new control. This can be confusing if you cut and paste a control. It seems as if nothing should have changed, but actually the control is no longer attached to any event handlers.*

ADDING AND REMOVING EVENT HANDLERS IN CODE

At design time, you can use the Properties window or the Code Editor to attach event handlers to events. Occasionally, you may want to attach or detach an event handler from code at run time. For example, suppose a drawing program needs to track the mouse's position while the user is drawing a curve but not while the user is clicking to select an existing curve. In that case, it might be useful to attach and detach a `MouseMove` event handler depending on what the user is doing.

The following code shows a simple `Button Click` event handler that is not attached to any event. When this event handler executes, it displays a message to the user.

```
' Display a message box.
Private Sub btnClickMe_Click(ByVal sender As System.Object,
 ByVal e As System.EventArgs)
    MessageBox.Show("You clicked me!")
End Sub
```

Suppose you have written this event handler but have not attached it to any control at design time. The following code attaches the event handler to the `btnClickMe` control's `Click` event:

```
AddHandler btnClickMe.Click, AddressOf btnClickMe_Click
```

The `AddHandler` command makes Visual Basic register the event handler so it can handle the event. The command's two parameters provide the event to handle and the address of the code that will handle it.

After running this code, if the user clicks the button, the event handler executes.

The following code removes the event handler from the button's `Click` event:

```
RemoveHandler btnClickMe.Click, AddressOf btnClickMe_Click
```

The DynamicEvents example program, which is available in the Ex4-1 folder of this lesson's code download, lets you add and remove event handlers at run time. Initially the Click Me button does nothing. Click the Attach button to attach an event handler to the Click Me button. Click the Detach button to remove the event handler.

USEFUL EVENTS

Table 4-1 lists some of the more useful events raised by various controls.

TABLE 4-1

EVENT	MEANING
CheckedChanged	A CheckBox's or RadioButton's checked state has changed.
Click	The user has clicked the control.
FormClosing	The form is about to close. Set the e.Cancel parameter to true to cancel the closing and force the form to remain open.
KeyDown	The user pressed a key down while this control had focus.
KeyPress	The user pressed and released a key while this control had focus.
KeyUp	The user released a key while this control had focus.
Load	The form is loaded but not yet visible. This is the last place you can change the form's appearance before the user sees it.
MouseClick	The user pressed and released a mouse button over the control. Unlike the Click event, this event has parameters that indicate the click's location.
MouseDown	The user pressed a mouse button down over the control.
MouseEnter	The mouse has entered the control.
MouseHover	The mouse has hovered over the control.
MouseLeave	The mouse has left the control.
MouseMove	The mouse has moved while over the control.
MouseUp	The user released a mouse button over the control.
Move	The control has moved.
Paint	The control needs to be redrawn. This is useful for drawing graphics.
Resize	The control has resized.
Scroll	The slider on a TrackBar or scrollbar was moved by the user.
SelectedIndexChanged	A ComboBox's or ListBox's selection has changed.
TextChanged	The control's Text property has changed. This is particularly useful for TextBoxes.
Tick	A Timer control's Interval has elapsed.
ValueChanged	The value of a TrackBar or scrollbar was changed (whether by the user or by code).

TRY IT

In this Try It, you use event handlers to display color samples as the user adjusts red, green, and blue `TrackBars`.

Figure 4-4 shows the finished program in action. When you change a `TrackBar`'s value, the label to the right shows the new value, and the large label on the far right shows a sample of the color with the selected red, green, and blue color components (although you can't really see the color in this grayscale figure).

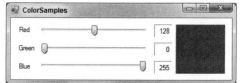

FIGURE 4-4

> *You can download the code and resources for this Try It from the book's web page at* www.wrox.com *or* www.vb-helper.com/24hourvb.html. *You can find them in the Lesson04 folder in the download.*

Lesson Requirements

In this lesson:

➤ Create the form shown in Figure 4-4, and arrange the controls and set their `Anchor` properties.

➤ Make an event handler for the red `TrackBar` that displays all three color values and the color sample.

➤ Attach the event handler to the green and blue `TrackBars`, in addition to the red one.

Hints

This Try It requires a few techniques that haven't been covered yet, but it's not too hard to build with a couple of hints.

➤ A `TrackBar`'s `Value` property is an integer. To convert it into a string so you can display it in the labels, call its `ToString` method. For example, the following code makes the `lblRed` control display `trkRed`'s `Value` property:

```
lblRed.Text = trkRed.Value.ToString()
```

➤ The `Color` class's `FromArgb` method returns a color with given red, green, and blue color components between 0 and 255. For example, `Color.FromArgb(255, 128, 0)` returns the color orange (red = 255, green = 128, and blue = 0). Pass this method the values selected by the `TrackBars` (returned by their `Value` properties) and assign the result to the sample label's `BackColor` property.

Step-by-Step

➤ Create the form shown in Figure 4-4. Arrange the controls and set their Anchor properties.

1. Create the controls as shown in Figure 4-4. For the TrackBars, set the properties Minimum = 0, Maximum = 255, TickStyle = None, and Anchor = Top, Left, Right.

➤ Make an event handler for the red TrackBar that displays all three color values and the color sample.

1. Double-click the red TrackBar to create an empty event handler for the control's Scroll event. You will use this event handler for all three TrackBars so change its name to trk-Color_Scroll so it doesn't imply that it handles only the red TrackBar's Scroll event. Then type the bold lines in the following code so the event handler looks like this:

```
' Display the numeric values and a sample.
Private Sub trkColor_Scroll(ByVal sender As System.Object,
ByVal e As System.EventArgs) _
Handles trkRed.Scroll, trkGreen.Scroll, trkBlue.Scroll
    ' Display numeric values.
    lblRed.Text = trkRed.Value.ToString()
    lblGreen.Text = trkGreen.Value.ToString()
    lblBlue.Text = trkBlue.Value.ToString()

    ' Display a sample.
    lblSample.BackColor = Color.FromArgb(
        trkRed.Value,
        trkGreen.Value,
        trkBlue.Value)
End Sub
```

If you use relaxed delegates to remove the event handler's parameters, the Properties window won't realize that this subroutine is a valid event handler for the TrackBars' Scroll events in the next step so don't remove the parameters now. If you like, you can remove them later after the event handler is connected to the controls' events.

➤ Attach the event handler to the green and blue TrackBars, in addition to the red one.

1. In the Form Designer, click the green TrackBar. In the Properties window, click the event button (the lightning bolt). Then click the control's Scroll event, click the drop-down arrow to the right, and select the event handler.

2. Repeat the previous steps for the blue TrackBar.

Run the program and experiment with it.

Please select Lesson 4 on the DVD to view the video that accompanies this lesson.

EXERCISES

1. Build the DynamicEvents example program described earlier in this lesson. What happens if you click Attach twice? Three times? What happens if you then click Detach once? Five times?

2. Create a form with one `Button` labeled "Stop" and two `Timers`. Set the `Timers'` `Interval` properties to 1000 (this is in milliseconds). At design time, set the first `Timer's` `Enabled` property to `True`.

➤ In each `Timer's` `Tick` event handler, disable that `Timer` and enable the other one.

➤ Make one `Timer's` `Tick` event handler move the `Button` to `(10, 10)` by setting its `Left` and `Top` properties.

➤ Make the other `Timer's` `Tick` event handler move the `Button` to `(200, 200)`.

➤ In the `Button's` `Click` event handler, set `Enabled = false` for both `Timers`.

Run the program. Experiment with different values for the `Timers'` `Interval` properties. What happens if `Interval = 10`?

3. Make a program similar to the one shown in Figure 4-5. When the user changes the scrollbar values, the program should set the `PictureBox's` `Left` and `Top` properties. Use `Anchor` properties to keep the scrollbars at the form's edges and make the background `Panel` fill most of the form. (Hint: When the form loads and when the `Panel` resizes, set the scrollbars' `Maximum` properties so they match the `Panel's` size. You can use the same event handler for both.)

FIGURE 4-5

4. Make a program similar to the one shown in Figure 4-6.

➤ Use `Anchor` properties to make the buttons stick to the form's lower-right corner. Make the `Buttons` be the form's accept and cancel buttons, and make them display message boxes saying "OK" and "Cancel."

➤ Make the `CheckBoxes'` `CheckedChanged` events enable or disable the corresponding `GroupBoxes`.

FIGURE 4-6

Hint: If you drag a `CheckBox` onto a `GroupBox`, it falls into the `GroupBox`. (Try it and run the program to see why that's bad.) To prevent this, position the `CheckBoxes` first and then position the `GroupBoxes` on top of them. Right-click a `GroupBox` and select Send to Back to move it behind its `CheckBox`.

Hint: Set the GroupBoxes' Text properties to a blank value.

Hint: Set a GroupBox's Enabled property equal to the corresponding CheckBox's Checked value.

 You can find solutions to this lesson's exercises in the Lesson04 folder inside the download available on the book's web site at www.wrox.com *or* www.vb-helper.com/24hourvb.html.

5

Making Menus

In addition to buttons, labels, and textboxes, menus are one of the most common user interface elements in interactive programs.

This lesson explains how to add menus and context menus to forms, and catch their events so your program can take action when the user selects menu items.

CREATING MENUS

To create a menu, simply drop a MenuStrip control on a form. By default, the MenuStrip is docked to the top of the form so you don't really need to position it carefully. Just double-click the Toolbox's MenuStrip tool and you're set.

Unlike most controls, the MenuStrip appears in the *Component Tray* below the form in addition to on the form itself. Figure 5-1 shows the SimpleEdit program in the Form Designer. Below the form you can see the Component Tray containing a MenuStrip and a StatusStrip.

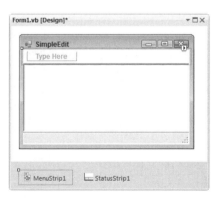

FIGURE 5-1

When you select a MenuStrip in the Form Designer, the menu bar at the top of the form displays a Type Here box. Click that box and type the menu's caption to create a main menu.

If you create a main menu entry and select it, the Form Designer displays a new Type Here box to let you create menu items below it, as shown in Figure 5-2.

The Form Designer also displays a new Type Here box to the right of the main menu item so you can create other main menus.

Continue entering text in the Type Here boxes to build the whole menu structure. Figure 5-3 shows the Format menu for a new version of the SimpleEdit program. Notice that the menu contains several cascading submenus. The Offset submenu is expanded in Figure 5-3.

FIGURE 5-2

You can use the Type Here boxes to create submenus to any depth, although in practice three levels (as in Format ⇨ Offset ⇨ Subscript) are about all the user can stomach.

In addition to menu items, you can place separators, text-boxes, and combo boxes in menus. Textboxes and combo boxes are unusual in menus so I won't cover them here. Separators, however, are quite useful for grouping related menu items.

To create a separator, right-click an item, open the Insert submenu, and select Separator. Alternatively, you can create a normal menu item and set its `Text` to a single dash (-).

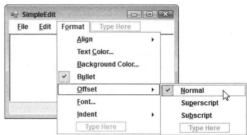

FIGURE 5-3

SETTING MENU PROPERTIES

The items in a menu are `ToolStripMenuItems`, and like other controls, they have properties that determine their appearance and behavior.

Table 5-1 summarizes the most useful `ToolStripMenuItem` properties.

TABLE 5-1

PROPERTY	PURPOSE
Checked	Determines whether the item is checked. In Figure 5-3, the Bullet and Normal items are checked. (See also `CheckOnClick`.)
CheckOnClick	If you set this to `True`, the item automatically toggles its checked state when the user selects it.
Enabled	Indicates whether the item is enabled.
Name	The `ToolStripMenuItem`'s name. Try to provide a descriptive name for any menu item that makes the program do something at run time so your code can refer to it. (My naming convention is `mnu` followed by the names of the menus leading to the item. For example, `mnuFormatOffsetNormal`.)

PROPERTY	PURPOSE
ShortcutKeys	Indicates the item's shortcut key combination (if any). Either type a value such as **Ctrl+C** or click the drop-down arrow to the right to display the shortcut editor shown in Figure 5-4.
Text	The text that the item displays. Place an ampersand (&) before the character that you want to use as the item's accelerator. For example, if you set an item's Text to &Edit, the item appears as Edit in its menu and the user can activate it by pressing [Alt]+E while the menu is open.

For the ShortcutKeys row, the following appears at the right:

> Modifiers:
> ☑ Ctrl ☐ Shift ☐ Alt
> Key:
> C ▾ Reset
>
> **FIGURE 5-4**

ESSENTIAL ELLIPSES

By convention, if a menu item opens a dialog or requires some other feedback from the user before proceeding, its Text should end with an ellipsis (...). If the menu item starts an action immediately, it should not include an ellipsis.

For example, the Open... menu item displays a file open dialog, so its caption ends with an ellipsis. In contrast, the Edit menu's Copy item immediately copies the selected text so it doesn't need an ellipsis.

Accelerators allow the user to navigate menus with the keyboard instead of the mouse. When the user presses [Alt], the menu's items display underlines below their accelerator keys. For example, the File menu might appear as File. The user can then press the accelerator key to open that menu and then use other accelerators to select the menu's items.

Recent versions of the Windows operating system typically don't underline menu accelerators until you press the [Alt] key.

You should assign accelerators to most if not all of your program's menus, submenus, and menu items. Experienced users can often navigate a menu system faster by using accelerators than they can by using the mouse.

Be sure not to assign the same accelerator character to two menu items in the same menu. For example, in the File menu, don't have Save and Save As menu items.

Shortcuts allow the user to instantly activate a menu item even if the menu isn't open. For example, in many programs [Ctrl]+O opens a file and [Ctrl]+S saves the current file. (I can remember the difference between accelerators and shortcuts because "accelerator" and the [Alt] key both begin with the letter "a.")

 Be extra *sure not to give two menu items the same shortcut!*

HANDLING MENU EVENTS

When the user clicks a menu item, its control raises a Click event exactly as a clicked Button does, and you can handle it in the same way. You can even create default event handlers in the same way: by double-clicking the control.

CREATING CONTEXT MENUS

A context menu appears when you right-click a particular control. In Visual Basic, building a context menu is almost as easy as building a form's main menu.

Start by dropping a ContextMenuStrip on the form. Like a MenuStrip, a ContextMenuStrip appears below the form in the Component Tray so you can just double-click the Toolbox's ContextMenuStrip tool and not worry about positioning the menu.

Unlike a MenuStrip, a ContextMenuStrip does not appear at the top of the form. In the Form Designer, you can click a MenuStrip either on the form or in the Component Tray to select it. To select a ContextMenuStrip, you must click it in the Component Tray. (Immediately after you add a ContextMenuStrip to a form, it is selected so you can see it on the form.)

After you select the ContextMenuStrip, it appears at the top of the form and you can edit it much as you can a MenuStrip. The big difference is that a ContextMenuStrip does not have top-level menus, just submenu items.

Figure 5-5 shows the Form Designer with a ContextMenuStrip selected. By now the menu editor should look familiar.

After you create a ContextMenuStrip, you need to associate it with the control that should display it. To do that, select the control's ContextMenuStrip property in the Properties window, click the drop-down arrow on the right, and select the ContextMenuStrip. The rest is automatic.

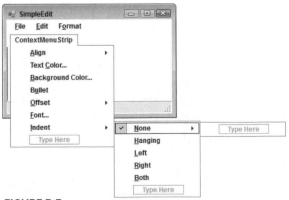

FIGURE 5-5

When the user right-clicks the control at run time, the control automatically displays the ContextMenuStrip.

TRY IT

In this Try It, you create a main menu and a context menu. The main menu includes an Exit command that closes the form. Both menus contain commands that let you change the appearance of a TextBox on the form. Figure 5-6 shows the finished program displaying its context menu.

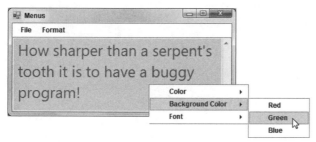

FIGURE 5-6

 You can download the code and resources for this Try It from the book's web page at www.wrox.com or www.vb-helper.com/24hourvb.html. You can find them in the Lesson05 folder in the download.

Lesson Requirements

In this lesson:

➤ Create the form shown in Figure 5-6.

➤ Create the following main menu structure (note the accelerator keys and shortcuts):

File

    Exit

Format

    Color

        Red   Ctrl+R

        Green   Ctrl+G

        Blue   Ctrl+B

        <u>B</u>ackground Color

          <u>R</u>ed

          <u>G</u>reen

          <u>B</u>lue

        <u>F</u>ont

          <u>S</u>mall   Ctrl+S

          <u>N</u>ormal Ctrl+N

          <u>L</u>arge   Ctrl+L

➤ Add code behind the main menu items.

➤ Make the context menu duplicate the main menu's Format submenu.

➤ Attach the context menu items to the event handlers used by the main menu.

➤ Attach the context menu to the `TextBox`.

Hints

➤ The E<u>x</u>it menu item can close the program's form with the code `Me.Close()`.

➤ Creating a font isn't trivial (and I haven't covered that yet). It's much easier to keep a sample of a font in a control somewhere on the form and then set the `TextBox`'s `Font` property equal to that control's `Font` property. And what better control to store the font than the menu item itself?

Step-by-Step

➤ Create the form shown in Figure 5-6.

   1. Create the main menu by double-clicking the Toolbox's `MenuStrip` tool.

   2. Add a `TextBox` to the form. Type some text into its `Text` property and set its other properties as follows: `Name = txtContents`, `MultiLine = True`, `Dock = Fill`, `ScrollBars = Both`.

   3. Create the context menu by double-clicking the Toolbox's `ContextMenuStrip` tool. Name it `ctxFormat`.

➤ Create the main menu structure.

   1. Select the `MenuStrip` and use the Type Here boxes to build the menu structure.

By convention, the E<u>x</u>it command uses X as its accelerator. It never has a short-cut because it would be too easy to accidentally close the program while banging your head on the keyboard (or if you fat-finger the keys, the keyboard is hit by a flying tennis ball, your cat walks across the keyboard, and so on).

2. Use the Properties window to set the font sizes for the Font menu's Small, Normal, and Large items to 6, 9, and 20, respectively.

3. If you like, set the `ForeColor` properties of the color menu items to their respective colors.

4. Give the menu items that take action appropriate names. For example, name the Font submenu's Small item `mnuFormatFontSmall`.

➤ Add code behind the main menu items.

1. Double-click the Exit menu item, remove the event handler's parameters, and type the bold line in the following code so the event handler looks like this:

```
Private Sub mnuFileExit_Click() Handles mnuFileExit.Click
    Me.Close()
End Sub
```

The keyword `Me` means "the object currently executing this code," which in this case means the current form, so this line of code tells the current form to close itself.

2. Double-click the Format ➪ Color ➪ Red menu item, remove the event handler's parameters, and type the bold line in the following code so the event handler looks like this:

```
Private Sub mnuFormatColorRed_Click() _
 Handles mnuFormatColorRed.Click
    txtContents.ForeColor = Color.Red
End Sub
```

3. Repeat step 2 for the Green and Blue menu items.

4. Repeat step 2 for the Format ➪ Background Color menu items, setting the `TextBox`'s `BackColor` property to `Pink`, `LightGreen`, and `LightBlue`.

5. Double-click the Format ➪ Font ➪ Small menu item, remove the event handler's parameters, and type the bold line in the following code so the event handler looks like this:

```
Private Sub mnuFormatFontSmall_Click() _
 Handles mnuFormatFontSmall.Click
    txtContents.Font = mnuFormatFontSmall.Font
End Sub
```

6. Repeat step 5 for the Normal and Large menu items.

➤ Make the context menu duplicate the main menu's Format submenu.

Do either 1 or 2:

1. Build the structure from scratch. (This is straightforward but slow.)

   a. Click the `ContextMenuStrip` in the Component Tray to open it for editing.

   b. Use steps similar to the ones you used to build the main menu's structure to build the context menu's structure. (I use the prefix `ctx` instead of `mnu` for context menu items, as in `ctxColorRed`.)

    2. Copy the Format menu's structure. (This is sneakier and faster, and therefore much cooler!)

        a. Click the `MenuStrip` in the Component Tray to open it for editing. Expand the Format menu. Click the Color item and then [Shift]+click the Font item to select all of the menu's items and their sub-items. Press [Ctrl]+C to copy the menu items into the clipboard.

        b. Click the `ContextMenuStrip` in the Component Tray to open it for editing. Press [Ctrl]+V to paste the menu items into the context menu.

        c. Give appropriate names to the new menu items.

➤ Attach the context menu items to the event handlers used by the main menu.

    1. Open the `ContextMenuStrip` for editing. Expand the Color submenu and click the Red item. In the Properties window, click the Events button (the lightning bolt) to see the menu item's events. Select the `Click` event, click the drop-down arrow to the right, and select `mnuFormatColorRed_Click`.

    2. Repeat step 1 for the `ContextMenuStrip`'s other items, attaching them to the correct event handlers.

➤ Attach the context menu to the `TextBox`.

    1. Click the `TextBox`. In the Properties window, set its `ContextMenuStrip` property to `ctxFormat`.

 Please select Lesson 5 on the DVD to view the video that accompanies this lesson.

EXERCISES

1. (SimpleEdit) Copy the SimpleEdit program you started in Lesson 3, Exercise 1 (or download Lesson 3's version from the book's web site at www.wrox.com) and add the menu structure. The following list shows the menu items. The items that display a dash (-) are separators. Note the shortcuts and underlined accelerator keys. Add the code behind the Exit item, but don't worry about the other items yet.

File

    New   Ctrl+N

    Open   Ctrl+O

    Save   Ctrl+S

    Save As...

    -

    Print Preview   Ctrl+P

Print...

-

E<u>x</u>it

<u>E</u>dit

    <u>U</u>ndo   Ctrl+Z

    <u>R</u>edo   Ctrl+Y

    -

    <u>C</u>opy   Ctrl+C

    Cu<u>t</u>   Ctrl+X

    <u>P</u>aste   Ctrl+V

    <u>D</u>elete   Del

    -

    Select <u>A</u>ll

F<u>o</u>rmat

    <u>A</u>lign

        <u>L</u>eft

        <u>R</u>ight

        <u>C</u>enter

    <u>C</u>olor...

    <u>B</u>ackground Color...

    B<u>u</u>llet

    <u>O</u>ffset

        <u>N</u>ormal

        Su<u>b</u>script

        Su<u>p</u>erscript

    <u>F</u>ont...

    <u>I</u>ndent

        <u>N</u>one

        <u>H</u>anging

        <u>L</u>eft

        <u>R</u>ight

        <u>B</u>oth

Eventually the user will be able to use the Bullet menu item to toggle whether a piece of text is bulleted. To allow Visual Basic to toggle this item for you, set the menu item's `CheckOnClick` property to `True`.

Add a `ContextMenuStrip` that duplicates the Format menu and use it for the `TextBox`'s `ContextMenuStrip` property.

2. (SimpleEdit) Copy the SimpleEdit program you built for Exercise 1 and add images to its menu items. (You can find suitable image files in the `PngFiles` directory of the Lesson 5 download available on the book's web site.) Figure 5-7 shows what the menus should look like when you're finished.

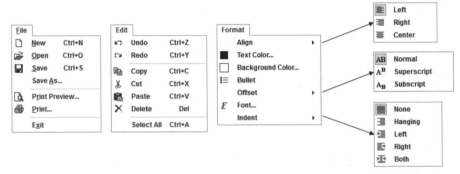

FIGURE 5-7

3. (SimpleEdit) Copy the SimpleEdit program you built for Exercise 2 and add placeholder routines for the menu items' event handlers. The routines should display simple message boxes indicating what they should do. For example, the following code shows the File menu's `Save` event handler:

```
Private Sub mnuFileSave_Click() Handles mnuFileSave.Click
    MessageBox.Show("Save")
End Sub
```

Add placeholders for all menu items (except separators) that do not have submenus. For example, add a placeholder for the Format ⇨ Align ⇨ Left item but not for Format ⇨ Align because it has a submenu.

Attach the context menu's items to the same event handlers but give the context menu's Bullet item its own event handler. (If you make these two share the same event handler, they interfere with each other in Exercise 4 because of their toggling behavior.)

4. (SimpleEdit) Copy the SimpleEdit program you built for Exercise 3 and add code to manage exclusive selections in the Format menu's Align, Offset, and Indent submenus. For example, the user can select only one of the Align submenu's options at a time.

Modify the items' placeholder code so when the user selects an option, the code:

a. Checks the selected submenu item.

b. Unchecks the other submenu items.

c. Checks the corresponding context menu item.

d. Unchecks the corresponding context menu item.

For example, the following code executes when the user selects the Align submenu's Left option:

```
Private Sub mnuFormatAlignLeft_Click() _
 Handles mnuFormatAlignLeft.Click, ctxAlignLeft.Click
    mnuFormatAlignLeft.Checked = True
    mnuFormatAlignRight.Checked = False
    mnuFormatAlignCenter.Checked = False
    ctxAlignLeft.Checked = True
    ctxAlignRight.Checked = False
    ctxAlignCenter.Checked = False

    MessageBox.Show("Align Left")
End Sub
```

5. (SimpleEdit) Make the Format ➪ Bullet menu item and the Bullet context menu item check and uncheck each other.

 You can find solutions to this lesson's exercises in the Lesson05 folder inside the download available on the book's web site at www.wrox.com *or* www.vb-helper.com/24hourvb.html.

6

Making Tool Strips and Status Strips

Not every program needs a tool strip or status strip, but they can make the user's life easier, particularly for complicated programs. This lesson explains how to add tool strips and status strips to your applications.

USING TOOL STRIPS

Usually a tool strip sits below a form's menu bar and displays a series of small buttons that enable the user to easily perform frequently executed tasks. The buttons typically duplicate functions that are also available in menus, but placing them on the tool strip makes it easier for the user to find and use them.

Place only the most frequently used commands in the tool strip so it doesn't become cluttered.

Recall from Lesson 5 that you should also give most if not all of your menu items accelerators, and you can give the most important commands shortcuts. That means the user can access the most important and useful commands in at least four ways: mouse menu navigation, accelerators, shortcuts, and tool strip buttons.

To create a single tool strip, simply double-click the Toolbox's `ToolStrip` tool. By default, the `ToolStrip` docks to the top of the form so you don't need to position it manually.

 Recall from Lesson 3 that docked controls are drawn in their stacking order, which by default is the same as their creation order. To avoid confusion, if a form should contain a main menu and a tool strip, create the menu first so the tool strip appears below it and not above it.

When you select a `ToolStrip`, the Form Designer displays a little icon with a drop-down arrow. Click the arrow to display a list of items that you might want to add to the `ToolStrip`, as shown in Figure 6-1.

As you can see from Figure 6-1, you can add the following types of objects to a `ToolStrip`:

FIGURE 6-1

➤ Button

➤ Label

➤ SplitButton

➤ DropDownButton

➤ Separator

➤ ComboBox

➤ TextBox

➤ ProgressBar

The `SplitButton` and `DropDownButton` are new controls that you haven't seen before in the Toolbox so they deserve a little explanation.

The `SplitButton` normally displays a button holding an icon and a drop-down arrow. (You can change its `DisplayStyle` property to make it display text instead of an image, both, or neither.) If the user clicks the button, its `Click` event fires. If the user clicks the drop-down arrow, a menu appears. As is the case with all menus, if the user selects an item, that item's `Click` event fires.

One way you might use a `SplitButton` would be to have the menu items perform some action and then change the button's icon to match the action. Clicking the button would perform the action again.

In other words, you can think of the button as representing a tool, and clicking it activates the current action. Selecting an item from the drop-down menu selects a new tool and activates it.

The `DropDownButton` is similar to the `SplitButton` except it doesn't provide a button that the user can click to repeat the previous command. It's basically a drop-down menu.

Although they can contain many different kinds of controls, `ToolStrips` look best when they are not too cluttered and confusing. For example, a `ToolStrip` that contains only `Buttons` and `Separators` is easy to understand and use. `DropDownButtons` and `SplitButtons` are the next easiest controls to understand and they don't clutter things up too much so you can add them if necessary.

Avoid using `Labels` in a `ToolStrip` to provide status information. Instead, place status information in a `StatusStrip`.

USING TOOL STRIP CONTAINERS

A `ToolStripContainer` displays areas on a form's top, left, bottom, and right edges that can hold `ToolStrips`. At run time, the user can drag `ToolStrips` back and forth within and among these areas.

The center of the `ToolStripContainer` is a content panel that can hold one or more other controls.

In a typical configuration for these controls, a form optionally contains a `MenuStrip` and `StatusStrip` docked to the form's top and bottom, respectively. A `ToolStripContainer` is docked to fill the rest of the form, and its content panel contains the rest of the program's controls.

Figure 6-2 shows a form that contains a `MenuStrip` at the top, a `StatusStrip` at the bottom, and a `ToolStripContainer` filling the rest of the form. The `ToolStripContainer` holds three `ToolStrips` and a `RichTextBox` docked to fill its content panel.

FIGURE 6-2

Figure 6-3 shows this program at run time. Here, I have dragged two of the `ToolStrips` to the `ToolStripContainer`'s left and right edges.

Two things in Figure 6-2 are of particular note. First, notice the thin rectangles holding arrows on the middle of the content panel's sides. If you click one of these, the control adds room on that edge so you can insert another `ToolStrip`.

The second thing of note in Figure 6-2 is the smart tag, which looks like a little square holding an arrow in the control's upper-right corner. If you click the smart tag, the smart tag panel shown in Figure 6-4 appears.

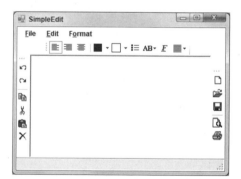

FIGURE 6-3

In general, smart tags provide quick ways to perform common tasks for a control. In this example, the smart tag panel lets you decide which panels the control should allow. If you uncheck one of the panels, at run time the user cannot drag `ToolStrips` to that edge of the `ToolStripContainer`.

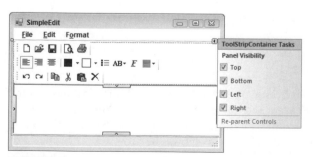

FIGURE 6-4

> *You can also determine which panels are available by setting the control's LeftToolStripPanelVisible, RightToolStripPanelVisible, TopToolStripPanelVisible, and BottomToolStripPanelVisible properties in the Properties window, but using the smart tag is easier.*

After you build the `ToolStripContainer`, simply place `ToolStrips` on it and build their items as usual.

USING STATUS STRIPS

A status strip is normally docked to a form's bottom edge and displays labels, icons, and other controls to give the user a quick summary of the application's status. This area should be reserved for status information and should generally not include buttons and other controls that make the application perform an action. Those commands belong in menus and tool strips.

To create a status strip, simply double-click the Toolbox's `StatusStrip` tool. By default, the `StatusStrip` docks to the bottom of the form so you don't need to position it manually.

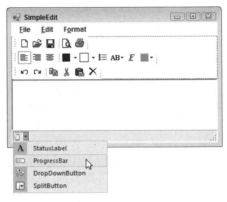

FIGURE 6-5

When you select a `StatusStrip`, the Form Designer displays a little icon with a drop-down arrow similar to the one it displays for a `ToolStrip`. Click the arrow to display a list of items that you might want to add to the `StatusStrip`, as shown in Figure 6-5.

As you can see from Figure 6-5, you can add the following types of objects to a `ToolStrip`:

➤   `StatusLabel`

➤   `ProgressBar`

➤   `DropDownButton`

➤   `SplitButton`

The only new control, `StatusLabel`, behaves like a normal `Label`.

TRY IT

In this Try It, you create a `MenuStrip` (covered in Lesson 5) and a `ToolStrip`, both containing commands to change a `RichTextBox` control's `ForeColor` and `BackColor` properties. You also create a `StatusStrip` to show the currently selected colors. (Yes, I know this is redundant because the values are shown in the `ToolStrip` and in the text itself.) Figure 6-6 shows the program.

You can download the code and resources for this Try It from the book's web page at www.wrox.com *or* www.vb-helper.com/24hourvb.html. *You can find them in the* Lesson06 *folder in the download.*

Lesson Requirements

In this lesson:

➤ Create the form shown in Figure 6-6.

➤ Create the MenuStrip. The menu's hierarchy should be:

File

    Exit

Format

    Text Color

        Black

        Red

        Green

        Blue

    Background Color

        White

        Pink

        Green

        Blue

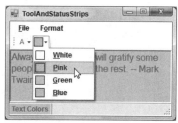

FIGURE 6-6

➤ Initially check the Text Color menu's Black option and the Background Color menu's White option.

➤ Give the Background Color menu items Images that display samples of the color.

➤ Create the ToolStrip with buttons that duplicate the menu hierarchy. The ToolStrip should hold two ToolStripDropDownButtons.

➤ Give the StatusStrip a ToolStripStatusLabel named lblColor with Text = Text Colors.

➤ Add event handlers.

Make the File menu's Exit item close the form.

Make the event handlers for each of the Text Color menu items set the appropriate properties for the `RichTextBox`, menu items, toolbar buttons, and status label. Check the selected menu and toolbar items and uncheck the others.

DUPLICATE CODE

As you will probably notice, this lesson's Try It includes event handlers that duplicate the same code with minor differences. In general, if large pieces of code do almost the same things with minor changes, then there's probably something wrong with the program's design.

In cases such as this, you should extract the common code into a separate procedure. You can use `If`, `Select Case`, and other Visual Basic statements to have the code take different actions for different situations, enabling the same procedure to handle multiple situations.

Unfortunately, you don't know how to do any of that yet. Lesson 20 explains how to write procedures, and Lesson 18 describes statements such as `If` and `Select Case`. Until then, you're stuck with some duplicate code.

After you read Lessons 18 and 20, you can revisit this section if you would like to remove the redundant code, making it easier to maintain in the future. (The process of restructuring existing code to make it more reliable, easier to read, easier to maintain, or otherwise better without changing its functionality is called *refactoring*.)

Hints

➤ Recall that the E<u>x</u>it menu item can close the program's form by calling `this.Close()`.

➤ Use the menu items' event handlers for the corresponding tool strip button event handlers.

Step-by-Step

➤ Create the form shown in Figure 6-6.

   1. Start a new project.

   2. Add a `MenuStrip` to the form.

   3. Add a `StatusStrip` to the form.

   4. Add a `ToolStripContainer` to the form.

   5. Add a `RichTextBox` named `rchContent` inside the `ToolStripContainer`'s content panel.

➤ Create the `MenuStrip`.

   1. Add the indicated menu items to the `MenuStrip`. Remember to give them descriptive names and appropriate accelerator keys.

➤ Initially check the Text Color menu's Black option and the Background Color menu's White option.

1. Set the Text Color ➪ Black menu item's Checked property to True.

2. Set the Background Color ➪ White menu item's Checked property to True.

➤ Give the Background Color menu items Images that display samples of the color.

1. Set the Image properties of these menu items to samples of their colors. (Use Microsoft Paint or some other graphical editor to make small, colored images.)

➤ Create the ToolStrip with buttons that duplicate the menu hierarchy. The ToolStrip should hold two ToolStripDropDownButtons.

Name the first tool ToolStripDropDownButton btnTextColor and make it display the text "A." Give it the items Black, Red, Green, and Blue. Each item should have ForeColor property set to its color.

1. Create the ToolStripDropDownButton.

2. Below that item, add the items Black, Red, Green, and Blue.

3. Set the ForeColor property for each of these items to show its color (for example, set the Black item's ForeColor property to black).

Name the second tool ToolStripDropDownButton btnBackColor and make it initially display a white color sample. Give it the items White, Pink, Green, and Blue. Make each of these display an Image showing a sample of the color.

1. Create the ToolStripDropDownButton.

2. Below that item, add the items White, Pink, Green, and Blue.

3. Set the Image property for each of these items to show samples of their colors.

➤ Give the StatusStrip a ToolStripStatusLabel named lblColor with Text = Text Colors.

1. Create the ToolStripStatusLabel. Set its Name and Text properties.

➤ Add event handlers.

Make the File menu's Exit item close the form.

1. Type the following bold line of code so the event handler looks like this:

```
Private Sub fileExitMenuItem_Click() Handles mnuFileExit.Click
    Me.Close()
End Sub
```

Make the event handlers for each of the Text Color menu items set the appropriate properties for the `RichTextBox`, menu items, toolbar buttons, and status label. Check the selected menu and toolbar items and uncheck the others.

1. For the Format ⇨ Text Color ⇨ Black menu item, type the following bold code so the event handler looks like this:

```
' Set the text color.
Private Sub mnuFormatTextColorBlack_Click() _
 Handles mnuFormatTextColorBlack.Click, btnTextColorBlack.Click
    rchContents.ForeColor = Color.Black
    btnTextColor.ForeColor = Color.Black
    lblColor.ForeColor = Color.Black

    mnuFormatTextColorBlack.Checked = True
    mnuFormatTextColorRed.Checked = False
    mnuFormatTextColorGreen.Checked = False
    mnuFormatTextColorBlue.Checked = False

    btnTextColorBlack.Checked = True
    btnTextColorRed.Checked = False
    btnTextColorGreen.Checked = False
    btnTextColorBlue.Checked = False
End Sub
```

2. Enter similar code for the other Text Color menu items.

3. Enter similar code for the other Background Color menu items.

4. Use the menu items' event handlers for the corresponding tool strip button event handlers.

    a. Click the Properties window's Events button.

    b. For each tool strip button:

    Click the button in the Form Designer.

    On the Properties window, select the `Click` event. Then click the drop-down arrow to the right.

    Select the appropriate menu event handler. For example, for the `btnTextColorBlack` tool strip button, select the `mnuFormatTextColorBlack _Click` event handler.

 Please select Lesson 6 on the DVD to view the video that accompanies this lesson.

EXERCISES

1. (SimpleEdit) Copy the SimpleEdit program you built in Lesson 5, Exercise 5 (or download Lesson 5's version from the book's web site) and add the tool strips, buttons, and separators shown in Figure 6-7. Delete the `RichTextBox` control, add a `ToolStripContainer`, and then re-add the `RichTextBox` inside the `ToolStripContainer`'s content panel.

The black button (fourth from the left on the second tool strip row) is a `ToolStripSplitButton` that lets the user pick a text color. It contains the options Black, White, Red, Green, and Blue.

The white button next to the text color button is another `ToolStripSplitButton`. This button lets the user pick a background color. It contains the options Black, White, Pink, Green, Blue, and Yellow.

The button that says "AB" is a `ToolStripDropDownButton` that provides the same options as the Format menu's Offset submenu: Normal, Superscript, and Subscript.

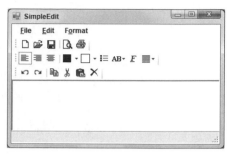

FIGURE 6-7

2. (SimpleEdit) Copy the SimpleEdit program you built for Exercise 1 and add menu item code to manage the new tool strip buttons. Add code to synchronize corresponding menu, context menu, and tool strip button items. For example, the following shows the new code for the Align Left menu item:

```
Private Sub mnuFormatAlignLeft_Click() _
  Handles mnuFormatAlignLeft.Click, ctxAlignLeft.Click
    mnuFormatAlignLeft.Checked = True
    mnuFormatAlignRight.Checked = False
    mnuFormatAlignCenter.Checked = False
    ctxAlignLeft.Checked = True
    ctxAlignRight.Checked = False
    ctxAlignCenter.Checked = False
    btnAlignLeft.Checked = True
    btnAlignRight.Checked = False
    btnAlignCenter.Checked = False

    MessageBox.Show("Align Left")
End Sub
```

3. (SimpleEdit) Copy the SimpleEdit program you built for Exercise 2 and attach the tool strip buttons to the corresponding event handlers. Write new event handlers for tool strip buttons that don't have corresponding menu items.

4. (SimpleEdit) Copy the SimpleEdit program you built for Exercise 3 and add code to display the appropriate image in the Background, Text Color, Offset, and Indent tool strip buttons. For example, when the user selects Offset Subscript, the `btnOffset` button and the `mnuFormatOffset` menu item should show the subscript image.

5. (SimpleEdit) Copy the SimpleEdit program you built for Exercise 4 and add appropriate tool-tips to the program's menu items and tool strip buttons. For example, set the `btnAlignLeft` button's `ToolTipText` property to "Align the selected text on the left."

6. Build the Scribbler program shown in Figure 6-8. Give it a `ToolStripContainer` and two `ToolStrips`. Give the first `ToolStrip` buttons representing arrow, line, rectangle, ellipse, scribble, and star tools. Use code to make these tools exclusive options so if the user selects one, the others are deselected. Give the second `ToolStrip` two `ToolStripDropDownButtons` to represent foreground and background colors. Use code to make the entries in each drop-down exclusive options so if the user selects one, the others are deselected. Give the color buttons appropriate images when the user picks a color. Give all of the tool strip buttons appropriate tooltips.

FIGURE 6-8

 You can find solutions to this lesson's exercises in the Lesson06 folder inside the download available on the book's web site at www.wrox.com *or* www.vb-helper .com/24hourvb.html.

7

Using RichTextBoxes

The `TextBox` control lets the user enter text and that's about it. It can display its text in different colors and fonts, but it cannot give different pieces of text different properties. The `TextBox` is intended to let the user enter a simple string, like a name or street address, and little more.

The `RichTextBox` is a much more powerful control. It can display different pieces of text with different colors, fonts, and styles. It can adjust paragraph indentation and make bulleted lists. It can even include pictures. It's not as powerful as a full-featured word processor, such as Microsoft Word or OpenOffice's Writer, but it can produce a much more sophisticated result than the `TextBox`.

In this lesson you learn more about the `RichTextBox` control and how to use it. You have a chance to experiment with the control, and you use it to add enough functionality to the SimpleEdit program to finally make the program useful.

USING RICHTEXTBOX PROPERTIES

To change the appearance of the text inside a `RichTextBox`, you first select the text that you want to change, and then you set one of the control's properties to modify the text.

To select the text, you use the control's `SelectionStart` and `SelectionLength` properties to indicate where the text begins and how many letters it includes. Note that the letters are numbered starting with 0. (In fact, almost all numbering starts with 0 in Visual Basic.) For example, setting `SelectionStart` = 0 and `SelectionLength` = 1 selects the control's first letter.

After you select the text, you set one of the `RichTextBox`'s properties to the value that you want the text to have.

For example, the following code makes the `RichTextBox` named `rchContent` display some text and color the word "red":

```
rchContent.Text = "Some red text"
rchContent.SelectionStart = 5
rchContent.SelectionLength = 3
rchContent.SelectionColor = Color.Red
```

Table 7-1 lists properties that you can use to change the text's appearance.

TABLE 7-1

PROPERTY	PURPOSE
SelectionAlignment	Aligns the selection's paragraph on the left, center, or right.
SelectionBackColor	Sets the selection's background color.
SelectionBullet	Determines whether the selection's paragraph is bulleted.
SelectionCharOffset	Determines whether the selection is superscript (offset > 0), subscript (offset < 0), or normal (offset = 0).
SelectionColor	Sets the selection's color.
SelectionFont	Sets the selection's font.
SelectionHangingIndent	The first line in the selection's paragraph is indented normally and then subsequent lines in the paragraph are indented by this amount.
SelectionIndent	All lines are indented by this amount.
SelectionProtected	Marks the selected text as protected so the user cannot modify it.
SelectionRightIndent	All lines are indented on the right by this amount.

The FontFeatures example program shown in Figure 7-1 demonstrates properties that change the appearance of text within a paragraph. These include the `SelectionBackColor`, `SelectionCharOffset`, `SelectionColor`, and `SelectionFont`.

The ParagraphFeatures program shown in Figure 7-2 demonstrates properties that change

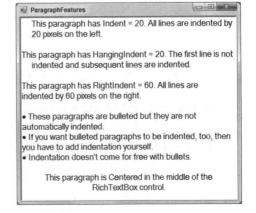

FIGURE 7-1

FIGURE 7-2

the way paragraphs are displayed. These include `SelectionIndent`, `SelectionHangingIndent`, `SelectionRightIndent`, `SelectionBullet`, and `SelectionAlignment`.

 Both the FontFeatures and ParagraphFeatures sample programs are available as part of the Lesson07 download at www.wrox.com *or* www.vb-helper .com/24hourvb.html.

Table 7-2 summarizes four additional properties that change the text displayed by the control that deserve special mention.

TABLE 7-2

PROPERTY	PURPOSE
Text	Gets or sets the control's complete text without any formatting properties.
Rtf	Gets or sets the control's Rich Text Format (RTF) contents. This includes the text plus RTF formatting codes that define how the text should be displayed.
SelectedText	Gets or sets the selection's text.
SelectedRtf	Gets or sets the selection's text and RTF codes.

GIVING THE USER CONTROL

Allowing the user to change text settings is easy. When the user selects text in the control, the `RichTextBox` sets its `SelectionStart` and `SelectionLength` properties accordingly. All you need to do is set the appropriate property (for example, `SelectionColor`) and the selected text is updated.

The SetTextProperties example program shown in Figure 7-3 (and available as part of the Lesson 7 code download) uses this technique to let the user control text color, character offset, and paragraph alignment. Select text and then click the tool strip buttons to change the text's properties.

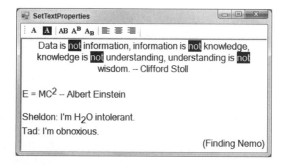

FIGURE 7-3

The following code shows how the program changes the currently selected text to have a black background and white foreground:

```
Private Sub btnReversedColors_Click() Handles btnReversedColors.Click
    rchContent.SelectionColor = Color.White
```

```
        rchContent.SelectionBackColor = Color.Black
    End Sub
```

The program's other buttons work similarly.

USING RICHTEXTBOX METHODS

Lesson 2 briefly described properties, methods, and events. Other lessons have also worked with many properties and events. In fact, most of the event handlers I've discussed in the lessons so far catch an event and change a property in response.

Though you've worked with many properties and events, the only method you've seen is the form's `Close` method, which makes the form go away. For example, the following code closes the form that executes it:

```
    Me.Close()
```

The `RichTextBox` provides many new methods that are helpful for building a text editing program. Table 7-3 summarizes some of the most useful.

TABLE 7-3

METHOD	PURPOSE
Clear	Clears all text from the control.
Copy	Copies the current selection into the clipboard.
Cut	Cuts the current selection onto the clipboard.
DeselectAll	Deselects all text by setting `SelectionLength` = 0.
LoadFile	Loads the control's text from a file with one of various formats such as RTF or plain text.
Paste	Pastes whatever is in the clipboard into the current selection. This can be anything that the `RichTextBox` understands, such as text, RTF formatted text, or an image.
Redo	Redoes the previously undone command.
SaveFile	Saves the control's text into a file in one of various formats, such as RTF or plain text.
SelectAll	Selects all of the control's text by setting `SelectionStart` = 0 and `SelectionLength` equal to the text's length.
Undo	Undoes the most recent change.

The following code shows how a program can use the `LoadFile` method. The first parameter gives the name of the file, which can be relative to the program's current directory or a full path. The second parameter gives the type of file.

```
rchContent.LoadFile("Test.rtf", RichTextBoxStreamType.RichText)
```

TYPING TIPS

When you type `rchContent.LoadFile`, IntelliSense displays a popup showing the parameters that the `LoadFile` method expects, as shown in Figure 7-4.

FIGURE 7-4

There are several different *overloaded* versions of the method to choose from. Overloaded versions of a method have the same name but take different parameters.

Use the up and down arrow keys to scroll through the method's available versions.

As you enter parameters, IntelliSense updates to describe the next parameter that it expects. For example, after you enter a filename, IntelliSense updates to indicate that it expects a file type next.

The following code shows how a program can use the `SaveFile` method. As with `LoadFile`, the first parameter gives the file's name and the second gives its type.

```
rchContent.SaveFile("Test.rtf", RichTextBoxStreamType.RichText)
```

 TRY IT

Available for
download on
Wrox.com

In this Try It, you add functionality to some of the SimpleEdit program's menu items and tool strip buttons. You use the `RichTextBox` properties and methods to implement the commands in the Edit menu: Undo, Redo, Copy, Cut, Paste, Delete, and Select All. (This also makes the corresponding buttons work at no extra charge.)

> *You can download the code and resources for this Try It from the book's web page at* www.wrox.com *or* www.vb-helper.com/24hourvb.html. *You can find them in the Lesson07 folder in the download.*

Lesson Requirements

In this lesson:

➤ Copy the SimpleEdit program you built in Lesson 6, Exercise 5.

➤ Add code to handle the Edit menu's commands.

    ➤ Add Undo code.

    ➤ Add Redo code.

    ➤ Add Copy code.

    ➤ Add Cut code.

    ➤ Add Paste code.

    ➤ Add Delete code.

    ➤ Add Select All code.

Hints

➤ For the Delete menu item, simply set the control's SelectedText property to an empty string (" ").

Step-by-Step

➤ Copy the SimpleEdit program you built in Lesson 6, Exercise 5 (or download Lesson 6's version from the book's web site).

➤ Add code to handle the Edit menu's commands.

1. Open the program's form in the Form Designer. Click the MenuStrip, expand the Edit menu, and double-click the Undo menu item.

2. Replace the placeholder call to MessageBox.Show with the following line of code so the event handler looks like this:

```
Private Sub mnuEditUndo_Click() _
 Handles mnuEditUndo.Click, btnUndo.Click
    rchDocument.Undo()
End Sub
```

3. Repeat the previous two steps for the other Edit menu items invoking the Redo, Copy, Cut, Paste, and SelectAll commands.

4. For the Delete menu item, set the control's SelectedText property to an empty string (" ").

When you finish, test the program's new features. One of the RichTextBox's more remarkable features is its ability to paste different kinds of items from the clipboard. For example, copy a picture to the clipboard and then use the program to paste it into the RichTextBox.

Please select Lesson 7 on the DVD to view the video that accompanies this lesson.

EXERCISES

1. (SimpleEdit) Copy the SimpleEdit program you built for the Try It and add simple code to handle the File menu's New, Open, and Save commands. For the New command, simply clear the RichTextBox. For the Open and Save commands, just load and save the file Test.rtf. (The program will create the file the first time you save. If you try to open the file before it exists, the program will crash, so don't use Open before you use Save.) Lesson 8 explains how to use File Open and Save dialogs to let the user pick the file that should be opened or saved.

2. (SimpleEdit) Copy the SimpleEdit program you built for Exercise 1 and add code to handle the Format menu's commands (except for the Font command, which is covered in Lesson 8). Remove the placeholder MessageBox.Show commands.

    Hints:

    ➤ Keep the code that manages the menu items and tool strip buttons. For example, keep the code that ensures only one alignment menu item and button are selected at a time.

    ➤ When the user clicks a color button, copy the appropriate color to the btnTextColor and btnBackgroundColor buttons' ForeColor and BackColor properties.

    ➤ To set the foreground color, use the color stored in btnTextColor.ForeColor.

    ➤ To set the background color, use the color stored in btnBackgroundColor. BackColor.

    ➤ Set the control's SelectionBullet property to the value of the bullet button's Checked property like this:

    ```
    rchDocument.SelectionBullet = btnBullet.Checked
    ```

    ➤ Make the indentation commands (None, Hanging, Left, Right, and Both) reset any other indentations. For example, the Hanging command should set the SelectionIndent and SelectionRightIndent properties to 0 as in the following code:

    ```
    rchDocument.SelectionIndent = 0
    rchDocument.SelectionRightIndent = 0
    rchDocument.SelectionHangingIndent = 0
    ```

3. The SimpleEdit program allows only the indentation styles None, Hanging, Left, Right, and Both. It doesn't allow other combinations such as Hanging plus Left. Build a program that uses tool strip buttons to let the user select each of the indentation properties (Hanging, Left, and Right) individually. Provide a fourth button to clear all the indentation properties.

You can find solutions to this lesson's exercises in the Lesson07 folder inside the download available on the book's web site at www.wrox.com *or* www.vb-helper .com/24hourvb.html.

8

Using Standard Dialogs

A huge number of applications need to display dialogs to enable users to select certain standard pieces of information. Two of the most common dialogs enable users to select a file to open and select a file to save into. Other dialogs enable users to select colors, filesystem folders, fonts, and printers for printing.

Closely related to the Print dialog are the Print Preview dialog (which enables users to see a preview of a document before sending it to the printer, possibly saving paper if the user then cancels the document) and the Page Setup dialog (which enables users to modify things like margins before printing).

You could build all of these dialogs yourself (or you will be able to once you've finished reading this book), but fortunately you don't need to do that. Because many programs need the exact same features, Microsoft has provided standard dialogs that everyone can use.

Visual Basic comes with the following standard dialogs that handle these common tasks:

- ➤ ColorDialog
- ➤ FolderBrowserDialog
- ➤ FontDialog
- ➤ OpenFileDialog
- ➤ PageSetupDialog
- ➤ PrintDialog
- ➤ PrintPreviewDialog
- ➤ SaveFileDialog

You might remember that in Lesson 1 I said that normally you don't need to worry about whether a feature is provided by Visual Studio, the Visual Basic language, or the .NET Framework. That's true here as well, but it's informative to note that these dialogs are actually provided by the .NET Framework, not Visual Basic. That doesn't change the way you use them, but it means they're the same dialogs used by all .NET languages such as C#, Visual C++, or JScript.

In this lesson you learn how to display these standard dialogs. You learn how to initialize them to show users the program's current settings, how to tell whether the user clicked the dialog's OK or Cancel button, and how to respond to the user's selection.

This lesson actually cheats a bit on the printing dialogs. Although it explains how to display these dialogs, you can't do anything really useful with them until you know how to print, which is a much more complicated topic. Lesson 33 covers the details of how to print.

USING DIALOGS IN GENERAL

You use all of the standard dialogs in more or less the same way. The only differences are how you initialize the dialogs so they show colors, fonts, files, or whatever, and how you handle the results.

You use a standard dialog by following these four steps:

1. Add the dialog to the form.
2. Initialize the dialog to show current settings.
3. Display the dialog and check the return result.
4. Process the results.

Adding the Dialog to the Form

You add a dialog to a form just as you add any other component such as a `Timer`. Like other components, the dialog appears below the form in the component tray.

The control Toolbox has a Dialogs tab that contains most of the standard dialogs, so they are easy to find. The printing-related dialogs are contained in the Printing tab, so they're also easy to find (if you know to look there). Figure 8-1 shows the Toolbox's Printing and Dialogs tabs.

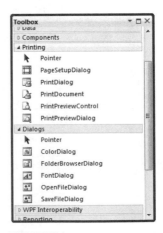

FIGURE 8-1

Initializing the Dialog

Most of the standard dialogs start with some initial selection. The FontDialog starts with a font selected, the ColorDialog starts with a color selected, and so forth. Normally you should initialize the dialog so it shows the program's current settings. For example, a FontDialog should show the program's current font.

Usually making these initial selections is easy. Simply set the dialog's key property (Font, Color, Filename) to the value you want to display.

For example, the following code sets a ColorDialog's Color property to the form's current BackColor value. (Recall that Me means the form or other object that is currently executing the code.)

```
cdBackColor.Color = Me.BackColor
```

The only real trick here is knowing what properties to set. Table 8-1 lists the key properties for the different kinds of dialogs.

TABLE 8-1

DIALOG	KEY PROPERTY
ColorDialog	Color
FolderBrowserDialog	SelectedPath
FontDialog	Font
OpenFileDialog	FileName
SaveFileDialog	FileName

The PageSetupDialog, PrintDialog, and PrintPreviewDialog are a bit different from the others so I won't say anything more about them here. Printing is covered in more detail in Lesson 33.

I just said that you should initialize the dialogs to show current values, but the file open and save dialogs have a special feature that enables you to skip this step. When you use these dialogs, they remember the directories they displayed last. That means if the user opens one of these dialogs again, it opens in the same directory it was in the last time. In fact, if the user closes and restarts the program, the dialogs still remember where they were last.

The only reason you might want to initialize these dialogs is if you want the program to separately track more than one file (perhaps different places to save text files, bitmaps, and RTF files).

Displaying the Dialog and Checking the Return Result

You display all of the standard dialogs by calling their ShowDialog methods. ShowDialog displays the dialog modally and then returns a value to tell you whether the user clicked OK, Cancel, or some other button.

Note that the OK buttons on some of the dialogs don't actually say "OK." The `OpenFileDialog`'s *OK button says "Open," the* `SaveFileDialog`'s *OK button says "Save," and the* `PrintDialog`'s *OK button says "Print." As far as the program is concerned, however, they're all OK buttons, and you test for them all in the same way.*

Your code should test the returned result; and if the user clicked OK, it should do something with the user's selection.

Unfortunately, to make that test, you need to use an `If` statement, and `If` statements aren't covered until Lesson 18. Luckily, this particular use of `If` statements is quite simple, so I only feel a little guilty about showing it to you now.

The following code shows how a program can display a `ColorDialog` named `cdBackColor`. The code calls the `ShowDialog` method. It then compares the value that `ShowDialog` returns to the value `DialogResult.OK`. If the values are equal, the program does whatever is between the `Then` keyword and `End If` statement (which I've omitted here).

```
If (cdBackColor.ShowDialog() = DialogResult.OK) Then
    ...
End If
```

If the user clicks the Cancel button, then `ShowDialog` returns the value `DialogResult.Cancel`, so the `If` test fails and the program skips the code up to the `End If` statement.

Processing the Results

Finally, if the user clicks OK, the program should do something with whatever the user selected in the dialog. Often this means doing the inverse of the step where you initialized the dialog. For example, suppose a program uses the following code to initialize its `ColorDialog`:

```
cdBackColor.Color = Me.BackColor
```

In this case, it would use the following code to set the form's `BackColor` property to the color that the user selected:

```
Me.BackColor = cdBackColor.Color
```

Putting It All Together

The following code shows the whole sequence for a `ColorDialog`. The program initializes the dialog, displays it and checks the return value, and processes the result.

```
cdBackColor.Color = Me.BackColor
If (cdBackColor.ShowDialog() = DialogResult.OK) Then
    Me.BackColor = cdBackColor.Color
End If
```

This looks a bit more complicated than previous code examples but it's not too bad. The only new part is the If test. The other statements simply set the dialog's Color property equal to the form's BackColor property and vice versa, and you've been setting properties for quite a while now.

USING DIALOG PROPERTIES

Table 8-1, earlier in this lesson, listed the dialogs' key properties, but some of the dialogs have other useful properties, too.

For example, the ColorDialog has an AllowFullOpen property that determines whether the user can click the dialog's Define Custom Colors button to display an area where the user can create new colors. Figure 8-2 shows a ColorDialog displaying this area.

You can learn more about these extra properties by reading the online help. For example, Microsoft's help page for the ColorDialog is msdn.microsoft.com/en-us/library/system .windows.forms.colordialog.aspx. You can replace *colordialog* in this URL with the name of another dialog to find its web page.

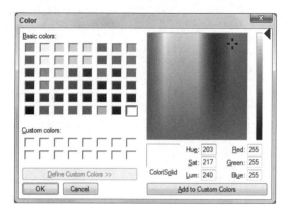

FIGURE 8-2

Table 8-2 summarizes the ColorDialog's most useful properties.

TABLE 8-2

PROPERTY	PURPOSE
AllowFullOpen	Determines whether the user can create custom colors
Color	The selected color
FullOpen	Determines whether the custom color area is displayed when the dialog appears

Table 8-3 summarizes the FolderBrowserDialog's most useful properties.

TABLE 8-3

PROPERTY	PURPOSE
RootFolder	The root folder where the dialog starts browsing. This can take values such as Desktop, Favorites, History, and MyComputer. The Properties window lets you pick from those values.
SelectedPath	The selected folder.

Table 8-4 summarizes the FontDialog's most useful properties.

TABLE 8-4

PROPERTY	PURPOSE
FixedPitchOnly	Determines if the dialog allows the user to select only fixed-width fonts. This is useful, for example, if you are going to use the font to build a report and you need all the characters to have the same width so columns line up properly.
Font	The selected font.
FontMustExist	Determines whether or not the dialog raises an error if the selected font doesn't exist (for example, if the user types "ExtraBold" for the font style and that style isn't available for the selected font).
MaxSize	The largest allowed size for the font.
ShowColor	Determines whether or not the dialog lets the user select a font color. If you set this to True, use the dialog's Color property to determine which color the user selected.
ShowEffects	Determines whether or not the dialog lets the user select under-line, strikeout, and font color. (To select font color, ShowColor and ShowEffects must both be True.)

Table 8-5 summarizes the OpenFileDialog's most useful properties.

TABLE 8-5

PROPERTY	PURPOSE
AddExtension	If this is True and the user selects a filename without an extension, the dialog adds the default extension to the name.
CheckFileExists	If this is True, the dialog won't let the user pick a file that doesn't exist.
CheckPathExists	If this is True, the dialog won't let the user pick a file path that doesn't exist.
DefaultExt	The default file extension.
FileName	The selected file's name.
Filter	The file selection filter. (See the section "Using File Filters" later in this lesson for details.)
FilterIndex	The index of the currently selected filter. (See the section "Using File Filters" later in this lesson for details.)

PROPERTY	PURPOSE
InitialDirectory	The directory in which the dialog initially opens.
ReadOnlyChecked	Indicates whether the user checked the dialog's Read Only box.
ShowReadOnly	Determines whether the dialog displays its Read Only box.
Title	The text displayed in the dialog's title bar.

The `SaveFileDialog` has many of the same properties as the `OpenFileDialog`. See Table 8-5 for descriptions of the properties `AddExtension`, `CheckFileExists`, `CheckPathExists`, `DefaultExt`, `FileName`, `Filter`, `FilterIndex`, `InitialDirectory`, and `Title`.

Table 8-6 summarizes the `SaveFileDialog` properties that are not shared with the `OpenFileDialog`.

TABLE 8-6

PROPERTY	PURPOSE
CreatePrompt	If this is `True` and the user selects a file that doesn't exist, the dialog asks if the user wants to create the file.
OverwritePrompt	If this is `True` and the user selects a file that already exists, the dialog asks if the user wants to overwrite it.
ValidateNames	Determines whether the dialog verifies that the filename doesn't contain any invalid characters.

Table 8-7 summarizes the `PrintDialog`'s most useful property.

TABLE 8-7

PROPERTY	PURPOSE
Document	This property tells the dialog what document object to print. Lesson 33 has more to say about this.

Table 8-8 summarizes the `PrintPreviewDialog`'s most useful property.

TABLE 8-8

PROPERTY	PURPOSE
Document	This property tells the dialog what document object to preview. Lesson 33 has more to say about this.

USING FILE FILTERS

Most of the dialogs' properties are fairly easy to understand. Two properties that are particularly confusing and important, however, are the `Filter` and `FilterIndex` properties provided by the `OpenFileDialog` and `SaveFileDialog`.

The `Filter` property is a list of text prompts and file matching patterns separated by the pipe (|) character. The items alternate between text prompts and their corresponding filters. The dialog provides a drop-down list from which the user can select one of the text prompts. When the user selects a prompt, the dialog uses the corresponding filter to decide which files to display.

For example, consider the following `Filter` value:

```
Bitmap Files|*.bmp|Graphic Files|*.bmp;*.gif;*.png;*.jpg|All Files|*.*
```

This value represents three file types:

➤ The text prompt "Bitmap Files" with filter `*.bmp`.

➤ The text prompt "Graphic Files" with filter `*.bmp;*.gif;*.png;*jpg`. That filter matches files ending with .bmp, .gif, .png, or .jpg.

➤ The text prompt "All Files" with filter `*.*`.

Figure 8-3 shows an `OpenFileDialog`. The filter drop-down (just above the Open and Cancel buttons) has the text prompt "Graphics Files" selected. (The dialog automatically added the filter in parentheses.) The dialog is listing the files in this directory that match the filter. In this case, the directory contains only a few `.png` files (some other nongraphical files are not listed because they don't match the filter).

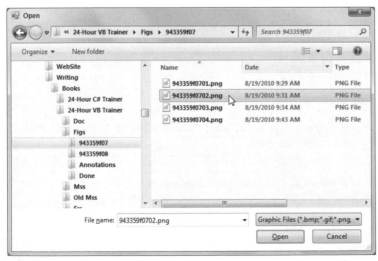

FIGURE 8-3

Once you understand the `Filter` property, the `FilterIndex` property is simple. `FilterIndex` is simply the index of the selected filter, where 1 means the first filter. (Remember in Lesson 7 when I said that "almost all numbering starts with 0 in Visual Basic?" This is one of the rare exceptions.) You can use `FilterIndex` to initially select the filter that you think will be most useful for the user.

The `OpenFileDialog` and `SaveFileDialog` both use the same type of `Filter` and `FilterIndex` properties. In fact, usually if a program displays both of these dialogs, they should use the same `Filter` value. If a program can load .txt and .rtf files, it should probably be able to save .txt and .rtf files.

> To carry this idea one step further, you could set the `SaveFileDialog`'s `FilterIndex` property to the value selected by the user in the `OpenFileDialog` under the assumption that a user who loads a .txt file is later likely to want to save it as a .txt file.

TRY IT

In this Try It, you get to experiment with all the standard dialogs except the `PageSetupDialog` (which is hard to use until you're doing actual printing). You initialize, display, and process the results of the dialogs (if the user clicks the OK button).

> You can download the code and resources for this Try It from the book's web page at www.wrox.com or www.vb-helper.com/24hourvb.html. You can find them in the Lesson08 folder in the download.

Lesson Requirements

In this lesson:

➤ Use `Labels`, `TextBoxes`, and `Buttons` to make a form similar to the one shown in Figure 8-4.

➤ Add `ColorDialog`, `FontDialog`, `FolderBrowserDialog`, `OpenFileDialog`, `SaveFileDialog`, `PrintDialog`, and `PrintPreviewDialog` components to the form.

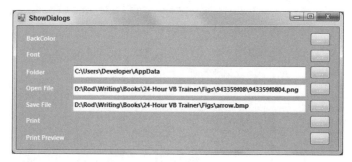

FIGURE 8-4

➤ When the user clicks the BackColor button, display the `ColorDialog` but don't allow the user to define custom colors. If the user clicks OK, set the form's `BackColor` property to the dialog's `Color` value.

➤ When the user clicks the Font button, display the `FontDialog`, allowing the user to select the font's color. If the user clicks OK, set the form's `Font` property to the dialog's `Font` value and its `ForeColor` property to the dialog's `Color` property.

➤ When the user clicks the Folder button, display the `FolderBrowserDialog`. Make the dialog start browsing at MyComputer. If the user clicks OK, make the Folder `TextBox` display the dialog's `SelectedPath` property.

➤ When the user clicks the Open File button, display the `OpenFileDialog`. Use a filter that lets the user select text files, RTF files, or all files. If the user clicks Open, make the Open File `TextBox` display the dialog's `FileName` property and set the `SaveFileDialog`'s `FilterIndex` equal to the `OpenFileDialog`'s `FilterIndex`.

➤ When the user clicks the Save File button, display the `SaveFileDialog`. Use a filter similar to the one used by the `OpenFileDialog`. If the user clicks Save, make the Save File `TextBox` display the dialog's `FileName` property and set the `OpenFileDialog`'s `FilterIndex` equal to the `SaveFileDialog`'s `FilterIndex`.

➤ When the user clicks the Print button, display the `PrintDialog`. Ignore the return result.

➤ When the user clicks the Print Preview button, display the `PrintPreviewDialog`. Ignore the return result.

Hints

➤ Be sure to initialize each of the dialogs before displaying them.

Step-by-Step

➤ Use `Labels`, `TextBoxes`, and `Buttons` to make a form similar to the one shown in Figure 8-4.

1. Add the controls to the form.

2. Use `Anchor` properties to make the `TextBoxes` grow when the form grows.

➤ Add `ColorDialog`, `FontDialog`, `FolderBrowserDialog`, `OpenFileDialog`, `SaveFileDialog`, `PrintDialog`, and `PrintPreviewDialog` components to the form.

1. Add the dialogs.

2. Give the dialogs descriptive names.

➤ When the user clicks the BackColor button, display the `ColorDialog` but don't allow the user to define custom colors. If the user clicks OK, set the form's `BackColor` property to the dialog's `Color` value.

1. To prevent the user from defining custom colors, set the `ColorDialog`'s `AllowFullOpen` property to `False`.

2. Use code similar to the following:

```
cdBackColor.Color = Me.BackColor
If (cdBackColor.ShowDialog() = DialogResult.OK) Then
    Me.BackColor = cdBackColor.Color
End If
```

➤ When the user clicks the Font button, display the FontDialog, allowing the user to select the font's color. If the user clicks OK, set the form's Font property to the dialog's Font value and its ForeColor property to the dialog's Color property.

1. To allow the user to select the font's color, set the dialog's ShowColor property to True.

2. Use code similar to the following:

```
fdFont.Color = Me.ForeColor
fdFont.Font = Me.Font
If (fdFont.ShowDialog() = DialogResult.OK) Then
    Me.Font = fdFont.Font
    Me.ForeColor = fdFont.Color
End If
```

➤ When the user clicks the Folder button, display the FolderBrowserDialog. Make the dialog start browsing at MyComputer. If the user clicks OK, make the Folder TextBox display the dialog's SelectedPath property.

1. To start browsing at MyComputer, set the dialog's RootFolder property to MyComputer at design time.

2. Use code similar to the following:

```
If (fbdFolder.ShowDialog() = DialogResult.OK) Then
    txtFolder.Text = fbdFolder.SelectedPath
End If
```

➤ When the user clicks the Open File button, display the OpenFileDialog. Use a filter that lets the user select text files, RTF files, or all files. If the user clicks Open, make the Open File TextBox display the dialog's FileName property and set the SaveFileDialog's FilterIndex equal to the OpenFileDialog's FilterIndex.

1. Use the filter:

```
Text Files|*.txt|RTF Files|*.rtf|All Files|*.*
```

2. Use code similar to the following:

```
If (ofdOpenFile.ShowDialog() = DialogResult.OK) Then
    txtOpenFile.Text = ofdOpenFile.FileName
    sfdSaveFile.FilterIndex = ofdOpenFile.FilterIndex
End If
```

➤ When the user clicks the Save File button, display the SaveFileDialog. Use a filter similar to the one used by the OpenFileDialog. If the user clicks Save, make the Save File TextBox display the dialog's `FileName` property and set the `OpenFileDialog`'s `FilterIndex` equal to the `SaveFileDialog`'s `FilterIndex`.

1. Use the same filter you used for the `OpenFileDialog`.

2. Use code similar to the following:

```
If (sfdSaveFile.ShowDialog() = DialogResult.OK) Then
    txtSaveFile.Text = sfdSaveFile.FileName
    ofdOpenFile.FilterIndex = sfdSaveFile.FilterIndex
End If
```

➤ When the user clicks the Print button, display the `PrintDialog`. Ignore the return result.

1. Use code similar to the following:

```
pdPrint.ShowDialog()
```

➤ When the user clicks the Print Preview button, display the `PrintPreviewDialog`. Ignore the return result.

1. Use code similar to the following:

```
ppdPrintPreview.ShowDialog()
```

 Please select Lesson 8 on the DVD to view the video that accompanies this lesson.

EXERCISES

1. (SimpleEdit) Copy the SimpleEdit program you built in Lesson 7, Exercise 2 (or download Lesson 7's version from the book's web site) and add the Open File and Save File dialogs for the File menu's Open and Save As commands. Use `Filter` properties that let the user select RTF files, text files, or all files. Continue using the `RichTextBox`'s `LoadFile` and `SaveFile` methods even though they won't really work properly for non-RTF files.

2. (SimpleEdit) Copy the SimpleEdit program you built for Exercise 1 and add a font selection dialog for the Format menu's Font item, and the font tool strip button. If the user selects a font and clicks OK, set the form's font to the selected font.

3. (SimpleEdit) Copy the SimpleEdit program you built for Exercise 2 and add color selection dialogs for the Format menu's Text Color and Background Color items. At design time, remove the images displayed by the color menu and context menu items. Also remove any code that sets those images.

 You can find solutions to this lesson's exercises in the Lesson08 folder inside the download available on the book's web site at www.wrox.com *or* www.vb-helper .com/24hourvb.html.

Creating and Displaying New Forms

So far, this book has dealt mostly with building forms. Previous lessons explained how to add, arrange, and handle the events of controls on a single form.

In this lesson you learn how to display multiple forms in a single program. You learn how to add new forms to the project and how to display one or more instances of those forms. Once you've mastered these techniques, you can make programs that display any number of forms for all kinds of different purposes.

ADDING NEW FORMS

To add a new form to a project, open the IDE's Project menu and select Add Windows Form. Leave the Windows Form template selected, enter a descriptive name for the new type of form, and click Add. After you click Add, Visual Studio adds the new form type to the project. Figure 9-1 shows the new form in Solution Explorer.

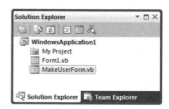

FIGURE 9-1

Now you can add Labels, TextBoxes, Buttons, MenuStrips, and any other controls you want to the new form.

 Remember that to open a form in the Form Designer, double-click it in Solution Explorer.

UNDERSTANDING CLASSES AND INSTANCES

When you add a new form to the project, you're really adding a new *type* of form, not a new instance of that type. If you add the `MakeUserForm` type to a project and then run the program, you still see only the original startup form (with the catchy name `Form1`), and `MakeUserForm` is nowhere to be seen.

Form types such as `Form1` and `MakeUserForm` are examples of *classes*. A class is like a blueprint for making items based on that class. The items themselves are called *instances* of the class. These are important and sometimes confusing topics so I'm going to explain them briefly now and then explain them again in greater detail later in the book in the lessons in Section IV.

A class defines the characteristics of any objects from that class. Your code can use the `New` keyword to create objects of the class. Once you define the class, you can make as many copies (instances) as you like, and every copy is identical in structure to all the others. Different instances may have different property values but their overall features are the same.

For example, suppose you define a `MakeUserForm` that has FirstName, LastName, Street, City, State, and ZIP labels and textboxes. Now suppose your program displays two instances of this class. Both of the forms will have the same labels and textboxes, so they have basically the same structure. However, the user can type different values into the two forms.

Your code can also change different instances in various ways. For example, menu items, buttons, and other controls could invoke event handlers that modify the form: change its colors, move controls around, resize the form, or whatever. Here's one of the more potentially confusing features of classes: The code in the event handlers modifies only the form that is currently running the code.

For example, suppose you build a form that has three `Buttons` that change the form's `BackColor` property to red, green, and blue, and then you display three instances of the form. When the user clicks the first form's Red button, the event handler makes the first form red but the other forms are unchanged. The code in the event handler is running in the first form's instance so that's the only instance of the form it affects.

Hopefully, by now you think I've beaten this topic into the ground and you understand the difference between the class (`MakeUserForm`) and the instance (a copy of `MakeUserForm` visible on the screen). If so, you're ready to learn how to actually display forms.

DISPLAYING FORMS

The `New` keyword creates a new instance of a form (or other class). If you want to do anything useful with the form, your code needs a way to refer to the instance it just created. It can do that with a *variable*. I'm jumping the gun a bit by discussing variables (they're covered in detail in Lesson 11) but, as was the case when I introduced the `If` statement in Lesson 8, this particular use of the concept is very useful and not too confusing, so I only feel a little guilty about discussing it now.

To declare a variable to refer to a form instance, you use the `Dim` keyword, followed by the name that you want to give the variable, the `As` keyword, and the variable's data type, which in this case is the form's type. For example, the following code declares a variable named `frmMakeUser` of type `MakeUserForm`:

```
Dim frmMakeUser As MakeUserForm
```

At this point, the program has a variable that *could* refer to a `MakeUserForm` object but right now it doesn't refer to anything. The variable contains the special value `Nothing`, which basically means it refers to no object.

To make the variable refer to a form instance, the code uses the `New` keyword to create the instance and then sets the variable equal to the result. For example, the following code creates a new `MakeNewUser` form and makes the `frmMakeUser` variable point to it:

```
frmMakeUser = New MakeUserForm()
```

Now the variable refers to the new form. The final step is to display that form. You can do that by calling the new form's `ShowDialog` or `Show` method.

> *Technically, the variable doesn't hold or contain the form. Instead it contains a reference to the form. The reference is like an address that points to where the form actually resides in memory. When your code says something like* `frmMakeUser.Show()`, *it hunts down the actual form instance and invokes its* `Show` *method.*
>
> *For now the distinction is small and you don't need to worry too much about it, but later it will be useful to know that some variables are value types that actually hold their values (`Integer`, `Long`, `Double`) and some are reference types that hold references to their values (object references and, interestingly, `String`). Lesson 17 says a bit more about this when it discusses structures.*

The `ShowDialog` method displays the form *modally*. That means the form appears on top of the program's other forms and the user cannot interact with the other forms until this form closes.

This is the way dialogs normally work. For example, when you open the IDE's Project menu and select Add Windows Form, the Add New Item dialog displays modally so you cannot interact with other parts of the IDE (the Properties window, Solution Explorer, the menus) until you close the dialog by clicking Add or Cancel.

The following code displays the form referred to by the variable `frmMakeUser` modally:

```
frmMakeUser.ShowDialog()
```

The `Show` method displays the form *nonmodally*. That means the form appears and the user can interact with it or with the program's other forms.

The following code displays the form referred to by the variable `frmMakeUser` nonmodally:

```
frmMakeUser.Show()
```

Visual Basic allows two other syntaxes for defining and instantiating objects. First, you can declare and initialize the object all in one line as in the following code:

```
Dim frmMakeUser As MakeUserForm = New MakeUserForm()
```

You can use similar code to declare and initialize other kinds of variables, too.

The final syntax for defining and instantiating an object declares the variable as a new instance of the class as in the following code:

```
Dim frmMakeUser As New MakeUserForm()
```

These two versions are concise, easy to understand, and keep the definition of the variable close to where it is initialized. Contrast this with the case where the code declares a variable and initializes it much later. At that point, you may not remember how the variable was declared.

Because of these considerations, the last syntax is preferred by most developers.

The UserForms example program shown in Figure 9-2 (and available as part of this lesson's code download at `www.wrox.com` or `www.vb-helper.com/24hourvb.html`) displays a main form with a New User button. Each time you click the button, the program displays a new `MakeUserForm`. In Figure 9-2, you can see the main form and two `MakeUserForms`.

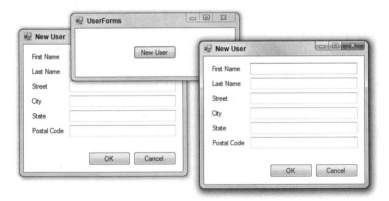

FIGURE 9-2

The following code shows how the UserForms program displays a new `MakeUserForm` when you click its button. The code declares and initializes a new form and displays it nonmodally.

```
' Make and display a new MakeUserForm.
Private Sub btnNewUser_Click() Handles btnNewUser.Click
    Dim frmMakeUser As New MakeUserForm()
    frmMakeUser.Show()
End Sub
```

Each time you click the button, the event handler executes again. Each time it runs, the event handler creates a new version of the variable named `frmMakeUser`, makes a new instance of the `MakeUserForm`, and displays that instance; so each time you click the button, you get a new form.

FLOOD OF FORMS

The startup form's type `Form1` is just like any other form type, so a program can make new instances of it. That means you can create more forms that look just like the startup form if you want.

However, though all forms look about the same to the user, the startup form has a special position in the application. The program keeps running only as long as the startup form exists. If you close that form, all of the others close too.

To avoid confusion, you should generally make the startup form look different from other forms so the user knows that it is special.

CONTROLLING REMOTE FORMS

When you create a new form and make a variable to refer to it, you can later use that variable to manipulate the form. There's just one catch: the techniques described so far don't keep the new form variable around long enough to be useful.

For example, the following code creates and displays a new form:

```
' Make and display a new MakeUserForm.
Private Sub btnNewUser_Click() Handles btnNewUser.Click
    Dim frmMakeUser As New MakeUserForm()
    frmMakeUser.Show()
End Sub
```

When the code finishes executing the event handler, the event handler stops running. If the user clicks the button again, the event handler springs back into action.

Unfortunately, when the event handler stops running, it loses its grip on the `frmMakeUser` variable. The next time the event handler runs, it creates a new variable named `frmMakeUser` and works with that one.

This is bad for a program that wants to manipulate the new form later. Because the variable is gone, it cannot refer to it to manipulate the form.

The good news is that this is fairly easy to fix. If you move the variable's declaration out of the event handler, the variable exists throughout the program's lifetime. The event handler can make the variable point to a new form, and it can then use the variable later to manipulate that form.

The following code demonstrates this technique. The main form's `Load` event handler creates and displays a new `ColorForm`. When the user clicks the main form's Red button, its event handler changes the remote form's `BackColor` and `ForeColor` properties. The startup form also contains green and blue buttons that have similar event handlers.

```
' The remote form we will manipulate.
Dim frmRemoteColor As ColorForm
```

```
' Make the new ColorForm and display it.
Private Sub Form1_Load() Handles MyBase.Load
    frmRemoteColor = New ColorForm()
    frmRemoteColor.Show()
End Sub

' Set the ColorForm's colors.
Private Sub btnRed_Click() Handles btnRed.Click
    frmRemoteColor.BackColor = Color.Red
    frmRemoteColor.ForeColor = Color.Pink
    frmRemoteColor.lblMessage.Text = "I'm red!"
End Sub
```

Here the `frmRemoteColor` variable is declared outside of the event handlers. The form's `Load` event handler initializes the variable and displays the remote form. The `btnRed_Click` event handler uses it. Because the variable is declared outside of the event handlers, they can all use it. (Lesson 13 has more to say about when and where variables are available to the code.)

Just as you can declare and initialize a variable in a single statement inside an event handler, you can do the same outside of an event handler. In that case, the program's Load *event handler doesn't need to initialize the variable, although the program still needs the event handler to display the new form.*

The following code shows the new version of the preceding code.

```
' Declare and initialize the remote form we will manipulate.
Dim frmRemoteColor As New ColorForm()

' Display the ColorForm.
Private Sub Form1_Load() Handles MyBase.Load
    frmRemoteColor.Show()
End Sub

' Set the ColorForm's colors.
Private Sub btnRed_Click() Handles btnRed.Click
    frmRemoteColor.BackColor = Color.Red
    frmRemoteColor.ForeColor = Color.Pink
    frmRemoteColor.lblMessage.Text = "I'm red!"
End Sub
```

The RemoteForm example program shown in Figure 9-3 (and available as part of this lesson's code download at www.wrox.com or www.vb-helper.com/24hourvb.html) uses similar code to make its `ColorForm` red, green, or blue.

FIGURE 9-3

In addition to modifying a remote form's properties, you can change the properties of the controls on that form. You refer to a control by using the form variable, followed by a dot, followed by the control's name.

For example, the bold line in the following code accesses the form referred to by the `frmRemoteColor` variable. It locates that form's `lblMessage` control and changes its `Text` property to "I'm red!"

```
' Set the ColorForm's colors.
Private Sub btnRed_Click() Handles btnRed.Click
    frmRemoteColor.BackColor = Color.Red
    frmRemoteColor.ForeColor = Color.Pink
    frmRemoteColor.lblMessage.Text = "I'm red!"
End Sub
```

Allowing one form direct access to a second form's controls is considered bad practice by some developers because it potentially lets the first form mess up the contents of the second. In technical terms, this weakens the second form's encapsulation, its ability to hide its internal details from the outside world.

A more restrictive approach would be to add a public SetCaption procedure to the ColorForm. *Then other code would call that procedure instead of setting the label's text directly. You learn how to build procedures such as this one in Lesson 20.*

TRY IT

In this Try It, you create an application similar to the one shown in Figure 9-4. When the user clicks the main form's buttons, the program displays the other forms nonmodally.

You can download the code and resources for this Try It from the book's web page at www.wrox.com *or* www.vb-helper.com/24hourvb.html. *You can find them in the Lesson09 folder in the download.*

FIGURE 9-4

Lesson Requirements

In this lesson:

➤ Create the forms shown in Figure 9-4.

➤ Declare and initialize the form variables outside of any event handler.

➤ Add code to the main form's Button event handlers to display the corresponding secondary forms nonmodally.

Hints

➤ Normally every form appears in the taskbar. To avoid cluttering the taskbar with all the secondary forms, set their ShowInTaskbar properties to False.

Step-by-Step

➤ Create the forms shown in Figure 9-4.

  1. Create the main form as shown in Figure 9-4.

  2. Create the GettingThereForm.

   a. Open the Project menu and select Add **Windows** Form. Enter the form type name GettingThereForm and click Add.

   b. Set the form's ShowInTaskbar property to False.

   c. Add the Label, ListBox, and Buttons as shown in Figure 9-4. Set the Anchor properties appropriately.

3. Repeat step 2 to create the `GettingAroundForm`.

4. Repeat step 2 to create the `LodgingForm`.

5. Repeat step 2 to create the `FunStuffForm`.

➤ Declare and initialize the form variables outside of any event handler.

1. Add the following to the main form's code module outside of any event handlers:

```
' Declare and initialize the forms but don't display them.
Dim frmGettingThere As New GettingThereForm()
Dim frmGettingAround As New GettingAroundForm()
Dim frmLodging As New LodgingForm()
Dim frmFunStuff As New FunStuffForm()
```

➤ Add code to the main form's `Button` event handlers to display the corresponding secondary forms nonmodally.

1. Use code similar to the following:

```
' Display the getting there form.
Private Sub gettingThereButton_Click() Handles btnGettingThere.Click
    frmGettingThere.Show()
End Sub

' Display the getting around form.
Private Sub gettingAroundButton_Click() Handles btnGettingAround.Click
    frmGettingAround.Show()
End Sub

' Display the lodging form.
Private Sub lodgingButton_Click() Handles btnLodging.Click
    frmLodging.Show()
End Sub

' Display the fun stuff form.
Private Sub funStuffButton_Click() Handles btnFunStuff.Click
    frmFunStuff.Show()
End Sub
```

 Please select Lesson 9 on the DVD to view the video that accompanies this lesson.

EXERCISES

1. Make a program that displays a `Button` that says "New Form." When the user clicks the `Button`, display a new nonmodal instance of the same kind of form. (What happens when you click the new form's button? What happens if you close the new form? What happens if you make several forms and close the original one?)

2. Copy the program you made for Exercise 1 and add a `TextBox` named `txtValue` to the form. Before you display the new form, copy the main form's `TextBox` value into the new form's `TextBox`.

3. Make a program that displays a `TextBox` and a "New Form" `Button`. When the user clicks the `Button`, display a new form of type `MessageForm` modally.

   Give the `MessageForm` two `Labels`. Make the first `Label` say "You entered" and leave the second `Label` blank. When the main program displays the `MessageForm`, it should copy whatever is in its `TextBox` into the `MessageForm`'s second label.

4. Build the PickAPicture program shown in Figure 9-5. When the user clicks one of the thumbnail images on the main form, the program should display a `PictureForm` showing the image at full scale. Use whatever images you like. (Hints: Display the thumbnail images in `PictureBoxes` with `ScaleMode` set to `Zoom`. Set the `PictureForm`'s `BackgroundImage` property equal to the `PictureBox`'s `Image` value.)

FIGURE 9-5

5. **Extra Credit:** As I've mentioned before, redundant code is usually a sign that the program's structure can be improved. The PickAPicture program from Exercise 4 uses four practically identical event handlers. The only difference is the image that they assign to the `PictureForm`'s background.

You can improve this program by making all four PictureBoxes use the same event handler and making the event handler figure out which image to use.

The event handler's sender parameter is the control that raised the event — in this case, the PictureBox that the user clicked. The data type of that parameter is Object, but you can get a variable of type PictureBox that refers to the same object by using the DirectCast statement. DirectCast takes two parameters: an object and the type into which you want to convert that object. In this example, it takes an Object that happens to refer to a PictureBox and returns a PictureBox variable referring to the same object. The following code shows how you can get a variable that treats the sender parameter as a PictureBox:

```
Dim pic As PictureBox = DirectCast(sender, PictureBox)
```

Of course you cannot use the sender parameter if you use relaxed delegates to remove it, so don't.

Copy the program you built for Exercise 4. Modify the first event handler so it uses DirectCast to get a reference to the PictureBox that the user clicked, and then uses that PictureBox to set the PictureForm's background. Delete the other event handlers and make all the PictureBoxes share the modified one. Rename the event handler to Picture_Click so its name doesn't imply that it only handles the first PictureBox's Click event.

 You can find solutions to this lesson's exercises in the Lesson09 folder inside the download available on the book's web site at www.wrox.com *or* www.vb-helper.com/24hourvb.html.

10

Building Custom Dialogs

The standard dialogs described in Lesson 8 make it easy to perform typical chores such as picking files, folders, colors, and fonts. Those dialogs can get you pretty far, but sometimes you may want a dialog that is customized for your application.

For example, you might want to display a dialog in which the user can enter a new customer's contact information (name, address, phone number, hat size, and so on). It's unlikely that any predefined standard dialog exists for that exact situation.

Fortunately, it's easy to build custom dialogs. All you need to do is build a new form as described in Lesson 9, add a few buttons, and set a few properties.

In this lesson you learn how to build custom dialogs and make them as easy to use as the standard dialogs that come with Visual Basic.

MAKING CUSTOM DIALOGS

Building a custom dialog is pretty easy. Simply add a new form to your project as described in Lesson 9 and give it whatever controls you need.

FIGURE 10-1

To allow the user to finish using the dialog, add one or more buttons. Some dialogs have a single OK button. Others have OK and Cancel buttons, or some other combination of buttons. Because you're creating the dialog, you can give it whatever buttons you like.

By convention, the buttons go at the bottom of the dialog in the right corner. Figure 10-1 shows a very simple dialog that contains a single textbox where the user can enter a name.

To make using the dialog easier, you can set the form's `AcceptButton` and `CancelButton` properties. These determine which button is triggered if the user presses [Enter] and [Esc], respectively. Typically the `AcceptButton` triggers the dialog's OK or Yes button, and the `CancelButton` triggers the Cancel or No button.

Often dialogs set other properties to make them behave more like standard dialogs. Some of these include the following:

➤ Setting `FormBorderStyle` to `FixedDialog` so the user cannot resize the dialog

➤ Setting `MinimumSize` and `MaximumSize` to keep the dialog a reasonable size

➤ Setting `MinimizeBox` and `MaximizeBox` to `False` so the user cannot maximize or minimize the dialog

➤ Setting `ShowInTaskbar` to `False` so the dialog doesn't clutter up the taskbar

You can make the dialog even easier to use if you set the tab order so the focus starts at the top of the form and works its way down. For example, if the dialog contains Name, Street, City, State, and ZIP textboxes, the focus should move through them in that order.

SETTING THE DIALOG RESULT

A program uses the `ShowDialog` method to display a dialog. This method returns a value that indicates which button the user clicked. As explained in Lesson 8, the program can check that return value to see what it should do with the dialog's results. The examples in Lesson 8 checked that `ShowDialog` returned the value `DialogResult.OK` before processing the user's selections.

A form's `DialogResult` property determines what value the call to `ShowDialog` returns. For example, you could use the following code to make the dialog's OK `Button` set the form's `DialogResult` property to `DialogResult.OK` to tell the calling program that the user clicked the OK button:

```
' Return OK to ShowDialog.
Private Sub btnOk_Click() Handles btnOk.Click
    Me.DialogResult = DialogResult.OK
End Sub
```

Setting the form's `DialogResult` property not only determines the return result, but also closes the dialog so the call to `ShowDialog` returns and the calling code can continue.

That means you can set the dialog's return result and close the dialog in a single line of code. Typing one line of code should be no real hardship, but believe it or not there's an even easier way to close the dialog.

If you set a `Button`'s `DialogResult` property, the `Button` automatically sets the form's `DialogResult` property when it is clicked. For example, suppose you set the `btnCancel`'s `DialogResult` property to `DialogResult.Cancel`. When the user clicks the `Button`, it automatically sets the form's `DialogResult` property to `DialogResult.Cancel` so the form automatically closes. That enables you to set the return value and close the form without typing any code at all.

If you think setting one Button property is still too much work, you can even avoid that, at least for the Cancel button. When you set a form's CancelButton property, Visual Basic automatically sets that Button's DialogResult property to DialogResult.Cancel.

Note that when you set the form's AcceptButton property, Visual Basic does not automatically set the Button's DialogResult property. The assumption is that the OK Button might need to validate the data on the form before it decides whether to close the dialog. For example, if the user doesn't fill in all required fields, the OK Button might display a message asking the user to fill in the remaining fields instead of closing the dialog.

If you don't want to perform any validation, you can simply set the OK Button's DialogResult property to DialogResult.OK yourself in the Properties window.

USING CUSTOM DIALOGS

A program uses a custom dialog in exactly the same way that it uses a standard dialog. It creates, initializes, and displays the dialog. It checks the return result and takes whatever action is appropriate.

There's a slight difference in how the program creates the dialog because you can add standard dialogs to a form at run time, something you can't do with custom dialogs. To use a custom dialog, the code needs to create a new instance of the dialog's form as described in Lesson 9.

The following code shows how a program might display a new customer dialog:

```
' Display the new customer form.
Private Sub btnNew_Click() Handles btnNew.Click
    ' Create and display a NewCustomerForm dialog.
    Dim dlgNewCustomer As New NewCustomerForm()

    If (dlgNewCustomer.ShowDialog() = DialogResult.OK) Then
        ' ... Create the new customer here ...
    End If
End Sub
```

The code declares a variable to refer to the dialog and makes a new dialog. It displays the dialog by using its ShowDialog method and checks the return result. If the user clicks OK, the program takes whatever steps are needed to create the new customer, such as adding a record to a database.

 TRY IT

In this Try It, you build and use a simple custom dialog. The dialog lets you enter a name. If you enter a nonblank value and click OK, the main form adds the name you entered to a ListBox.

This Try It also gives you a little practice using the ListBox control, showing how to add and remove items.

You can download the code and resources for this Try It from the book's web page at www.wrox.com *or* www.vb-helper.com/24hourvb.html. *You can find them in the Lesson10 folder in the download.*

Lesson Requirements

In this lesson:

➤ Create the main form shown on the upper left in Figure 10-2. Make the New Comedian `Button` be the form's `AcceptButton` and the Delete Comedian `Button` be the form's `CancelButton`.

➤ Create the dialog shown on the lower right in Figure 10-2. Set the `AcceptButton` and `CancelButton` properties in the obvious way.

➤ Make the New Comedian `Button` display the dialog. If the dialog returns `DialogResult.OK`, add the new comedian's name to the `ListBox`.

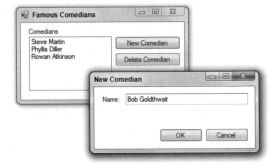

➤ Make the Delete Comedian `Button` remove the currently selected comedian from the `ListBox`.

➤ When the user clicks the dialog's Cancel button, close the form and return `DialogResult.Cancel`.

FIGURE 10-2

➤ When the user clicks the dialog's OK `Button`, check the entered name's length. If the length is 0, display a message asking the user to enter a name. If the length is greater than 0, close the form and return `DialogResult.OK`.

Hints

➤ Use the `ListBox`'s `Items.Add` method to add a new item.

➤ Use the `ListBox`'s `Items.Remove` method to remove the selected item (identified by the `SelectedItem` property).

➤ Check `txtName.Text.Length = 0` to see whether the name entered on the dialog is blank. You can use code similar to the following to take one action if the length is 0 and another if it is not. Notice the new `Else` part of the `If` statement. If the condition is true, then the statements after the `If` clause are executed. If the condition is false, then the statements after the `Else` clause are executed. (Lesson 18 covers `If` and `Else` in more detail.)

```
If (txtName.Text = "") Then
    ' ... Display a message here ...
Else
    ' ... Return DialogResult.OK here ...
End If
```

Step-by-Step

➤ Create the main form shown on the upper left in Figure 10-2. Make the New Comedian `Button` be the form's `AcceptButton` and the Delete Comedian `Button` be the form's `CancelButton`.

   1. Start a new project and build a form similar to the one shown in Figure 10-2.

   2. Set the form's `AcceptButton` property to the New Comedian `Button`. Set its `CancelButton` property to the Delete Comedian `Button`.

➤ Create the dialog shown on the lower right in Figure 10-2. Set the `AcceptButton` and `CancelButton` properties in the obvious way.

   1. Add a new form and make it look roughly as shown in Figure 10-2.

   2. Set the form's `AcceptButton` property to the OK `Button`. Set its `CancelButton` property to the Cancel `Button`.

➤ Make the New Comedian `Button` display the dialog. If the dialog returns `DialogResult.OK`, add the new comedian's name to the `ListBox`.

   1. Create an event handler for the New Comedian `Button`. Use code similar to the following:

```
' Make a new comedian entry.
Private Sub btnNewComedian_Click() Handles btnNewComedian.Click
    Dim dlgNewComedian As New NewComedianForm()
    If (dlgNewComedian.ShowDialog() = DialogResult.OK) Then
        lstComedians.Items.Add(dlgNewComedian.txtName.Text)
    End If
End Sub
```

➤ Make the Delete Comedian `Button` remove the currently selected comedian from the `ListBox`.

   1. Create an event handler for the Delete Comedian `Button`. Use code similar to the following:

```
' Delete the selected comedian.
Private Sub btnDeleteComedian_Click() _
 Handles btnDeleteComedian.Click
    lstComedians.Items.Remove(lstComedians.SelectedItem)
End Sub
```

This makes the `ListBox` remove the currently selected item. Fortunately, if there is no selected item, the `ListBox` does nothing instead of crashing.

➤ When the user clicks the dialog's Cancel button, close the form and return `DialogResult.Cancel`.

   1. You don't need to do anything else to make this work. When you set the dialog's `CancelButton` property to this `Button`, Visual Basic sets the `Button`'s `DialogResult` property to `DialogResult.Cancel` so the button automatically sets the return result and closes the dialog.

➤ When the user clicks the dialog's OK `Button`, check the entered name's length. If the length is 0, display a message asking the user to enter a name. If the length is greater than 0, close the form and return `DialogResult.OK`.

1. Create an event handler for the dialog's OK `Button`. Use code similar to the following:

```
' The user clicked OK.
Private Sub btnOk_Click() Handles btnOk.Click
    If (txtName.Text = "") Then
        MessageBox.Show("Please enter a name")
    Else
        Me.DialogResult = DialogResult.OK
    End If
End Sub
```

 Please select Lesson 10 on the DVD to view the video that accompanies this lesson.

EXERCISES

1. Make a program that has First Name, Last Name, Street, City, State, and ZIP `Labels` as shown on the Contact Information form in Figure 10-3. When the user clicks the Edit `Button`, the program should display the Edit Contact Information dialog shown in Figure 10-3 to let the user change the values. If the user clicks OK, the program copies the new values back into the main form's `Labels`.

Hint: As you would with a standard dialog, initialize the custom dialog before you display it.

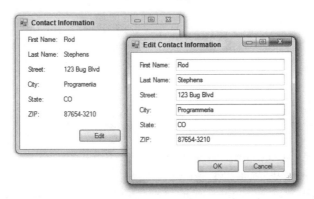

FIGURE 10-3

2. Sometimes the standard message box provided by `MessageBox.Show` is adequate but you'd like to change the buttons' text. Create a program that defines the message dialog shown in Figure 10-4.

FIGURE 10-4

The main program should set the `Label`'s text, the dialog's title, and the buttons' text. Make the Accept `Button` return `DialogResult.OK` and make the Decline `Button` return `DialogResult.Cancel`. Make the main form display different messages depending on whether the user clicked Accept or Decline.

Hints:

➤ The light gray area around the buttons at the bottom of Figure 10-4 is a blank label with `AutoSize = False` and `Dock = Bottom`. It's just for decoration.

➤ The question mark image is displayed in a `PictureBox`.

3. Create a color selection dialog like the one shown in Figure 10-5. The main program's `Buttons` should display the same dialog to let the user select foreground and background colors. Update the main form's colors only if the user clicks OK. Don't worry about initializing the dialog to show the current values before displaying it. (Hint: You built a program that lets the user select colors with scrollbars for Lesson 4's Try It.)

FIGURE 10-5

4. Make a background selection dialog like the one shown in Figure 10-6. When the user clicks the main form's Select Background `Button`, the form displays the dialog. When the user clicks one of the thumbnail images, the dialog displays a border around that image's `PictureBox`. If the user clicks OK, the dialog closes and the main form displays the selected image at full scale.

Hints:

➤ When the user clicks an image, set the `BorderStyle` property to `Fixed3D` for that `PictureBox` and `None` for the others.

➤ To remember which image was selected, place a hidden `PictureBox` on the dialog and set its `Image` property equal to that of the clicked `PictureBox`.

➤ Use a single event handler for all four `PictureBox`es.

FIGURE 10-6

You can find solutions to this lesson's exercises in the Lesson10 folder inside the download available on the book's web site at www.wrox.com *or* www.vb-helper.com/24hourvb.html.

SECTION II
Variables and Calculations

You may have noticed that the lessons up to this point haven't done much with numbers, dates, text (other than to just display it), or any other pieces of data. They've mostly dealt with controls and their properties, methods, and events.

Although you can do some fairly impressive things with controls alone, most programs also need to manipulate data. They need to do things like add purchase costs, calculate sales tax, sort appointments by time, and search text for keywords.

The lessons in this section explain how to perform these kinds of tasks. They explain the variables that a program uses to represent data in code, and they show how to manipulate variables to calculate new results.

▶ **LESSON 11:** Using Variables and Performing Calculations

▶ **LESSON 12:** Debugging Code

▶ **LESSON 13:** Understanding Scope

▶ **LESSON 14:** Working with Strings

▶ **LESSON 15:** Working with Dates and Times

▶ **LESSON 16:** Using Arrays and Collections

▶ **LESSON 17:** Using Enumerations and Structures

11

Using Variables and Performing Calculations

Variables hold values in memory so a program can manipulate them. Different kinds of variables hold different types of data: numbers, text, pictures, Halo scores, even complex groups of data such as employee records.

In this lesson you learn what variables are and how to use them. You learn how to define variables, put data in them, and use them to perform simple calculations.

WHAT ARE VARIABLES?

Technically speaking, a *variable* is a named piece of memory that can hold some data of a specific type. For example, a program might allocate 4 bytes of memory to store an integer. You might name this memory "payoffs" so you can easily refer to it in the program's code.

Less technically, you can think of a variable as a named place to put a piece of data. The program's code can use variables to store values and perform calculations. For example, a program might store two values in variables, add the values together, and store the result in a third variable.

DATA TYPES

Every variable has a particular *data type* that determines the kind of data that it can hold. In general, you cannot place data of one type in a variable of another. For example, if `price` is a variable that can hold a number in dollars and cents, you cannot put the string "Hello" in it.

If you like, you can think of a variable as an envelope with a name written on the outside that can hold some data, but each type of data requires a differently shaped envelope. Integers need relatively small envelopes, singles (which hold numbers with decimal points) need envelopes that are long and thin, and strings need big fat envelopes.

BITS AND BYTES

A *bit* is a single binary digit of memory that can have the value 0 or 1. (The name "bit" comes from "BInary digiT." Or is it "Binary digIT?") Generally, bits are grouped into bytes, and a program doesn't work with bits directly.

A *byte* is a chunk of memory holding 8 bits. If you view the bits as digits in a binary number, then a byte can hold values between 0 (00000000 in binary) and 255 (11111111 in binary). Groups of bytes make up larger data types such as integers and strings.

A *nibble* is half a byte. Way back in the old days when memory was expensive and computers fit in warehouses rather than pockets, some programs needed to split bytes and consider the nibbles separately to save space. Now that memory is as cheap as day-old lottery tickets, the nibble is a historical curiosity.

Bigger units of memory include the kilobyte (KB) = 1,024 bytes, megabyte (MB) = 1,024 KB, gigabyte (GB) = 1,024 MB, and terabyte (TB) = 1,024 GB. These are often used to measure the size of files, computer memory, flash drives, and disk drives, although in some contexts people use powers of 1,000 instead of 1,024. (For example, most disk drive manufacturers define a gigabyte as 1,000,000,000 bytes.)

Sometimes the line between two data types is a bit fuzzy. For example, if a variable should hold a number, you cannot put in the string "ten." The fact that "ten" is a number is obvious to a human but not to a Visual Basic program.

You can't even place a string containing the characters "10" in a variable that holds a number. Though it should be obvious to just about anyone that "10" is a number, Visual Basic just knows it's a string containing the two characters 1 and 0; it doesn't try to determine that the characters in the string represent a number.

Programs often need to convert a value from one data type to another (particularly switching between strings and numbers), so Visual Basic provides an assortment of data conversion functions to do just that. The section "Type Conversions" later in this lesson describes these functions.

Table 11-1 summarizes Visual Basic's built-in data types. The signed types can store values that are positive or negative, whereas the unsigned types can hold only positive values.

TABLE 11-1

DATA TYPE	MEANING	RANGE
Byte	Byte	0 to 255
SByte	Signed byte	−128 to 127
Short	Small signed integer	−32,768 to 32,767
UShort	Unsigned short	0 to 65,535

DATA TYPE	MEANING	RANGE
Integer	Integer	−2,147,483,648 to 2,147,483,647
UInteger	Unsigned integer	0 to 4,294,967,295
Long	Long integer	−9,223,372,036,854,775,808 to 9,223,372,036,854,775,807
ULong	Unsigned long	0 to 18,446,744,073,709,551,615
Single	Single-precision floating point	Roughly −3.4e38 to 3.4e38
Double	Double-precision floating point	Roughly −1.8e308 to 1.8e308
Decimal	Higher precision and smaller range than floating-point types	See the following section, "Single, Double, and Decimal Data Types."
Char	Character	A single Unicode character. (Unicode characters use 16 bits to hold data for text in scripts such as Arabic, Cyrillic, Greek, and Thai.)
String	Text	A string of Unicode characters
Boolean	Boolean	Can be True or False
Object	An object	Can point to almost anything

Some of these data types are a bit confusing but the most common data types (Integer, Long, Single, Double, and String) are fairly straightforward, and they are the focus of most of this lesson. Before moving on to further details, however, it's worth spending a little time comparing the Single, Double, and Decimal data types.

Single, Double, and Decimal Data Types

The computer represents values of every type in binary using bits and bytes, so some values don't fit perfectly in a particular data type. In particular, real numbers such as 1/7 don't have exact binary representations, so the Single, Double, and Decimal data types often introduce slight rounding errors.

For example, a Single represents 1/7 as approximately 0.142857149. Usually the fact that this is not exactly 1/7 isn't a problem, but once in a while if you compare two Single values to determine whether they are exactly equal, rounding errors make them appear to be different even though they should be the same.

The Decimal data type helps reduce this problem for decimal values such as 1.5 (but not non-decimal real values such as 1/7) by storing an exact representation of the decimal value. Instead of storing a value as a binary number the way Single and Double do, Decimal stores the number's digits and its exponent separately as integral data types with no rounding. That lets it hold 28 or 29 significant digits (depending on the exact value) for numbers between roughly −7.9e28 and 7.9e28.

Note that rounding errors can still occur when you combine Decimal values. For example, if you add 1×10^{28} plus 1×10^{-28}, the result would have more than the 28 or 29 significant digits that a Decimal can provide so it rounds off to 1×10^{28}.

The moral of the story is that you should always use the Decimal data type for values when you need great accuracy and the values won't get truly enormous. In particular, you should always use Decimal for currency values. Unless you're Bill Gates' much richer uncle, you'll never get close to the largest value a Decimal can represent, and the extra precision can prevent rounding errors during some fairly complex calculations.

 Another interesting feature of the Decimal *type is that, due to the way it stores its significant digits, it remembers zeros on the right. For example, if you add the values 1.35 and 1.65 as* Singles, *you get the value 3. In contrast, if you add the same values as* Decimals, *you get 3.00. The* Decimal *result remembers that you were working with two digits to the right of the decimal point so it stores the result that way, too.*

DECLARING VARIABLES

To declare a variable in Visual Basic code, use the Dim keyword, followed by the name that you want to give the variable, the As keyword, and the data type. For example, the following code creates a variable named numMistakes. The variable's data type is Integer, so it can hold an integer between −2,147,483,648 and 2,147,483,647.

```
Dim numMistakes As Integer
```

After you declare the variable, you can use the equals symbol to assign a value to a variable. For example, the following code sets numMistakes to 1337:

```
numMistakes = 1337
```

As an added convenience, you can declare a variable and give it a value at the same time:

```
Dim numMistakes As Integer = 1337
```

You can declare several variables of the same type all at once by separating them with commas as in the following code:

```
Dim x, y, z As Single
```

LITERAL VALUES

A *literal value* is a piece of data stuck right in the code. For example, in the following statement, numMistakes is a variable and 1337 is a literal integer value:

```
Dim numMistakes As Integer = 1337
```

Usually Visual Basic is pretty smart about using the correct data types for literal values. For example, in the preceding statement Visual Basic knows that `numMistakes` is an integer and `1337` is an integer, so it can safely put an integer value in an integer variable.

You should use double quotes to surround or *delimit* `Strings` and `Chars`, as in the following code:

```
Dim firstName As String = "William"
Dim lastName As String = "Gates"
Dim middleInitial As Char = "H"
```

You should use number signs (#) to delimit dates and times, as shown here:

```
Dim birthday As Date = #8/20/2011#
Dim partyTime As DateTime = #5:30:00 PM#
```

 You must use American formats in date and time literals in your code even if your system uses other settings such as the day/month/year date format. Visual Basic code understands only these formats.

TYPE CONVERSIONS

As I mentioned earlier, you can think of a variable as an envelope of a certain size that can only hold one kind of data. For example, you can't put a string value in an `Integer` variable.

However, programs often do need to store one kind of value in a different kind of variable. For example, suppose a user wants to buy five rare Pokémon cards for $1.50 each. Before it can calculate the total cost, the program needs to get the values 5 and 1.50 into numeric variables such as `Integers` or `Decimals`.

Other times a program may have a value stored in a variable of one type, such as `Integer`, and need to copy it into a variable of another type, such as `Double`.

In these cases, the program must perform a *type conversion* to convert a value from one data type to another. Your program can use one of two basic types of conversion: *implicit* or *explicit*.

Implicit Type Conversions

In an implicit type conversion, Visual Basic converts a value from one type to another automatically, often without you even being aware of it.

Visual Basic will convert any data from one type to another if it understands how to make such a conversion. For example, if you assign a `Single` variable equal to an `Integer` value, Visual Basic will very happily convert the `Integer` into a `Single`.

In fact, any valid `Integer` value will fit without any loss of precision in a `Single` variable so this is even a safe type conversion.

Returning to the earlier analogy of data types as envelopes, you might imagine `Integer` as a thin envelope because it holds a relatively small range of values. In contrast, `Single` can hold a much bigger range of values so it is a wider envelope. Keeping this analogy in mind, converting an `Integer` into a `Single` is called a *widening conversion* because you are going from a relatively thin data type to a wider one.

In contrast, suppose you need to convert a `Single` value into an `Integer`. This is called a *narrowing conversion* because you are going from a "wider" data type to a "narrower" one. In this case, some precision may be lost. For example, if you store the `Single` value 1.23 in an `Integer`, you get the result 1.

Visual Basic is quite creative at both widening and narrowing implicit conversions and will perform them automatically if necessary. For example, all of the following conversions are legal in a Visual Basic program:

```
Dim i As Integer
Dim s As Single

' Copy the Integer value 123 into a Single.
i = 123
s = i

' Copy the Single value 1.23 into an Integer (giving 1).
s = 1.23
i = s

' Copying strings holding numbers into numeric variables.
i = "321"
s = "3.21"

' Set a Boolean from a string.
Dim ready As Boolean = "True"
```

There are limits to what Visual Basic can do, however. For example, it can convert the string values `True` and `False` into the `Boolean` data type but it doesn't understand `Yes`, `No`, `Sure`, `Negatory`, or any other string value.

For simple programs, implicit conversions are typically fine and they do the right thing, but it's not always obvious where they occur and that can sometimes lead to problems.

For example, suppose a program contains the following statement:

```
total = subtotal
```

This may look like a perfectly safe statement but suppose `total` is an `Integer` and `subtotal` is a `Long`. In that case, this is a narrowing conversion because not all `Long` values can fit in an `Integer`, so the program may sometimes crash. To make matters worse, many `Long` values do fit so you may not notice the problem until specific inputs make the value really large. For example, if `subtotal` is the number of items in a customer's order, then it will probably fit in an `Integer`; but, if it represents the total population of the world, then it won't fit in an `Integer`.

For an even trickier example, suppose the user enters a purchase quantity in a `TextBox`. If the user enters a number such as "10," then the following code works:

```
Dim quantity As Integer = txtQuantity.Text
```

However, if the user enters "ten," the program crashes with the error message "Conversion from string "ten" to type 'Integer' is not valid."

Possibly even more troubling, if the user enters the value 12.34, the program does not crash! Instead, it silently converts the string into the Double value 12.34 and then converts that into an Integer. You might prefer to have the program warn you somehow that the user didn't enter an Integer, rather than silently treat it like one.

One way you can minimize these unexpected problems is to prohibit implicit narrowing conversions. Then you can't give an Integer variable a Long value, and you can't save a String value into an Integer.

To prohibit implicit narrowing conversions, add the following line to the very top of a code module:

```
Option Strict On
```

BEST PRACTICE

To prohibit narrowing conversions globally throughout the project without having to edit each code file, open the Project menu and select Properties. On the Compile tab, set the Option Strict option to On.

To make new programs always set Option Strict On, open the Tools menu and select Options. Expand the Projects and Solutions entry, select VB Defaults, and set Option Strict to On.

Explicit Type Conversions

Prohibiting implicit narrowing conversions prevents some kinds of errors but what if you really need to perform a narrowing conversion? For example, suppose the user enters an order quantity in a TextBox. How do you convert the value into an Integer so you can perform calculations?

The answer is to use an *explicit* conversion. In an explicit conversion, you use code to convert the value. This works more or less the same way an implicit conversion would work except you are doing it on purpose. By making an explicit conversion, you are acknowledging that you know there's a risk and you are willing to take responsibility.

There are five main ways you can perform an explicit conversion: using Visual Basic conversion functions, using CType, using DirectCast and TryCast, using Convert, and using Parsing.

Using Visual Basic Conversion Functions

Visual Basic provides a set of functions for explicitly converting values into new data types. For example, the following code uses the CDec function to convert the text entered by the user in the txtCost TextBox into a Decimal and then saves it in the variable cost:

```
Dim cost As Decimal = CDec(txtCost.Text)
```

Table 11-2 lists Visual Basic's conversion functions.

TABLE 11-2

FUNCTION	CONVERTS TO
CBool	Boolean
CByte	Byte
CChar	Char
CDate	Date
CDbl	Double
CDec	Decimal
CInt	Integer
CLng	Long
CObj	Object
CShort	Short
CSng	Single
CStr	String

The integer functions round floating-point values off to the nearest integer. For example, CInt(1.7) returns 2.

Another function, Int, truncates floating-point values. For example, Int(1.7) returns 1. Note that the result returned by Int has the same data type as its parameter; so, for example, if you pass Int a Double, it returns a Double. Often you will want to use CInt to convert that result into an Integer.

The Fix function is similar to Int except it truncates towards 0. That means for negative numbers Int decreases the value (Int(-8.5) = -9.0) but Fix increases the value (Fix(-8.5) = -8.0).

Each of these functions causes an error if it cannot convert the value. For example, CInt("1x3") causes an error because "1x3" is not a valid number.

Visual Basic also includes a special-purpose Val function that converts a value into a Double. If Val cannot convert the value into a Double, it silently returns 0. For example, if you use Val to convert a value typed by the user into a number and the user types "six," then Val ignores the error and returns 0.

This makes Val useful for converting values typed by the user into numbers if 0 is a reasonable default value. If 0 is not a reasonable default value, then your program should use some other method for converting the string into a number, such as parsing, which is described shortly.

Using CType

The CType function takes a value and a data type as parameters and returns the value converted into the data type. For example, the following code converts the text entered by the user in the txtCost TextBox into a Decimal and saves it in the variable cost:

```
Dim cost As Decimal = CType(txtCost.Text, Decimal)
```

Like the Visual Basic conversion functions, CType works only if the conversion is possible. For example, if the user types "eleven" in the TextBox, CType will cause an error.

Using DirectCast and TryCast

The DirectCast operator converts an object from one type to another. For example, event handlers have a sender parameter of type Object that holds a reference to the control that raised the event. If you know that the control is actually a Button, you can use DirectCast to convert sender into a variable of type Button as shown in the following code:

```
Private Sub btnSetColor_Click()
    Dim btn As Button = DirectCast(sender, Button)
    . . .
End Sub
```

This is particularly handy when you want one event handler to catch events raised by multiple controls. After converting sender into a Button, the program can use the Button's properties to decide how to proceed.

The DirectCast operator fails if the object you are trying to convert doesn't have the correct data type. For example, if the preceding event handler were invoked by a PictureBox, then sender would not be a Button so the call to DirectCast would fail.

The TryCast operator attempts to convert an object from one data type to another much as DirectCast does but if there is a problem TryCast returns Nothing instead of throwing an exception. The following code shows the previous event handler rewritten so it doesn't crash if the sender that raised the event isn't a Button.

```
Private Sub btnSetColor_Click()
    Dim btn As Button = TryCast(sender, Button)
    If btn IsNot Nothing Then
        . . .
    End If
    . . .
End Sub
```

This code uses TryCast to convert sender into a Button. It then uses IsNot to see if the result is Nothing. (The IsNot operator is described later in the section "Comparison Operators.") If the result isn't Nothing, the code executes whatever is inside the If Then block.

Using Convert

The Convert class provides methods that convert from one data type to another. For example, the following code converts the text entered by the user in the txtCost TextBox into a Decimal and saves it in the variable cost:

```
Dim cost As Decimal = Convert.ToDecimal(txtCost.Text)
```

 A method is simply a function or subroutine provided by a class as opposed to in a separate code module. In this case, the Convert class provides these methods.

Table 11-3 lists the Convert class's conversion methods.

TABLE 11-3

METHOD	CONVERTS TO
ToBoolean	Boolean
ToByte	Byte
ToChar	Char
ToDateTime	DateTime
ToDecimal	Decimal
ToDouble	Double
ToInt16	16-bit integer (Short)
ToInt32	32-bit integer (Integer)
ToInt64	64-bit integer (Long)
ToSByte	SByte
ToSingle	Single
ToString	String
ToUInt16	Unsigned 16-bit integer (UShort)
ToUInt32	Unsigned 32-bit integer (UInteger)
ToUInt64	Unsigned 64-bit integer (ULong)

One drawback to the Convert methods is that they require you to remember how long the integer data types are in bits. For example, you need to use ToInt32 to convert to a 32-bit Integer.

Using Parsing

Trying to find structure and meaning in text is called *parsing*. All the simple data types (Integer, Double, Decimal) provide a Parse method that converts text into that data type. For example, the Integer data type's Parse method takes a string as a parameter and returns an Integer; at least it does if the string contains an integer value.

For example, the following code parses the text entered by the user in the txtCost TextBox to get a Decimal value and saves it in the variable cost:

```
Dim cost As Decimal = Decimal.Parse(txtCost.Text)
```

Like the previous methods, this works only if the text can reasonably be converted into a decimal. If the user types "12,345.67," the parsing works. If the user types "ten" or "1.2.3," the parsing fails.

> *Unfortunately, Visual Basic's conversion and parsing methods are confused by some formats that you might expect them to understand. For example, they can't handle currency characters, so they fail on strings like "$12.34" and "€54.32."*
>
> *You can tell the* Decimal *class's* Parse *method to allow currency values by passing it a second parameter as shown in the following code:*
>
> ```
> Dim cost As Decimal =
>     Decimal.Parse(txtCost.Text,
>     System.Globalization.NumberStyles.Any)
> ```

All the parsing methods described so far have one really big problem: if the value they are converting cannot be converted into the desired data type, they cause an error that crashes your program (at least until you read Lesson 21 on handling errors).

One way to avoid this problem is to use TryParse. A data type's TryParse method is a lot like Parse except it returns a Boolean value indicating whether it succeeded. It takes a second parameter to hold the parsed value.

For example, consider the following code:

```
Dim cost As Decimal
If Decimal.TryParse(txtCost.Text, cost) Then
    ' Perform some calculations...
Else
    MessageBox.Show("Please enter a valid cost.")
End If
```

The first statement calls TryParse, passing it the value to convert (txtCost.Text) and the variable (cost) that should receive the Decimal value. TryParse attempts to convert the user's text into a Decimal and returns True if it succeeds. The code then uses an If Then Else statement to either process the value or display an error message.

Like `Parse`, `TryParse` doesn't automatically understand text with a currency format. To make it allow currency formats, you can add extra parameters as shown in the following code:

```
Dim cost As Decimal
If Decimal.TryParse(txtCost.Text,
 System.Globalization.NumberStyles.Any, Nothing, cost) Then
    MessageBox.Show("OK")
Else
    MessageBox.Show("Failed")
End If
```

This syntax is the most cumbersome of the conversion methods described here, but it is also the most robust.

> *Which of these methods you use to convert between data types is largely a matter of preference. Many developers prefer the Visual Basic conversion functions such as* `CInt` *and* `CDec` *because they're short and easy to read (once you get used to them). Others prefer* `CType`.
>
> *For parsing user-entered values, however, you should generally use* `TryParse` *so you can easily detect errors (although I often use* `Parse` *in examples because it's easier to read, even if it isn't as robust).*

PERFORMING CALCULATIONS

You've already seen several pieces of code that assign a value to a variable. For example, the following code converts the text in the `txtSalary` TextBox into a `Decimal` and saves it in the variable `salary`:

```
Dim salary As Decimal = Decimal.Parse(txtSalary.Text)
```

You can also save a value that is the result of a more complex calculation into a variable on the left side of an equals sign. Fortunately, the syntax for these kinds of calculations is usually easy to understand. The following code calculates the value 2736 + 7281 / 3 and saves the result in the variable named `result`:

```
Dim result As Double = 2736 + 7281 / 3
```

The operands (the values used in the expression) can be literal values, values stored in variables, or the results of methods. For example, the following code calculates the sales tax on a purchase's subtotal. It multiplies the tax rate stored in the `taxRate` variable by the `Decimal` value stored in the `txtSubtotal` TextBox and saves the result in the variable `salesTax`:

```
salesTax = taxRate * Decimal.Parse(txtSubtotal.Text)
```

Note that a variable can appear on both sides of the equals sign. In that case, the value on the right is the variable's current value; and after the calculation, the new result is saved back in the same variable.

For example, the following code takes x's current value, doubles it, adds 10, and saves the result back in variable x. If x started with the value 3, then when this statement finishes, x holds the value 16.

```
x = 2 * x + 10
```

A variable may appear more than once on the right side of the equals sign but it can appear only once on the left.

The following sections provide some additional details about performing calculations.

Promotion

If an expression uses two different data types, Visual Basic *promotes* the one with the narrower data type. For example, if you try to divide an Integer by a Single, Visual Basic promotes the Integer to a Single before it performs the division.

Visual Basic also performs this promotion if the operation would lead to a wider data type. For example, if you divide two integers, the result might not be an integer. To allow for fractional results, Visual Basic promotes the values to Doubles before performing the division. The result is a Double so you need to treat it as one. For example, the following code is not allowed (if you have Option Strict turned on) because you cannot save a Double result in an Integer:

```
Dim result As Integer = 8 / 4
```

Operator Summary

Visual Basic has many operators for manipulating variables of different data types. The following sections describe the most commonly used operators grouped by operand type (arithmetic, string, logical, and so forth).

Arithmetic Operators

The arithmetic operators perform calculations on numbers. Table 11-4 summarizes these operators. The Example column shows sample results.

TABLE 11-4

OPERATOR	MEANING	EXAMPLE
^	Exponentiation	3 ^ 2 is 9
+	Addition	3 + 2 is 5
-	Negation	-3 is -3
-	Subtraction	3 - 2 is 1
*	Multiplication	3 * 2 is 6
\	Division (integer)	3 \ 2 is 1
/	Division (floating point)	3.0 / 2.0 is 1.5
Mod	Modulus	3 Mod 2 is 1

Integer division drops any remainder and returns the integer quotient. The modulus operator does the opposite: It drops the quotient and returns the remainder. For example, 17 Mod 5 returns 2 because 17 divided by 5 is 3 with a remainder of 2.

Logical Operators

The logical operators perform calculations on Boolean (True or False) values. They let you combine logical statements to form new ones.

Lesson 18 explains how to use these values to perform tests that let a program take action only under certain circumstances. For example, a program might pay an employee overtime if the employee is paid hourly and works more than 40 hours in a week.

Table 11-5 summarizes these operators.

TABLE 11-5

OPERATOR	RETURNS TRUE WHEN...
And	Both operands are True
AndAlso	Both operands are True
Or	One or both operands is True
OrElse	One or both operands is True
Xor	One operand is True and the other is False
Not	The single operand is False

The *exclusive or* operator Xor is perhaps the most confusing. It returns True if one of its operands is True and the other is False. For example, you and Ann will get a single lunch check and pay each other back later if either Ann forgot her money and you brought yours, *or* Ann remembered her money and you forgot yours. If neither of you forgot your money, you can get separate checks. If you both forgot your money, you're both going hungry today.

```
singleCheck = annForgotMoney Xor youForgotMoney;
```

AndAlso and OrElse are called *conditional operators* or *short-circuit operators*. They work just like the regular And and Or operators except they don't evaluate their second operand unless necessary. For example, consider the following AndAlso statement:

```
mustBuyLunch = isLunchTime AndAlso forgotToBringLunch
```

Suppose it's only 9:00 a.m., so isLunchTime is false. When the program sees this expression, evaluates isLunchTime, and sees the AndAlso operator, it already knows that mustBuyLunch must be false no matter what value follows the `AndAlso` (in this case `forgotToBringLunch`), so it doesn't bother to evaluate `forgotToBringLunch`, which saves a tiny amount of calculation time.

Similarly, consider the following "or" statement:

```
canAffordLunch = haveEnoughMoney OrElse haveCreditCard
```

If you have enough money, `haveEnoughMoney` is `True`, so the program doesn't need to evaluate `haveCreditCard` to know that the result `canAffordLunch` is also `True`.

Because the conditional `AndAlso` and `OrElse` operators are slightly faster, most developers use them when they can instead of `And` and `Or`.

> *There is one case where the conditional operators may cause problems. If the second operand is not a simple value but the returned result from some sort of subroutine call, then if you use a conditional operator, you cannot always know whether the subroutine was called. This might matter if the subroutine has side effects, consequences that last after the subroutine has finished, such as opening a database or creating a file. In that case, you cannot know later whether the database is open or the file is created, so the code might not work properly.*
>
> *This is seldom a problem, and you can avoid it completely by avoiding side effects.*

String Operators

The only string operator Visual Basic provides is &. This operator concatenates (joins) two strings together. For example, suppose the variable `username` contains the user's name. The following code concatenates the text "Hello " (note the trailing space) with the user's name and displays the result in a message box:

```
MessageBox.Show("Hello " & username)
```

> *Actually the + operator will also concatenate strings but it can make the code hard to read and the results aren't always obvious, for example, if you use + to combine an `Integer` and a `String`. Concatenating strings with + is a bad practice.*

Lesson 14 explains methods that you can use to manipulate strings: find substrings, replace text, check length, and so forth.

One very non-obvious fact about string operations is that a string concatenation does not really save the results in the same memory used by the variable on the left side of an assignment statement. Instead, it creates a new string holding the result of the calculation and makes the variable refer to that.

For example, consider the following code:

```
String greeting = txtUserName.Text
greeting = "Hello" + username
```

This code looks like it saves a user's name in the variable username *and then tacks "Hello " onto the front. Actually, the second statement creates an entirely new string that holds "Hello " plus the user's name and then makes* greeting *refer to the new string.*

For most practical applications, the difference is small, and you can ignore it. However, if you're performing many concatenations (perhaps in one of the loops described in Lesson 19), then your program may have performance issues. The StringBuilder *class can help address this issue, but it's a bit more advanced so I'm not going to cover it here. See* msdn.microsoft.com/library/2839d5h5 .aspx *for more information.*

Comparison Operators

The comparison operators compare two values and return True or False depending on the values' relationship. For example, x < y returns True if x is less than y.

Table 11-6 summarizes these operators.

TABLE 11-6

OPERATOR	MEANING	EXAMPLE
=	Equals	2 = 3 is False
<>	Not equals	2 <> 3 is True
<	Less than	2 < 3 is True
<=	Less than or equal to	2 <= 3 is True
>	Greater than	2 > 3 is False
>=	Greater than or equal to	2 >= 3 is False
Is	Returns True if two object variables represent the same object	person1 Is person2 is True if these are the same Person object
IsNot	Returns True if two object variables do not represent the same object	person1 IsNot person2 is True if these are different Person objects

The `Is` and `IsNot` operators are a bit unusual because they work only on reference variables that refer to objects not on more ordinary data types such as `Integers` and `Doubles`.

These operators compare variables to see if they refer to the same object. They don't compare the values in two different objects. For example, suppose you have two `Person` objects, `person1` and `person2`, that happen to have the same `FirstName`, `LastName`, and other property values. Even if their properties are identical, they are two distinct objects so `person1 Is person2` would return `False`.

Assignment Operators

The assignment operators set a variable (or property or whatever) equal to something else. The simplest of these is the = operator, which you have seen several times before. This operator simply assigns whatever value is on the right to the variable on the left.

The other assignment operators, known as *compound assignment operators*, combine the variable's current value in some way with whatever is on the right. For example, the following code adds 3 to whatever value x currently holds:

```
x += 3
```

This has the same effect as the following statement that doesn't use the += operator:

```
x = x + 3
```

Table 11-7 summarizes these operators.

TABLE 11-7

OPERATOR	MEANING	EXAMPLE	MEANS
=	Assign	x = 10	x = 10
+=	Add and assign	x += 10	x = x + 10
-=	Subtract and assign	x -= 10	x = x - 10
*=	Multiply and assign	x *= 10	x = x * 10
\=	Integer-point divide and assign	x \= 10	x = x \ 10
/=	Floating-point divide and assign	x /= 10	x = x / 10
&=	Concatenate and assign	x &= "A"	x = x & "A"

There are no compound assignment operators for `Mod` or the logical operators.

Bitwise Operators

The bitwise operators enable you to manipulate the individual bits in integer values. For example, the bitwise `Or` operator combines the bits in two values, so the result has a bit equal to 1 wherever either of the two operands has a bit equal to one.

For example, suppose x and y are the byte values, with bits 10000000 and 00000001. Then x Or y has bits 10000001.

These are fairly advanced operators so I'm not going to do much with them, but Table 11-8 summarizes them. The shift operators are not "bitwise" because they don't compare two operands one bit at a time, but they are bit-manipulation operators so they're included here.

TABLE 11-8

OPERATOR	MEANING	EXAMPLE
And	Bitwise *and*	11110000 And 00111100 = 00110000
Or	Bitwise *or*	11110000 Or 00111100 = 11111100
Xor	Bitwise *xor*	11110000 Xor 00111100 = 11001100
Not	Bitwise complement	Not 11110000 = 00001111
<<	Left shift	11100111 << 2 = 10011100
>>	Right shift (for signed types)	11100111 >> 2 = 11111001
>>	Right shift (for unsigned types)	11100111 >> 2 = 00111001

If the operand has a signed type (SByte, Integer, Long), then >> makes new bits on the left copies of the value's sign bit (its leftmost bit). If the operand has an unsigned type (Byte, UInteger, ULong), then >> makes new bits 0.

The shift operators also have corresponding compound assignments operators <<= and >>=.

Precedence

Sometimes the order in which you evaluate the operators in an expression changes the result. For example, consider the expression 2 + 3 * 5. If you evaluate the + first, you get 5 * 5, which is 25; but if you evaluate the * first, you get 2 + 15, which is 17.

To prevent any ambiguity, Visual Basic defines *operator precedence* to determine which operation is evaluated first.

Table 11-9 lists the operators in order of decreasing precedence. In other words, the operators listed at the beginning of the table are applied before those listed later. Operators listed at the same level have the same precedence and are applied left to right in the order in which they appear in the expression.

TABLE 11-9

CATEGORY	OPERATORS
Exponentiation	^
Unary	+, -
Multiplication and floating-point division	*, /
Integer division	\
Modulus	Mod
Addition, subtraction, concatenation	+, -, &
Bit shift	<<, >>
Comparison	=, <>, <, <=, >, >=, Is, IsNot
Logical negation	Not
Logical And	And, AndAlso
Logical Or	Or, OrElse
Logical Xor	Xor

The compound assignment operators (+=, *=, ^=, and so forth) always have lowest precedence. The program evaluates the expression on the right, combines it with the original value of the variable on the left, and then saves the result in that variable.

By carefully using the precedence rules, you can always figure out how a program will evaluate an expression, but sometimes the expression can be confusing enough to make figuring out the result difficult. Trying to determine precedence in confusing expressions can be a great party game (the programmer's version of "Pictionary"), but it can make understanding and debugging programs hard.

Fortunately, you can always use parentheses to change the order of evaluation, or to make the default order obvious. For example, consider the following three statements:

```
x = 2 + 3 * 5
y = 2 + (3 * 5)
z = (2 + 3) * 5
```

The first statement uses no parentheses so you need to use the precedence table to figure out which operator is applied first. The table shows that * has higher precedence than +, so * is applied first and the result is 2 + 15, which is 17.

The second statement uses parentheses to emphasize the fact that the * operator is evaluated first. The result is unchanged but the code is easier to read.

The third statement uses parentheses to change the order of evaluation. In this case the + operator is evaluated first, so the result is 5 * 5, which is 25.

> *Parentheses are useful tools for making your code easier to understand and debug. Unless an expression is so simple that it's obvious how it is evaluated, add parentheses to make the result clear.*

CONSTANTS

A constant is a lot like a variable except you must assign it a value when you declare it and you cannot change the value later.

Syntactically, a constant's declaration is similar to a variable except it uses the keyword Const instead of Dim.

For example, the following code declares a Decimal constant named taxRate and assigns it the value 0.09D. It then uses the constant in a calculation.

```
Const taxRate As Decimal = 0.09D

Dim subtotal As Decimal = Decimal.Parse(txtSubtotal.Text)
Dim salesTax As Decimal = taxRate * subtotal
Dim grandTotal As Decimal = subtotal + salesTax
```

The D character in the code tells Visual Basic that 0.09 is a Decimal value. Without this character, Visual Basic thinks 0.09 is a Double and complains when you try to assign it to a Decimal constant.

Constants work just like literal values so you could replace the constant taxRate with the literal value 0.09D in the preceding calculation. Using a constant makes the code easier to read, however. When you see the value 0.09D, you need to remember or guess that this is a tax rate. In contrast, the meaning of the constant taxRate is obvious.

Not only can it be hard to remember what this kind of "magic number" means, but it can also make changing the value difficult if it appears in many places throughout the program. Suppose the code uses the value 0.09D in several places. If the tax rate goes up, you need to hunt down all of the occurrences of that number and change them. If you miss some of them, you could get very confusing results.

Note that constants can contain calculated values as long as Visual Basic can perform the calculation before the program actually runs. For example, the following code declares a constant that defines the number of centimeters per inch. It then uses that value to define the number of centimeters per foot.

```
Const cmPerInch As Double = 2.54
Const cmPerFoot As Double = cmPerInch * 12
```

TRY IT

In this Try It you perform some simple calculations. You take values entered by the user, convert them into numbers, do some multiplication and addition, and display the results.

> *You can download the code and resources for this Try It from the book's web page at* www.wrox.com *or* www.vb-helper.com/24hourvb.html. *You can find them in the Lesson11 folder in the download.*

Lesson Requirements

In this lesson:

➤ Create the form shown in Figure 11-1.

➤ Make the program do the following when the user clicks the Calculate Button:

➤ Multiply each item's Quantity value by its Price Each value and display the result in the corresponding Ext. Price textbox.

➤ Add up the Ext. Price values and display the result in the Subtotal textbox.

➤ Multiply the Subtotal by the Tax Rate and display the result in the Sales Tax textbox.

➤ Add the Subtotal, Sales Tax, and Shipping values and display the result in the Grand Total textbox.

FIGURE 11-1

Hints

➤ It is often helpful to perform this kind of calculation in three separate phases:

1. Gather input values from the user and store them in variables.

2. Perform calculations.

3. Display results.

➤ Use the Decimal data type for all the variables because they represent currency.

➤ Lesson 14 has more to say about manipulating and formatting strings, but for this Try It it's helpful to know that all data types provide a ToString method that converts a value into a string. An optional parameter string indicates the format to use. For this Try It, use the format "C" (including the quotes) to indicate a currency format, as in:

```
txtGrandTotal.Text = grandTotal.ToString("C")
```

Step-by-Step

➤ Create the form shown in Figure 11-1.

1. Create the controls. Use `NumericUpDown` controls for the Quantity values.

2. Set `ReadOnly` to `True` for the `TextBoxes` that display results (Subtotal, Sales Tax, and Grand Total).

➤ Make the program do the following when the user clicks the Calculate button:

➤ Multiply each item's Quantity value by its Price Each value and display the result in the corresponding Ext. Price textbox.

➤ Add the Ext. Price values and display the result in the Subtotal textbox.

➤ Multiply the Subtotal value by the entered Tax Rate and display the result in the Sales Tax textbox.

➤ Add the Subtotal, Sales Tax, and Shipping values and display the result in the Grand Total textbox.

This is easy to do in three steps:

1. Gather input values from the user and store them in variables. Because they are already numeric, the code doesn't need to parse the values that come from the `NumericUpDown` control's `Value` properties. The program *does* need to parse the values in `TextBoxes` to convert them into `Decimal` values. The following code snippet shows how the program can read the Quantity and Price Each values for the first item. Read the other values similarly.

```
' Get input values.
Dim quantity1 As Decimal = nudQuantity1.Value
...
Dim priceEach1 As Decimal = Decimal.Parse(txtPriceEach1.Text)
...
```

2. Perform calculations. In this Try It, the calculations are pretty simple. Notice that the code uses a separate variable for each result, instead of trying to add them all at once, to keep the code simple and easy to read:

```
' Calculate results.
Dim extPrice1 As Decimal = quantity1 * priceEach1
Dim extPrice2 As Decimal = quantity2 * priceEach2
Dim extPrice3 As Decimal = quantity3 * priceEach3
Dim extPrice4 As Decimal = quantity4 * priceEach4
Dim subtotal As Decimal =
    extPrice1 + extPrice2 + extPrice3 + extPrice4
Dim salesTax As Decimal = subtotal * taxRate
Dim grandTotal As Decimal = subtotal + salesTax + shipping
```

3. Display results. The program uses `ToString("C")` to display values in a currency format:

```
' Display results.
txtExtPrice1.Text = extPrice1.ToString("C")
txtExtPrice2.Text = extPrice2.ToString("C")
txtExtPrice3.Text = extPrice3.ToString("C")
txtExtPrice4.Text = extPrice4.ToString("C")
txtSubtotal.Text = subtotal.ToString("C")
txtSalesTax.Text = salesTax.ToString("C")
txtGrandTotal.Text = grandTotal.ToString("C")
```

 Please select Lesson 11 on the DVD to view the video that accompanies this lesson.

EXERCISES

1. Make a program similar to the one shown in Figure 11-2. When the user checks or unchecks either of the A or B `CheckBoxes`, the program should check or uncheck the result `CheckBoxes` appropriately. For example, if A and B are both checked, the A and B `CheckBox` should also be checked.

The last `CheckBox` is checked at the same time as one of the others. Which one? Does that make sense?

2. There are many ways for a program to get information about the operating system. The following lists three useful values:

➤ `Environment.UserName` — The current user's name

➤ `DateTime.Now.ToShortTimeString()` — The current time in short format

➤ `DateTime.Now.ToShortDateString()` — The current date in short format

Make a program that greets the user when it starts by displaying a message box similar to the one shown in Figure 11-3. (Hint: You'll need to concatenate several strings together.)

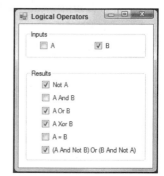

FIGURE 11-2

FIGURE 11-3

3. Make a program to determine whether 12345 * 54321 > 22222 * 33333. In three `Labels`, display the result of 12345 * 54321, the result of 22222 * 33333, and the Boolean value 12345 * 54321 > 22222 * 33333. The final value should be true or false. (Hint: Use `ToString` to convert the Boolean result into a string.)

4. Make a program that converts degrees Celsius to degrees Fahrenheit. It should have two TextBoxes with associated Buttons. When the user enters a value in the Celsius TextBox and clicks its Button, the program converts the value into degrees Fahrenheit and displays the result in the other TextBox. Make the other Button convert from Fahrenheit to Celsius. (Hint: °F = °C * 9 / 5 + 32 and °C = (°F – 32) * 5 / 9.) (What's special about the temperature –40° Celsius?)

5. Make a money converter that converts between U.S. dollars, British pounds, euros, Japanese yen, Indian rupees, and Swiss francs. Make constants for the following conversion factors (or go online and look up the current exchange rates):

```
' Exchange rates in USD.
Const eurPerUsd As Decimal = 0.79D
Const gbpPerUsd As Decimal = 0.64D
Const jpyPerUsd As Decimal = 84.64D
Const inrPerUsd As Decimal = 46.82D
Const chfPerUsd As Decimal = 1.03D
```

To make the constants usable by every event handler in the program, place these declarations outside of any event handler.

Make a TextBox and Button for each currency. When the user clicks the Button, the program should:

➤ Get the value in the corresponding TextBox.

➤ Convert that value into U.S. dollars.

➤ Use the converted value in U.S. dollars to calculate the other currency values.

Display the results. (Note that these event handlers contain a lot of duplicated code, which is not good programming practice. Lesson 20 explains how you can make a subroutine to perform the duplicated work for the event handlers.)

6. Make a program similar to the one you made for Exercise 5 but make this one convert between inches, feet, yards, miles, centimeters, meters, and kilometers.

You can find solutions to this lesson's exercises in the Lesson11 folder inside the download available on the book's web site at www.wrox.com *or* www.vb-helper .com/24hourvb.html.

12

Debugging Code

A *bug* is a programming error that makes a program fail to produce the correct result. The program might crash, display incorrect data, or do something completely unexpected such as delete the wrong file.

In this lesson you learn how to use the excellent debugging tools provided by Visual Studio's IDE to find bugs in Visual Basic. You learn about different kinds of bugs and you get to practice debugging techniques on some buggy examples that you can download from the book's web site.

DEFERRED TECHNIQUES

Unfortunately, at this point in the book you don't know enough about writing code to be able to understand and fix certain kinds of bugs. For example, a program crashes if it tries to access an array entry that is outside of the array, but you won't learn about arrays until Lesson 16.

So why does this lesson cover debugging when you don't even know all of what can cause bugs or the techniques that you need to fix certain kinds of bugs? It makes sense for two reasons.

First, the previous lesson was the first part of the book in which you were likely to encounter bugs. Whenever I teach beginning programming, students start seeing bugs as soon as they write code that performs calculations like those covered in Lesson 11. These kinds of bugs are easy to fix if you know just a little bit about debugging but can be extremely frustrating if you don't.

Second, it turns out that you don't need to know more advanced techniques to learn simple debugging. Once you learn how to track down simple bugs, you can use the same techniques to find more advanced bugs. (If you learn to swim in 3 feet of water, you can use the same techniques to swim in 10 feet or 100 feet of water.)

Later, when you know more about Visual Basic programming and deal with more advanced bugs, that same knowledge will help you fix those bugs. When you know enough to have array indexing errors, you'll also know enough to fix them.

DEBUGGING THEN AND NOW

Back in the bad old days, programmers often fixed bugs by staring hard at the code, making a few test changes, and then running the program again to see what happened. This trial-and-error approach was extremely slow because the programmer didn't really know exactly what was going on inside the code. If the programmer didn't have a good understanding of what was really happening, the test changes often didn't help and sometimes made the problem worse.

Visual Studio's IDE provides excellent tools for debugging code. In particular, it lets you stop a program while it is running and see what it's doing. It lets you follow the program as it executes its code one line at a time, look at variable values, and even change those values while the program is still running.

The following sections describe some of Visual Studio's most useful debugging tools.

SETTING BREAKPOINTS

A *breakpoint* stops code execution at a particular piece of code. To set a breakpoint, open the Code Editor and click the gray margin to the left of the code where you want to stop. Alternatively, you can place the cursor on the line and press F9. The IDE displays a red circle to show that the line has a breakpoint.

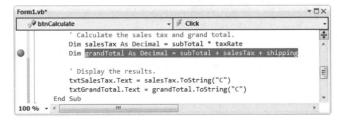

FIGURE 12-1

Figure 12-1 shows a breakpoint set on the following line of code:

```
Dim grandTotal As Decimal = subTotal + salesTax + shipping
```

If you run the program now, execution stops when it reaches that line. You can then study the code as described in the following sections.

The debugger provides an *edit-and-continue* feature that lets you modify a stopped program's code. You can add new statements, remove existing statements, declare new variables, and so forth. Unfortunately, some changes confuse the debugger, and you'll have to restart your program. But sometimes you can make small changes without restarting.

To remove a breakpoint, click the red breakpoint circle or press F9 again.

> Note that edit-and-continue isn't supported when you're building a 64-bit program, but you can test a 32-bit program built on a 64-bit system. In Solution Explorer, right-click on the solution and select Properties. Expand the Configuration Properties folder, select the Configuration tab, and set Platform to "x86." After you finish testing, you can switch the program back to 64 bits.

SPONTANEOUS STOP

If you need to stop a program while it is running and you haven't set any breakpoints, you can select the Debug menu's Break All command or press [Ctrl]+[Break]. The debugger will halt the program in the middle of whatever it is doing and enter break mode.

This technique is particularly useful for interrupting long tasks or infinite loops.

READING VARIABLES

It's easy to read a variable's value while execution is stopped. Simply hover the mouse over a variable and its value appears in a popup window.

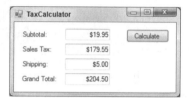

For example, consider the TaxCalculator program shown in Figure 12-2. The program is supposed to add a subtotal, 9% sales tax, and shipping costs to get a grand total. It doesn't take Stephen Hawking to realize that something's wrong. If you're really paying $204.50 for a $19.95 purchase, you need to find a new place to shop.

FIGURE 12-2

To debug this program, you could place a breakpoint on a line of code near where you know the bug occurs. For example, the line of code containing the breakpoint in Figure 12-1 calculates the grand total. Because the total displayed in Figure 12-2 is wrong, this seems like a good place to begin the bug hunt. (You can download the TaxCalculator program from the book's web site and follow along if you like.)

When the code is stopped, you can hover the mouse over a variable to learn its value. If you hover the mouse over the variables in that line of code, you'll find that subTotal is 19.95 (correct), shipping is 5 (correct), and salesTax is 179.55 (very much incorrect). Figure 12-3 shows the mouse hovering over the salesTax variable to display its value.

Now that you know the bug is lurking in the variable salesTax, you can hover the mouse over other variables to see how that value was calculated. If you hover the mouse over the variables in the previous line of code, you'll find that subTotal is 19.95 (still correct), and taxRate is 9.

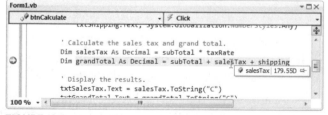

FIGURE 12-3

You may need to think about that for a bit to realize what's going wrong. To apply a tax rate such as 9%, you divide by 100 and then multiply. In this case, taxRate should be 0.09, not 9.

Having figured out the problem, you can stop the program by opening the Debug menu and selecting the Stop Debugging command or by clicking the Stop Debugging button on the toolbar (see Figure 12-4).

Now you can fix the code and run the program again to see if it works. The following line shows the incorrect line of code (I scrolled it out of view in Figure 12-3 so it wouldn't be a complete giveaway):

```
Const taxRate As Decimal = 9D
```

If you change this to 0.09D and run the program again, you should get the correct a sales tax $1.80 and the grand total $26.75. In a more complicated program, you would need to perform a lot more tests to ensure that the program behaved properly for different inputs, including weird ones such as when the user enters "ten dollars" for the subtotal or leaves the shipping cost blank. This example isn't robust enough to handle those problems.

STEPPING THROUGH CODE

Once you've stopped the code at a breakpoint, you can step through the execution one statement at a time to see what happens. The Debug menu provides four commands that control execution:

➤ **Continue (F5)** — Makes the program continue running until it finishes or reaches another breakpoint. Use this to run the program normally after you're done looking at the code.

➤ **Step Into (F8)** — Makes the program execute the current statement. If that statement contains a call to a subroutine, function, or other executable piece of code (these are covered in Lesson 20), execution stops inside that code so you can see how it works.

➤ **Step Over ([Shift]+F8)** — Makes the program execute the current statement. If that statement contains a call to another piece of executable code, the program runs that code and returns without stopping inside that code (unless it contains a breakpoint).

➤ **Step Out ([Ctrl]+[Shift]+F8)** — Makes the program run the current routine until it finishes and returns to the calling routine (unless it hits another breakpoint first).

 When it is stopped, the debugger highlights the next line of code that it will execute in yellow.

In addition to using the Debug menu or shortcut keys, you can invoke these commands from the toolbar. Figure 12-4 shows the debugging-related buttons in the Standard toolbar.

Stop Debugging   Step Over

Continue —   — Step Out

Break All   Step Into

FIGURE 12-4

Normally the program steps through its statements in order, but there is a way to jump to a particular line of code if you feel the need. Right-click the line that you want the code to execute next and select Set Next Statement from the context menu. Alternatively you can place the cursor on the line and press [Ctrl]+F9. When you let the program continue, it starts executing from this line.

Setting the next statement to execute is useful for replaying history to see where an error occurred, re-executing a line after you change a variable's value (described in the "Using the Immediate Window" section later in this lesson), or jumping forward to skip some code.

Note that you can jump only to certain lines of code. For example, you can't jump to a comment or other line of code that doesn't actually do anything (you can't set a breakpoint there either), you can't jump to a different method, you can't jump at all if an error has just occurred, you can't jump to a variable declaration unless it also initializes the variable, and so forth. Visual Basic does its best, but it has its limits.

USING WATCHES

Sometimes you may want to check a variable's value frequently as you step through the code one line at a time. In that case, pausing between steps to hover over a variable could slow you down, particularly if you have a lot of code to work through.

To make monitoring a variable easier, the debugger provides watches. A *watch* displays a variable's value whenever the program stops.

To create a watch, break execution, right-click a variable, and select Add Watch from the context menu. Figure 12-5 shows watches set on the variables `salesTax` and `subTotal`. Each time the program executes a line of code and stops, the watches update to display the variables' current values.

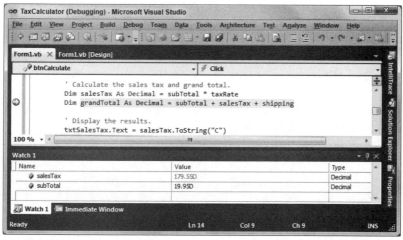

FIGURE 12-5

The Watch window also highlights, in red, any variables that have just changed. If you're tracking a lot of watches, this makes it easy to find the values that have changed.

The Locals window is similar to the Watch window except it shows the values of all the local variables (and constants). This window is handy if you want to view many of the variables at once. It also highlights recently changed values in red so you can see what's changing.

USING THE IMMEDIATE WINDOW

While the program is stopped, the Immediate window lets you execute simple commands. The four most useful commands that this window supports let you view variable values, evaluate expressions, set variable values, and call subroutines.

To find the Immediate window if it's missing, open the Debug menu, expand the Windows submenu, and select Immediate.

To view a variable's value, type a question mark followed by the variable's name and press [Enter].

The following code shows the contents of the Immediate window after I asked for the value of the `salesTax` variable:

```
?salesTax
179.55D
```

To evaluate an expression, type a question mark followed by the expression and press [Enter]. You can include literal values, variables, properties, constants, and just about anything else that you can normally include inside an expression in the code.

The following text shows the Immediate window after I typed an expression and pressed [Enter]:

```
?taxRate * subTotal
179.55D
```

To set a variable's value, simply type the variable's name, an equals sign, and the value that you want to give it. The new value can be a literal value or it can be the result of an expression. After you press [Enter], the Immediate window evaluates whatever is on the right of the equals sign and saves it in the variable.

The same technique lets you set new values for properties. For example, you can change a control's `Location`, `Text`, `Visible`, `BackColor`, *and other properties on-the-fly.*

Finally, to call a subroutine, simply type the subroutine call into the Immediate window and press [Enter]. Don't forget to add parentheses and parameters if they are required. If the method has a return value, start with a question mark to make the Immediate window display the result.

TRY IT

If you look closely at Figure 12-6, you'll see that this program has a serious problem. One tofu dinner at $13.95 each doesn't add up to $142.65. If you look a little more closely, you'll also see that the grand total doesn't add up properly.

In this Try It, you debug this program. You set breakpoints and use the debugger to figure out where the code is going wrong.

FIGURE 12-6

 You can download the code and resources for this Try It from the book's web page at www.wrox.com *or* www.vb-helper.com/24hourvb.html. *You can find them in the Lesson12 folder in the download. Note that the download contains both the version of the program that isn't working right and the corrected version (named "TryIt12" and "TryIt12Solution," respectively).*

Lesson Requirements

In this lesson:

➤ Use the debugger to fix this program. To follow along in the debugger, download this lesson's material from the book's web site and open the TryIt12 project.

➤ Run the program and experiment with it for a bit to see what seems to work and what seems to be broken. This should give you an idea of where the problem may lie.

➤ Set a breakpoint in the code near where you think there might be a problem. In this case, the tofu dinner cost calculation is wrong so you might set a breakpoint on this line:

```
Dim priceTofu As Decimal = tofuCost * numTofu
```

➤ Run the program so it stops at that breakpoint. Hover the mouse over different variables to see whether they look like they make sense.

➤ Step through the code watching each line closely to see what's wrong.

➤ Fix the error.

➤ Run the program again and test it to make sure the change you made works. Try setting two of the quantities to 0 and the third to 1 to see if the program can correctly calculate the non-zero value.

➤ If the program still has problems, run through these steps again.

Step-by-Step

The first two lesson requirements for this Try It are fairly straightforward so they aren't repeated here. The following paragraphs discuss the solution to the mystery, so if you want to try to debug the program yourself, do so before you read any further.

Ready? Let's go.

The following code shows how the program works. The bold line is where I set my breakpoint. If you stare at the code long enough, you'll probably find the bug so don't look too closely. Remember, the point is to practice using the debugger (which will be your only hope in more complicated programs), not to simply fix the program by staring at the code.

```
' Calculate the prices for each entree and the total price.
Private Sub btnCalculate_Click() Handles btnCalculate.Click
    Const costChicken As Decimal = 15.95D
    Const costSteak As Decimal = 18.95D
    Const costTofu As Decimal = 13.95D

    ' Get inputs.
    Dim numChicken As Integer = Integer.Parse(txtNumChicken.Text)
    Dim numSteak As Integer = Integer.Parse(txtNumSteak.Text)
    Dim numTofu As Integer = Integer.Parse(txtNumTofu.Text)

    ' Calculate results.
    Dim total As Decimal = 0

    Dim priceChicken As Decimal = costChicken * numChicken
    total += priceChicken

    Dim priceSteak As Decimal = costSteak * numSteak
    total += priceSteak

    Dim priceTofu As Decimal = costTofu * numTofu
    total += priceTofu

    ' Display results.
    txtPriceChicken.Text = priceChicken.ToString("C")
    txtPriceSteak.Text = priceSteak.ToString("C")
    txtPriceTofu.Text = priceTofu.ToString("C")
    txtTotal.Text = total.ToString("C")
End Sub
```

➤ Run the program so it stops at that breakpoint. Hover the mouse over different variables to see whether they look like they make sense.

    1. If you run to the breakpoint and hover the mouse over the variables, you'll find that most of them make sense: the values `numChicken = 9`, `priceChicken = 142.65`, and so forth.

➤ Step through the code watching each line closely to see what's wrong.

    1. While the program is stopped on the breakpoint, the variable `priceTofu` has the value 0 because the code hasn't yet executed the line that sets its value. Press [F8] to step over that line and you'll see that `priceTofu` is `13.95` as it should be. So far, you haven't found the bug.

If you continue stepping through the code, watching each line carefully, you'll eventually see the problem in this line:

```
txtPriceTofu.Text = priceChicken.ToString("C")
```

Here the code is making the tofu price `TextBox` display the value of `priceChicken`!

This is a fairly typical copy-and-paste error. The programmer wrote one line of code, copied and pasted it several times to perform similar tasks (displaying the values in the `TextBoxes`), but then didn't update each pasted line correctly.

➤ Fix the error.

1. This bug is easy to fix. Simply change the offending line to this:

```
txtPriceTofu.Text = priceTofu.ToString("C")
```

➤ Run the program again and test it to make sure the change you made works. Try setting two of the quantities to 0 and the third to 1 to see if the program can correctly calculate the non-zero value.

1. If you run the program again, everything should initially look okay. If you reproduce some calculations by hand, however, you may find a small discrepancy in the chicken prices.

2. You can see the problem more easily if you set the quantities of steak and tofu to 0 and the quantity of chicken to 1. Then the program calculates that the price of one chicken dinner (at $15.95 each) is $15.85.

➤ If the program still has problems, run through these steps again.

1. Having found another bug, run through the debugging process again. Set a breakpoint on the line that calculates `priceChicken` and hover over the variables to see if their values make sense.

   If you're paying attention, you'll see that the value of the constant `costChicken` is `15.85`, not `15.95` as it should be.

2. Fix the constant declaration and test the program again.

Please select Lesson 12 on the DVD to view the video that accompanies this lesson.

It's extremely common for a program to contain more than one bug. In fact, it's an axiom of software development that any nontrivial program contains at least one bug.

A consequence of this axiom is that even after you fix the program's "last" bug, it still contains another bug. Sometimes fixing the bug introduces a new bug. (That's not as uncommon as you might think in a complex program.) Other times more bugs are hiding; you just haven't found them yet.

In complex projects, the goal is still to eradicate every single bug; but the reality is that often the best you can do is to fix bugs until the odds of the user finding one in everyday use are extremely small.

EXERCISES

Putting debugging exercises in a book can be a bit strange. If the code is included in the book, you can stare at that code until you see the bugs without using the debugger, which defeats the purpose.

For that reason, this section only describes the programs containing the bugs; you'll have to download the broken programs from the book's web site at www.wrox.com *or* www.vb-helper.com/24hourvb.html. *You can find the programs and corrected versions in the Lesson12 folder. The corrected versions are named after their exercises — for example, Ex12-1Solution. Modified lines are marked with comments.*

1. Debug this CelsiusToFahrenheit conversion program that produces incorrect results. (Hint: 0°C = 32°F and 100°C = 212°F.)

2. Debug this FeetToMiles program that produces incorrect results. (After you fix this one, notice that using constants instead of magic numbers and the approach taken by Exercises 5 and 6 in Lesson 11 would make fixing these bugs easier and might have avoided them from the start. Also note again that the duplicated code is a bad thing, which you'll learn how to fix in Lesson 20.)

3. The ResizePicture program is supposed to zoom in on a picture when you adjust its `TrackBar`. Unfortunately, when you move the `TrackBar`, the picture seems to shrink and move to a new location. Debug the program.

4. Debug the TaxForm program, which performs a fictitious tax calculation based on a real one. It's an ugly little program, but it's probably the most realistic one in this lesson. (Hint: For the program's initial inputs, the tax due should be $290.00.)

13

Understanding Scope

A variable's *scope* is the code that can "see" or access that variable. It determines whether a piece of code can read the variable's value and give it a new value.

In this lesson you learn what scope is; why restricting scope is a good thing; and how to determine a variable's scope.

SCOPE WITHIN A CLASS

A Visual Basic class (and note that Form types are classes, too) contains three main kinds of scope: class scope, method scope, and block scope. (If you have trouble remembering what a class is, review Lesson 9's section "Understanding Classes and Instances.")

➤ Variables with **class scope** are declared inside the class but outside of any of its methods. (A method is a routine containing statements, such as an event handler or a subroutine that you write.) These variables are visible to all of the code throughout the instance of the class and are known as *fields*.

➤ Variables with **method scope** are declared within a method. They are usable by all of the code that follows the declaration within that method.

➤ Variables with **block scope** are declared inside a block of code defined by some other program element such as an If Then statement or a For loop. The section "Block Scope" later in this lesson says more about this.

For example, consider the following code that defines a field, and some variables inside event handlers:

```
Public Class Form1
    ' A field.
    Dim a As Integer = 1
```

```
        Private Sub btnClickMe_Click() Handles btnClickMe.Click
            ' A method variable.
            Dim b As Integer = 2
            MessageBox.Show("a = " & a.ToString() & ", b = " & b.ToString())
        End Sub

        Private Sub btnClickMeToo_Click() Handles btnClickMeToo.Click
            ' A method variable.
            Dim c As Integer = 3
            MessageBox.Show("a = " & a.ToString() & ", c = " & c.ToString())
        End Sub
    End Class
```

The field a is declared outside of the two methods (btnClickMe_Click and btnClickMeToo_Click), so it has class scope. That means the code in any of the methods can see and use this variable. In this example, the two Click event handlers each display the value.

The variable b is declared within btnClickMe_Click, so it has method scope. Only the code within this method that comes after the declaration can use this variable. In particular, the code in the other methods cannot see it.

Similarly, the code in the btnClickMeToo_Click event handler that comes after the c declaration can see that variable.

Two variables with the same name cannot have the same scope. For example, you cannot create two variables named a at the class level, nor can you create two variables named b inside the same method.

Same-Named Variables

Although you cannot give two variables the same name within the same scope, you can give them the same name if they are in different methods or one is a field and the other is declared inside a method. For example, the following code defines three variables, all named count:

```
    Public Class Form1
        ' A field.
        Dim count As Integer = 0

        Private Sub btnClickMe_Click() Handles btnClickMe.Click
            ' A method variable.
            Dim count As Integer = 1
            MessageBox.Show(count.ToString())
        End Sub

        Private Sub btnClickMeToo_Click() Handles btnClickMeToo.Click
            ' A method variable.
            Dim count As Integer = 2
            MessageBox.Show(count.ToString())
        End Sub
    End Class
```

In this example, the method-level variable hides the class-level variable with the same name. For example, within the btnClickMe_Click event handler, its local version of count is visible and has the value 1. The class-level field with the value 0 is hidden.

You can still get the class-level value if you prefix the variable with the executing object. Recall that the special keyword Me *means "the object that is currently executing this code." That means you could access the class-level field while inside the* btnClickMe_Click *event handler like this:*

```
' A method variable.
Dim count As Integer = 1
MessageBox.Show(count.ToString())
MessageBox.Show(Me.count.ToString())
```

Usually it's better to avoid potential confusion by giving the variables different names in the first place.

Method Variable Lifetime

A variable with method scope is created when its method is executed. Each time the method is called, a new version of the variable is created. When the method exits, the variable is destroyed. If its *value* is referenced by some other variable, the value might still exist, but this variable is no longer available to manipulate it.

One consequence of this is that the variable's value resets each time the method executes. For example, consider the following code:

```
Private Sub btnClickMe_Click() Handles btnClickMe.Click
    ' A method variable.
    Dim count As Integer = 0
    count += 1
    MessageBox.Show(count.ToString())
End Sub
```

Each time this code executes, it creates a variable named count, adds 1 to it, and displays its value. The intent may be to have the message box display an incrementing counter but the event handler uses a new version of count each time, so the result is actually the value 1 every time the user clicks the button.

To save a value between method calls, you can change the variable into a field declared outside of any method. The following version of the preceding code displays the values 1, 2, 3, and so on when the user clicks the button multiple times:

```
' A field.
Dim count As Integer = 0

Private Sub btnClickMe_Click() Handles btnClickMe.Click
    ' A method variable.
    count += 1
    MessageBox.Show(count.ToString())
End Sub
```

Note that a parameter declared in a method's declaration counts as having method scope. For example, the preceding event handler has two parameters named `sender` and `e`. That means you cannot declare new variables within the event handler with those names.

Block Scope

A method can also contain nested blocks of code that define other variables that have scope limited to the nested code. This kind of variable cannot have the same name as a variable declared at a higher level of nesting within the same method.

Later lessons explain some of these kinds of nesting used to make decisions (Lesson 18), loops (Lesson 19), and error handlers (Lesson 21).

One example that you've seen before is the `If Then Else` statement. For example, consider the following code:

```
Private Sub btnClickMeToo_Click() Handles btnClickMeToo.Click
    ' A method variable.
    Dim count As Integer = 1
    MessageBox.Show(count.ToString())

    If count = 1 Then
        Dim i As Integer = 2
        MessageBox.Show(i.ToString())
    Else
        Dim i As Integer = 3
        MessageBox.Show(i.ToString())
    End If
End Sub
```

This method declares the variable `count` at the method level and displays its value.

The code then uses an `If Then Else` structure. It declares the variable `i` between the `Then` and `Else`, and displays its value. Note that the code could not create a second variable named `count` inside this block because the higher-level method code contains a variable with that name.

After the first block ends, the code contains a second block between the `Else` and `End If` statements. It makes a new variable `i` within that block and displays its value. Because the two inner blocks are not nested (neither contains the other), it's okay for both blocks to define variables named `i`.

ACCESSIBILITY

A field's scope determines what parts of the code can see the variable. So far I've focused on the fact that all of the code in a class can see a field declared at the class level outside of any methods. In fact, a field may also be visible to code running in other classes depending on its accessibility.

A field's *accessibility* determines which code is allowed to access the field. For example, a class might contain a public field that is visible to the code in any other class. It may also define a private field that is visible only to code within the class that defines it. The following code shows how a class might declare a public variable named `NumberOfUsers`:

```
Public NumberOfUsers As Integer
```

*Most developers use Pascal casing for public items declared at the class level,
so in this case the variable is* NumberOfUsers *instead of* numberOfUsers. *Many
developers even use Pascal casing for all items declared at the class level, even if
they are not public.*

*Also note that declaring fields to be public is considered bad programming style.
It's better to make a public property instead. Lesson 23 explains why and tells
how to make properties. Public fields do work, however, and are good enough
for this discussion of accessibility.*

Accessibility is not the same as scope, but the two work closely together to determine what code can
access a field.

Table 13-1 summarizes the field accessibility values. Later when you learn how to build properties and
methods, you'll be able to use the same accessibility values to determine what code can access them.

TABLE 13-1

ACCESSIBILITY VALUE	MEANING
Public	Any code can see the variable.
Private	Only code in the same class can see the variable.
Protected	Only code in the same class or a derived class can see the variable. For example, if the Manager class inherits from the Person class, a Manager object can see a Person object's Protected variables. (You'll learn more about deriving one class from another in Lesson 25.)
Friend	Only code in the same assembly can see the variable. For example, if the variable's class is contained in a library (which is its own assembly), a main program that uses the library cannot see the variable.
Protected Friend	The variable is visible to any code in the same assembly or any derived class in another assembly.

If you omit the accessibility value for a field, it defaults to Private. You can still include the
Private keyword, however, to make the field's accessibility obvious. (In fact, I recommend always
using an accessibility keyword to make the code easier to understand.)

The Private keyword sometimes causes confusion. A Private field is visible to any code in *any
instance* of the same class, not just to the *same instance* of the class.

*You cannot use accessibility keywords with variables defined inside a method.
For example, you cannot declare a public variable inside an event handler. No
code outside the event handler can ever see its variables.*

For example, suppose you build a `Person` class with a private field named `Salary`. Not only can all of the code in an instance see its own `Salary` value, but *any* `Person` object can see any other `Person` object's `Salary` value.

RESTRICTING SCOPE AND ACCESSIBILITY

It's a good programming practice to restrict a field's scope and accessibility as much as possible to limit the code that can access it. For example, if a piece of code has no business using a form's field, there's no reason to give it the opportunity. This not only reduces the chances that you will use the variable incorrectly, but also removes the variable from IntelliSense so it's not there to clutter up your options and confuse things.

If you can use a variable declared locally inside an event handler or other method, do so. In fact, if you can declare a variable within a block of code inside a method, such as in an `If Then` statement, do so. That gives the variable very limited scope so it won't get in the way when you're working with unrelated code. It also keeps the variable's declaration closer to the code that uses it so it's easier to see the connection.

If you need multiple methods to share the same value or you need to preserve a value between method calls, use a private field. Only make a field public if code in another form (or other class) needs to use it.

TRY IT

In this Try It, you build the program shown in Figure 13-1. You use fields to allow two forms to communicate and to perform simple calculations. You also get to try out a new control: `ListView`.

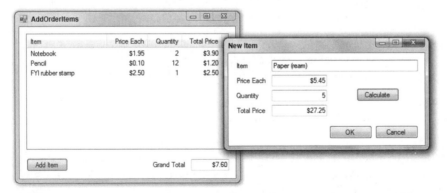

FIGURE 13-1

You can download the code and resources for this Try It from the book's web page at www.wrox.com or www.vb-helper.com/24hourvb.html. You can find them in the Lesson13 folder in the download.

Lesson Requirements

In this lesson:

➤ Create the `NewItemForm` shown on the right in Figure 13-1.

    ➤ Make the OK button initially disabled.

    ➤ Provide public fields to let the main form get the data entered by the user.

    ➤ Calculate and display Total Price when the user clicks the Calculate button, and enable the OK button.

➤ Create the main form shown on the left in Figure 13-1.

➤ Make the program display the `NewItemForm` when the user clicks the Add Item button. If the user clicks OK, display the entered values in the `ListView` control and update the Grand Total.

Hints

➤ Because the main form's Grand Total must retain its value as the user adds items, it must be a field.

➤ To let the main form see the values entered by the user on the `NewItemForm`, use public fields.

Step-by-Step

➤ Create the `NewItemForm` shown on the right in Figure 13-1.

1. Arrange the controls as shown in Figure 13-1.

2. Set the form's `AcceptButton` property to the OK button and its `CancelButton` property to the Cancel button. The OK button will always close the form, so set its `DialogResult` property to `OK`.

    ➤ Make the OK button initially disabled.

    1. Set the OK button's `Enabled` property to `False`.

    ➤ Provide public fields to let the main form get the data entered by the user.

    1. Declare public fields for the program to use in its calculations:

```
' Public fields. (They should really be properties.)
Public ItemName As String
Public PriceEach, Quantity, TotalPrice As Decimal
```

    ➤ Calculate and display Total Price when the user clicks the Calculate button, and enable the OK button.

    1. Use the techniques described in Lesson 11 to get the values entered by the user and calculate the item's Total Price. Use the fields you created in the previous step.

    2. Set the OK button's `Enabled` property to `True`.

➤ Create the main form shown on the left in Figure 13-1.

1. Create the controls shown in the figure.

2. To make the ListView display its items in a list:

    a. Set its View property to Details.

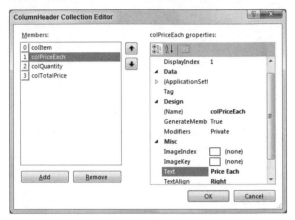

    b. Select its Columns property and click the ellipsis to the right to open the ColumnHeader Collection Editor shown in Figure 13-2. Click the Add button four times to make the four columns. Use the property editor on the right to set each column's Name and Text properties, and to set TextAlign to Right for the numeric columns.

FIGURE 13-2

➤ Make the program display the NewItemForm when the user clicks the Add Item button. If the user clicks OK, display the entered values in the ListView control and update the Grand Total.

1. Use code similar to the following.

```
' A private field to keep track of grand total
' across multiple calls to the event handler.
Private GrandTotal As Decimal = 0

' Let the user add a new item to the list.
Private Sub btnAddItem_Click() Handles btnAddItem.Click
    Dim frm As New NewItemForm()
    If (frm.ShowDialog() = DialogResult.OK) Then
        ' Get the new values.
        Dim lvi As ListViewItem = lvwItems.Items.Add(frm.ItemName)
        lvi.SubItems.Add(frm.PriceEach.ToString("C"))
        lvi.SubItems.Add(frm.Quantity.ToString())
        lvi.SubItems.Add(frm.TotalPrice.ToString("C"))

        ' Add to the grand total and display the new result.
        GrandTotal += frm.TotalPrice
        txtGrandTotal.Text = GrandTotal.ToString("C")
    End If
End Sub
```

 Please select Lesson 13 on the DVD to view the video that accompanies this lesson.

EXERCISES

1. Use a design similar to the one used in the Try It to let the user fill out an appointment calendar. The main form should contain a `ListView` with columns labeled Subject, Date, Time, and Notes. The `NewAppointmentForm` should provide textboxes for the user to enter these values and should have the public fields `AppointmentSubject`, `AppointmentDate`, `AppointmentTime`, and `AppointmentNotes` to let the main form get the entered values. Instead of a grand total, the main form should display the number of appointments.

2. Build a form that contains a `ListBox`, `TextBox`, and `Button`. When the user clicks the `Button`, display a dialog that lets the user enter a number. Give the dialog a public field to return the value to the main form.

If the user enters a value and clicks OK, the main form should add the number to its `ListBox`. It should then display the average of its numbers.

3. Build the conference schedule designer shown in Figure 13-3. Give the main form (on the left in Figure 13-3) the following features:

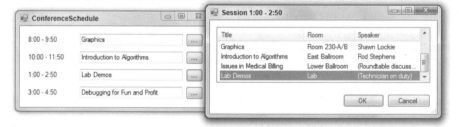

FIGURE 13-3

➤ Create private fields named `SessionIndex1`, `SessionIndex2`, and so forth to hold the indexes of the user's choices.

➤ When the user clicks an ellipsis button, display the session selection dialog shown on the right in Figure 13-3.

➤ After creating the dialog but before displaying it, set its `Text` property to indicate the session time in the dialog's title bar as shown in the figure.

➤ Also before displaying the dialog, use code similar to the following to tell the dialog about the user's previous selection for this session. (The `SessionIndex` and `SessionTitle` variables are public fields defined by the dialog and are discussed shortly.)

```
frm.SessionIndex = SessionIndex1
```

➤ If the user clicks OK, use code similar to the following to save the index of the user's choice and to display the session's title:

```
SessionIndex1 = frm.SessionIndex
txtChoice1.Text = frm.SessionTitle
```

Give the dialog the following features:

➤ Set the `ListView`'s `FullRowSelect` property to `True` and set its `MultiSelect` property to `False`.

➤ Use the Properties window to define the `ListView`'s column headers.

➤ Use the Properties window's editors to define the `ListView`'s items. Select the `ListView`, click its `Items` property, click the ellipsis to the right, and use the editor to define the items. Set the `Text` property to determine an item's text. Click the `SubItems` property and then click the ellipsis to the right to define the sub-items (Room and Speaker).

➤ Use the following code to create public fields to communicate with the main form:

```
' Public fields to communicate with the main form.
Public SessionIndex As Integer
Public SessionTitle As String
```

➤ Create a `Load` event handler that uses the following code to initialize the dialog. This code selects the proper session in the `ListView` control and then makes the control scroll if necessary so the session is visible:

```
' Initialize the selection.
Private Sub PickSessionForm_Load() Handles MyBase.Load
    lvwSessions.SelectedIndices.Add(SessionIndex)

    ' Ensure that the selection is visible.
    lvwSessions.SelectedItems(0).EnsureVisible()
End Sub
```

➤ In the OK button's `Click` event handler, use the following code to save the selected item's index and title for the main form to use:

```
' Save the user's selection.
Private Sub btnOk_Click() Handles btnOk.Click
    SessionIndex = lvwSessions.SelectedIndices(0)
    SessionTitle = lvwSessions.SelectedItems(0).Text
End Sub
```

You can find solutions to this lesson's exercises in the Lesson13 folder inside the download available on the book's web site at www.wrox.com *or* www.vb-helper.com/24hourvb.html.*

14

Working with Strings

Previous lessons provided a sneak peek at some of the things that a Visual Basic program can do with strings. Lesson 11 explained how you can use the & operator to concatenate two strings. Several lessons show how to use the ToString method to convert numeric values into strings that you can then display to the user.

In this lesson, you learn a lot more about strings. You learn about String class methods that let you search strings, replace parts of strings, and extract pieces of strings. You also learn new ways to format numeric and other kinds of data to produce strings.

STRING METHODS

The String class provides a lot of useful methods for manipulating strings. For example, the EndsWith method returns True if a string ends with a particular substring. The following code determines whether a string ends with the substring dog:

```
Dim str As String = "The quick brown fox jumps over the lazy dog"
MessageBox.Show("Ends with dog: " & str.EndsWith("dog"))
```

Table 14-1 summarizes the String class's most useful methods.

TABLE 14-1

METHOD	PURPOSE
Contains	Returns True if the string contains a target string.
EndsWith	Returns True if the string ends with a target string.
IndexOf	Returns the index of a target character or string within the string.

continues

TABLE 14-1 *(continued)*

METHOD	PURPOSE
IndexOfAny	Returns the index of the first occurrence of any of a set of characters in the string.
Insert	Inserts text in the middle of the string.
LastIndexOf	Returns the index of the last occurrence of a target character or string within the string.
LastIndexOfAny	Returns the index of the last occurrence of any of a set of characters in the string.
PadLeft	Pads the string to a given length by adding characters on the left if necessary.
PadRight	Pads the string to a given length by adding characters on the right if necessary.
Remove	Removes a piece of the string.
Replace	Replaces occurrences of a string or character with new values within the string.
Split	Splits the string apart at a delimiter (for example, commas) and returns an array containing the pieces.
StartsWith	Returns True if the string starts with a target string.
Substring	Returns a substring.
ToLower	Returns the string converted to lowercase.
ToUpper	Returns the string converted to uppercase.
Trim	Removes leading and trailing characters from the string. A version that takes no parameters removes whitespace characters (space, tab, newline, and so on).
TrimEnd	Removes trailing characters from the string.
TrimStart	Removes leading characters from the string.

 Remember that string indexing starts with 0 so the first letter has index 0, the second has index 1, and so forth.

In addition to all of these methods, the String class provides a very useful Length property. As you can probably guess, Length returns the number of characters in the string.

The String class also provides the useful shared methods Format and Join. A shared method is one that is provided by the class itself rather than an instance of the class. You invoke a static method using the class's name instead of a variable's name.

The Format method formats a series of parameters according to a format string and returns a new string. For example, the following code uses the String class's Format method to display the values in the variables x and y surrounded by parentheses and separated by a comma:

```
Dim x As Integer = 10
Dim y As Integer = 20
Dim txt As String = String.Format("({0}, {1})", x, y)
MessageBox.Show(txt)
```

The next section says more about the Format method.

The Join method does the opposite of the Split method: it joins a series of strings, separating them with a delimiter.

FORMAT AND TOSTRING

The String class's Format method builds a formatted String. Its first parameter is a format string that tells how the method should display its other parameters. The format string can contain literal characters that are displayed as they appear, plus formatting fields.

Each field has the following syntax:

```
{index[,alignment][:formatString]}
```

The curly braces are required. The square brackets indicate optional pieces.

The key pieces of the field are:

> index — The zero-based index of the Format method's parameters that should be displayed by this field.

> alignment — The minimum number of characters that the field should use. If this is negative, the field is left-justified.

> formatString — The format string that indicates how the field's value should be formatted. The following format sections describe some of the many values that you can use here in addition to literal characters.

For example, the following code defines a String and two Decimal values. It then displays the result in a message box.

```
Dim itemName As String = "Fiendishly Difficult Puzzles"
Dim quantity As Decimal = 2D
Dim price_each As Decimal = 9.99D

MessageBox.Show(
    String.Format("You just bought {1} {0} at {2:C} each.",
    itemName, quantity, price_each))
```

The format string is `"You just bought {1} {0} at {2:C} each."`

The first field is `{1}`. This displays parameter number 1 (the second parameter — remember they're zero-based).

The second field is `{0}`. This displays the first parameter.

The third field is `{2:C}`. This displays the third parameter with the format string `C`, which formats the value as currency.

The result is:

```
You just bought 2 Fiendishly Difficult Puzzles at $9.99 each.
```

The following code shows an example that uses field widths to make values line up in columns. Before the code executes, assume that `itemName1`, `quantity1`, and the other variables have already been initialized. (The `Console.WriteLine` statement writes output into the Output window.)

```
Console.WriteLine(
    String.Format("{0,-20}{1,5}{2,10}{3,10}",
    "Item", "Qty", "Each", "Total")
)
Console.WriteLine(
    String.Format("{0,-20}{1,5}{2,10:C}{3,10:C}",
    itemName1, quantity1, priceEach1, quantity1 * priceEach1)
)
Console.WriteLine(
    String.Format("{0,-20}{1,5}{2,10:C}{3,10:C}",
    itemName2, quantity2, priceEach2, quantity2 * priceEach2)
)
Console.WriteLine(
    String.Format("{0,-20}{1,5}{2,10:C}{3,10:C}",
    itemName3, quantity3, priceEach3, quantity3 * priceEach3)
)
```

Notice that the code begins with a line that defines the column headers. Its formatting string uses the same indexes and alignment values as the other formatting strings so the headers line up with the values below.

The following shows the result:

```
Item                  Qty    Each     Total
Pretzels (dozen)        4   $5.95    $23.80
Blue laser pointer      1 $149.99   $149.99
Titanium spork          2   $8.99    $17.98
```

Because the format string is just a string, you could define it in a constant or variable and then use that variable as the first argument to the Format *method. That way you are certain that all of the* Format *statements use the same string. This also makes it easier to change the format later if necessary.*

Every object provides a `ToString` method that converts the object into a string. For simple data types such as numbers and dates, the result is the value in an easy-to-read string.

The `ToString` method for some objects can take a format parameter that tells how you want the item formatted. For example, the following statement displays the variable `cost` formatted as a currency value in the Output window:

```
Console.WriteLine(cost.ToString("C"))
```

The following sections describe standard and custom format strings for numbers, dates, and times. You can use these as arguments to the `ToString` method or as format strings passed to `String.Format`.

Standard Numeric Formats

Formatting characters tell `String.Format` and `ToString` how to format a value. For the characters discussed in this section, you can use either an uppercase or lowercase letter. For example, you can use `C` or `c` for the currency format.

Table 14-2 summarizes the standard numeric formatting characters.

TABLE 14-2

CHARACTER	MEANING	EXAMPLE
C	Currency with a currency symbol, thousands separators, and a decimal point.	$12,345.67
D	Decimal. Integer types only.	12345
E	Scientific notation.	1.234567E+004
F	Fixed-point.	12345.670
G	General. Either fixed-point or scientific notation, whichever is shorter.	12345.67
N	Similar to currency except without the currency symbol.	12,345.67
P	Percent. The number is multiplied by 100 and a percent sign is added appropriately for the computer's locale. Includes thousands separators and a decimal point.	123.45 %
R	Round trip. The number (double or float only) is formatted in a way that guarantees it can be parsed back into its original value.	1234.567
X	Hexadecimal.	3A7

You can follow several of these characters with a *precision specifier* that affects how the value is formatted. How this value works depends on the format character that it follows.

For the D and X formats, the result is padded on the left with zeros to have the length given by the precision specifier. For example, the format D10 produces a decimal value padded with zeros to 10 characters.

For the C, E, F, N, and P formats, the precision specifier indicates the number of digits after the decimal point.

Custom Numeric Formats

If the standard numeric formatting characters don't do what you want, you can use a custom numeric format. Table 14-3 summarizes the custom numeric formatting characters.

TABLE 14-3

CHARACTER	MEANING
0	Digit or zero. A digit is displayed here or a zero if there is no corresponding digit in the value being formatted.
#	Digit or nothing. A digit is displayed here or nothing if there is no corresponding digit in the value being formatted.
.	Decimal separator. The decimal separator goes here. Note that the actual separator character may not be a period depending on the computer's regional settings, although you still use the period in the format string.
,	Thousands separator. The thousands separator goes here. The actual separator character may not be a comma depending on the computer's regional settings, although you still use the comma in the format string.
%	Percent. The number is multiplied by 100 and the percent sign is added at this point. For example, %0 puts the percent sign before the number and 0% puts it after.
E+0	Scientific notation. The number of 0s indicates the number of digits in the exponent. If + is included, the exponent always includes a + or − sign. If + is omitted, the exponent only includes a sign if the exponent is negative. For example, the format string #.##E+000 used with the value 1234.56 produces the result 1.23E+003.
\	Escape character. Whatever follows the \ is displayed without any conversion. For example, the format 0.00\% would add a percent sign to a number without scaling it by 100 as the format 0.00% does.
'ABC'	Literal string. Characters enclosed in single quotes are displayed without any conversion.
;	Section separator. See the following text.

You can use a section separator to divide a formatting string into two or three sections. If you use two sections, the first applies to values greater than or equal to zero, and the second section applies to values less than zero. If you use three sections, they apply to values that are greater than, less than, and equal to zero, respectively.

For example, Table 14-4 shows the result produced by the three-section custom formatting string `"{0:$#,##0.00;($#,##0.00);— zero —}"` for different values.

TABLE 14-4

VALUE	FORMATTED RESULT
12345.678	$12,345.68
-12345.678	($12,345.68)
0.000	— zero —

Standard Date and Time Formats

Just as numeric values have standard and custom formatting strings, so too do dates and times.

Table 14-5 summarizes the standard date and time formatting patterns. The examples are those produced for 1:23 PM August 20, 2011 on my computer set up for US English. Your results will depend on how your computer is configured. Note that for many of the characters in this table, the uppercase and lowercase versions have different meanings.

TABLE 14-5

CHARACTER	MEANING	EXAMPLE
d	Short date	8/20/2011
D	Long date	Friday, August 20, 2011
f	Full date, short time	Friday, August 20, 2011 1:23 PM
F	Full date, long time	Friday, August 20, 2011 1:23:00 PM
g	General date/time, short time	8/20/2011 1:23 PM
G	General date/time, long time	8/20/2011 1:23:00 PM
M or m	Month day	August 20
O	Round trip	2011-08-20T13:23:00.0000000
R or r	RFC1123	Fri, 20 Aug 2011 13:23:00 GMT
s	Sortable date/time	2011-08-20T13:23:00
t	Short time	1:23 PM
T	Long time	1:23:00 PM

continues

TABLE 14-5 *(continued)*

CHARACTER	MEANING	EXAMPLE
u	Universal sortable short date/time	2011-08-20 13:23:00Z
U	Universal sortable full date/time	Friday, August 20, 2011 1:23:00 PM
Y or y	Month, year	August, 2011

The `DateTime` class also provides several methods that return the date's value as a string formatted in the most common date and time formats. Table 14-6 summarizes the most useful of these methods and shows the results on my computer set up for US English. Your results will depend on how your computer is configured.

TABLE 14-6

METHOD	FORMAT	EXAMPLE
ToLongDateString	Long date (D)	Friday, August 20, 2010
ToLongTimeString	Long time (T)	1:23:00 PM
ToShortDateString	Short date (d)	8/20/2010
ToShortTimeString	Short time (t)	1:23 PM
ToString	General date and time (G)	8/20/2010 1:23:00 PM

Custom Date and Time Formats

If the standard date and time formatting characters don't do the trick, you can use a custom format. Table 14-7 summarizes the custom date and time formatting strings. Note that for many of the characters in this table, the uppercase and lowercase versions have different meanings.

TABLE 14-7

CHARACTER	MEANING
d	Day of month between 1 and 31.
dd	Day of month between 01 and 31.
ddd	Abbreviated day of week (Mon, Tue, and so on).
dddd	Full day of week (Monday, Tuesday, and so on).
f	Digits after the decimal for seconds. For example, ffff means use four digits.
F	Similar to f but trailing zeros are not displayed.

CHARACTER	MEANING
g	Era specifier. For example, A.D.
h	Hours between 1 and 12.
hh	Hours between 01 and 12.
H	Hours between 0 and 23.
HH	Hours between 00 and 23.
m	Minutes between 0 and 59.
mm	Minutes between 00 and 59.
M	Month between 1 and 12.
MM	Month between 01 and 12.
MMM	Month abbreviation (Jan, Feb, and so on).
MMMM	Month name (January, February, and so on).
s	Seconds between 0 and 59.
ss	Seconds between 00 and 59.
t	First character of AM/PM designator.
tt	AM/PM designator.
y	One- or two-digit year. If the year has fewer than two digits, is it not zero padded.
yy	Two-digit year, zero padded if necessary.
yyy	Three-digit year, zero padded if necessary.
yyyy	Four-digit year, zero padded if necessary.
yyyyy	Five-digit year, zero padded if necessary.
z	Signed time zone offset from GMT. For example, Pacific Standard Time is −8.
zz	Signed time zone offset from GMT in two digits. For example, Pacific Standard Time is −08.
zzz	Signed time zone offset from GMT in hours and minutes. For example, Pacific Standard Time is −08:00.
:	Hours, minutes, and seconds separator.
/	Date separator.
'ABC'	Literal string. Characters enclosed in single quotes are displayed without any conversion.

Table 14-8 shows some example formats and their results. The date used was 1:23:45.678 PM August 20, 2011 on my computer set up for US English. Your results will depend on how your computer is configured.

TABLE 14-8

FORMAT	RESULT
M/d/yy	8/20/11
d MMM yy	20 Aug 11
HH:mm 'hours'	13:23 hours
h:mm:ss.ff, M/d/y	1:23:45.67, 8/20/11
dddd 'at' h:mmt	Friday at 1:23P
ddd 'at' h:mmtt	Fri at 1:23PM

TRY IT

In this Try It, you build a program that displays the current date and time in a `Label` when it starts, as shown in Figure 14-1.

It is 9:21AM on Fri, Apr 01 2011

FIGURE 14-1

Lesson Requirements

In this lesson:

➤ Start a new project and add a `Label` to its form.

➤ Give the form a `Load` event handler that sets the `Label`'s text as shown in Figure 14-1.

> *You can download the code and resources for this Try It from the book's web page at* www.wrox.com *or* www.vb-helper.com/24hourvb.html. *The programs can be found within the Lesson14 folder.*

Hints

➤ The `DateTime.Now` property returns the current date and time.

➤ Either use `String.Format` or the value's `ToString` method to format the result.

Step-by-Step

➤ Start a new project and add a `Label` to its form.

1. Create the new project and its `Label`. Dock the label to the form and make it center its text.

➤ Give the form a `Load` event handler that sets the `Label`'s text as shown in Figure 14-1.

1. Use code similar to the following:

```
' Display the current date and time.
Private Sub Form1_Load() Handles MyBase.Load
    lblDateAndTime.Text = DateTime.Now.ToString(
        "'It is' h:mmtt 'on' ddd, MMM dd yyyy")
End Sub
```

 Please select Lesson 14 on the DVD to view the video that accompanies this lesson.

EXERCISES

1. Lesson 13's Try It reads and displays currency values, but it displays quantities without thousands separators. If you ordered 1,200 pencils, the program would display 1200.

Copy that program (or download the Lesson 13 Try It from the book's web site) and modify it so quantities are displayed with thousands separators.

2. Make a program that displays the time every second. (Hint: Use a `Timer`.)

3. Copy the program that you built for Exercise 1 and modify it so the main form displays items in a `ListBox` instead of a `ListView`. Make the program use `string.Format` to add items to the `ListBox` in a format similar to the following:

```
1,200 Gummy slugs at $0.02 each = $24.00
```

4. Make a program that replaces all occurrences of the letter e in a string entered by the user with the character -.

 You can find solutions to this lesson's exercises in the Lesson14 folder inside the download available on the book's web site at www.wrox.com *or* www.vb-helper.com/24hourvb.html.

15

Working with Dates and Times

One of Visual Basic's more confusing data types is Date. A Date represents a date, a time, or both. For example, a Date variable might represent Thursday April 1, 2011 at 9:15 a.m.

In this lesson, you learn how to work with dates and times. You learn how to create Date variables, find the current date and time, and calculate elapsed time.

 The DateTime *data type is a synonym for* Date.

CREATING DATE VARIABLES

You can initialize a Date variable to a literal value by surrounding it in number signs as shown here:

```
Dim dueDate As Date = #10/31/2011 1:23:00 PM#
```

You can also initialize a Date by using the New keyword as in the following code:

```
Dim dueDate As New Date(2011, 10, 31)
```

The preceding code uses a year, month, and day to initialize its Date variable, but the Date type lets you use many different kinds of values. The three most useful combinations of arguments specify the following (all as integers):

➤ Year, month, day

➤ Year, month, day, hour, minute, second

➤ Year, month, day, hour, minute, second, milliseconds

You can also add a `kind` parameter to the end of the second and third of these combinations to indicate whether the value represents local time or UTC time. (Local and UTC times are explained in the next section.) For example, the following code creates a `Date` representing 12 noon on March 15, 2010 in the local time zone:

```
Dim idesOfMarch As New Date(2010, 3, 15, 12, 0, 0, DateTimeKind.Local)
```

LOCAL AND UTC TIME

Windows has several different notions of dates and times. Two of the most important of these are *local time* and *Coordinated Universal Time (UTC)*.

➤ **Local time** is the time on your computer as it is configured for a particular locale. It's what you and a program's user typically think of as time.

➤ **UTC time** is basically the same as Greenwich Mean Time (GMT), the time at the Royal Academy in Greenwich, London.

For most everyday tasks, local time is fine. If you need to compare data on computers running in different time zones, however, UTC time can make coordination easier. For example, if you want to know whether a customer in New York created an order before another customer created an order in San Salvador, UTC enables you to compare the times without worrying about the customers' time zones.

A `Date` object's `Kind` property indicates whether the object represents local time, UTC time, or an unspecified time. When you create a `Date`, you can indicate whether you are creating a local time or UTC time. If you do not specify the kind of time, Visual Basic assumes you are making an unspecified time.

After you create a `Date`, the type provides a couple of methods for converting it between local and UTC values. The `ToLocalTime` method converts a `Date` object to local time. Conversely, the `ToUniversalTime` method converts a time to UTC time.

 The `ToLocalTime` *and* `ToUniversalTime` *methods don't affect a* Date *if it is already in the desired format. For example, if you call* `ToLocalTime` *on a variable that already uses local time, the result is the same as the original variable.*

DATE PROPERTIES AND METHODS

The `Date` type provides many useful properties and methods for manipulating dates and times. Table 15-1 summarizes some of `Date`'s most useful methods. It indicates which methods are shared, meaning you invoke them using the type name, rather than a variable name, as in `Date.IsLeapYear(2012)`.

TABLE 15-1

METHOD	PURPOSE
Add	Adds a `TimeSpan` to the `Date`. The following section of this lesson describes `TimeSpan`.
AddDays	Adds a specified number of days to the `Date`.
AddHours	Adds a specified number of hours to the `Date`.
AddMinutes	Adds a specified number of minutes to the `Date`.
AddMonths	Adds a specified number of months to the `Date`.
AddSeconds	Adds a specified number of seconds to the `Date`.
AddYears	Adds a specified number of years to the `Date`.
IsDaylightSavingsTime	Returns `True` if the date and time are within the Daylight Savings Time period for the local time zone.
IsLeapYear	(Shared) Returns `True` if the indicated year is a leap year.
Parse	(Shared) Parses a string and returns the corresponding `Date`.
Subtract	Subtracts another `Date` from this one and returns a `TimeSpan`. The following section of this lesson says more about `TimeSpan`.
ToLocalTime	Converts the `Date` to a local value.
ToLongDateString	Returns the `Date` in long date format.
ToLongTimeString	Returns the `Date` in long time format.
ToShortDateString	Returns the `Date` in short date format.
ToShortTimeString	Returns the `Date` in short time format.
ToString	Returns the `Date` in general format.
ToUniversalTime	Converts the `Date` to a UTC value.

Table 15-2 summarizes the `Date`'s most useful properties.

TABLE 15-2

PROPERTY	PURPOSE
Date	Gets the `Date`'s date without the time
Day	Gets the `Date`'s day of the month between 1 and 31
DayOfWeek	Gets the `Date`'s day of the week

continues

TABLE 15-2 *(continued)*

PROPERTY	PURPOSE
DayOfYear	Gets the Date's day of the year between 1 and 366 (leap years have 366 days)
Hour	Gets the Date's hour between 0 and 23
Kind	Returns the Date's kind: Local, Utc, or Unspecified
Millisecond	Gets the Date's millisecond
Minute	Gets the Date's minute between 0 and 59
Month	Gets the Date's month between 1 and 12
Now	(Shared) Gets the current date and time
Second	Gets the Date's second between 0 and 59
TimeOfDay	Gets the Date's time of day as a TimeSpan
Today	(Shared) Gets the current date without a time
UtcNow	(Shared) Gets the current UTC date and time
Year	Gets the Date's year

TIMESPANS

A Date represents a point in time (July 20, 1969 at 20:17:40). A TimeSpan represents an elapsed period of time (1 day, 17 hours, 27 minutes, and 12 seconds).

One of the more useful ways to make a TimeSpan is to subtract one Date from another to find the amount of time between them. For example, the following code calculates the time that elapsed between the first and last manned moon landings:

```
Dim firstLanding As New Date(1969, 7, 20, 20, 17, 40)
Dim lastLanding As New Date(1972, 12, 11, 19, 54, 57)
Dim elapsed As TimeSpan = lastLanding - firstLanding
MessageBox.Show(elapsed.ToString())
```

The code creates Date values to represent the times of the two landings. It then subtracts the first date from the second to get the elapsed time and uses the resulting TimeSpan's ToString method to display the duration. The following text shows the code's output in the format days. hours:minutes:seconds.

```
1239.23:37:17
```

Table 15-3 summarizes the `TimeSpan`'s most useful properties and methods.

TABLE 15-3

PROPERTY	MEANING
Days	The number of days.
Hours	The number of hours.
Milliseconds	The number of milliseconds.
Minutes	The number of minutes.
Seconds	The number of seconds.
ToString	Converts the `TimeSpan` into a string in the format `days.hours:minutes:seconds.fractionalSeconds`
TotalDays	The entire `TimeSpan` represented as days. For a 36-hour duration, this would be 1.5.
TotalHours	The entire `TimeSpan` represented as hours. For a 45-minute duration, this would be 0.75.
TotalMilliseconds	The entire `TimeSpan` represented as milliseconds. For a 1-second duration, this would be 1,000.
TotalMinutes	The entire `TimeSpan` represented as minutes. For a 1-hour duration, this would be 60.
TotalSeconds	The entire `TimeSpan` represented as seconds. For a 1-minute `TimeSpan`, this would be 60.

Note that you can use the + and – operators to add and subtract `TimeSpans`, getting a new `TimeSpan` as a result. This works in a fairly obvious way. For example, a 90-minute `TimeSpan` minus a 30-minute `TimeSpan` results in a 60-minute `TimeSpan`.

TRY IT

In this Try It, you use `Date` and `TimeSpan` variables to build the stopwatch application shown in Figure 15-1. When the user clicks the Start button, the program starts its counter. When the user clicks the Stop button, the program stops the counter.

Normally the `TimeSpan`'s `ToString` method displays a value in the format `d.hh:mm:ss.fffffff`. In this example, you use `String.Format` to display the elapsed time in the format `hh:mm:ss.ff`.

FIGURE 15-1

You can download the code and resources for this Try It from the book's web page at www.wrox.com *or* www.vb-helper.com/24hourvb.html. *You can find them within the Lesson15 folder.*

Lesson Requirements

In this lesson:

➤ Create the form shown in Figure 15-1. In addition to the controls that are visible, give the form a `Timer` with `Interval` = 1. Initially disable the Stop button.

➤ When the user clicks the Start button, start the `Timer`, disable the Start button, and enable the Stop button.

➤ When the user clicks the Stop button, stop the `Timer`, enable the Start button, and disable the Stop button.

➤ When the `Timer`'s `Tick` event fires, display the elapsed time in the format `hh:mm:ss.ff`.

Hints

➤ `TimeSpan` doesn't use the same formatting characters as a `Date`; for example, you can't simply use a format string such as `hh:mm:ss.ff`. Instead, use the `TimeSpan` properties to get the elapsed hours, minutes, seconds, and milliseconds and then format those values.

Step-by-Step

➤ Create the form shown in Figure 15-1. In addition to the controls that are visible, give the form a `Timer` with `Interval` = 1. Initially disable the Stop button.

1. Add the Start and Stop buttons and a `Label` to the form as shown in Figure 15-1. Set the Stop button's `Enabled` property to `False`.

2. Add a `Timer` and set its `Interval` property to 1 millisecond. (This is much faster than your computer can actually fire the `Timer`'s `Click` event, so the `Timer` will run as quickly as it can.)

➤ When the user clicks the Start button, start the `Timer`, disable the Start button, and enable the Stop button.

1. To remember the time when the user clicked the Start button, create a `Date` field named `StartTime`:

   ```
   ' The time when the user clicked Start.
   Private StartTime As Date
   ```

2. Add the following code to the Start button's `Click` event handler:

   ```
   StartTime = Date.Now
   btnStart.Enabled = False
   btnStop.Enabled = True
   tmrElapsed.Enabled = True
   ```

➤ When the user clicks the Stop button, stop the Timer, enable the Start button, and disable the Stop button.

1. Add the following code to the Stop button's Click event handler:

```
btnStart.Enabled = True
btnStop.Enabled = False
tmrElapsed.Enabled = False
```

➤ When the Timer's Tick event fires, display the elapsed time in the format hh:mm:ss.ff.

1. Use code similar to the following. Notice that the code divides the number of milliseconds by 10 to convert it into hundredths of seconds.

```
' Subtract the start time from the
' current time to get elapsed time.
Dim elapsed As TimeSpan = Date.Now - StartTime

' Display the result.
lblElapsed.Text = String.Format(
    "{0:00}:{1:00}:{2:00}.{3:00}",
    elapsed.Hours,
    elapsed.Minutes,
    elapsed.Seconds,
    elapsed.Milliseconds / 10)
```

 Please select Lesson 15 on the DVD to view the video that accompanies this lesson.

EXERCISES

1. Make a program with a Birth Date TextBox and a Calculate button. When the user enters a birth date and clicks the button, calculate the person's current age and add items to a ListBox that display the age converted into each of days, hours, minutes, and seconds.

2. Make a program that displays the days of the week for your next 10 birthdays in a ListBox.

3. Make a program with two TextBoxes for dates and a Button. When the user clicks the Button, the program should calculate the time between the dates and display it in a message box.

4. Modify the program you built for Exercise 3 to use DateTimePicker controls instead of TextBoxes. To keep things simple, just display the total number of days between the dates. Use the controls' Value properties to get the selected dates. (This control prevents the user from entering invalid dates. Preventing the user from making mistakes is generally a good idea.)

 You can find solutions to this lesson's exercises in the Lesson15 folder inside the download available on the book's web site at www.wrox.com or www.vb-helper .com/24hourvb.html.

16

Using Arrays and Collections

The data types described in previous lessons each hold a single piece of data. A variable might hold an integer, a string, or a point in time.

Sometimes it's convenient to work with a group of related values all at once. For example, suppose you're the CEO of a huge company that just posted huge losses. In that case, you might want to give each hourly employee a 10 percent pay cut and give each executive a 15 percent bonus.

In cases like this, it would be handy to be able to store all the hourly employee data in one variable so you could easily work with it. Similarly, you might like to store the executives' data in a second variable so it's easy to manage.

In this lesson, you learn how to make variables that can hold more than one piece of data. You learn how to make arrays and different kinds of collections such as `Lists`, `Dictionaries`, `Stacks`, and `Queues`.

This lesson explains how to build these objects and add and remove items from them. Lesson 19 explains how to get the full benefit of them by looping through them to perform some action on each of the items they contain.

ARRAYS

An *array* is a group of values that all have the same data type and that all share the same name. Your code uses an *index*, which is an integer greater than or equal to 0, to pick a particular item in the array.

An array is analogous to the mailboxes in an apartment building. The building has a single bank of mailboxes that all have the same street address (the array's name). You use the apartment numbers to pick a particular cubbyhole in the bank of mailboxes.

Figure 16-1 shows an array graphically. This array is named `values`. It contains eight entries with indexes 0 through 7.

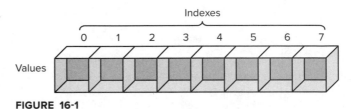

FIGURE 16-1

 An array's smallest and largest indexes are called its lower bound and upper bound, respectively. In Visual Basic, the lower bound is always 0, and the upper bound is always one less than the length of the array.

Creating Arrays

The following code shows how you might create an array of integers. The parentheses and the number 8 mean this should be an array with bounds 0 and 8, giving it 9 items.

```
Dim values(8) As Integer
```

You can optionally include the phrase "0 To" before the upper bound to emphasize the fact that array has 0 for its lower bound, as in the following code:

```
Dim values(0 To 8) As Integer
```

 Don't get confused and think the number inside the array declaration (in this case, 8) is the array's length. That number is the array's upper bound, so its length is one greater than this number. Adding "0 To" may make this easier to remember.

Alternatively, you can declare an array without giving it an upper bound. Later you can use the `ReDim` statement to *redimension* the array and give it bounds. For example, the following code declares an array of strings named `employees`. Later it uses `ReDim` to give the array 100 entries.

```
Dim employees() As String
...
ReDim employees(0 To 99)
```

If you include the optional `Preserve` keyword, then the array retains any old values when it resizes. If you don't include `Preserve`, then all of the entries in the array are reset to default values such as 0 for numbers and a blank string for strings.

For example, the following code shrinks the `employees` array to hold only 50 values, keeping the entries in positions 0 through 49:

```
ReDim Preserve employees(0 To 49)
```

After you have created an array, you can access its members by using the array's name followed by an index inside parentheses. For example, the following code initializes the `values` array by setting the Nth entry equal to N squared:

```
values(0) = 0 * 0
values(1) = 1 * 1
values(2) = 2 * 2
values(3) = 3 * 3
values(4) = 4 * 4
values(5) = 5 * 5
values(6) = 6 * 6
values(7) = 7 * 7
values(8) = 8 * 8
```

 Most programmers pronounce `values(5)` *as "values of 5," "values sub 5," or "the fifth element of values."*

After you have placed values in an array, you can read the values using the same parentheses syntax. The following code displays a message box that uses one of the array's values:

```
MessageBox.Show("7 * 7 is " & values(7).ToString())
```

To make initializing arrays easier, Visual Basic provides an abbreviated syntax that lets you declare an array and set its values all in one statement. Simply set the variable equal to the values you want separated by commas and surrounded by braces, as shown in the following code:

```
Dim values() As Integer = {0, 1, 1, 2, 3, 5, 8, 13, 21, 34}
```

Note that you cannot include an upper bound when you initialize an array in this way. Visual Basic figures out the upper bound based on the number of values you provide.

A FIBONACCI ARRAY

The Fibonacci program shown in Figure 16-2 (and available as part of this lesson's code download) uses an array to display Fibonacci numbers. The Nth Fibonacci number Fib(N) is defined by the equations:

➤ Fib(0) = 0

➤ Fib(1) = 1

➤ Fib(N) = Fib(N − 1) + Fib(N − 2)

The first few Fibonacci values are 0, 1, 1, 2, 3, 5, 8, 13, 21.

FIGURE 16-2

Use the program's `NumericUpDown` control to select a number and click Calculate to see the corresponding Fibonacci number.

When the user clicks Calculate, the program executes the following code:

```
' Display a Fibonacci number.
Private Sub btnCalculate_Click() Handles btnCalculate.Click
    Dim values(0 To 20) As Integer
    values(0) = 0
    values(1) = 1
    values(2) = values(0) + values(1)
    values(3) = values(1) + values(2)
    ...

    Dim index As Integer = CInt(nudIndex.Value)
    txtResult.Text = values(index).ToString()
End Sub
```

The code starts by initializing the values array to hold the first 21 Fibonacci numbers. It uses the following definition of the numbers to calculate the values:

```
Fibonacci(i) = Fibonacci(i - 1) + Fibonacci(i - 2)
```

After initializing the array, the program gets the value selected by the NumericUpDown control, converts it from a Decimal to an Integer, uses it as an index into the values array, and displays the result in txtResult.

Multi-Dimensional Arrays

The arrays described in the previous section hold a single row of items but Visual Basic also enables you to define multi-dimensional arrays. You can think of these as higher dimensional sequences of apartment mailboxes.

Figure 16-3 shows a graphic representation of a two-dimensional array with four rows and eight columns.

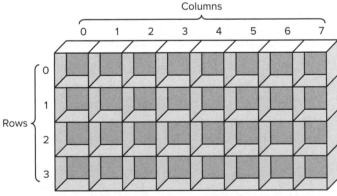

FIGURE 16-3

The following code shows how you could declare, allocate, and initialize this array to hold a multiplication table with values up to 3 times 7:

```
Dim values(0 To 3, 0 To 7) As Integer
values(0, 0) = 0 * 0
values(0, 1) = 0 * 1
values(0, 2) = 0 * 2
...
values(1, 0) = 1 * 0
values(1, 1) = 1 * 1
...
values(3, 7) = 3 * 7
```

The following code shows the Visual Basic syntax for quickly defining and initializing a two-dimensional array:

```
Dim values(,) As Integer =
{
    {0, 1, 2},
    {3, 4, 5},
    {6, 7, 8}
}
```

You can use similar syntax to make and initialize even higher-dimensional arrays. For example, the following code makes a four-dimensional array of strings:

```
Dim employeeData(0 To 9, 0 To 19, 0 To 29, 0 To 39) As String
```

Array Properties and Methods

All arrays have a Length property that your code can use to determine the number of items in the array. All arrays have a lower bound of 0, so for one-dimensional arrays, Length − 1 gives an array's upper bound.

Arrays also have GetLowerBound and GetUpperBound methods that return the lower and upper bounds, respectively, for a particular dimension in an array.

For example, the following code creates a 5-by-10 array. It then displays the lower and upper bounds for the two dimensions. (As usual, the dimension numbers start at 0.)

```
Dim x(4, 9) As Integer
MessageBox.Show("The first dimension runs from " &
    x.GetLowerBound(0) & " to " & x.GetUpperBound(0))
MessageBox.Show("The second dimension runs from " &
    x.GetLowerBound(1) & " to " & x.GetUpperBound(1))
```

The Array class also provides several useful static methods that you can use to manipulate arrays. For example, the following code sorts the array named salaries:

```
Array.Sort(salaries)
```

To sort an array, the array must contain things that can be compared in a meaningful way. For example, Integer and String data have a natural order, so it's easy to say that the string "Jackson" should come before the string "Utah."

If an array holds Employee objects, however, it's unclear how you would want to compare two items. In fact, it's likely that you couldn't define an order that would always work because sometimes you might want to sort employees by name and other times you might want to sort them by employee ID or even salary.

You can solve this problem in a couple of ways, including the IComparer interface (mentioned briefly in Lesson 29's Exercise 2) and making the Employee class implement IComparable (mentioned in Lesson 30). These are slightly more advanced topics, so they aren't covered in great depth here.

The Sort method has many overloaded versions that perform different kinds of sorting. For example, instead of passing it a single array, you can pass it an array of keys and an array of items. In that case the method sorts the keys, moving the items so they remain matched up with their corresponding keys.

Table 16-1 summarizes the most useful methods provided by the Array class.

TABLE 16-1

METHOD	PURPOSE
BinarySearch	Uses binary search to find an item in a sorted array
Clear	Resets a range of items in the array to the default value for the array's data type (for example, 0, False, or Nothing)
Copy	Copies a range of items from one array to another
IndexOf	Returns the index of a particular item in the array
LastIndexOf	Returns the index of the last occurrence of a particular item in the array
Resize	Resizes the array, preserving any items that fit in the new size
Reverse	Reverses the order of the items in the array
Sort	Sorts the array's items

COLLECTION CLASSES

An array holds a group of items and lets you refer to them by index. The .NET Framework also provides an assortment of *collection classes* that you can use to store and manipulate items in other ways. For example, a Dictionary stores items with keys and lets you very quickly locate an item from its key. You could use a `Dictionary` to make an employee phone book and very quickly look up a phone number by employee name.

Generic Classes

The following sections describe some particular kinds of classes that are included pre-built by the .NET Framework. These are generic classes so before you learn about them you should know a little about what a generic class is.

A *generic class* is one that is not tied to a particular data type. For example, suppose you built a `StringList` class that can store a list of strings. Now suppose you decided you wanted an `IntegerList` class to store lists of integers. The two classes would be practically identical, just for different data types.

I've mentioned several times that duplicated code is a bad thing. Having two nearly identical classes means debugging and maintaining two different sets of code that are practically the same.

One solution to this dilemma is to make a more general `AnythingList` class that uses the general `Object` data type to store items. An `Object` can hold any kind of data, so this class could hold lists of integers, strings, or `Customer` objects. Unfortunately, this solution has two big problems.

First, you would do a lot of work converting the items with the general `Object` data type stored in the list into the `Integer`, `String`, or `Customer` type of the items that you put in there. This is annoying because it gives you more work to do, and it makes your code more complicated and harder to read.

A bigger problem is that a list that can hold anything can hold *anything*. If you make a list intended to hold customer data, it could still hold `Integers`, `Strings`, and `PurchaseOrder` objects. Your code would need to do a lot of work to protect against potentially invalid data.

A much better approach is to use generic classes. These classes take data types in their declarations so they know what kind of data they will manipulate. Using this kind of class, you can use the same class to build a list of integers, strings, or what have you.

The following code declares and initializes a generic `List` class:

```
Dim names As New List(Of String)
```

The `(Of String)` part of the declaration indicates that the class will work with strings. You can put strings into the list and take strings out of it. You cannot add an integer to the list, just as you can't set a string variable equal to an integer. Visual Studio knows that the list works with strings and not with anything else.

Note that IntelliSense recognizes generic classes and provides help. If you begin a declaration with `List`, IntelliSense displays `List(Of T)` to let you know that it is a generic class.

Now, with some understanding of generic classes, you're ready to look at some generic collection classes.

Lists

A `List` is a simple ordered list of items. You can declare and initialize a `List` as shown in the following code:

```
Dim names As New List(Of String)
```

The `List` class provides several methods for manipulating the items it contains. The three most important are `Add`, `Remove`, and `RemoveAt`:

➤ The `Add` method adds a new item to the end of the `List`, automatically resizing the `List` if necessary. This is easier than adding an item to an array, which requires you to resize the array first.

➤ The `Remove` method removes a particular item from the `List`. Note that you pass the target item to `Remove`, not the index of the item that you want to remove. If you know that the string `"Zaphod"` is in the `List` names, the following code removes the first instance of that name from the `List`:

```
names.Remove("Zaphod")
```

 The `Remove` *method removes only the first occurrence of an item from the* `List`.

➤ The `RemoveAt` method removes an item from a particular position in the `List`. It then compacts the `List` to remove the hole where the item was. This is much easier than removing an item from an array, which requires you to shuffle items from one part of the array to another and then resize the array to reduce its size.

In addition to these methods, you can use parentheses to get and set a `List`'s entries much as you can with an array. For example, the following code sets and then displays the value of the first entry in a `List`:

```
names(0) = "Mickey"
MessageBox.Show("The first name is " & names(0))
```

Note that this works only if the index you use exists in the `List`. If the list holds 10 names and you try to set the 14th, the program crashes.

SortedLists

A `SortedList` stores a list of key/value pairs, keeping the list sorted by the keys. The types of the keys and values are generic parameters; for example, you could make a list that uses numbers (such as employee IDs) for keys, and strings (such as names) for values.

Note that the list will not allow you to add two items with the same key. Multiple items can have the same value, but if you try to add two with the same key, the program crashes.

Table 16-2 summarizes useful methods provided by the `SortedList` class.

TABLE 16-2

METHOD	PURPOSE
Add	Adds a key and value to the list
Clear	Empties the list
Contains	Returns True if the list contains a given value
ContainsKey	Returns True if the list contains a given key
ContainsValue	Returns True if the list contains a given value
GetKeyList	Returns a list holding the keys
GetValueList	Returns a list holding the values
Remove	Removes the item with a specific key from the list

In addition to these methods, you can use parentheses to index into the list, using the items' keys as indexes.

The following code demonstrates a `SortedList`:

```
Dim addresses As New SortedList(Of String, String)

addresses.Add("Dan", "4 Deer Dr, Bugville VT, 01929")
addresses.Add("Bob", "8273 Birch Blvd, Bugville VT, 01928")

addresses("Cindy") = "32878 Carpet Ct, Bugville VT, 01929"
addresses("Alice") = "162 Ash Ave, Bugville VT, 01928"
addresses("Bob") = "8273 Bash Blvd, Bugville VT, 01928"

MessageBox.Show("Bob's address is " & addresses("Bob"))
```

The code starts by declaring and initializing the list. It uses the `Add` method to add some entries and then uses parentheses to add some more. Notice that the `SortedList` doesn't need to already contain a key before the code can set its value. In this example, there is no entry for Cindy until the code sets `addresses("Cindy")`.

Next, the code uses the parentheses syntax to update Bob's address. Finally, the code displays Bob's new address.

You can't see it from this example, but unlike the `List` class, `SortedList` actually stores its items ordered by key. For example, you could use the `GetKeyList` and `GetValueList` methods to get the `SortedList`'s keys and values in order.

Dictionaries

The `Dictionary` and `SortedDictionary` classes provide features similar to the `SortedList` class, manipulating key/value pairs. The difference is in the data structures the three classes use to store their items.

Without getting into technical details, the result is that the three classes use different amounts of memory and work at different speeds. In general, `SortedList` is the slowest but takes the least memory, while `Dictionary` is the fastest but takes the most memory.

For small programs, the difference is insignificant. For big programs that work with thousands of entries, you might need to be more careful about picking a class. (Personally, I like `Dictionary` for most purposes because speed is nice, memory is relatively cheap, and the name is suggestive of the way you use the class: to look up something by key.)

Queues

A `Queue` is a collection that enables you to add items at one end and remove them from the other. It's like the line at a bank; you stand at the back of the line and the teller helps the person at the front of the line until eventually it's your turn.

 Because a queue retrieves items in first-in-first-out order, queues are sometimes called FIFO lists or FIFOs. ("FIFO" is pronounced fife-o.)

Table 16-3 summarizes the `Queue`'s most important methods.

TABLE 16-3

METHOD	PURPOSE
Clear	Removes all items from the `Queue`
Dequeue	Returns the item at the front of the `Queue` and removes it
Enqueue	Adds an item to the back of the `Queue`
Peek	Returns the item at the front of the `Queue` without removing it

Stacks

A `Stack` is a collection that enables you to add items at one end and remove them from the same end. It's like a stack of books on the floor: You can add a book to the top of the stack and remove a book from the top, but you can't pull one out of the middle or bottom without risking a collapse.

Because a stack retrieves items in last-in-first-out order, stacks are sometimes called LIFO lists or LIFOs. ("LIFO" is pronounced life-o.)

The top of a stack is also sometimes called its head. The bottom is sometimes called its tail.

Table 16-4 summarizes the Stack's most important methods.

TABLE 16-4

METHOD	PURPOSE
Clear	Removes all items from the Stack
Peek	Returns the item at the top of the Stack without removing it
Pop	Returns the item at the top of the Stack and removes it
Push	Adds an item to the top of the Stack

 ## TRY IT

In this Try It, you use a Dictionary to build the order lookup system shown in Figure 16-4. When the user clicks the Add button, the program adds a new item with the given order ID and items. If the user enters an order ID and clicks Find, the program retrieves the corresponding items. If the user enters an order ID and some items and then clicks Update, the program updates the order's items.

FIGURE 16-4

 You can download the code and resources for this Try It from the book's web page at www.wrox.com *or* www.vb-helper.com/24hourvb.html. *You can find them in the Lesson16 folder in the download.*

Lesson Requirements

In this lesson:

➤ Create the form shown in Figure 16-4.

➤ Add code that creates a Dictionary field named Orders. Set its generic type parameters to Integer (for order ID) and String (for items).

➤ Add code to the Add button that creates the new entry in the dictionary.

➤ Add code to the Find button that retrieves the appropriate entry from the dictionary.

➤ Add code to the Update button to update the indicated entry.

 This program will be fairly fragile and will crash if you don't enter an order ID, enter an ID that is not an integer, try to enter the same ID twice, try to find a nonexistent ID, and so forth. Don't worry about these problems. You learn how to handle them later, notably in Lessons 18 and 21.

Step-by-Step

➤ Create the form shown in Figure 16-4.

  1. This is relatively straightforward. The only tricks are to set the Items TextBox's MultiLine and AcceptsReturn properties to True.

➤ Add code that creates a Dictionary named orders. Set its generic type parameters to Integer (for order ID) and String (for items).

  1. Use code similar to the following to make the Orders field:

```
' The dictionary to hold orders.
Private Orders As New Dictionary(Of Integer, String)()
```

➤ Add code to the Add button that creates the new entry in the dictionary.

  1. This code should call the Dictionary's Add method, passing it the order ID and items entered by the user. Use Integer.Parse to convert the ID entered by the user into an Integer.

Optionally, you can add code to clear the textboxes to get ready for the next entry. The code could be similar to the following:

```
' Add the order data.
Orders.Add(Integer.Parse(txtOrderId.Text), txtItems.Text)

' Get ready for the next one.
txtOrderId.Clear()
txtItems.Clear()
txtOrderId.Focus()
```

➤ Add code to the Find button that retrieves the new appropriate entry from the dictionary.

  1. Use code similar to the following:

```
txtItems.Text = Orders(Integer.Parse(txtOrderId.Text))
```

➤ Add code to the Update button to update the indicated entry.

1. Use code similar to the following:

```
Orders(Integer.Parse(txtOrderId.Text)) = txtItems.Text
```

 Please select Lesson 16 on the DVD to view the video that accompanies this lesson.

EXERCISES

1. Make a program similar to the Fibonacci program that looks up factorials in an array. When the program starts, make it create the array to hold the first 20 factorials. Use the following definition for the factorial (where N! means the factorial of N):

```
0! = 1
N! = N * (N - 1)!
```

2. Make a program that demonstrates a stack of strings. The program should display a textbox and two buttons labeled Push and Pop. When the user clicks Push, add the current text to the stack. When the user clicks Pop, remove the next item from the stack and display it in the textbox.

3. Make a program that demonstrates a queue of strings. The program should display a textbox and two buttons labeled Enqueue and Dequeue. When the user clicks Enqueue, add the current text to the queue. When the user clicks Dequeue, remove the next item from the queue and display it in the textbox.

4. Make a program similar to the one you built for this lesson's Try It except make it store appointment information. The `Dictionary` should use the `Date` type for keys and the `String` type for values. Let the user pick dates from a `DateTimePicker`.

   Hint: When the `DateTimePicker` first starts, it defaults to the current time, which may include fractional seconds. After the user changes the control's selection, however, the value no longer includes fractional seconds. That makes it hard to search for the exact same date and time later, at least if the user enters a value before changing the control's initial value.

   To avoid this problem, when the form loads, initialize the `DateTimePicker` to a value that doesn't include fractional seconds. Use the properties provided by `Date.Now` to create a new `Date` without fractional seconds and set the `DateTimePicker`'s value to that.

5. Make a day planner application. The code should make an array of 31 strings to hold each day's plan. Initialize the array to show fake plans such as "Day 1."

   Use a `ComboBox` to let the user select a day of the month. When the `ComboBox`'s value changes, display the corresponding day's plan in a large `TextBox` on the form.

Hint: Use the ComboBox's SelectedIndex property as an index into the array. Note that this program doesn't let the user enter or modify the plan, it just displays hardcoded values. To let the user modify the plan, you would need Find and Update buttons similar to those used in other exercises.

Hint: To make the DateTimePicker display date and time, set its Format property to Custom and set its CustomFormat property to ddd dd MMM yyyy h:mm tt.

 You can find solutions to this lesson's exercises in the Lesson16 folder inside the download available on the book's web site at www.wrox.com *or* www.vb-helper.com/24hourvb.html.

17

Using Enumerations and Structures

The data types you've learned about so far hold strings, integers, dates, and other predefined kinds of information, but sometimes it would be nice to define your own data types. You might like to be able to make a data type that can hold only certain values, such as a `MealType` data type that can hold the values `Breakfast`, `Lunch`, and `Dinner`. You might also like to define a type to hold related pieces of data (such as name, address, and phone number) in a single variable.

Enumerations and structures enable you to do these things. An *enumeration* (or *enumerated type*) enables you to define a new data type that can take only one of an allowed list of values. A *structure* enables you to define a group of related pieces of data that should be kept together.

In this lesson, you learn how to define and use enumerations and structures to make your code easier to understand and debug.

ENUMERATIONS

An enumeration is simply a data type that allows only specific values. The following code defines a `ContactMethod` enumeration that can hold the values `None`, `Email`, `Phone`, or `SnailMail`:

```
' Define possible contact methods.
Private Enum ContactMethod As Integer
    None = 0
    Email
    Phone
    SnailMail
End Enum
```

Internally, an enumeration is stored as an integral data type, by default an `Integer`. A number after a value tells Visual Basic explicitly which integer to assign to that value. In the preceding code, `None` is explicitly assigned the value 0.

If you don't specify a value for an enumeration's item (and often you don't care what these values are), its value is one greater than the previous item's value (the first item gets the value 0). In this example, `None` is 0, `Email` is 1, `Phone` is 2, and `SnailMail` is 3.

You create an instance of an enumerated type just as you make an instance of a primitive type such as `Integer`, `Decimal`, or `String`. The following code declares a variable of type `ContactMethod`, assigns it the value `ContactMethod.Email`, and then displays its value in a message box:

```
Dim method As ContactMethod = ContactMethod.Email
MessageBox.Show(method.ToString())
```

An enumeration's `ToString` method returns the value's name, in this case "Email."

STRUCTURES

Defining a structure is easy. The following code defines a simple structure named `Address` that holds name and address information:

```
' Define a structure to hold addresses.
Private Structure Address
    Public Name As String
    Public Street As String
    Public City As String
    Public State As String
    Public Zip As String
    Public Email As String
    Public Phone As String
    Public PreferredMethod As ContactMethod
End Structure
```

The structure begins with a `Structure` statement that defines the structure's name and ends with an `End Structure` statement. The lines in between define the pieces of data that the structure holds together. The `Public` keywords in this example mean that the fields inside the structure (`Name`, `Street`, and so on) are visible to any code that can see an `Address`.

Notice that the structure can use an enumeration. In this example, the `Address` structure's `PreferredMethod` field has type `ContactMethod`.

In many ways structures behave like simple built-in types such as `Integer` and `Single`. In particular, when you declare a variable with a structure type, the code not only declares it but also creates it. That means you don't need to use the `New` keyword to create a structure.

After defining a structure variable, you can access its fields using syntax similar to the way you access a control's properties. Start with the variable's name, follow it with a dot, and then add the field's name.

The following code creates and initializes a new `Address` structure named `homeAddress`:

```
Dim homeAddress As Address
homeAddress.Name = txtName.Text
homeAddress.Street = txtStreet.Text
homeAddress.City = txtCity.Text
homeAddress.State = txtState.Text
homeAddress.Zip = txtZip.Text
homeAddress.Email = txtEmail.Text
homeAddress.Phone = txtPhone.Text
homeAddress.PreferredMethod =
    CType(cboMethod.SelectedIndex, ContactMethod)
```

This code fills in the text fields using values entered by the user in textboxes.

The final field is a `ContactMethod` enumeration. The user selects a value for this field from the cboMethod `ComboBox`. The code takes the index of the `ComboBox`'s selected item, uses `CType` to convert it from an integer into a `ContactMethod`, and saves the result in the structure's `PreferredMethod` field.

 To correctly convert a `ComboBox` *selection into an enumeration value, the* `ComboBox` *must display the choices in the same order in which they are defined by the enumeration. In this example, the* `ComboBox` *must contain the items None, Email, Phone, and SnailMail, in that order, to match up with the enumeration's items.*

STRUCTURES VERSUS CLASSES

In many ways structures are very similar to classes. Lessons 23 through 30 say a lot more about classes and the sorts of things you can do with them, and many of the same techniques apply to structures.

For example, both can contain properties, methods, and events. Both can also have constructors, special methods that are executed when you use `New` to create a new one.

While structures and classes have many things in common, they also have many differences. A lot of these differences are outside the scope of this book, so I won't cover them here, but one very important difference that you should understand is that structures are *value types,* whereas classes are *reference types.*

➤   A **reference type** variable doesn't actually hold an instance of a class. Instead it holds a reference to an instance. For example, the following code creates a reference to an object of type `NewUserForm`. The second statement actually creates that instance and then the third statement displays it. If you tried to display the form without the second statement, the program would crash because the variable wouldn't be referring to an instance yet.

```
Dim userForm As NewUserForm
userForm = New NewUserForm()
userForm.ShowDialog()
```

➤ In contrast, a **value type** variable actually contains its data instead of referring to it. For example, the following code declares an Address variable. After the first statement, the variable already contains an Address structure, its fields have default values, and it is ready for use.

```
Dim homeAddress As Address
homeAddress.Name = "Benjamin"
```

One other important difference between value and reference types is that when you set a variable with a value type equal to another, the first variable receives a copy of the second variable's value. For example, if x and y are integers, then the statement x = y makes x hold the same value as y.

Similarly, if ann and ben are variables of the structure type Person, then ben = ann makes all of the fields in ben have the same values as all of the fields in ann, but they are still two separate Person structures.

In contrast, if you set a reference type variable equal to another, the first variable now refers to *the same object* as the other, not just a copy of that object. For example, suppose cindy and dan are two variables that hold references to Student objects. The statement dan = cindy makes the variable dan refer to the same object to which cindy refers. If you change one of dan's properties, cindy also sees the change because they point to the same object.

The StructureVersusClass example program that is available in the Lesson 17 download demonstrates this difference.

So which should you use, a structure or a class? In many programs the difference doesn't matter much. As long as you are aware of the relevant differences, you can often use either.

Microsoft's "Classes and Structs (C# Programming Guide)" web page at msdn.microsoft.com/library/ms173109.aspx gives the following advice (though that page is discussing C# programming, its advice also applies to Visual Basic):

> *In general, classes are used to model more complex behavior, or data that is intended to be modified after a class object is created. Structs are best suited for small data structures that contain primarily data that is not intended to be modified after the struct is created.*

TRY IT

In this Try It, you use an enumeration and a structure to make the address book shown in Figure 17-1. When the user clicks the Add button, the program saves the entered address values. If the user enters a name and clicks Find, the program retrieves the corresponding address data.

FIGURE 17-1

You can download the code and resources for this Try It from the book's web page at www.wrox.com *or* www.vb-helper.com/24hourvb.html. *You can find them in the Lesson17 folder in the download.*

Lesson Requirements

In this lesson:

➤ Create the form shown in Figure 17-1.

➤ Define the ContactMethod enumeration with values None, Email, Phone, and SnailMail.

➤ Define an Address structure to hold the entered address information.

➤ Create a Dictionary(Of String, Address) field to hold the address data.

➤ Add code to initially select the ComboBox's None entry when the form loads (just so something is selected).

➤ Add code to the Add button that creates the new entry in the Dictionary.

➤ Add code to the Find button that retrieves the appropriate entry from the Dictionary and displays it.

Hints

➤ Remember to add the choices to the ComboBox in the same order they are defined in the ContactMethod enumeration.

➤ Use CType to convert from a ComboBox's selected index to a ContactMethod.

➤ Use CInt to convert from a ContactMethod to a ComboBox's selected index.

Step-by-Step

➤ Create the form shown in Figure 17-1.

   1. This is relatively straightforward.

➤ Define the ContactMethod enumeration with values None, Email, Phone, and SnailMail.

   1. Use code similar to the following:

```
' Define possible contact methods.
Private Enum ContactMethod
    None = 0
    Email
    Phone
    SnailMail
End Enum
```

➤ Define an `Address` structure to hold the entered address information.

  1. Use code similar to the following:

```
' Define a structure to hold addresses.
Private Structure Address
    Public Name As String
    Public Street As String
    Public City As String
    Public State As String
    Public Zip As String
    Public Email As String
    Public Phone As String
    Public PreferredMethod As ContactMethod
End Structure
```

➤ Create a `Dictionary(Of String, Address)` field to hold the address data.

  1. Use code similar to the following:

```
' Make a Dictionary to hold addresses.
Private Addresses As New Dictionary(Of String, Address)()
```

➤ Add code to initially select the `ComboBox`'s `None` entry when the form loads.

  1. Use code similar to the following:

```
cboMethod.SelectedIndex = 0
```

➤ Add code to the Add button that creates the new entry in the `Dictionary`.

  1. Use code similar to the following. Optionally, you can clear the `TextBoxes` to get ready for the next address.

```
' Add a new address.
Private Sub btnAdd_Click() Handles btnAdd.Click
    Dim newAddress As Address
    newAddress.Name = txtName.Text
    newAddress.Street = txtStreet.Text
    newAddress.City = txtCity.Text
    newAddress.State = txtState.Text
    newAddress.Zip = txtZip.Text
    newAddress.Email = txtEmail.Text
    newAddress.Phone = txtPhone.Text
    newAddress.PreferredMethod =
        CType(cboMethod.SelectedIndex, ContactMethod)

    ' Add the name and address to the dictionary.
    Addresses.Add(txtname.Text, newAddress)

    ' Get ready for the next one.
    txtName.Clear()
    txtStreet.Clear()
    txtCity.Clear()
    txtState.Clear()
    txtZip.Clear()
```

```
                    txtEmail.Clear()
                    txtPhone.Clear()
                    cboMethod.SelectedIndex = 0

                    txtname.Focus()
            End Sub
```

➤ Add code to the Find button that retrieves the appropriate entry from the `Dictionary` and displays it.

1. Use code similar to the following:

```
' Look up an address.
Private Sub btnFind_Click() Handles btnFind.Click
    ' Get the Address.
    Dim selectedAddress As Address = Addresses(txtName.Text)

    ' Display the Address's values.
    txtname.Text = selectedAddress.Name
    txtStreet.Text = selectedAddress.Street
    txtCity.Text = selectedAddress.City
    txtState.Text = selectedAddress.State
    txtZip.Text = selectedAddress.Zip
    txtEmail.Text = selectedAddress.Email
    txtPhone.Text = selectedAddress.Phone
    cboMethod.SelectedIndex =
        CInt(selectedAddress.PreferredMethod)
End Sub
```

 Please select Lesson 17 on the DVD to view the video that accompanies this lesson.

EXERCISES

1. Copy the program you built for this lesson's Try It. Add a Remove button that removes an item by calling the `Dictionary`'s `Remove` method.

2. Copy the program you built for Exercise 1. Modify it by adding a new integer `Id` field to the structure. Then create a second `Dictionary` that uses `Id` as its key. Allow the user to click the Find by Name or Find by ID buttons to locate an item using either the customer's name or ID. Also provide Remove buttons that remove by name or ID. (Hint: When the user clicks a Remove button, be sure to remove the item from both `Dictionaries`.)

3. Make a program to store appointment data similar to the program you built for Exercise 1. Use a structure with the following fields: `Time`, `Attendees`, `Type`, `Topic`, and `Notes`. Make `Type` come from the `AppointmentType` enumeration that includes the values `None`, `Work`, `Home`, and `Other`. (Hint: See Lesson 16's Exercise 4 for tips on how to use a `DateTimePicker` control's values as keys.)

You can find solutions to this lesson's exercises in the Lesson17 folder inside the download available on the book's web site at www.wrox.com *or* www.vb-helper.com/24hourvb.html.

SECTION III
Program Statements

The lessons in Section II focused on working with variables. They explained how to declare variables, set their values, and perform calculations.

Those techniques let you do some fairly complex things, but they're still relatively straightforward things that you could do yourself by hand if you really had to. For example, you could easily calculate line item totals, sales tax, shipping, and a grand total for a purchase order.

With what you know so far, you really can't write a program that takes full advantage of the computer's power. You can't make the program add up an unknown number of values stored in a ListBox, perform the same task (such as calculating an account balance) for thousands of customers, or take different actions depending on the user's inputs. You can't even write a program that can tell if the user entered "seventy-eight" in a TextBox that should contain a number.

The lessons in this section explain how to perform these kinds of tasks. They explain ways you can make a program take different courses of action depending on circumstances, repeat a set of actions many times, break code into manageable pieces to make it easier to write and debug, and handle unexpected errors. After you finish reading these lessons, you'll be able to write applications that are much more powerful than those you can write now.

18

Making Choices

All the code used in the preceding lessons has been completely linear. The program follows a series of steps in order with no deviation.

For example, a sales program could multiply a unit price by quantity desired, add several items' values, multiply to get sales tax and shipping costs, and calculate a grand total.

So far there's been no way to perform different steps under different circumstances. For example, the sales program couldn't charge different prices for different quantities purchased or waive shipping charges for orders over $100. It couldn't even check quantities to see if they make sense. In fact, a clever customer could order –1,000 items to get a huge credit!

In this lesson you learn how a program can make decisions. You learn how the program can take different actions based on user inputs and other circumstances.

DECISION STATEMENTS

Programs often need to decide between two or more courses of action. For example:

➤ If it's before 4:00 p.m., ship today. Otherwise, ship tomorrow.

➤ If the user enters an order quantity less than zero, make the user fix it.

➤ If a word processor has unsaved changes, refuse to exit.

➤ Calculate shipping based on order total: $5 if total < $20, $7.50 if total < $50, $10 if total < $75, and free if total ≥ $75.

The basic idea is the same in all of these cases. The program examines a value and takes one of several different actions depending on the value.

The following sections describe the different statements that Visual Basic provides for making this sort of decision.

IF STATEMENTS

The `If` statement examines a condition and takes action only if the condition is true. The basic syntax for the `If` statement is as follows:

```
If condition Then statement
```

Here, `condition` is a Boolean expression that evaluates to either `True` or `False`, and `statement` is a statement that should be executed if `condition` is true.

Suppose you are writing an order entry program and shipping should be $5 for orders under $100 and free for orders of at least $100. Suppose also that the program has already calculated the variable `total`. The following code shows how the program might handle this:

```
Dim shipping As Decimal = 5D           ' Default shipping cost.
If (total >= 100) Then shipping = 0D   ' Free shipping if total >= 100.
```

The code starts by setting the variable `shipping` to $5. Then if the `total` (which is calculated in code not shown here) is at least $100, the program sets `shipping` to $0.

If `total` is less than $100, the code inside the `If` block is not executed and `shipping` keeps its original value of $5.

If you want to execute more than one statement when `condition` is true, you can use a multi-line `If Then` statement as shown in the following code:

```
Dim shipping As Decimal = 5D     ' Default shipping cost.
Dim giveFreeGift As Boolean = False
If (total >= 100) Then
    shipping = 0D                ' Free shipping if total >= 100.
    giveFreeGift = True          ' Free gift if total >= 100.
End If
```

You can place as many statements as you like between the `Then` and `End If` statements, and they are all executed if `condition` is true.

To make the code more consistent and easier to read, some programmers always use multi-line `If` statements even if the program should execute only one statement. The following code shows an example:

```
If (total >= 100) Then
    shipping = 0D    ' Free shipping if total >= 100.
End If
```

IF THEN ELSE

The previous examples set shipping to a default value and then changed it if total was at least $100.

Another way to think about this problem is to imagine taking one of two actions depending on total's value. If total is less than $100, the program should set shipping to $5. Otherwise, the program should set shipping to $0.

The If Then Else construct lets a program follow this approach, taking one of two actions depending on some condition.

The syntax for If Then Else is as follows:

```
If condition Then
    statementsIfTrue
Else
    statementsIfFalse
End If
```

If condition is true, the first block statementsIfTrue is executed. Otherwise, if condition is false, the second block statementsIfFalse is executed.

Using the Else keyword, the preceding code could be rewritten like this:

```
Dim shipping As Decimal
If (total < 100) Then
    shipping = 5D              ' Shipping is $5 if total < 100.
Else
    shipping = 0D              ' Free shipping if total >= 100.
End If
```

ELSEIF STATEMENTS

The If Then Else construct performs one of two actions depending on whether the condition is true or false. Often a program may need to perform one of a series of actions depending on several conditions.

For example, suppose an order entry program calculates shipping charges depending on the total purchase amount according to this schedule:

➤ If total < $20, shipping is $5.00.

➤ Otherwise, if total < $50, shipping is $7.50.

➤ Otherwise, if total < $75, shipping is $10.00.

➤ Otherwise, shipping is free.

You can make a program perform each of these tests one after another by adding `ElseIf` statements after the initial `If` statement. The following code shows how you can calculate shipping according to the preceding schedule:

```
Dim shipping As Decimal
If (total < 20) Then
    shipping = 5D
ElseIf (total < 50) Then
    shipping = 7.5D
ElseIf (total < 75) Then
    shipping = 10D
Else
    shipping = 0D
End If
```

The D character in this code indicates that the 7.5 is a `Decimal` *value. Without the D, Visual Basic thinks 7.5 is a* `Double` *and then refuses to save a* `Double` *value in a* `Decimal`.

When the program encounters a series of `If ElseIf` statements, it executes each in turn until it finds one with a true condition.

For example, consider the previous code and suppose `total` is $60. The code evaluates the first condition and determines that `(total < 20)` is false, so it does not execute the first code block.

The program skips to the `ElseIf` statement and performs the next test. The program determines that `(total < 50)` is also not true, so it skips to the next `ElseIf` test.

The program executes the third `ElseIf` test and finds that `(total < 75)` is true, so it executes the statement `shipping = 10D`.

Because the program found an `ElseIf` statement with a true condition, it skips any following `ElseIf` or `Else` statements without evaluating their conditions.

NESTED IF STATEMENTS

Another common arrangement of `If` statements nests one inside another. The inner `If` statement is executed only if the first statement's condition allows the program to reach it.

For example, suppose you charge customers 5 percent state sales tax. If a customer lives within your county, you also charge a county transportation tax. Finally, if the customer also lives within city limits, you charge a city sales tax. (Taxes where I live are at least this confusing.)

The following code performs these checks, where the variables `inCounty` and `inCity` indicate whether the customer lives within the county and city:

```
If (inCounty) Then
    If (inCity) Then
        salesTaxRate = 0.09D
```

```
        Else
            salesTaxRate = 0.07D
        End If
    Else
        salesTaxRate = 0.05D
    End If
```

You can nest `If` statements as deeply as you like, although at some point the code gets hard to read.

> *There are always ways to rearrange code by using the* And, AndAlso, Or, *and* OrElse *operators to remove nested* If *statements. For example, the following code does the same thing as the previous version without nesting:*

```
If (inCounty AndAlso inCity) Then
    salesTaxRate = 0.09D
ElseIf (inCounty) Then
    salesTaxRate = 0.07D
Else
    salesTaxRate = 0.05D
End If
```

SELECT CASE STATEMENTS

The `Select Case` statement provides an easy-to-read equivalent to a series of `If Then ElseIf` statements that compare one value to a series of other values.

The syntax of the `Select Case` statement is as follows:

```
Select Case testValue
    Case test1
        statements1
    Case test2
        statements2
    ...
    Case Else
        statementsElse
End Select
```

Here, *testValue* is the value that you are testing; *test1*, *test2*, and so on are the values to which you are comparing *testValue*; and *statements1*, *statements2*, and so on are statements that you want to execute for each case.

If you include the optional `Case Else` section, its statements execute if no other `Case` applies.

Note that a `Case`'s code block doesn't need to include any statements. You can use that fact to make the code take no action when a particular `Case` occurs.

For example, suppose you build a form in which the user selects a hotel from a combo box. The program uses that selection to initialize an enumerated variable named `hotel`. The following code sets the `lodgingPrice` variable according to which hotel the user selected:

```
Select Case hotel
    Case HotelChoice.LuxuryLodge
        lodgingPrice = 45D

    Case HotelChoice.HamiltonArms
        lodgingPrice = 80D

    Case HotelChoice.InvernessInn
        lodgingPrice = 165D

    Case Else
        MessageBox.Show("Please select a hotel")
        lodgingPrice = 0D
End Select
```

The `Case` statements check for the three expected choices and set `lodgingPrice` to the appropriate value. If the user doesn't select any hotel, the `Case Else` section's code displays a message box and sets `lodgingPrice` to 0 to indicate a problem.

A `Select Case` statement is most robust (less prone to bugs and crashes) if its cases can handle every possible value. That makes them work very well with enumerated types because you can list each of the enumeration's values explicitly.

Even then, it's good practice to include a `Case Else` section just in case another value sneaks into the code. For example, a bug in the code could convert an integer into an enumeration value that doesn't exist, or you could later add a new value to the enumeration and forget to add a corresponding `Case` statement. In those cases, the `Case Else` statement can catch the bug or change, take some default action, and warn you that something is wrong.

When you use other data types for the switch's value, be sure to consider unexpected values, particularly if the user entered the value. For example, don't assume the user will always enter a valid string. Allowing the user to select a string from a combo box is safer, but you should still include a `Case Else` statement.

CASE TESTS

The `Case` statements in the previous examples are simple values. The program compares the test value to those values to see if they are the same.

However, a `Case` statement's test can be more than a simple value. It can include a comma-separated list of tests that can use the following:

➤ A simple value (as before)

➤ A range of values indicated by the `To` keyword, as in `1 To 100`

➤ The `Is` keyword followed by a comparison operator such as `<`, `=`, or `<>` and a comparison value

For example, the following code generates a message corresponding to a student's test average. It demonstrates comma-separated tests, ranges, and the `Is` keyword.

```
Dim message As String
Select Case average
    Case Is < 60, Is > 98
        message = "Please see instructor"
    Case 60 To 69
        message = "You got a D"
    Case 70 To 79
        message = "You got a C"
    Case 80 To 89
        message = "You got a B"
    Case Is >= 90
        message = "You got an A"
End Select
```

The first `Case` statement applies if the average is less than 60 or greater than 98. If the average is less than 60, then the student should talk to the instructor about doing some extra-credit work to avoid failing. If the average is greater than 98, then the student should talk to the instructor about becoming a teaching assistant.

The second `Case` statement applies if the average is between 60 and 69 inclusive. If the average falls into this range, the student is getting a D.

Similarly, the next two `Case` statements produce messages for students getting Cs and Bs.

The final `Case` statement applies if the average is at least 90, and produces a message indicating that the student is getting an A.

Note that the `Cases` are processed in order until one applies, after which the program skips the rest. For example, if the student has an average of 99, the first `Case` statement applies, so the program skips the final `Case` statement, which would otherwise apply.

TRY IT

In this Try It, you build the OrderForm program shown in Figure 18-1. The program uses a series of `If` and `ElseIf` statements to calculate shipping cost based on the subtotal.

FIGURE 18-1

You can download the code and resources for this Try It from the book's web page at www.wrox.com *or* www.vb-helper.com/24hourvb.html. *You can find them in the Lesson18 folder in the download.*

Lesson Requirements

In this lesson:

➤ Build the form shown in Figure 18-1.

➤ Write the code for the Calculate button so it calculates the subtotal, sales tax, shipping, and grand total. The sales tax should be 7 percent of the subtotal, and shipping should be as follows: $5 if subtotal < $20, $7.50 if subtotal < $50, $10 if subtotal < $75, and free if subtotal ≥ $75.

Hints

➤ Make the sales tax rate a constant, giving it the most limited scope you can.

Step-by-Step

➤ Build the form shown in Figure 18-1.

1. This is relatively straightforward.

➤ Write the code for the Calculate button so it calculates the subtotal, sales tax, shipping, and grand total. The sales tax should be 7 percent of the subtotal, and shipping should be as follows: $5 if subtotal < $20, $7.50 if subtotal < $50, $10 if subtotal < $75, and free if subtotal ≥ $75.

1. Get the inputs from the user.

2. Calculate the total costs for each of the four items. Add them together to get the subtotal.

3. Calculate sales tax by multiplying the tax rate by the subtotal.

4. Use a series of If and ElseIf statements to calculate the shipping cost based on the subtotal as in the following code:

```
' Calculate shipping cost.
Dim shipping As Decimal
If (subtotal < 20D) Then
    shipping = 5D
ElseIf (subtotal < 50D) Then
    shipping = 7.5D
ElseIf (subtotal < 75D) Then
    shipping = 10D
Else
    shipping = 0D
End If
```

5. Add the subtotal, tax, and shipping cost to get the grand total.

 Please select Lesson 18 on the DVD to view the video that accompanies this lesson.

EXERCISES

1. Build the ConferenceCoster program shown in Figure 18-2.

When the user clicks the Calculate button, first check each ListBox's SelectedIndex property. If any SelectedIndex is less than zero (indicating the user didn't make a choice), display an error message.

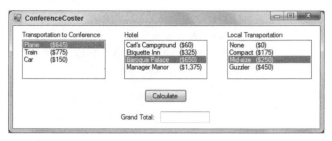

FIGURE 18-2

If the user made a choice for all of the ListBoxes, create a variable total to hold the total cost. Use three Select Case statements to add the appropriate amounts to total and display the result. (Hint: Add a Case Else statement to each Select Case statement to catch unexpected selections, even though none should occur in this program. Try adding a new hotel and see what happens if you select it.)

2. (SimpleEdit) Copy the SimpleEdit program you built in Lesson 8, Exercise 3 (or download Lesson 8's version from the book's web site) and add code to protect the user from losing unsaved changes.

The basic idea is to check whether the document has been modified before you do anything that will lose the changes, such as starting a new document, opening another file, or exiting the program.

a. In the File menu's New, Open, and Exit event handlers, check the RichTextBox's Modified property to see if the document has unsaved changes.

b. If there are unsaved changes, ask if the user wants to save them. Display a message box with the buttons Yes, No, and Cancel.

c. If the user clicks Yes, save the changes and continue the operation.

d. If the user clicks No, don't save the changes (do nothing special) and let the operation continue.

e. If the user clicks Cancel, don't perform the operation. For example, don't open a new file.

f. After starting a new document, saving an old one, or opening an existing one, set the RichTextBox control's Modified property to false to indicate that there are no unsaved changes anymore.

3. (SimpleEdit) Copy the SimpleEdit program you built for Exercise 2. That program protects against lost changes if the user opens the File menu and selects Exit, but there are several other ways the user can close the program, such as pressing [Alt]+F4, clicking the "X" button in the program's title bar, and opening the system menu in the form's upper-left corner and selecting Close. Currently, the program doesn't guard unsaved changes for any of those.

To fix this, give the form a `FormClosing` event handler. When the form is about to close, it raises this event. If you set the event's `e.Cancel` parameter to `True`, the form cancels the close and remains open. Add code to this event handler to protect unsaved changes.

Now that the `FormClosing` event handler is protecting against lost changes, you don't need to perform the same checks in the Exit menu item's event handler. Make that event handler simply call `Me.Close`, and `FormClosing` will do the rest.

 You can find solutions to this lesson's exercises in the Lesson18 folder inside the download available on the book's web site at www.wrox.com *or* www.vb-helper.com/24hourvb.html.

19

Repeating Program Steps

One of the computer's greatest strengths is its ability to perform an action repeatedly without getting bored or making careless mistakes. It can calculate the average test scores for a dozen students, print 100 party invitations, or compute the monthly bills for a million customers with no trouble or complaining.

The lessons you've read so far, however, don't tell you how to do these things. Until this point, every step the computer takes requires a separate line of code. To add 10 numbers, you would need to write 10 lines of code (or one long one).

In this lesson you learn how to make the computer execute the same lines of code many times. You learn how to loop through arrays and collections of items to take action or perform calculations on them.

The following sections describe the kinds of loops provided by Visual Basic. The final section describes two statements you can use to change the way a loop works: Exit and Continue.

FOR LOOPS

A For loop uses a variable to control the number of times it executes a series of statements. The For loop's syntax is as follows:

```
For variable [As datatype] = start To stop [Step amount]
    statements...
Next [variable]
```

Where:

➤ *variable* — This is the looping variable that controls the loop.

➤ [As *datatype*] — If present, this declares the looping variable's data type. This gives the variable the loop's scope so it is not visible outside the loop. Usually the data type is Integer.

➤ *start* — This is the looping variable's initial value.

➤ *stop* — The loop continues until the looping passes this value.

➤ [Step *amount*] — By default, the looping variable increases by 1 each time through the loop, but this statement can change that. The *amount* is the value by which the looping variable changes each time through the loop. Note that *amount* can be negative.

➤ *statements* — These are the statements that you want the loop to execute.

➤ Next [*variable*] — The Next keyword ends the loop. The looping variable's name is optional but recommended because it makes the code easier to read.

For example, the following code displays the numbers 0 through 9, followed by their squares, in the Output window:

```
For i As Integer = 0 To 9
    Console.WriteLine(i & ": " & i * i)
Next i
```

This code is relatively straightforward. It uses the looping variable i declared as part of the loop. The value i starts at 0 and increases by 1 each time through the loop until it reaches 9. After the final pass through the loop with i = 9, the loop ends.

Here's a slightly more complicated example that calculates factorials. The program converts the value selected in the NumericUpDown control named nudNumber into a long integer and saves it in variable n. It initializes the variable factorial to 1 and then uses a loop to multiply factorial by each of the numbers between 2 and n. The result is 1 * 2 * 3 * ... * n, which is n!.

```
' Get the input value n.
Dim n As Long = CLng(nudNumber.Value)

' Calculate n!.
Dim factorial As Long = 1
For i As Long = 2 To n
    factorial *= i
Next i

' Display the result.
txtResult.Text = factorial.ToString()
```

 *The Factorials program available as part of the Lesson19 download on the book's web site (*www.wrox.com *or* www.vb-helper.com/24hourvb.html*) demonstrates this code.*

You may recall that Lesson 16 used code to calculate Fibonacci numbers, and in that lesson's Exercise 1 you calculated factorials. Those programs used 20 lines of code to calculate and store 20 values that the program then used as a kind of lookup table.

The factorial calculation code shown here is more efficient. It doesn't require a large array to hold values. It also doesn't require that you know ahead of time how many values you might need to calculate (20 for the earlier programs), although the factorial function grows so quickly that this program can only calculate values up to 20! before the result won't fit in a long integer.

 The For *loop is often the best choice if you know exactly how many times you need the loop to execute.*

FOR EACH LOOPS

A For Each loop executes a block of code once for each item in an array or list. The syntax of the For Each loop is as follows:

```
For Each variable [As datatype] In items
    statements...
Next [variable]
```

Where:

➤ variable — This is the looping variable that controls the loop.

➤ [As datatype] — If present, this declares the looping variable's data type. This gives the variable the loop's scope so it is not visible outside the loop. This should be a data type compatible with whatever is in the array or collection.

➤ items — This is the array or list of items over which you want to loop.

➤ statements — These are the statements that you want the loop to execute.

➤ Next [variable] — The Next keyword ends the loop. The looping variable's name is optional but recommended because it makes the code easier to read.

For example, the following code calculates the average of the test scores stored in the ListBox named lstScores.

```
' Make sure the list isn't empty.
If (lstScores.Items.Count = 0) Then
    MessageBox.Show("There are no items to average.")
Else
    ' Add up the values.
    Dim total As Integer = 0
    For Each value As Integer In lstScores.Items
        total += value
    Next value

    ' Calculate the average.
    Dim average As Double = total / lstScores.Items.Count
```

```
            ' Display the result.
            MessageBox.Show("Average: " & average.ToString("0.00"))
        End If
```

After confirming that the ListBox isn't empty, the code creates a variable named total and sets it equal to 0. It then loops through the items in the ListBox, adding each value to total.

> *This code loops over the items in a ListBox, treating those items as integers. If the ListBox contains something other than integers, such as file names or other strings, the program will crash.*

The code finishes by dividing total by the number of items in the ListBox.

> *When you need to perform an operation on all the items in an array or list, a For Each loop is often your best choice.*

WHILE LOOPS

A While loop executes as long as some condition is true. The syntax for a While loop is as follows:

```
While condition
    statements...
End While
```

Where:

➤   condition — The loop executes as long as this Boolean expression is true.

➤   statements — These are the statements that you want the loop to execute.

For example, the following code calculates a number's prime factors:

```
' Get the input number.
Dim number As Long = Long.Parse(txtNumber.Text)

' Find the factors.
Dim result As String = "1"

' Consider factors between 2 and the number.
For factor As Long = 2 To CLng(Math.Sqrt(number))
    ' Pull out as many copies of this factor as possible.
    While (number Mod factor = 0)
        result &= " * " & factor
        number \= factor
    End While
Next factor
```

```
' Add whatever is left.
If number <> 1 Then result &= " * " & number

' Display the result.
txtResult.Text = result
```

 *The PrimeFactors program available as part of the Lesson19 download on the book's web site (*www.wrox.com *or* www.vb-helper.com/24hourvb.html*) demonstrates this code.*

The code starts by getting the user's input number. It builds a result string and initializes it to "1."

Next, the code users a `For` loop to consider the numbers between 2 and the square root of the user's number as possible factors.

For each of the possible factors, it uses a `While` loop to remove that factor from the number. As long as the factor divides evenly into the remaining number, the program adds the factor to the result and divides the user's number by the factor.

The code finishes by adding any remaining value and displaying its result.

 Loops that use incrementing integers to decide when to stop are often easier to write using For *loops instead of* While *loops. A* While *loop is particularly useful when the stopping condition occurs at a less predictable time, as in the factoring example.*

DO LOOPS

Visual Basic provides two forms of `Do` loops. The first is similar to a `While` loop but with different syntax. The second is also similar to a `While` loop except it checks its stopping condition at the end of the loop instead of the beginning (so it executes its code at least once).

The syntax of the first kind of `Do` loop is as follows:

```
Do While condition
    statements...
Loop
```

The syntax of the second kind of `Do` loop is as follows:

```
Do
    statements...
Loop While condition
```

In both versions:

➤ `statements` — These are the statements that you want the loop to execute.

➤ `condition` — The loop continues to execute as long as this Boolean expression is true.

The following code uses a Do loop to calculate the greatest common divisor (GCD) of two numbers, the largest number that divides them both evenly:

```
' Get the input values.
Dim a As Long = Long.Parse(txtA.Text)
Dim b As Long = Long.Parse(txtB.Text)

' Calculate the GCD.
Dim remainder As Long
Do
    remainder = a Mod b
    If (remainder <> 0) Then
        a = b
        b = remainder
    End If
Loop While (remainder > 0)

txtResult.Text = b.ToString()
```

The GCD program available as part of the Lesson19 download on the book's web site (www.wrox.com or www.vb-helper.com/24hourvb.html) demonstrates this code.

Notice that the variable remainder *used to end the loop is declared outside of the loop even though it doesn't really do anything outside of the loop. Normally, to restrict scope as much as possible you would want to declare this variable inside the loop if you could.*

However, the loop ending test executes in a scope that lies outside of the loop, so any variables declared inside the loop are hidden from the test.

EUCLID'S ALGORITHM

This algorithm was described by the Greek mathematician Euclid (circa 300 b.c.), so it's called the *Euclidean algorithm* or *Euclid's algorithm*. I won't explain why the algorithm works because it's nontrivial and irrelevant to this discussion of loops (you can find a good discussion at primes.utm.edu/glossary/xpage/ EuclideanAlgorithm.html).

It's important that any loop eventually ends, and in this code it's not completely obvious why that happens. It turns out that each time through the loop (with the possible exception of the first time), a and b get smaller. If you run through a few examples, you'll be able to convince yourself.

If the loop runs long enough, b eventually reaches 1. At that point b must evenly divide a no matter what a is so the loop ends. If b does reach 1, then 1 is the greatest common divisor of the user's original numbers and those numbers are called *relatively prime*.

A Do *loop with the test at the end always executes its code at least once because it doesn't check its condition until the end. That's why you should pick a* Do *loop over a* While *loop or vice versa. If you might not want the loop to execute even once, use a* While *loop or a* Do While *loop. If you need to run the loop once before you can tell whether to stop, use a* Do *loop with the test at the end.*

EXIT AND CONTINUE

The Exit and Continue statements change the way a loop works.

The Exit statement makes the code exit a loop immediately without executing any more statements inside the loop. A second keyword after Exit determines the kind of loop that exits. That second keyword can be For, Do, or While to exit the corresponding kind of loop.

If the Exit *statement is inside a nested series of loops, it exits the closest enclosing loop of the appropriate type.*

For example, the following code searches the selected items in a ListBox for the value Carter. If it finds that value, it sets the Boolean variable carterSelected to true and breaks out of the loop. If the ListBox has many selected items, breaking out of the loop early may enable the program to skip many loop iterations and save some time.

```
' See if Carter is one of the selected names.
Dim carterSelected As Boolean = False
For Each name As String In lstNames.SelectedItems
    If (name = "Carter") Then
        carterSelected = True
        Exit For
    End If
Next name

MessageBox.Show(carterSelected.ToString())
```

The Continue statement makes a loop jump to its looping statement early, skipping any remaining statements inside the loop after the Continue statement. Like the Exit statement, the Continue statement takes a second keyword that indicates what kind of loop should continue.

If the Continue *statement is inside a nested series of loops, it continues the closest enclosing loop of the appropriate type.*

For example, the following code uses a For Each loop to display the square roots of the numbers in an array. The Math.Sqrt function cannot calculate the square root of a negative number, so to avoid trouble the code checks each value. If it finds a value less than zero, it uses the Continue statement to skip the rest of that trip through the loop so it doesn't try to take the number's square root. It then continues with the next number in the array.

```
' Display square roots.
Dim values() As Single = {4, 16, -1, 60, 100}
For Each value As Single In values
    If (value < 0) Then Continue For
    Console.WriteLine(String.Format(
        "The square root of {0} is {1:0.00}",
        value, Math.Sqrt(value)))
Next value
```

The following shows this program's results:

```
The square root of 4 is 2.00
The square root of 16 is 4.00
The square root of 60 is 7.75
The square root of 100 is 10.00
```

The Break *and* Continue *statements make loops work in nonstandard ways, which sometimes makes the code harder to read, debug, and maintain. Use them if it makes the code easier to read, but ask yourself whether there's a simpler way to write the loop that avoids these statements. For example, the following code does the same things as the previous code but without a* Continue *statement:*

```
' Display square roots.
Dim values() As Single = {4, 16, -1, 60, 100}
For Each value As Single In values
    If (value >= 0) Then
        Console.WriteLine(String.Format(
            "The square root of {0} is {1:0.00}",
            value, Math.Sqrt(value)))
    End If
Next value
```

TRY IT

FIGURE 19-1

In this Try It, you make the simple login form shown in Figure 19-1. When the program's startup form loads, it enters a loop that makes it display this form until the user enters the correct username and password or clicks the Cancel button.

> *You can download the code and resources for this Try It from the book's web page at* www.wrox.com *or* www.vb-helper.com/24hourvb.html. *You can find them in the Lesson19 folder in the download.*

Lesson Requirements

In this lesson:

➤ Build a main form that displays a success message.

➤ Build the login dialog shown in Figure 19-1.

➤ In the main form's `Load` event handler, create an instance of the login dialog. Then enter a `While` loop that displays the dialog and doesn't stop until the user enters a username and password that match values in the code. If the user clicks Cancel, close the main form.

Hints

➤ Use a `Boolean` variable named `tryingToLogin` to control the loop. Initialize it to `True` before the loop and set it to `False` when the user either cancels or enters the right username and password.

➤ To determine whether the user entered a valid username and password, compare them to the strings "User" and "Secret." (A real application would validate these values against a database or by using some other authentication method.)

Step-by-Step

➤ Build a main form that displays a success message.

   1. Place labels on the form to display the message.

➤ Build the login dialog shown in Figure 19-1.

   1. Create the controls shown in Figure 19-1.

   2. Set the password `TextBox`'s `PasswordChar` property to `X`.

➤ In the main form's `Load` event handler, create an instance of the login dialog. Then enter a `While` loop that displays the dialog and doesn't stop until the user enters a username and password that match values in the code. If the user clicks Cancel, close the main form and break out of the loop.

1. The following code shows one possible solution:

```
' Make the user log in.
Private Sub Form1_Load() Handles MyBase.Load
    ' Create a LoginForm.
    Dim frm As New LoginForm()

    ' Repeat until the user successfully logs in.
    Dim tryingToLogin As Boolean = True
    While tryingToLogin
        ' Display the login dialog and check the result.
        If (frm.ShowDialog() = DialogResult.Cancel) Then
            ' The user gives up. Close and exit the loop.
            Me.Close()
            tryingToLogin = False
        Else
            ' See if the user entered valid values.
            If ((frm.txtUsername.Text = "User") AndAlso
                (frm.txtPassword.Text = "Secret")) Then
                ' Login succeeded. Stop trying to log in.
                tryingToLogin = False
            Else
                ' Login failed. Display a message and
                ' let the loop continue.
                MessageBox.Show("Invalid username and password.")
            End If
        End If
    End While

    ' If we get here, we're done trying to log in.
End Sub
```

 Please select Lesson 19 on the DVD to view the video that accompanies this lesson.

EXERCISES

1. Make a program that calculates the sum $1 + 2 + 3 + ... + N$ for a number N entered by the user.

2. Make a program that calculates the Nth Fibonacci number for a number N entered by the user. The Fibonacci sequence is defined as follows:

```
Fibonacci(0) = 0
Fibonacci(1) = 1
Fibonacci(N) = Fibonacci(N - 1) + Fibonacci(N - 2)
```

Hint: Use a loop. Define variables `fiboN`, `fiboNMinus1`, and `fiboNMinus2` outside the loop. Inside the loop, make the variables hold Fibonacci(N), Fibonacci(N - 1), and Fibonacci(N - 2). (To test your code, Fibonacci(10) = 55 and Fibonacci(20) = 6,765.)

3. Make a program that lets the user enter test scores into a `ListBox`. After adding each score, display the minimum, maximum, and average values. (Hint: Before you start the loop, initialize `minimum` and `maximum` variables to the value of the first score. Then loop through the rest of the list revising the variables as needed.)

4. Copy the program you built for Lesson 14's Exercise 1 (or download Lesson 14's version from the book's web site) and add the List Items button shown in Figure 19-2. When the user clicks the button, display the items and their values in the Output window as a semicolon-separated list similar to the following:

```
**********
Pencil;$0.10;12;$1.20;
Pen;$0.25;12;$3.00;
Notebook;$1.19;3;$3.57;
**********
```

FIGURE 19-2

Hint: The `ListView` control's `Items` property is a collection of `ListViewItem` objects. Loop through that collection to get information about each row.

Hint: Each `ListViewItem` has a `SubItems` property that is a collection of `ListViewItem.ListViewSubItem` objects. Loop through each item's `SubItems` collection to get the values for that row. Use `Console.Write` to add data to the Output window without adding a carriage return.

5. Make a program that uses a `ListBox` to display all possible four-letter words using the letters A, B, C, and D. (Hint: Make an array containing the letters A, B, C, and D. Use a `For Each` loop to loop through the letters. Inside that loop, use another loop to loop through the letters again. After four nested loops, concatenate the looping variables to get the word.)

 You can find solutions to this lesson's exercises in the Lesson19 folder inside the download available on the book's web site at www.wrox.com *or* www.vb-helper.com/24hourvb.html.

20

Reusing Code with Procedures

Sometimes a program needs to perform the same action in several places. For example, suppose you're using a simple editor such as WordPad, you make some changes, and then you select the File menu's New command. The program realizes that you have unsaved changes and asks if you want to save them. Depending on whether you click Yes, No, or Cancel, the program saves the changes, discards the changes, or cancels the attempt to create a new file.

Now consider what happens when you try to open a file while you have unsaved changes. The program goes through basically the same steps, asking if you want to save the changes. It does practically the same thing if you select the File menu's Exit command, or click the X in the program's upper-right corner, or open the window's system menu and select Close, or press [Alt]+F4. In all of these cases, the program performs the same checks.

Instead of repeating code to handle unsaved changes everywhere it might be needed, it would be nice if you could centralize the code in a single location and then invoke that code when you need it. In fact, you can do exactly that by using a procedure.

A *procedure* is a group of programming statements wrapped in a neat package so you can invoke it as needed. A procedure can take parameters that the calling code can use to give it information, it can perform some actions, and then it can return a single value to pass information back to the calling code.

In this lesson, you learn how to use procedures. You learn why they are useful, how to write them, and how to call them from other places in your code.

PROCEDURE ADVANTAGES

The file-editing scenario described in the previous section illustrates one of the key advantages of procedures: code reuse. By placing commonly needed code in a single procedure, you can reuse that code in many places. Clearly, that saves you the effort of writing the code several times.

Much more important, it also saves you the trouble of debugging the code several times. Often, debugging a piece of complex code takes much longer than typing in the code in the first place, so being able to debug the code in only one place can save you a lot of time.

Reusing code also greatly simplifies maintenance. If you later find a bug in the code, you only need to fix it in one place. If you have several copies of the code scattered around, you need to fix each one individually and make sure that all of the fixes are the same. That may sound easy enough, but making synchronized changes is actually pretty hard, particularly for larger projects. It's just too easy to miss one change or to make a slightly different change that later causes a big problem.

Procedures can sometimes make finding and fixing bugs much easier. For example, suppose you're working on an inventory program that can remove items from inventory for one of many reasons: external sales, internal sales, ownership transfer, spoilage, and so forth. Unfortunately, the program occasionally removes items that don't exist, leaving you with negative inventory. If the program has code in many places that can remove items from inventory, figuring out which place is causing the problem can be tricky. Conversely, if all the code uses the same procedure to remove items, you can set breakpoints inside that procedure to see what's going wrong. When you see the problem occurring, you can trace the program's flow to determine where the problem originated.

A final set of advantages to using procedures is that it makes the pieces of the program easier to understand and use. Breaking a complex calculation into a series of simpler procedure calls can make the code easier to understand. No one can keep all the details of a large program in mind at once. Breaking the program into procedures makes it possible to understand the pieces separately.

To provide the most benefit, a procedure should encapsulate its task at an abstract level so other developers don't need to know the details. For example, you could write a `FindItemForPurchase` procedure that searches through a database of vendors to find the best possible deal on a particular item. This enables developers writing other parts of the program to call that procedure without needing to understand exactly how the search works. The procedure might perform an amazingly complex search to minimize price and long-term expected maintenance costs but the programmer calling the procedure doesn't need to know or care how it works.

In summary, key benefits of using procedures include the following:

➤ **Code reuse** — You write the code once and use it many times.

➤ **Centralized debugging** — You only need to debug the shared code once.

➤ **Centralized maintenance** — If you need to modify or fix the code, you only need to do so in the procedure, not everywhere it is used.

➤ **Problem decomposition** — Procedures can break complex problems into simple pieces.

➤ **Encapsulation** — Procedures can hide complex details from developers.

PROCEDURE SYNTAX

Visual Basic provides several different kinds of procedures that have slightly different syntax:

➤ A **subroutine, subprocedure,** or simply **sub** is a procedure that performs some action but does not return any value.

➤   A **function** is a procedure that returns a value.

➤   A **method** is a subroutine or function provided by a class. This term is used to emphasize the fact than a class provides the method. Lesson 24 says more about class methods.

➤   A **property procedure** is a procedure used to implement a property for a class. Lesson 23 says more about defining properties.

> *This book uses the terms* subroutine *and* function *when appropriate. When the difference doesn't matter, it uses the term* procedure.

Subroutine Syntax

The syntax for defining a subroutine is as follows:

```
[accessibility] Sub name([parameters])
    ...statements...
End Sub
```

Where:

➤   `accessibility` — This is an accessibility keyword such as `Public` or `Private`. This keyword determines what other code in the project can invoke the procedure. If you omit the accessibility, it defaults to `Public`.

➤   `name` — This is the name that you want to give the procedure. You can give the procedure any valid name, although by convention most developers use Pascal case. Valid names must start with a letter or underscore and include letters, underscores, and numbers. A valid name cannot be a keyword such as `If` or `While`.

➤   `parameters` — This is an optional parameter list that you can pass to the procedure. I'll say more about this shortly.

➤   `statements` — These are the statements that the procedure should execute.

For example, the following subroutine displays a message box that greets the user by name. This subroutine takes no parameters.

```
Public Sub SayHi()
    MessageBox.Show("Hello " & SystemInformation.UserName)
End Sub
```

> *You cannot define a procedure inside another procedure. (You can, however, make* anonymous methods *that are sort of like procedures inside other procedures. These are quite advanced so I won't discuss them in any depth.)*

The following code shows how the program might invoke the subroutine:

```
Private Sub Form1_Load() Handles MyBase.Load
    SayHi()
End Sub
```

 A subroutine need not be defined before the code that uses it in the file. It can be defined before or after the code that uses it, or even in another file as long as it has the right accessibility.

A subroutine executes its code until it reaches the `End Sub` statement, at which point control returns to the calling code.

You can also use one or more `Return` statements to make the subroutine return to the calling code early, skipping any code that comes later.

 A subroutine can also return to the calling code by using an `Exit Sub` statement instead of using `Return`.

For example, the following subroutine checks the username and password textboxes. If either is blank, the subroutine returns. If both are filled in, the subroutine continues to run other code to validate the user.

```
Public Sub ValidateUser ()
    If txtUsername.Text.Length < 1 Then Return
    If txtPassword.Text.Length < 1 Then Return

    ' Look up the user in the database.
    ...
End Sub
```

 If you have a long and complicated subroutine, noticing a `Return` statement buried in the middle can be hard, which can make debugging the code difficult. For that reason, some programmers prefer not to use `Return` statements in subroutines and always make them exit through the `End Sub` statement.

You should probably break a long and complicated subroutine into smaller pieces that are easier to understand anyway.

Function Syntax

The syntax for defining a function is similar to the syntax for defining a subroutine, with the addition of a return type:

```
[accessibility] Function name([parameters]) As returnType
    ...statements...
End Function
```

The only new piece (aside from using the keyword Function instead of Sub) is *returnType*. This indicates the data type returned by the function.

To exit a function, use the Return keyword followed by the value the function should return to the calling code.

For example, the following function examines the current hour of the day and builds a greeting message accordingly. The Return statement at the end makes the function return the message.

```
Public Function Greeting() As String
    Dim message As String
    Select Case Date.Now.Hour
        Case Is < 12
            message = "Good morning "
        Case Is < 17
            message = "Good afternoon "
        Case Else
            message = "Good evening "
    End Select

    Return message
End Function
```

You can use more than one Return statement to make the function return in several places. For example, you could rewrite the Greeting function like this:

```
Private Function Greeting() As String
    Select Case Date.Now.Hour
        Case Is < 12
            Return "Good morning "
        Case Is < 17
            Return "Good afternoon "
        Case Else
            Return "Good evening "
    End Select
End Function
```

Once you have defined a function, you can invoke it and treat its result just as you would treat any literal or variable value of that data type.

For example, the following version of the `SayHi` subroutine calls the `Greeting` function and concatenates its result to the value returned by `SystemInformation.UserName` to produce a greeting message:

```
Public Sub SayHi()
    MessageBox.Show(Greeting() & SystemInformation.UserName)
End Sub
```

Parameters

A procedure's declaration can include a comma-separated list of parameters that allow calling code to pass information into the procedure. Each parameter's declaration begins with the keyword `ByVal` or `ByRef`, followed by the parameter's name and its data type.

The following section says more about `ByVal` and `ByRef` but first it's worth looking at an example.

Recall the definition of the factorial function. The factorial of a number N is written N! and pronounced *N factorial*. The definition of N! is 1 * 2 * 3 * ... * N.

The following Visual Basic code implements the factorial function:

```
' Return value!
Public Function Factorial(ByVal value As Long) As Long
    Dim result As Long = 1
    For i As Long = 2 To value
        result *= i
    Next i
    Return result
End Function
```

This function's parameter list declares a parameter named `value` of type `Long`. The name `value` is the name that the parameter has inside the function. It behaves mostly like a variable declared within the function by using the `Dim` statement.

The following code invokes the `Factorial` function:

```
Dim number As Long = CLng(txtNumber.Text)
Dim result As Long = Factorial(number)
MessageBox.Show(result.ToString())
```

This code converts text entered by the user into a `Long` and saves it in the variable `number`. It then calls the `Factorial` function, passing `number` in as a parameter.

At this point control moves to the `Factorial` function. Inside that function, whatever value was passed to it (in this case, whatever was in the `number` variable) is known by the parameter name `value`. The function performs its calculations and returns a result.

Control then returns to the `Click` event handler, which saves the value returned by `Factorial` in the variable `result`. Finally, the code displays the result in a message box.

A procedure's parameter list can include zero, one, or more parameters separated by commas. For example, the following code defines the function Gcd, which returns the greatest common divisor (GCD) of two integers. (The GCD of two integers is the largest integer that evenly divides them both.)

```
' Calculate GCD(a, b).
Private Function Gcd(ByVal a As Long, ByVal b As Long) As Long
    Dim remainder As Long
    Do
        remainder = a Mod b
        If (remainder <> 0) Then
            a = b
            b = remainder
        End If
    Loop While (remainder > 0)

    Return b
End Function
```

The following code shows how you might call the Gcd function. The code initializes two integers and passes them to the Gcd function, saving the result. It then displays the result in a message box.

```
Dim a As Long = CLng(txtA.Text)
Dim b As Long = CLng(txtB.Text)
Dim result As Long = Gcd(a, b)
MessageBox.Show(result.ToString())
```

ByVal and ByRef

Parameter lists have one more feature that's confusing enough to deserve its own section. Parameters can be passed to a procedure by value or by reference.

When you pass a parameter *by value*, Visual Basic makes a copy of the value and passes the copy to the procedure. The procedure can then modify its copy without damaging the value used by the calling code.

In contrast, when you pass a value *by reference*, Visual Basic passes the location of the value's memory into the procedure. If the procedure modifies the parameter, the value is changed in the calling code as well.

Normally values are passed by value. That's less confusing because changes that are hidden inside the procedure cannot confuse the calling code. Sometimes, however, you may want to let a procedure modify a parameter. For example, suppose you want to write a function named GetMatchup that selects two chess players to play against each other. The method should return True if it can find a match and False if no other matches are possible (because they've all been played). The function can only return one value (True or False), so it returns the two players through parameters passed by reference.

The following code shows how the method might be structured:

```
Private Function GetMatchup(ByRef player1 As Integer,
 ByRef player2 As Integer) As Boolean
    ' Do complicated stuff to pick an even match.
    ...
```

```
      ' Somewhere in here the code sets player1 and player2.
      ...

      ' We found a match.
      Return True
End Function
```

The method takes two parameters, `player1` and `player2`, that are passed by reference. The method performs some complex calculations not shown here to assign values to `player1` and `player2`. It then returns `True` to indicate that it found a match.

The following code shows how a program might call this method:

```
Dim playerA, playerB As Integer
If (GetMatchup(playerA, playerB)) Then
    ' Announce this match.
    ...
Else
    ' No match is possible. We're done.
    '...
End If
```

This code declares variables `playerA` and `playerB` to hold the selected players' names. It calls the `GetMatchup` method, passing it the two player name variables. Depending on whether the method returns `True` or `False`, the program announces the match or does whatever it should when all the matches have been played.

Notice that there's no indication in the calling code that these parameters are being passed by reference. That can make understanding and debugging the code more confusing. Because of that potential for confusion, it's considered bad practice to return results from a procedure through parameters passed by reference.

A better approach is to use a function that takes input parameters by value and returns as a result a structure holding all the output values.

The `ByVal` and `ByRef` keywords are more confusing when the parameter is a reference. If you pass a reference variable `ByVal`, then the procedure can change the properties of the object to which it refers; it just cannot change the object to which the original variable points in the calling code.

For example, suppose a piece of code has a `Person` variable named `customer` and passes it `ByVal` to the `SendInvoice` subroutine. That subroutine could change the object's `FirstName` and `LastName` properties, and the changes will be visible in the calling code. However, if it changes the parameter so it points to a different `Person` object, the variable `customer` will still point to the original object when the code returns because `ByVal` prevents changes to the variable itself.

CODE MODULES

If you place a procedure in a form's code file, it is visible to all the other code inside that form. In fact, if you make the procedure public, then it is visible from the code in other forms, too. For example you could give a dialog a public subroutine that the main program could call to make the dialog perform some action.

But what if you have a procedure that doesn't really apply to a single type of form? For example, consider the Factorial and Gcd functions shown earlier in this lesson. They really don't have much to do with a particular kind of form so why should their code be specific to a particular type of form? Placing them inside a form's code would make it difficult to use them from another form's code.

To solve this problem, Visual Basic provides code modules. A *code module* is a code file that is not associated with any particular form or other class. All the code in the whole application can see the code in a module, at least if its accessibility allows.

To create a code module, open Visual Studio's Project menu and select Add Module. On the Add New Item dialog, give the module a meaningful name and click Add. Now you can enter procedures inside the module.

In addition to procedures, a code module can contain fields similar to those you can put in a form's code. If you declare a field with public accessibility, then the field is essentially a global variable that is visible from any code in the application.

The following code shows a complete module named MathTools. It defines a global constant named GoldenRatio and a Factorial function, both of which are accessible from any code in the application.

```
Module MathTools
    Public Const GoldenRatio As Double = 1.61803398874

    ' Return value!
    Private Function Factorial(ByVal value As Long) As Long
        Dim result As Long = 1
        For i As Long = 2 To value
            result *= i
        Next i
        Return result
    End Function
End Module
```

TRY IT

In this Try It, you make a procedure that calculates the minimum, maximum, and average values for an array of Doubles. You build the program shown in Figure 20-1 to test the procedure.

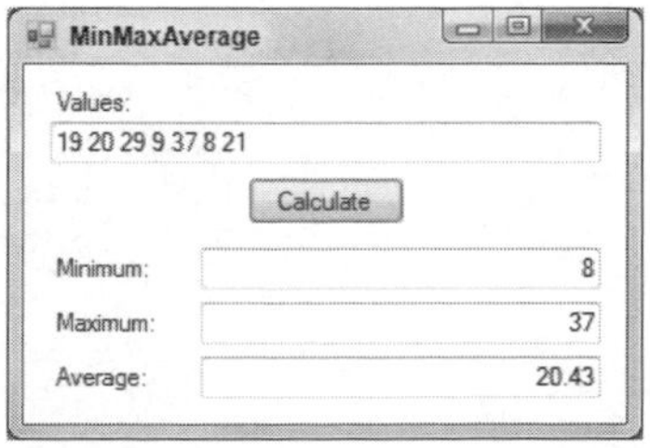

FIGURE 20-1

You can download the code and resources for this Try It from the book's web page at www.wrox.com *or* www.vb-helper.com/24hourvb.html. *You can find the code in the Lesson20 folder.*

Lesson Requirements

In this lesson:

➤ Build the program shown in Figure 20-1.

➤ Build a subroutine that takes four parameters: an array of Doubles, and three more Doubles passed by reference. It should loop through the array to find the minimum, maximum, and average.

➤ Make the form call the subroutine and display the results.

Hints

➤ Use Split to break the input string into pieces. Then loop through the strings, parsing them to make the array of Doubles.

Step-by-Step

➤ Build the program shown in Figure 20-1.

1. This is reasonably straightforward.

➤ Build a subroutine that takes four parameters: an array of Doubles, and three more Doubles passed by reference. It should loop through the array to find the minimum and maximum, and to calculate the average.

1. Initialize minimum and maximum variables to the first entry in the array. Create a total variable and initialize it to the first item, too.

2. Loop through the rest of the array (skipping the first entry), updating the minimum and maximum variables as needed, and adding the values in the array to the total.

3. Divide the total by the number of values to get the average.

The following code shows how you might build this subroutine:

```
' Calculate the minimum, maximum, and average values for the array.
Private Sub FindMinimumMaximumAverage(ByVal values() As Double,
 ByRef minimum As Double,
 ByRef maximum As Double,
 ByRef average As Double)
    ' Initialize the minimum, maximum, and total values.
    minimum = values(0)
    maximum = values(0)
    Dim total As Double = values(0)
```

```
        ' Loop through the rest of the array.
        For i As Integer = 1 To values.Length - 1
            If (values(i) < minimum) Then minimum = values(i)
            If (values(i) > maximum) Then maximum = values(i)
            total += values(i)
        Next i

        ' Calculate the average.
        average = total / values.Length
    End Sub
```

➤ Make the form call the subroutine and display the results.

1. The following code shows how you might use Split to break the inputs apart, loop through them to build the array of Doubles, and call the subroutine:

```
' Find and display the minimum, maximum, and average of the values.
Private Sub btnCalculate_Click() Handles btnCalculate.Click
    ' Get the values.
    Dim textValues() As String = valuesTextBox.Text.Split()
    Dim values(0 To textValues.Length - 1) As Double
    For i As Integer = 0 To textValues.Length - 1
        values(i) = Double.Parse(textValues(i))
    Next i

    ' Calculate.
    Dim smallest, largest, average As Double
    FindMinimumMaximumAverage(values, smallest, largest, average)

    ' Display the results.
    minimumTextBox.Text = smallest.ToString()
    maximumTextBox.Text = largest.ToString()
    averageTextBox.Text = average.ToString("0.00")
End Sub
```

This lesson mentions that returning values through parameters passed by reference isn't a good practice, so how could you modify this example to avoid that?

You could break the FindMinimumMaximumAverage *subroutine into three separate functions,* FindMinimum, FindMaximum, *and* FindAverage, *and have each return its result by using a* Return *statement. In addition to avoiding parameters passed by reference, that makes each routine perform a single, well-focused task, making them easier to understand and use. It also makes them easier to use separately in case you only wanted to find an array's minimum and not its maximum or average.*

(Also note that the Array *class provides methods that can find these values for you, so you really don't need to write these functions anyway. This Try It is here purely to demonstrate parameters passed by reference.)*

Please select Lesson 20 on the DVD to view the video that accompanies this lesson.

EXERCISES

1. Make a program that calculates the least common multiple (LCM) of two integers. (The LCM of two integers is the smallest integer that the two numbers divide into evenly.) Hints: LCM(a, b) = a * b \ GCD(a, b). Also, don't write the LCM function from scratch. Instead, make it call the GCD function described earlier in this lesson.

2. A *recursive procedure* is one that calls itself. Write a recursive factorial function by using the following definition:

   ```
   0! = 1
   N! = N * (N-1)!
   ```

   Hint: Be sure to check the stopping condition N = 0 so the function doesn't call itself forever.

3. Write a program that recursively calculates the Nth Fibonacci number using the following definition:

   ```
   Fibonacci(0) = 0
   Fibonacci(1) = 1
   Fibonacci(N) = Fibonacci(N - 1) + Fibonacci(N - 2)
   ```

4. (SimpleEdit) Copy the SimpleEdit program you built in Lesson 18, Exercise 3 (or download Lesson 18's version from the book's web site) and move the code that checks for unsaved changes into a function named IsDataSafe. The IsDataSafe function should perform the same checks as before and return True if it is safe to continue with whatever operation the user is about to perform (new file, open file, or exit).

   Other code that needs to decide whether to continue should call IsDataSafe. For example, the mnuFileNew_Click event handler can now look like this:

   ```
   Private Sub mnuFileNew_Click() _
    Handles mnuFileNew.Click, btnNew.Click
       ' See if it's okay to continue.
       If IsDataSafe() Then
           ' Make the new document.
           rchDocument.Clear()

           ' There are no unsaved changes now.
           rchDocument.Modified = False
       End If
   End Sub
   ```

5. Recursive procedures can be very confusing to understand and debug, so often it's better to write the procedure without recursion. Some problems have natural recursive definitions but usually a nonrecursive procedure is better and sometimes faster.

Copy the program you made for Exercise 3 and replace the `Fibonacci` function with this nonrecursive version:

```
' Calculate the n-th Fibonacci number recursively.
' Note that this value is only correct if n >= 0.
Private Function Fibonacci(ByVal n As Long) As Long
    ' Initialize the base cases.
    Dim fiboN As Long = 0           ' Initially Fibonacci(0).
    Dim fiboNMinus1 As Long = 0     ' Initially Fibonacci(0).
    Dim fiboNMinus2 As Long = 1     ' Initially Fibonacci(1).

    ' Calculate the result.
    For i As Long = 1 To n
        ' Calculate fiboN from fibo1 and fibo2.
        fiboN = fiboNMinus1 + fiboNMinus2

        ' Update fibo1 and fibo2 for the next loop.
        fiboNMinus2 = fiboNMinus1
        fiboNMinus1 = fiboN
    Next i

    Return fiboN
End Function
```

Compare the performance of this program and the one you wrote for Exercise 3 when N is around 35 or 40. Also notice that you don't need to modify the rest of the program to replace the `Fibonacci` function.

Many of the examples and exercises in earlier lessons use duplicated code. For further practice, rewrite some of them to move the duplicated code into procedures.

 You can find solutions to this lesson's exercises in the Lesson20 folder inside the download available on the book's web site at www.wrox.com *or* www.vb-helper.com/24hourvb.html.

21

Handling Errors

The best way to handle errors is to not give the user the chance to make them in the first place. For example, suppose a program can take purchase orders for between 1 and 100 reams of paper. If the program lets you specify the quantity by using a NumericUpDown control with Minimum = 1 and Maximum = 100, you cannot accidentally enter invalid values like –5 or 10,000.

Sometimes, however, it's hard to build an interface that protects against all possible errors. For example, if the user needs to type in a numeric value, you need to worry about invalid inputs such as 1.2.3 and "ten." If you write a program that works with files, you can't always be sure the file will be available when you need it. For example, it might be on a DVD, CD, or flash drive that has been removed, or it might be locked by another program.

In this lesson, you learn how to deal with these kinds of unexpected errors. You learn how to protect against invalid values, unavailable files, and other problems that are difficult or impossible to predict in advance.

ERRORS AND EXCEPTIONS

An *error* is a mistake. It occurs when the program does something incorrect. Sometimes an error is a bug — for example, the code adds the wrong numbers.

Sometimes an error is caused by circumstances outside of the program's control. If the program expects the user to enter a numeric value in a textbox but the user types 1.2.3, the program won't be able to continue its work until the user fixes the problem.

Sometimes you can predict when an error may occur. For example, if a program needs to open a file, there's a chance that the file won't exist. In predictable cases such as this one, the program should try to anticipate the error and protect itself. In this case, it should check to see if the file exists before it tries to open it. It can then display a message to the user and ask for help.

Other errors are hard or impossible to predict. Even if the file exists, it may be locked by another program. The user entering invalid data is another example. In those cases, the program may need to just try to do its job anyway. If the program tries to do something invalid, it will receive an exception.

An *exception* tells the program that something bad occurred such as trying to divide by zero, trying to access an entry in an array that doesn't exist (for example, setting `values(100) = 100` when `values` only holds 10 items), or trying to convert "ten" into an integer.

In cases like these, the program must *catch* the exception and deal with it. Sometimes it can figure out what went wrong and fix the problem. Other times it might only be able to tell the user about the problem and hope the user can fix it.

 In Visual Basic terms, the code that has the problem throws the exception. Code higher up in the call chain can catch *the exception and try to handle it.*

To catch an exception, a program uses a `Try Catch` block.

TRY CATCH BLOCKS

In Visual Basic, you can use a `Try Catch` block to catch exceptions. One common form of this statement has the following syntax:

```
Try
    ...codeToProtect...
Catch ex As ExceptionType1
    ...exceptionCode1...
Catch ex As ExceptionType2
    ...exceptionCode2...
Finally
    ...finallyCode...
End Try
```

Where:

➤ *codeToProtect* — The code that might throw the exception.

➤ *ExceptionType1, ExceptionType2* — These are exception types such as `FormatException` or `DivideByZeroException`. If this particular exception type occurs in the *codeToProtect*, the corresponding `Catch` block executes.

➤ *ex* — A variable that has the type *ExceptionType*. You pick the name for this variable (developers often just call it `ex`). If an error occurs, you can use this variable to learn more about what happened.

➤ *exceptionCode* — The code that the program should execute if the corresponding exception occurs.

➤ *finallyCode* — This code always executes when the `Try Catch` block ends whether or not an error occurs.

A `Try Catch Finally` block can include any number of `Catch` blocks with different exception types. If an error occurs, the program looks through the `Catch` blocks in order until it finds one that matches the error. It then executes that block's code and jumps to the `Finally` statement if there is one.

If you use a `Catch` statement without an exception type and variable, that block catches all exceptions.

If you omit the `Catch` *statement's exception type and variable, the code cannot learn anything about the exception that occurred. Sometimes that's okay if you don't really care what went wrong as long as you know that* something *went wrong.*

An alternative strategy is to catch a generic `Exception`, *which matches any kind of exception and provides more information. Then you can at least display an error message, as shown in the following code that tries to calculate a student's test score average assuming the variables* `totalScore` *and* `numTests` *are already initialized. If the code throws an exception, the* `Catch` *block displays the exception's default description.*

```
Try
    ' Calculate the average.
    Dim averageScore As Integer = totalScore \ numTests

    ' Display the student's average score.
    MessageBox.Show("Average Score: " &
        averageScore.ToString
    ("0.00"))
Catch ex As Exception
    ' Display a message describing the exception.
    MessageBox.Show("Error calculating average." & vbCrLf &
        ex.Message)
End Try
```

In this code the most likely error is a `DivideByZeroException`, *which is thrown if* `numTests` *is 0. Because that kind of error is predictable, the code should use a* `Catch` *statement to look specifically for it. The best strategy is to catch the most specific type of exception possible to get the most information. Then catch more generic exceptions in later* `Catch` *statements just in case.*

Better still, the code should check `numTests` *and not perform the calculation if* `numTests` *is 0. Then it can avoid the exception completely.*

A `Try Catch Finally` block must include at least one `Catch` block or the `Finally` block, although none of them needs to contain any code. For example, the following code catches and ignores all exceptions:

```
Try
    ...codeToProtect...
Catch
End Try
```

Simply ignoring exceptions is a bad practice. The code should do something with the exception, even if it can only notify the user.

The code in the `Finally` block executes whether or not an exception occurs. If an error occurs, the program executes a `Catch` block (if one matches the exception) and then executes the `Finally` block. If no error occurs, the program executes the `Finally` block after it finishes the `codeToProtect` code.

In fact, if the code inside the `Try` or `Catch` section breaks out early by using `Return`, `Exit For`, `Exit Do`, or some other statement, the `Finally` block still executes before the program actually leaves the `Try Catch` block!

THROWING ERRORS

Occasionally it's useful to be able to throw your own errors. For example, consider the factorial function you wrote in Lesson 20 and suppose the program invokes the function and passes the value –10 for its parameter. The value –10! is not defined, so what should the function do with the input of –10? It could just declare that –10! is 1 and return that, but that approach could hide a potential error in the rest of the program, which should not be calling the function with an input of –10.

A better solution is to throw an exception telling the program what's wrong. The calling code can then use a `Try Catch Finally` block to catch the error and tell the user what's wrong.

The following code shows an improved version of the factorial function described in Lesson 20. Before calculating the factorial, the code checks its parameter; if the parameter is less than zero, it throws a new `ArgumentOutOfRangeException`. The exception's constructor has several different versions. The one used here takes as parameters the name of the parameter that caused the problem and a description of the error.

```
' Calculate value!
Private Function Factorial(ByVal value As Long) As Long
    If value < 0 Then
        Throw New ArgumentOutOfRangeException(
            "value",
            "The Factorial parameter must be at least 0.")
    End If

    ' Calculate the factorial.
    Dim result As Long = 1
    For i As Long = 2 To value
        result *= i
    Next i
    Return result
End Function
```

The following code shows how the program might invoke the new version of the `Factorial` function. It uses a `Try Catch` block to protect itself in case the `Factorial` function throws an error. The block also protects against other errors such as the user entering invalid input in the textbox.

```
' Calculate the factorial.
Private Sub btnCalculate_Click() Handles btnCalculate.Click
    Try
        ' Get the input number.
        Dim number As Long = Long.Parse(txtNumber.Text)

        ' Calculate the factorial.
        Dim answer As Long = Factorial(number)

        ' Display the result.
        txtResult.Text = answer.ToString()
    Catch ex As Exception
        ' Display the error message.
        MessageBox.Show(ex.Message)
        txtResult.Clear()
    End Try
End Sub
```

The Factorial example program that is available in this lesson's download material demonstrates this code.

Exceptions take additional overhead and disrupt the natural flow of code, making it harder to read, so only throw exceptions to signal exceptional conditions.

If a method needs to tell the calling code whether it succeeded or failed, that isn't an exceptional condition, so use a return value instead of an exception. If a method has an invalid input parameter (such as a 0 in a parameter that cannot be 0), that's an error, so throw an exception.

TRY IT

In this Try It, you add validation and error-handling code to the program you built for Lesson 19's Exercise 4. When the user clicks the `NewItemForm`'s Calculate and OK buttons, the program should verify that the values make sense and protect itself against invalid input such as the user entering the quantity "one," as shown in Figure 21-1.

You can download the code and resources for this Try It from the book's web page at www.wrox.com or www.vb-helper.com/24hourvb.html. You can find the code in the Lesson21 folder.

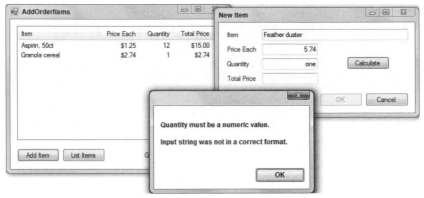

FIGURE 21-1

Lesson Requirements

In this lesson:

➤ Copy the program you built in Lesson 19, Exercise 4 (or download Lesson 19's version from the book's web site).

➤ The previous version of this program uses repeated code to perform calculations when the user clicks either Calculate or OK. Move that code into a new ValuesAreOk function that validates the user's inputs. In addition to protecting the form from format errors, the function should verify that:

    ➤ Item name is not blank.

    ➤ Price Each > 0.

    ➤ Quantity > 0.

➤ If ValuesAreOk finds a problem, it should:

    ➤ Tell the user.

    ➤ Set focus to the textbox that caused the problem.

    ➤ Return False.

➤ If ValuesAreOk finds that all of the values are okay, it should return True.

Hints

➤ If the user clicks the OK button, the form should close only if the user's inputs are valid. Be sure the OK button's DialogResult property doesn't automatically close the form.

➤ Use Try Catch blocks to protect against format errors.

Step-by-Step

➤ Copy the program you built in Lesson 19, Exercise 4 (or download Lesson 19's version from the book's web site).

1. This is straightforward.

➤ The previous version of this program uses repeated code to perform calculations when the user clicks either Calculate or OK. Move that code into a new ValuesAreOk function that validates the user's inputs. In addition to protecting the form from format errors, the function should verify that:

➤ Item name is not blank.

➤ Price Each > 0.

➤ Quantity > 0.

1. Copy the item name into a String variable and verify that its length is at least 1.

2. Parse Price Each and verify that it is greater than zero.

3. Parse Quantity and verify that it is greater than zero.

➤ If ValuesAreOk finds a problem, it should:

➤ Tell the user.

➤ Set focus to the textbox that caused the problem.

➤ Return False.

1. Whenever the function finds a problem, it should display a message box, set focus to the textbox containing the error, and return False. For example, the following code shows how you might verify the price each:

```
' Validate price each.
Try
    PriceEach = Decimal.Parse(
        txtPriceEach.Text,
        System.Globalization.NumberStyles.Any)

    If (PriceEach <= 0) Then
        MessageBox.Show("Price Each must be greater than 0.")
        txtPriceEach.Focus()
        Return False
    End If
Catch ex As Exception
    MessageBox.Show("Price Each must be a dollar amount." &
        vbCrLf & vbCrLf & ex.Message)
    txtPriceEach.Focus()
    Return False
End Try
```

➤ If ValuesAreOk finds that all of the values are okay, it should return True.

1. Each of the method's tests returns if there is a problem; therefore, if the code reaches the end of the routine, all the tests passed. At that point, simply return True.

Please select Lesson 21 on the DVD to view the video that accompanies this lesson.

EXERCISES

1. Copy the LCM program you built in Lesson 20, Exercise 1 (or download Lesson 20's version from the book's web site) and add error handling to it. If a value causes an error, display a message and set focus to its textbox. Hints: Validate both the GCD and LCM methods so they only allow inputs greater than zero. That way they're both covered if a different program uses GCD directly. Also, use a `Try Catch` block in the Calculate button's `Click` event handler to protect against format errors.

2. Copy the Fibonacci program you built in Lesson 19, Exercise 2 (or download Lesson 19's version from the book's web site). Move the calculation itself into a new function that throws an error if its input is less than zero. Add error handling and validation to the main program.

3. (SimpleEdit) Copy the SimpleEdit program you built in Lesson 20, Exercise 4 (or download Lesson 20's version from the book's web site) and add error handling to the functions that open and save files. To test the program, open the file `Test.rtf` in Microsoft Word. Make changes in the SimpleEdit program and try to save them into that file.

4. The quadratic equation finds solutions to equations with the following form, where *a*, *b*, and *c* are constants:

$$a * x^2 + b * x + c = 0$$

The solutions to this equation (the values of x that make it true) are given by the quadratic formula:

$$x = \frac{-b \pm \sqrt{b^2 - 4ac}}{2a}$$

Build a program similar to the one shown in Figure 21-2 that calculates solutions to quadratic equations. Use a `Try Catch` block to protect against format errors. Hints: Use `Math.Sqrt` to take square roots. The equation has zero, one, or two real solutions depending on whether the *discriminant* $b^2 - 4ac$ is less than, equal to, or greater than zero. Use `If` statements to avoid trying to take the square root of a negative number.

FIGURE 21-2

 You can find solutions to this lesson's exercises in the Lesson21 folder inside the download available on the book's web site at www.wrox.com *or* www.vb-helper.com/24hourvb.html.

22

Preventing Bugs

Many programmers believe that the way to make a program robust is to make it able to continue running even when it encounters errors. For example, consider the following version of the `Factorial` function:

```
' Recursively calculate n!
Private Function Factorial(ByVal n As Long) As Long
    If (n <= 1) Then Return 1
    Return n * Factorial(n - 1)
End Function
```

This function is robust in the sense that it can handle nonsensical inputs such as –10. The function cannot calculate –10!, but because it doesn't crash you might think this is a safe function.

Unfortunately, while the function doesn't crash on this input, nor does it return a correct result because –10! is not defined. That makes the program continue running even though it has produced an incorrect result.

In general, bugs that cause a program to crash are a lot easier to find and fix than bugs like this one that produce incorrect results but continue running.

In this lesson, you learn techniques for detecting and correcting bugs. You learn how to make bugs jump out so they're easy to fix instead of remaining hidden.

INPUT ASSERTIONS

In Visual Basic programming, an *assertion* is a statement that the code claims is true. If the statement is false, the program stops running so you can decide whether a bug occurred.

The .NET Framework provides a `Debug` class that makes checking assertions easy. The `Debug` class's static `Assert` method takes as a parameter a Boolean value. If the value is `False`, `Assert` stops the program and displays an error message showing the program's stack dump at the time so you can figure out where the error occurred.

The following code shows a new version of the factorial function that uses `Debug.Assert`. The optional second parameter to `Debug.Assert` defines a message that should be displayed if the assertion fails.

```
' Recursively calculate n!
Private Function Factorial(ByVal n As Long) As Long
    ' Validate the input.
    Debug.Assert((n >= 0) AndAlso (n <= 20),
        "Factorial parameter must be between 0 and 20.")

    If (n <= 1) Then Return 1
    Return n * Factorial(n - 1)
End Function
```

Normally, when you develop a program you make *debug builds*. These include extra debugging symbols so you can step through the code in the debugger. If you switch to a *release build*, those symbols are omitted, making the compiled program a bit smaller. The `Debug.Assert` method has no effect in release builds.

The idea is that you can use `Debug.Assert` to test the program but then skip the assertions after the program is debugged and ready for release to the user. Of course, this works only if the code is robust enough to behave correctly when a bug does slip past the testing process and appears in the release build. In the case of the `Factorial` function, this code must always protect itself against input errors, so it should throw an exception rather than use `Debug.Assert`.

> *If the program can continue to produce a usable (although possibly unusual) result, use* `Debug.Assert`.
>
> *If there's no way the program can produce a useful result, throw an exception.*

To switch from a debug build to a release build or vice versa, open the Build menu and select the Configuration Manager command to display the dialog shown in Figure 22-1. Select Debug or Release from the drop-down menu and click Close.

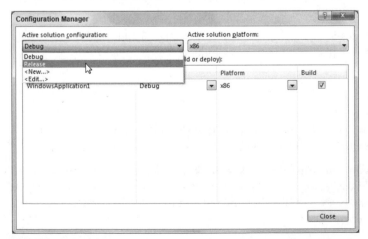

FIGURE 22-1

When you build the program, Visual Studio places the compiled executable in the project's bin\ Debug or bin\Release subdirectory. Be sure you use the correct version or you may find Debug. Assert statements displaying errors in what you thought was a release build.

The Debug *class provides some other handy methods in addition to* Assert. *The* WriteLine *method displays a message in the Immediate window. You can use it to display messages showing you what code is executing, to display parameter values, and to provide other information that you might otherwise need to learn by stepping through the code in the debugger.*

The Debug *class's* Indent *method lets you change the indentation of output produced by* Debug.WriteLine; *for example, you can indicate nesting of procedure calls.*

Like the other Debug *methods, these do nothing in release builds, so the end user never sees these messages.*

OTHER ASSERTIONS

In addition to input assertions, a program can make other assertions as it performs calculations. A program can use assertions to check intermediate results, and a function can use assertions to validate final results before returning them. A piece of code can even use assertions to validate the values it receives from a function.

Often these assertions cannot be as exact as those you can perform on inputs but you may still be able to catch some really ludicrous values.

For example, suppose an order processing form lets the user enter items for purchase and then calculates the total cost. You could use assertions to verify that the total cost is between $0.01 and $1 million. This is a pretty wide range so you are unlikely to catch any but the most egregious errors, but you may catch a few.

Note that you should not test user input errors with assertions. An assertion interrupts the program so you can try to find a bug. Your code should check for user input errors and handle them without interrupting the program. Remember, when you make a release build, Debug.Assert calls have no effect, so you cannot rely on them to help the user enter valid values.

One drawback to assertions is that it's hard to get into the habit of using them. When you're writing code, it's hard to convince yourself that the code could be wrong. After all, if you knew there was a bug in the code, you'd fix it.

Assertions are like seat belts, airbags, and bicycle helmets. You don't use them because you expect to need them today; you use them just on the off chance that you'll need them someday. Usually your assertions will just sit there doing nothing; but if a bug does rear its ugly head, a good set of assertions can make the difference between finding the bug in seconds, hours, or days.

TRY IT

In this Try It, you write a function to calculate a department's average salary. The interesting part is adding assertions to make sure the function is being called correctly.

To test the function, you build the program shown in Figure 22-2.

The focus of this Try It is the function that calculates the average, not the user interface. The assumption is that some other part of a larger program would call this function, so the user interface shown in Figure 22-2 is purely for testing purposes. A real program would not allow the user to enter invalid values.

FIGURE 22-2

You can download the code and resources for this Try It from the book's web page at www.wrox.com or www.vb-helper.com/24hourvb.html. You can find them in the Lesson22 folder in the download.

Lesson Requirements

In this lesson:

➤ Build a program similar to the one shown in Figure 22-2.

➤ When the user clicks Calculate, make the program split the values entered in the textbox apart, copy them into an array of `Decimals`, pass them to the `AverageSalary` function, and display the result.

➤ Make the `AverageSalary` function validate its inputs by asserting that the array has a reasonable number of elements and that the salaries are reasonable. Also validate the average.

Hints

➤ Assume you're not working on Wall Street, so salaries are at least $10,000 and less than $1 million.

➤ Think about how the program should react in a final release build for each of the input conditions.

For example, if the input array contains a salary of $1,600, what should the function do? In this case, that value is unusual but it could be valid (perhaps the company hired an intern for a week) so the function can calculate a meaningful (although unusual) result. The function should check this condition with `Debug.Assert` so it can calculate a result in the release version.

For another example, suppose the `values` array is empty. In this case the function *cannot* calculate a meaningful value so it should throw an exception so the code calling it can deal with the problem.

Step-by-Step

➤ Build a program similar to the one shown in Figure 22-2.

1. This is reasonably straightforward.

➤ When the user clicks Calculate, make the program split the values entered in the textbox apart, copy them into an array of `Decimals`, pass them to the `AverageSalary` function, and display the result.

1. You can use code similar to the following:

```
' Calculate and display the average salary.
Private Sub btnCalculate_Click() Handles btnCalculate.Click
    Try
        ' Copy the salaries into an array.
        Dim string_salaries() As String =
            salariesTextBox.Text.Split()
        Dim salaries(0 To string_salaries.Length - 1) As Decimal
        For i As Integer = 0 To string_salaries.Length - 1
            salaries(i) = Decimal.Parse(string_salaries(i),
                System.Globalization.NumberStyles.Any)
        Next i

        ' Calculate the average.
        Dim average As Decimal = AverageSalary(salaries)

        ' Display the result.
        averageTextBox.Text = average.ToString("C")
    Catch ex As Exception
        averageTextBox.Clear()
        MessageBox.Show(ex.Message)
    End Try
End Sub
```

Again, a real program shouldn't let the user enter salaries in a string like this because the user could enter invalid values.

➤ Make the `AverageSalary` function validate its inputs by asserting that the array has a reasonable number of elements and that the salaries are reasonable. Also validate the average.

1. You can use code similar to the following:

```
' Calculate the average of this array of salaries.
Private Function AverageSalary(ByVal salaries() As Decimal) _
As Decimal
    ' Sanity checks.
    If salaries Is Nothing Then
        Throw New ArgumentOutOfRangeException("salaries",
            "AverageSalary function: salaries parameter " &
            "must not be Nothing")
    End If
    If (salaries.Length = 1) Then
        Throw New ArgumentOutOfRangeException("salaries",
            "AverageSalary function cannot calculate average " &
            "salary for an empty array.")
```

```
            End If
            Debug.Assert(salaries.Length < 100, "Too many salaries.")
            For Each salary As Integer In salaries
                Debug.Assert(salary >= 10000, "Salary is too small.")
                Debug.Assert(salary < 1000000, "Salary is too big.")
            Next salary

            ' Calculate the result.
            Dim total As Decimal = 0
            For Each salary As Integer In salaries
                total += salary
            Next salary
            Dim result As Decimal = total / salaries.Length

            ' Validate the result.
            Debug.Assert(result >= 10000, "Average salary is too small.")
            Debug.Assert(result < 1000000, "Average salary is too big.")

            Return result
        End Function
```

 Please select Lesson 22 on the DVD to view the video that accompanies this lesson.

EXERCISES

1. Suppose you're writing a routine for sorting orders based on priority using the following `Order` structure:

```
' Define the Order structure.
Private Structure Order
    Public OrderId As Integer
    Public Priority As Integer
End Structure
```

Write the `SortOrders` subroutine that takes as a parameter an array of `Orders` and sorts them. Don't actually write the code that sorts the orders, just write assertions to validate the inputs and outputs.

2. Build a program to convert temperatures between the Fahrenheit, Celsius, and Kelvin scales. Write functions `FahrenheitToCelsius`, `KelvinToCelsius`, `CelsiusToFahrenheit`, and `CelsiusToKelvin` to perform the conversions using the following formulas:

$$C = (F - 32) * 5 / 9$$

$$C = K - 273.15$$

$$F = C * 9 / 5 + 32$$

$$K = C + 273.15$$

Use assertions to help the conversion functions ensure that Fahrenheit values are between −130 and 140, Celsius values are between −90 and 60, and Kelvin values are between 183 and 333.

3. Make a program that lets the user input miles and gallons of fuel and calculates miles per gallon using a `MilesPerGallon` function. Make the function protect itself against miles and gallons values that are too big or too small. Make it also validate its result so it doesn't return values that are too large or small.

 You can find solutions to this lesson's exercises in the Lesson22 folder inside the download available on the book's web site at www.wrox.com *or* www.vb-helper.com/24hourvb.html.

SECTION IV
Classes

The lessons in Section III focus on Visual Basic programming statements. They explain how to make decisions with `If` and `Select Case` statements, repeat program steps with loops, reuse code with procedures, and catch exceptions.

Procedures are particularly useful for programming at a higher level because they let you encapsulate complex behaviors in a tightly wrapped package. For example, you might write a `CalculateGrade` function that determines a student's grades. This method can hide all the details about how grades are calculated. (Are tests graded on a curve? Is the grade a weighted average of tests and homework assignments? How much is attendance worth?) The main program only needs to know how to call the function, not how it works.

Classes provide another even more powerful method for abstracting complex entities into manageable packages. For example, a `Student` class might embody the idea of a student and include basic information (name, address, phone number), the courses that the student is taking, grades (test scores, homework grades), and even attendance. It would also include methods such as `CalculateGrade` for manipulating the `Student` data.

The lessons in this section explain classes. They explain how you can build classes, make one class inherit the capabilities of another, and make a class override the features of its parent class.

23

Defining Classes and Their Properties

This book hasn't emphasized the fact, but you've been working with classes since the very beginning. The very first program you created in Lesson 1 included several classes, such as the program's main form and some behind-the-scenes classes that help get the program running. Since then, you've used all kinds of control classes — the MessageBox class, the Array class, collection classes, the Debug class, and more. You can even treat primitive data types such as Integer and String as classes under some circumstances.

In this lesson you learn how to create your own classes. You learn how to define a class and give it properties.

WHAT IS A CLASS?

A *class* defines a type of object. It defines the properties, methods, and events provided by its type of object. After you define a class, you can make as many *instances* of that class as you like.

For example, the Button class defines the properties and behaviors of a button user interface element. You can create any number of instances of Buttons and place them on your forms.

You can think of a class as a blueprint for making objects. When you create an instance of the class, you use the blueprint to make an object that has the properties and behaviors defined by the class. You can also think of a class as a cookie cutter. Once you've created the cookie cutter, you can make any number of cookies that all have the same shape.

Classes are very similar to the structures described in Lesson 17, and many of the techniques you learned there apply here as well. For example, you can give a class fields that the instance can use to perform calculations.

There are several important differences between structures and classes, but one of the most important is that structures are value types, whereas classes are reference types. Perhaps the most confusing consequence of this is that when you assign structure variable A equal to structure variable B, A becomes a *copy* of B. In contrast, if you assign class variable C equal to class variable D, then variable C now points to the same object that variable D does.

For a more detailed discussion of some of these differences, see the section "Structures versus Classes" in Lesson 17.

The rest of this lesson focuses on classes and doesn't really talk about structures.

 Note that the same techniques apply to both structures and classes: structures have the same benefits as classes described in the following section. Just because I'm describing those benefits or techniques here doesn't mean I'm implying that classes are better because they have these advantages and structures don't.

CLASS BENEFITS

The biggest benefit of classes is encapsulation. A well-designed class hides its internal workings from the rest of the program so the program can use the class without knowing how the class works.

For example, suppose you build a Turtle class to represent a turtle crawling across the screen, drawing lines as it moves. The class would need properties such as X, Y, and Direction to define the Turtle's location and direction. It might also provide methods such as Turn to make it change direction, and Move to make it move.

The Turtle class needs to know how to draw the Turtle's path as it moves, but the main program doesn't need to know how it works. It doesn't need to know about Graphics objects, Pens, or the trigonometric functions the Turtle uses to figure out where to go. The main program only needs to know how to set the Turtle's properties and call its methods.

 You can download the Turtle example program from the book's web site (at www.wrox.com *or* www.vb-helper.com/24hourvb.html*) as part of the Lesson23 folder and follow along in its code as you read through this lesson.*

Some other benefits of classes (and structures for that matter) include the following:

➤ **Grouping data and code** — The code that makes a Turtle move is contained in the same object as the data that determines the Turtle's position and direction.

➤ **Code reuse** — You only need to write the code for the Turtle class once and then all instances of the class get to use it. You get even more code reuse through inheritance, which is described in Lesson 25.

➤ **Polymorphism** — Polymorphism means you can treat an object as if it were another class as long as it inherits from that class. For example, a Student is a type of Person so you should be able to treat a `Student` object as if it were either a `Student` or a `Person`. Lesson 25 describes this further.

MAKING A CLASS

Now that you know a bit about what classes are for, it's time to learn how to build one.

Making a class in Visual Basic is simple. Open the Project menu and select Add Class. Give the class a meaningful name and click Add. The following code shows a newly created `Employee` class:

```
Public Class Employee

End Class
```

At this point, the class can't do anything. You can write code to create an instance of the class but it will just sit there. To make the class useful, you need to add properties, methods, and events.

➤ **Properties** are values associated with a class. For example, an `Employee` class might define `FirstName`, `LastName`, and `EmployeeId` properties.

➤ **Methods** are actions that an object can perform. For example, an `Employee` class might provide a `CalculateBonus` method that calculates the employee's end-of-year bonus based on performance during the year. (Methods are simply subroutines and functions provided by the class.)

➤ **Events** are *raised* by the class to tell the rest of the program that something interesting happened, sort of like raising a flag to draw attention to something. For example, the `Employee` class might raise a `TooManyHours` event if the program tried to assign an employee more than 40 hours of work in a week.

Properties, methods, and events allow a program to control and interact with objects. The following sections explain how you can add properties to a class. Lesson 24 explains how to give a class methods and events.

PROPERTIES

If you give a class a public variable, other pieces of code can get and set that variable's values. This kind of variable is called a *field*. A field is similar to a property but it has one big disadvantage: it provides unrestricted access to its value. That means other parts of the program could dump any old garbage into the field without the class being able to stop them.

In contrast, a class implements a property by using *property get* and *property set* methods that can include code to protect the class from garbage values. Because the program uses those methods to access the value, they are also called *accessor methods*. You'll learn more about this as you learn how to build properties.

The following sections describe the two most common approaches for implementing properties: auto-implemented properties and backing fields.

Auto-Implemented Properties

The easiest way to make a property is to use an auto-implemented property. The syntax for an auto-implemented property is as follows:

```
accessibility Property Name As dataType
```

Here *accessibility* determines what code can use the property. It can be Public, Private, and so forth. The *dataType* determines the property's data type and *Name* determines its name.

The following code creates a simple property named FirstName of type String:

```
Public Property FirstName As String
```

Creating an auto-implemented property is almost as easy as making a field but it's a tiny bit more work, so why should you bother? Making an auto-implemented property sets up the code so it will be easy to upgrade the property to use more complicated code later. For example, suppose you decide that the Turtle class's Direction property should only allow angles between 0 and 259 degrees. In that case you can convert the auto-implemented property into a property built using a backing field, as described in the next section. If you initially made Direction a simple field, then adding validation code would be more difficult.

Backing Fields

When you make an auto-implemented property, Visual Basic automatically generates property get and set procedures behind the scenes. You can use those procedures without needing to know the details about how they work (another example of encapsulation).

When you make a property that is not auto-implemented, you need to write the property get and set procedures yourself.

The following shows the basic syntax used to define a property that is not auto-implemented:

```
accessibility Property Name As dataType
    Get
        ...getCode...
    End Get
    Set(ByVal value As dataType)
        ...setCode...
    End Set
End Property
```

Here *accessibility*, *dataType*, and *Name* are the same as before. The *getCode* and *setCode* are the pieces of code that get and set the property's value.

One common way to implement this kind of property is with a backing field. A *backing field* is a field that stores data to represent the property. The *getCode* and *setCode* use the field to get and set the property's value.

The following Visual Basic code shows a version of the Direction property stored in the backing field named _Direction:

```
' The Turtle's direction in degrees.
Private _Direction As Integer = 0        ' Backing field.
```

```
Public Property Direction As Integer
    Get
        Return _Direction
    End Get
    Set(ByVal value As Integer)
        _Direction = value
    End Set
End Property
```

The code starts by defining the field _Direction to hold the property's value. The field is private so only the code inside the class can see it.

 Different programmers use different naming conventions for the backing field. Some use the same name as the property with an underscore in front as shown here. Others add m_ *to the name to indicate that the variable has module-level scope. Others add* Value *to the end of the property's name as in* DirectionValue. *As is usually the case with naming conventions, it doesn't matter too much what you do as long as you're consistent.*

The property's Get procedure simply returns the value of _Direction.

The property's Set procedure saves a new value in the backing field _Direction. The new value that the calling code is trying to assign to the property is stored in a parameter named value.

The preceding code simply copies values in and out of the backing field, so why bother doing this instead of using a public field? There are several reasons.

First, a property hides its details from the outside world, increasing the class's encapsulation. As far as the outside world is concerned, a description of the Direction property tells you *what* is stored (the direction) but not *how* it is stored (as an integer value in degrees).

This example stores the direction in degrees, but suppose you decided that the class would work better if you stored the direction in radians? If Direction is a field, then any code that uses it would now break because it is using degrees. However, if you use property procedures, they can translate between degrees and radians as needed so the code outside the class doesn't need to know that anything has changed.

The following code shows a new version of the Direction property that stores its value in radians. As far as the code outside the class is concerned, nothing has changed.

```
' Store Direction in radians but get and set in degrees.
Private _Direction As Double = 0       ' Backing field.
Public Property Direction As Integer
    Get
        Return CInt(_Direction * 180 / Math.PI)
    End Get
    Set(ByVal value As Integer)
        _Direction = value * Math.PI / 180
    End Set
End Property
```

Second, you can also add validation code to property procedures. For example, suppose the `Direction` property represents an angle in degrees and you only want to allow values between 0 and 359. The following code asserts that the new value is within that range. The program can continue correctly if the value is outside of this range so the code uses `Debug.Assert` instead of throwing an exception.

```
' The Turtle's direction in degrees.
Private _Direction As Integer = 0        ' Backing field.
Public Property Direction As Integer
    Get
        Return _Direction
    End Get
    Set(ByVal value As Integer)
        Debug.Assert((value >= 0) AndAlso (value <= 359),
            "Direction should be between 0 and 359 degrees")
        _Direction = value
    End Set
End Property
```

Finally, property procedures give you a place to set breakpoints if something is going wrong. For example, if you know that some part of your program is setting a `Turtle`'s `Direction` to 45 when it should be setting it to 60 but you don't know where, you could set a breakpoint in the property `Set` procedure to see where the change is taking place.

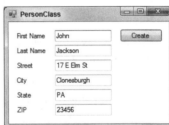

FIGURE 23-1

TRY IT

In this Try It, you create a simple `Person` class with `FirstName`, `LastName`, `Street`, `City`, `State`, and `Zip` properties, some having simple validations. You also build a simple test application, as shown in Figure 23-1.

 You can download the code and resources for this Try It from the book's web page at www.wrox.com *or* www.vb-helper.com/24hourvb.html. *You can find them in the Lesson23 folder in the download.*

Lesson Requirements

In this lesson:

➤   Build the program shown in Figure 23-1.

➤   Create a `Person` class.

➤   Make auto-implemented properties for `Street`, `City`, `State`, and `Zip`.

➤   For this application, assume that setting `FirstName` or `LastName` to a blank string is an error and add validation code to their property procedures.

Hints

➤ Don't allow `FirstName` or `LastName` to be set to `Nothing`, which is different from setting them equal to blank strings. If you don't check for these, the other code in the property procedures will throw an error anyway when it tries to manipulate the `Nothing` value, but if you check yourself, then you can provide a more meaningful exception.

Step-by-Step

➤ Build the program shown in Figure 23-1.

1. This is reasonably straightforward.

➤ Create a `Person` class.

1. Use the Project menu's Add Class item. Name the class `Person`.

➤ Make auto-implemented properties for `Street`, `City`, `State`, and `Zip`.

1. You can use code similar to the following:

```
' Auto-implemented properties.
Public Property Street As String
Public Property City As String
Public Property State As String
Public Property Zip As String
```

➤ For this application, assume that setting `FirstName` or `LastName` to a blank string is an error and add validation code to their property procedures.

1. The following code shows how you might implement the `FirstName` property. The code for the `LastName` property is similar.

```
' FirstName property.
Private _FirstName As String = ""
Public Property FirstName As String
    Get
        Return _FirstName
    End Get
    Set(ByVal value As String)
        If (value Is Nothing) Then
            Throw New ArgumentOutOfRangeException("FirstName",
                "Person.FirstName cannot be Nothing.")
        End If
        If (value.Length = 0) Then
            Throw New ArgumentOutOfRangeException("FirstName",
                "Person.FirstName cannot be blank.")
        End If

        ' Validations passed. Save the new value.
        _FirstName = value
    End Set
End Property
```

Please select Lesson 23 on the DVD to view the video that accompanies this lesson.

EXERCISES

1. Copy the program you built for this lesson's Try It or download the version available on the book's web site. Convert the auto-implemented `Zip` property into one that uses property get and set procedures. Notice that you don't need to change the main program.

    Make the property set procedure verify that the new value has the format #####. Hint: The following `Like` statement returns `True` if value has the correct format:

    ```
    value Like "#####"
    ```

2. Copy the program you built for Exercise 1 or download the version available on the book's web site. Modify the `Zip` property get procedure to allow either the format ##### or #####-####. Add a new `PhoneNumber` property that allows the formats ###-#### or ###-###-####.

    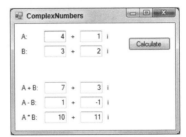

    FIGURE 23-2

3. Write a program similar to the one shown in Figure 23-2 to manipulate complex numbers. When you enter the complex numbers' real and imaginary parts in the textboxes and click Calculate, the program should display the sum, difference, and product of the two complex numbers.

    Make a `ComplexNumber` class with properties `Real` and `Imaginary` to hold a number's real and imaginary parts. Give the class `AddTo`, `MultiplyBy`, and `SubtractFrom` functions that combine the current `ComplexNumber` with another taken as a parameter and return the result as a new `ComplexNumber`.

    Hints: Recall from school these equations for calculating with complex numbers:

    ```
    (A + Bi) + (C + Di) = (A + C) + (B + D)i
    (A + Bi) - (C + Di) = (A - C) + (B - D)i
    (A + Bi) * (C + Di) = (A * C - B * D) + (A * D + B * C)i
    ```

    For more review of complex numbers, see en.wikipedia.org/wiki/Complex_numbers or mathworld.wolfram.com/ComplexNumber.html.

 You can find solutions to this lesson's exercises in the Lesson23 folder inside the download available on the book's web site at www.wrox.com *or* www.vb-helper.com/24hourvb.html.

24

Defining Class Methods and Events

Lesson 23 explains how to create a class and give it properties. In this lesson you learn how to add the remaining two key pieces of a class: methods and events.

METHODS

A method is simply a subroutine or function in the class that other parts of the program can execute. The following code shows how the Turtle drawing class described in Lesson 23 might implement its Move method:

```
' Make the Turtle move the indicated distance in its current direction.
Public Sub Move(ByVal distance As Integer)
    ' Calculate the new position.
    Dim radians As Double = Direction * Math.PI / 180
    Dim newX As Integer = CInt(X + Math.Cos(radians) * distance)
    Dim newY As Integer = CInt(Y + Math.Sin(radians) * distance)

    ' Draw to the new position.
    Using gr As Graphics = Graphics.FromImage(Canvas)
        gr.DrawLine(Pens.Blue, X, Y, newX, newY)
    End Using

    ' Save the new position.
    X = newX
    Y = newY
End Sub
```

 You can download the Turtle example program from the book's web site (at www.wrox.com or www.vb-helper.com/24hourvb.html) as part of the Lesson24 folder and follow along in its code as you read through this lesson.

The method takes as a parameter the distance it should move. It uses the `Turtle`'s current position and direction to figure out where this move will terminate. It uses some graphics code to draw a line from the current position to the new one (don't worry about the details) and finishes by saving the new position.

That's all there is to adding a method to a class. Simply give it a subroutine or function. The only detail worth mentioning is that you need to give the method an accessibility such as `Public` or `Friend` if you want code outside of the class to be able to use it. See Lesson 20 for more information on writing subroutines and functions.

EVENTS

Events enable the class to tell the rest of the program that something interesting is happening. For example, if a `BankAccount` object's balance falls below 0, it could raise an `AccountOverdrawn` event to notify the main program.

Declaring and using an event requires three steps: declaring the event, raising the event, and catching the event.

Declaring Events

Declaring an event in Visual Basic is easy. Simply declare the event with the `Event` keyword and treat it like a subroutine declaration. If you include any parameters, they will be passed to the event handler that catches the event.

For example, the following code declares an event named `TooManyAbsences` that includes a `daysAbsent` parameter:

```
Public Event TooManyAbsences(ByVal daysAbsent As Integer)
```

Microsoft recommends that you adopt the convention of giving an event handler two parameters. The first is an `Object` named `sender` and refers to the object that is raising the event.

Making `sender` an `Object` makes the code very general. That's handy if the same event handler might be able to handle events from more than one class. If you know that the event applies only to one class, you could give `sender` a more specific type such as `Student`.

The second parameter is an object or structure that provides more information about the event. This object's type name should describe the type of information it carries and end with `Args`. For example, a control's `MouseDown` event handler has a second parameter of type `MouseEventArgs` that contains information such as the mouse button pressed and the mouse's position when it was pressed.

The following code shows the declaration for the `Turtle` class's `OutOfBounds` event:

```
Public Class Turtle
    ' The TurtleOutOfBoundsEventArgs data type.
    Public Class TurtleOutOfBoundsEventArgs
        ' Where the Turtle would stop if this were not out of bounds.
        Public Property X As Integer
        Public Property Y As Integer
    End Class

    ' Declare the OutOfBounds event.
    Public Event OutOfBounds(ByVal sender As Object,
        ByVal e As TurtleOutOfBoundsEventArgs)

    ...
End Class
```

The code first defines the `TurtleOutOfBoundsEventArgs` class to hold information about the `Turtle` when it tries to move off its drawing area. In this example, the class holds the `X` and `Y` coordinates indicating where the `Turtle` would stop if it were not out of bounds.

Raising Events

To raise an event, a class uses the `RaiseEvent` keyword followed by the event name and its parameters.

The following code shows how an object could raise the `TooManyAbsences` event described in the previous section, passing it the parameter 10:

```
RaiseEvent TooManyAbsences(10)
```

The next bit of code shows how a `Turtle` object moves to a new position, possibly raising its `OutOfBounds` event:

```
' Make the Turtle move the indicated distance in its current direction.
Public Sub Move(ByVal distance As Integer)
    ' Calculate the new position.
    Dim radians As Double = Direction * Math.PI / 180
    Dim newX As Integer = CInt(X + Math.Cos(radians) * distance)
    Dim newY As Integer = CInt(Y + Math.Sin(radians) * distance)

    ' See if the new position is off the Bitmap.
    If ((newX < 0) OrElse (newY < 0) OrElse
        (newX >= Canvas.Width) OrElse (newY >= Canvas.Height)) Then

        ' Raise the OutOfBounds event, passing
        ' the event handler the new coordinates.
        Dim args As New TurtleOutOfBoundsEventArgs()
        args.X = newX
        args.Y = newY
        RaiseEvent OutOfBounds(Me, args)
        Return
    End If
```

```
    ' Draw to the new position.
    Using gr As Graphics = Graphics.FromImage(Canvas)
        gr.DrawLine(Pens.Blue, X, Y, newX, newY)
    End Using

    ' Save the new position.
    X = newX
    Y = newY
End Sub
```

The code first calculates the `Turtle`'s new position. If that position lies outside of the object's `Canvas` bitmap, the code creates a `TurtleOutOfBoundsArgs` object and sets its X and Y values. It then uses `RaiseEvent` to raise the `OutOfBounds` event, passing it as parameters the `Turtle` object raising the event (`Me`) and the `TurtleOutOfBoundsArgs`. The code then uses `Return` to break out of the `Move` method.

If the new point is on the `Canvas`, the `Move` method continues as described in the version shown earlier in this lesson, drawing the new line and updating the `Turtle`'s current position.

Catching Events

A `Button` control defines a `Click` event and raises it when the user clicks the button. Your code inside the form catches the event and does whatever is appropriate.

Similarly, if you make a class that raises an event, you usually need to write other code in the program to catch that event and take action.

The easiest way to catch an event is to declare the object that will raise it with the `WithEvents` keyword, as in the following code:

```
' The Turtle instance this program uses.
Private WithEvents MyTurtle As Turtle
```

 Your code still needs to initialize the variable somewhere with the New *keyword or it will never raise events.*

Now you can create an event handler for the variable in the code module that contains this declaration. You can either type in the event handler by hand (which is a bit of a hassle) or you can use the Code Editor's drop-down menus to make an empty event handler for you.

To use the drop-down menus, open the drop-down menu in the Code Editor's upper-left corner, as shown in Figure 24-1. Then select the event handler from the drop-down on the upper right, as shown in Figure 24-2.

The following code shows the initial blank event handler:

```
Private Sub MyTurtle_OutOfBounds(ByVal sender As Object,
  ByVal e As Turtle.TurtleOutOfBoundsEventArgs) Handles MyTurtle.OutOfBounds

End Sub
```

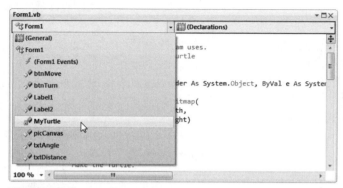

FIGURE 24-1

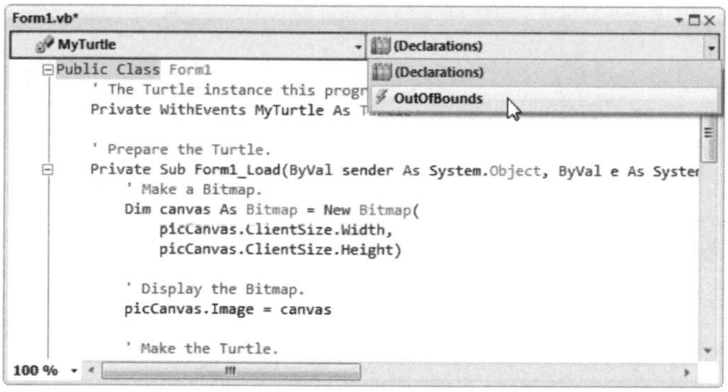

FIGURE 24-2

Now add whatever code you like to the event handler. The following code shows how the Turtle program handles the OutOfBounds event:

```
' Handle the OutOfBounds event.
Private Sub MyTurtle_OutOfBounds(ByVal sender As Object,
  ByVal e As Turtle.TurtleOutOfBoundsEventArgs) Handles MyTurtle.OutOfBounds
    MessageBox.Show(String.Format(
        "Oops! ({0}, {1}) is out of bounds.",
        e.X, e.Y))
End Sub
```

The WithEvents keyword makes building event handlers easier, but you can do without it if you wish. Declare the variable as before but without the WithEvents keyword. Define the event handler but without the Handles clause at the end. Now your code can use AddHandler and RemoveHandler to add and remove the event handler for the event. See Lesson 4 for more information about AddHandler and RemoveHandler.

TRY IT

In this Try It, you create a BankAccount class. You give it a Balance property and two methods, Credit and Debit. The Debit method raises an Overdrawn event if a withdrawal would give the account a negative balance.

You also build the test application shown in Figure 24-3.

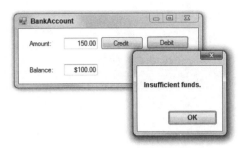

FIGURE 24-3

 You can download the code and resources for this Try It from the book's web page at www.wrox.com *or* www.vb-helper.com/24hourvb.html. *You can find them in the Lesson24 folder of the download.*

Lesson Requirements

In this lesson:

➤ Build the program shown in Figure 24-3.

➤ Create a BankAccount class. Give it a Balance property.

➤ Add Debit and Credit methods to add and remove money from the account.

➤ Define the AccountOverdrawnArgs class to pass the current and invalid balances to event handlers.

➤ Declare the Overdrawn event.

➤ Make the Debit method raise the event when necessary.

➤ In the main program, declare the MyAccount variable using the WithEvents keyword.

➤ In the main program, catch the Overdrawn event and display a message.

Hints

➤ This example doesn't do anything special with the Balance property so you can make it auto-implemented.

➤ Remember to declare the BankAccount variable with the WithEvents keyword.

Step-by-Step

➤ Build the program shown in Figure 24-3.

    1. This is reasonably straightforward.

➤ Create a `BankAccount` class. Give it a `Balance` property.

1. Use code similar to the following:

```
' The account balance.
Public Property Balance As Decimal
```

➤ Add `Debit` and `Credit` methods to add and remove money from the account.

1. Start with code similar to the following. You'll modify the `Debit` method later to raise the `Overdrawn` event.

```
' Add money to the account.
Public Sub Credit(ByVal amount As Decimal)
    Balance += amount
End Sub

' Remove money from the account.
Public Sub Debit(ByVal amount As Decimal)
    Balance -= amount
End Sub
```

➤ Define the `AccountOverdrawnArgs` class to pass the current and invalid balances to event handlers.

1. Use code similar to the following:

```
' Define the OverdrawnEventArgs type.
Public Class OverdrawnEventArgs
    Public Property CurrentBalance As Decimal
    Public Property InvalidBalance As Decimal
End Class
```

➤ Declare the `Overdrawn` event.

1. Use code similar to the following:

```
' Declare the Overdrawn event.
Public Event Overdrawn(ByVal sender As Object,
 ByVal e As OverdrawnEventArgs)
```

➤ Make the `Debit` method raise the event when necessary.

1. Modify the simple initial version of the method so it raises the event when necessary. Use code similar to the following:

```
' Remove money from the account.
Public Sub Debit(ByVal amount As Decimal)
    ' See if there is enough money.
    If (Balance >= amount) Then
        ' There is enough money. Just do it.
        Balance -= amount
    Else
        ' There's not enough money.
        ' Make an OverdrawnEventArgs to describe the event.
        Dim args As New OverdrawnEventArgs()
```

```
        args.CurrentBalance = Balance
        args.InvalidBalance = Balance - amount

        '  Raise the Overdrawn event.
        RaiseEvent Overdrawn(Me, args)
    End If
End Sub
```

➤ In the main program, declare the `MyAccount` variable using the `WithEvents` keyword.

1. Use code similar to the following:

```
' Declare an account.
Private WithEvents MyAccount As BankAccount
```

➤ In the main program, catch the `Overdrawn` event and display a message.

1. Use code similar to the following:

```
' We're overdrawn.
Private Sub MyAccount_Overdrawn(ByVal sender As Object,
 ByVal e As BankAccount.OverdrawnEventArgs) _
 Handles MyAccount.Overdrawn
    MessageBox.Show("Insufficient funds.")
End Sub
```

If you don't need to use the event handler's parameters, you can use relaxed delegates to remove them and make the code simpler as in the following code:

```
' We're overdrawn.
Private Sub MyAccount_Overdrawn() Handles MyAccount.Overdrawn
    MessageBox.Show("Insufficient funds.")
End Sub
```

Please select Lesson 24 on the DVD to view the video that accompanies this lesson.

EXERCISES

1. The version of the `BankAccount` class used by this lesson's Try It allows the main program to directly get and set the `Balance` property, and that could lead to errors. For example, if the program directly sets `Balance = -10`, the class would not have a chance to raise the `Overdrawn` event.

To fix this problem, copy the program you built for this lesson's Try It or download the version available on the book's web site. Convert the `Balance` property from an auto-implemented property to one implemented with a backing field. Add the keyword `ReadOnly` before the property's `Public` keyword and remove the property set procedure. Now the only way to set the balance is through the `Credit` and `Debit` methods. (Hint: You may need to fix some code that tries to set `Balance` directly. Inside the `BankAccount` class, use the backing field. Outside the class, use the `Credit` method.)

2. Make a `Student` class that has a `Name` property (a `String`) and a private `TestScores` field (a `List` of `Integers`). Give it a `ReadOnly Average` property that calculates and returns the `Student`'s test average. Also give it an `AddScore` method that adds a score to the list. If the `Student`'s new average is below 60, raise a `FailureWarning` event, passing the new average as a parameter. Hint: Initialize the `TestScores` field when you declare it, as in:

```
Private TestScores As New List(Of Integer)()
```

3. Make a `Player` class with `Name` and `Points` properties. Make a `ReadOnly` property `Level` that returns `Points \ 10`. In the `Points` property set procedure, raise a `LevelUp` or `LevelDown` event every time the `Level` changes.

You can find solutions to this lesson's exercises in the Lesson24 folder inside the download available on the book's web site at www.wrox.com *or* www.vb-helper.com/24hourvb.html.

25

Using Inheritance and Polymorphism

Subroutines and functions enable you to reuse code by packaging it so other pieces of code can call it easily. By using inheritance, you can reuse code in another way: by making one class reuse the properties, methods, and events of another class.

In this lesson you learn how to use inheritance to make one class reuse the code of another. You also learn how polymorphism enables a program to treat an object of one class as if it belonged to another.

INHERITANCE

One way to understand inheritance is to realize that real-world things of one type may also be of another type. For example, an employee is also a person (despite what some managers may think). That means whatever attributes a person has, an employee has also. A person has a name, address, birthday, and so forth. An employee also has those things, in addition to some new ones such as a salary, job title, office number, and employee ID number.

Similarly, a manager is a type of employee. That means a manager has everything an employee does, which in turn means the manager has everything a person does.

In Visual Basic, classes provide a similar structure through inheritance. One class such as `Employee` can *inherit* the properties, methods, and events of another class such as `Person`.

This kind of inheritance enables you to reuse code in a new way because it means you don't need to write the same properties, methods, and events for the `Employee` class that you already defined for the `Person` class.

When you make one class inherit from another one, you *derive* the new class from the existing class. In that case, the new class is called the *child class* and the class from which it inherits is called the *parent class*.

You could build a `Person` class with properties that all people have: `FirstName`, `LastName`, `Street`, `City`, `State`, and `Zip`. You could then derive the `Employee` class from `Person` and add the new properties `Salary`, `JobTitle`, `MailStop`, and `EmployeeId`.

Next, you could derive the `Manager` class from `Employee` and add new manager-related properties such as `DepartmentName` and `DirectReports`.

Syntactically, to make a class that inherits from another you add an `Inherits` statement immediately after the `Class` statement. For example, the following code shows definitions for a `Person` class, an `Employee` class that inherits from `Person`, and a `Manager` class that inherits from `Employee`:

```
Public Class Person
    Public Property FirstName As String
    Public Property LastName As String
    Public Property Street As String
    Public Property City As String
    Public Property State As String
    Public Property Zip As String
End Class

Public Class Employee
    Inherits Person

    Public Property Salary As Decimal
    Public Property JobTitle As String
    Public Property MailStop As String
    Public Property EmployeeId As Integer
End Class

Public Class Manager
    Inherits Employee

    Public Property DepartmentName As String
    Public Property DirectReports As New List(Of Person)
End Class
```

 Note that Visual Basic supports single inheritance only. That means a class can inherit from at most one parent class. For example, if you define a `House` *class and a* `Boat` *class, you cannot make a* `HouseBoat` *class that inherits from both.*

POLYMORPHISM

Polymorphism is a rather confusing concept that basically means a program can treat an object as if it were any class that it inherits. Another way to think of this is that polymorphism enables you to treat an object as if it were any of the classes that it *is*. For example, an `Employee` is a kind of `Person` so you should be able to treat an `Employee` as a `Person`.

Note that the reverse is not true. A `Person` is not necessarily an `Employee` (it could be a `Customer` or some other unrelated person such as a `Plumber`).

For a more detailed example, suppose you make the `Person`, `Employee`, and `Manager` classes, and they inherit from each other in the obvious way. Now suppose you write a method that takes a `Person` as a parameter. `Employee` inherits from `Person` so you should be able to pass an `Employee` into this method and the method should be able to treat it as a `Person`. This makes intuitive sense because an `Employee` *is* a `Person`, just a particular kind of `Person`.

Similarly, `Manager` inherits from `Employee`, so a `Manager` is a kind of `Employee`. If an `Employee` is a kind of `Person` and a `Manager` is a kind of `Employee`, then a `Manager` must also be a kind of `Person`, so the same method should be able to take a `Manager` as its parameter.

This feature enables you to reuse code in ways that make sense. For example, if you write a method that addresses letters for a `Person`, it can also address letters to `Employees` and `Managers`.

 ## TRY IT

Available for
download on
Wrox.com

In this Try It, you get to experiment with classes, inheritance, and polymorphism. You build `Person`, `Employee`, and `Manager` classes. To test the classes, you build a simple program that creates instances of each class and passes them to a method that takes a `Person` as a parameter.

> *You can download the code and resources for this Try It from the book's web page at* www.wrox.com *or* www.vb-helper.com/24hourvb.html. *You can find them in the Lesson25 folder of the download.*

Lesson Requirements

In this lesson:

➤ Create a `Person` class with properties `FirstName`, `LastName`, `Street`, `City`, `State`, and `Zip`. Give the class a `GetAddress` method that returns the `Person`'s name and address properties as a string of the following form:

```
Alice Archer
100 Ash Ave
Bugsville   CO    82010
```

➤ Derive an `Employee` class from `Person`. Add the properties `EmployeeId` and `MailStop`.

➤ Derive a `Manager` class from `Employee`. Add a `DepartmentName` property and a `DirectReports` property of type `List(Of Employee)`. Make a `GetDirectReportsList` method that returns the names of the `Manager`'s direct reports, separated by new lines.

➤ Make the main program create two `Employees` named Alice and Bob, a `Manager` named Cindy who has Alice and Bob in her department, and a `Person` named Dan.

➤ Make a `ShowAddress` method that takes a `Person` as a parameter and displays the `Person`'s address.

➤ On the main form, make buttons that call `ShowAddress` for each of the people, passing the method the appropriate object.

➤ Make a final button that displays Cindy's list of direct reports.

Hints

➤ This example doesn't do anything fancy with the class's properties, so you can use auto-implemented properties.

➤ The `ShowAddress` method should take a `Person` parameter even though some of the objects it will be passed are `Employees` or `Managers`.

Step-by-Step

➤ Create a `Person` class with properties `FirstName`, `LastName`, `Street`, `City`, `State`, and `Zip`. Give the class a `GetAddress` method that returns the `Person`'s name and address properties as a string of the following form:

```
Alice Archer
100 Ash Ave
Bugsville    CO    82010
```

1.   Make a new `Person` class with code similar to the following:

```
Public Class Person
    Public Property FirstName As String
    Public Property LastName As String
    Public Property Street As String
    Public Property City As String
    Public Property State As String
    Public Property Zip As String

    ' Display the person's address.
    ' A real application might print this on an envelope.
    Public Function GetAddress() As String
        Return FirstName & " " & LastName &
            vbCrLf & Street & vbCrLf & City &
            "    " & State & "    " & Zip
    End Function
End Class
```

➤ Derive an `Employee` class from `Person`. Add the properties `EmployeeId` and `MailStop`.

1.   Make the `Employee` class similar to the following:

```
Public Class Employee
    Inherits Person

    Public Property EmployeeId As Integer
    Public Property MailStop As String
End Class
```

➤ Derive a `Manager` class from `Employee`. Add a `DepartmentName` property and a `DirectReports` property of type `List(Of Employee)`. Make a `GetDirectReportsList` method that returns the names of the `Manager`'s direct reports, separated by new lines.

1. Make the `Manager` class similar to the following:

```
Public Class Manager
    Inherits Employee

    Public Property DepartmentName As String
    Public Property DirectReports As New List(Of Person)

    ' Return a list of this manager's direct reports.
    Public Function GetDirectReportsList() As String
        Dim result As String = ""
        For Each emp As Employee In DirectReports
            result &= emp.FirstName & " " & emp.LastName & vbCrLf
        Next emp
        Return result
    End Function
End Class
```

➤ Make the main program create two `Employees` named Alice and Bob, a `Manager` named Cindy who has Alice and Bob in her department, and a `Person` named Dan.

1. Because the program's buttons need to access the objects, these objects should be stored in fields as in the following code:

```
' Define some people of various types.
Private Dan As Person
Private Alice, Bob As Employee
Private Cindy As Manager
```

2. Add code to the main form's `Load` event handler to initialize the objects. The following code shows how the program might create Alice's `Employee` object:

```
' Make an Employee named Alice.
Alice = New Employee()
Alice.FirstName = "Alice"
Alice.LastName = "Archer"
Alice.Street = "100 Ash Ave"
Alice.City = "Bugsville"
Alice.State = "CO"
Alice.Zip = "82010"
Alice.EmployeeId = 1001
Alice.MailStop = "A-1"
```

3. Creating and initializing the other objects is similar. The only odd case is adding Alice and Bob as Cindy's employees as in the following code:

```
Cindy.DirectReports.Add(Alice)
Cindy.DirectReports.Add(Bob)
```

➤ Make a `ShowAddress` method that takes a `Person` as a parameter and displays the `Person`'s address.

1. Use code similar to the following:

```
' Display this Person's address.
Private Sub ShowAddress(ByVal per As Person)
    MessageBox.Show(per.GetAddress())
End Sub
```

➤ On the main form, make buttons that call `ShowAddress` for each of the people, passing the appropriate object to the method.

1. Create the buttons' `Click` event handlers. The following code shows the event handler that displays Cindy's address:

```
Private Sub btnCindyAddress_Click() Handles btnCindyAddress.Click
    ShowAddress(Cindy)
End Sub
```

Note that the variable `Cindy` is a `Manager` but the `ShowAddress` method treats it as a `Person`. That's okay because `Manager` inherits indirectly from `Person`.

➤ Make a final button that displays Cindy's list of direct reports.

1. This method simply calls the `Cindy` object's `GetDirectReportsList` method and displays the result:

```
Private Sub btnCindyReports_Click() Handles btnCindyReports.Click
    MessageBox.Show(Cindy.GetDirectReportsList)
End Sub
```

 Please select Lesson 25 on the DVD to view the video that accompanies this lesson.

EXERCISES

1. Make `Vehicle`, `Car`, `SportsCar`, and `Truck` classes, giving them appropriate properties.

2. Figure 25-1 shows an inheritance diagram that illustrates the relationships between the `Vehicle`, `Car`, `SportsCar`, and `Truck` classes. Arrows point from each child class to its parent class. Draw a similar diagram to show the relationships between the `Person`, `Employee`, `Manager`, `Secretary`, `Programmer`, `Executive`, and `Customer` classes.

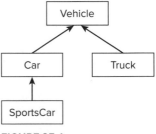

FIGURE 25-1

3. Implement the inheritance hierarchy you built in Exercise 2, giving each class a few reasonable properties. If you give the Executive class a ReportingManagers property that is a list of Managers, can an Executive have another Executive as a reporting Manager? (Look in the solution's Executive class for the answer.)

 You can find solutions to this lesson's exercises in the Lesson25 folder inside the download available on the book's web site at www.wrox.com *or* www.vb-helper .com/24hourvb.html.

26

Initializing Objects

Most of the time when you create an object, you need to initialize its properties. For example, you generally wouldn't create an `Employee` object without at least setting its `FirstName` and `LastName` properties. The following code shows how you might initialize an `Employee` object:

```
' Make an Employee named Alice.
Dim alice As New Employee()
alice.FirstName = "Alice"
alice.LastName = "Archer"
alice.Street = "100 Ash Ave"
alice.City = "Bugsville"
alice.State = "CO"
alice.Zip = "82010"
alice.EmployeeId = 1001
alice.MailStop = "A-1"
```

Though this is relatively straightforward, it is a bit tedious. Creating and initializing a bunch of `Employees` would take a lot of repetitive code. Fortunately, Visual Basic provides alternatives that make this task a little easier.

In this lesson you learn how to initialize an object's properties as you create it. You also learn how to make constructors that make initializing objects easier.

INITIALIZING OBJECTS

Visual Basic provides a simple syntax for initializing an object's properties as you create it. Create the object as usual with a `New` statement. Next add the keyword `With` and a pair of braces holding the property assignments. Each assignment should include a dot, a property name, an equals sign, and the value you want to give to the property.

For example, the following code creates an `Employee` object named `Bob`. The statements inside the braces initialize the object's properties.

```
' Make an Employee named Bob.
Dim bob As New Employee() With
{
    .FirstName = "Bob",
    .LastName = "Baker",
    .Street = "200 Beach Blvd",
    .City = "Bugsville",
    .State = "CO",
    .Zip = "82010",
    .EmployeeId = 1002,
    .MailStop = "B-2"
}
```

 An initializer can only initialize properties that the code can access. For example, if a property is private, the initializer cannot set its value.

CONSTRUCTORS

Initializers are handy and easy to use but sometimes you might like some extra control over how an object is created. Constructors give you that extra control.

A *constructor* is a subroutine named `New` that is executed when an object is created. The constructor executes before the code that creates the object gets hold of it. The constructor can perform any setup tasks that you want to get the object ready for use. It can look up data in databases, prepare data structures, and initialize properties.

The next two sections describe two kinds of constructors: parameterless constructors and parameterized constructors. The section after those explains how one constructor can invoke another to avoid duplicated work.

Parameterless Constructors

A constructor can take parameters just like any other method to help it in its setup tasks. A *parameterless constructor* takes no parameters, so it's somewhat limited in what it can do.

 Parameterless constructors are also sometimes called empty constructors.

For example, suppose the `Manager` class has a `DirectReports` property, which is a list of `Employees` that report to a given manager. A parameterless constructor cannot build that list because it doesn't know which employees to put in it. It can, however, initialize the `DirectReports` to an empty list as shown in the following code:

```
Public Class Manager
    Inherits Employee

    Public Property DirectReports As List(Of Employee)

    ' Initialize the DirectReports list.
    Public Sub New()
        DirectReports = New List(Of Employee)()
    End Sub
End Class
```

You implicitly invoke a parameterless constructor anytime you create an object without using any parameters. For example, the following code creates a new `Manager` object. When this code executes, control jumps briefly to the parameterless constructor so it can prepare the object for use.

```
Dim fred As New Manager()
```

Note that Visual Basic creates a default public parameterless constructor for you if you make a class that doesn't define any constructors explicitly. This code is hidden behind the scenes so you can't see it in any of your project's files.

If you give the class *any* constructors, Visual Basic doesn't create the default constructor. In that case, if you want a parameterless constructor, you must make it yourself.

Parameterized Constructors

Parameterless constructors are useful but fairly limited because they don't have much information to go by. To give a constructor more information, you can make it take parameters just like you can with any other method.

One simple type of parameterized constructor uses its parameters to initialize properties. For example, you could make a constructor for the `Person` class that takes the person's first and last names as parameters. The constructor could then set the object's `FirstName` and `LastName` properties.

Why would you bother doing this when you could use an initializer? First, the syntax for using a constructor is slightly more concise than initializer syntax. The following code uses a constructor that takes six parameters to initialize a `Person`'s properties:

```
Dim cindy As New Person("Cindy", "Carstairs",
    "300 Clam Ct", "Bugsville", "CO", "82010")
```

Compare this code to the earlier snippet that used initializers to initialize an `Employee` object. This version is more concise, although it's less self-documenting because it doesn't explicitly list the property names.

The second reason you might prefer to use a parameterized constructor instead of an initializer is that a constructor can perform all sorts of checks that an initializer cannot. For example, a constructor can validate its parameters against each other or against a database. An `Employee` class's constructor could take an employee ID as a parameter and check a database to verify that the employee really exists.

A constructor can also require that certain parameters be provided. For example, a `Person` constructor could require that the first name and last name parameters be provided. If you rely on initializers, the program could create a `Person` that has no first name or last name.

To make a constructor that takes parameters, simply add the parameters as you would for any other method. The following code shows a constructor for the `Person` class that uses its parameters to initialize the new `Person` object's properties:

```
' Initializing constructor.
Public Sub New(ByVal newFirstName As String,
 ByVal newLastName As String, ByVal newStreet As String,
 ByVal newCity As String, ByVal newState As String,
 ByVal newZip As String)

    ' Verify that FirstName and LastName are present.
    If newFirstName Is Nothing Then
        Throw New ArgumentException("FirstName is required")
    End If
    If newFirstName.Length = 0 Then
        Throw New ArgumentException("FirstName cannot be blank")
    End If
    If newLastName Is Nothing Then
        Throw New ArgumentException("LastName is required")
    End If
    If newLastName.Length = 0 Then
        Throw New ArgumentException("LastName cannot be blank")
    End If

    ' Initialize the properties.
    FirstName = newFirstName
    LastName = newLastName
    Street = newStreet
    City = newCity
    State = newState
    Zip = newZip
End Sub
```

INVOKING OTHER CONSTRUCTORS

You can give a class many different constructors as long as they have different parameter lists (so Visual Basic can tell them apart). For example, you might give the `Person` class a parameterless constructor; a second constructor that takes first name and last name as parameters; and a third constructor that takes first name and last name, street, city, state, and zip code as parameters.

Often when you give a class multiple constructors, some of them perform the same actions. In the `Person` example, the constructor that initializes first name, last name, street, city, state, and zip code probably does the same things that the second constructor does to initialize just first name and last name (plus more).

You can also find overlapping constructor functionality when one class inherits from another. For example, suppose the Person class has FirstName and LastName properties. The Employee class inherits from Person and adds some other properties such as EmployeeId and MailStop. The Person class's constructor initializes the FirstName and LastName properties, something that the Employee class's constructors should also do.

Having several methods perform the same tasks makes debugging and maintaining code harder. Fortunately, Visual Basic provides a way you can make one constructor invoke another.

To make a constructor use another constructor in the same class, simply invoke it as if it were any other subroutine. The only catch is that you need to call the constructor Me.New, not just New.

 Note that if constructor A invokes constructor B, then constructor A must do so before doing anything else.

For example, the following code shows three constructors for the Person class that invoke each other. The code that invokes other constructors is shown in bold.

```
' Parameterless constructor.
Public Sub New()
    ' General initialization if needed...
End Sub

' Initialize FirstName and LastName only.
Public Sub New(ByVal newFirstName As String, ByVal newLastName As String)
    ' Call the parameterless constructor.
    Me.New()

    ' Initialize the properties.
    FirstName = newFirstName
    LastName = newLastName
End Sub

' Initialize all properties.
Public Sub New(ByVal newFirstName As String, ByVal newLastName As String,
 ByVal newStreet As String, ByVal newCity As String,
 ByVal newState As String, ByVal newZip As String)
    ' Call the previous constructor to initialize FirstName and LastName.
    Me.New(newFirstName, newLastName)

    ' Initialize the other properties.
    Street = newStreet
    City = newCity
    State = newState
    Zip = newZip
End Sub
```

The first constructor is a parameterless constructor. In this example it doesn't do anything.

The second constructor takes first and last names as parameters. It invokes the parameterless constructor and then initializes the FirstName and LastName properties. This version doesn't verify that FirstName and LastName are present and nonblank because a program could use the parameterless constructor to get around that restriction anyway.

The third constructor takes name and address parameters. It invokes the previous constructor to initialize FirstName and LastName. (That constructor in turn invokes the parameterless constructor.) It then initializes the object's remaining properties.

You can use a similar syntax to invoke a parent class constructor by simply replacing Me.New with MyBase.New.

For example, the Employee class inherits from the Person class. The following code shows three of the class's constructors:

```
Public Sub New()
    ' Invoke the Person constructor.
    MyBase.New()
End Sub

Public Sub New(ByVal newFirstName As String, ByVal newLastName As String)
    ' Invoke the Person constructor.
    MyBase.New(newFirstName, newLastName)
End Sub

Public Sub New(ByVal newFirstName As String, ByVal newLastName As String,
 ByVal newStreet As String, ByVal newCity As String,
 ByVal newState As String, ByVal newZip As String,
 ByVal newEmployeeId As Integer, ByVal newMailStop As String)
    ' Invoke the Person constructor.
    MyBase.New(newFirstName, newLastName, newStreet,
        newCity, newState, newZip)

    ' Initialize the remaining properties.
    EmployeeId = newEmployeeId
    MailStop = newMailStop
End Sub
```

The first constructor is parameterless. It invokes its parent class's parameterless constructor by using MyBase.New().

The second constructor takes first name and last name parameters and invokes the Person class's constructor, which takes two strings as parameters.

The final constructor takes eight parameters, invokes the Person class's six-parameter constructor to initialize most of the object's properties, and then initializes the last two properties (which are not inherited from the Person class) itself.

> *Notice how the constructors invoke other constructors by using* Me.New *or* MyBase.New *followed by a parameter list. Visual Basic uses the parameter list to determine which constructor to invoke. That's why you cannot have more than one constructor with the same kinds of parameters. For example, if two constructors took a single* String *as a parameter, how would Visual Basic know which one to use?*

TRY IT

In this Try It, you enhance the Person, Employee, and Manager classes you built for the Try It in Lesson 25. In this Try It, you add constructors to make initializing objects easier.

> *You can download the code and resources for this Try It from the book's web page at* www.wrox.com *or* www.vb-helper.com/24hourvb.html. *You can find the files in the Lesson26 folder.*

Lesson Requirements

In this lesson:

➤ Copy the program you built for the Try It in Lesson 25 (or download the version that's available on the book's web site).

➤ Give the Person class a parameterless constructor. Make it print a message to the Output window indicating that a new Person is being created.

➤ Give the Person class a second constructor that initializes all of the class's properties. Make it invoke the parameterless constructor and display its own message.

➤ Make similar constructors for the Employee and Manager classes.

➤ Remove the buttons from the main form and make the program create Person, Employee, and Manager objects using each of the constructors.

➤ Run the program, close it, and examine the Output window messages to see if they make sense.

Hints

➤ Make the constructors invoke each other where possible to avoid duplicate work.

➤ When the main program uses parameterless constructors, use object initialization to set the objects' properties.

Step-by-Step

➤ Copy the program you built for the Try It in Lesson 25 (or download the version that's available on the book's web site).

1. This is relatively straightforward.

➤ Give the `Person` class a parameterless constructor. Make it print a message to the Output window indicating that a new `Person` is being created.

1. The `Person` class's parameterless constructor should look something like this:

```
' Constructors.
Public Sub New()
    Console.WriteLine("Person()")
End Sub
```

➤ Give the `Person` class a second constructor that initializes all of the class's properties. Make it invoke the parameterless constructor and display its own message.

1. This constructor should look something like this:

```
' Initialize all properties.
Public Sub New(ByVal newFirstName As String,
 ByVal newLastName As String, ByVal newStreet As String,
 ByVal newCity As String, ByVal newState As String,
 ByVal newZip As String)
    Me.New()

    ' Initialize the other properties.
    Street = newStreet
    City = newCity
    State = newState
    Zip = newZip
    Console.WriteLine("Person(parameters)")
End Sub
```

➤ Make similar constructors for the `Employee` and `Manager` classes.

1. The following code shows the `Employee` class's constructors:

```
' Constructors.
Public Sub New()
    MyBase.New()

    Console.WriteLine("Employee()")
End Sub

' Initialize all properties.
Public Sub New(ByVal newFirstName As String,
 ByVal newLastName As String,
 ByVal newStreet As String, ByVal newCity As String,
 ByVal newState As String, ByVal newZip As String,
```

```
        ByVal newEmployeeId As Integer, ByVal newMailStop As String)
            MyBase.New(newFirstName, newLastName, newStreet, newCity,
                newState, newZip)

            ' Initialize the other properties.
            EmployeeId = newEmployeeId
            MailStop = newMailStop
            Console.WriteLine("Employee(parameters)")
    End Sub
```

2. The following code shows the `Manager` class's constructors:

```
' Constructors.
Public Sub New()
    MyBase.New()

        Console.WriteLine("Manager()")
End Sub

' Initialize all properties.
Public Sub New(ByVal newFirstName As String,
 ByVal newLastName As String,
 ByVal newStreet As String, ByVal newCity As String,
 ByVal newState As String, ByVal newZip As String,
 ByVal newEmployeeId As Integer, ByVal newMailStop As String,
 ByVal newDepartmentName As String)
    MyBase.New(newFirstName, newLastName, newStreet, newCity,
        newState, newZip,
        newEmployeeId, newMailStop)

        ' Initialize the other properties.
        DepartmentName = newDepartmentName
        Console.WriteLine("Manager(parameters)")
End Sub
```

➤ Remove the buttons from the main form and make the main program create `Person`, `Employee`, and `Manager` objects using each of the constructors.

1. The following code creates objects in this way:

```
' Persons.
Console.WriteLine("Creating Paula")
Dim paula As New Person() With
{
    .FirstName = "Paula",
    .LastName = "Perch",
    .Street = "100 Ash Ave",
    .City = "Bugsville",
    .State = "CO",
    .Zip = "82010"
}

Console.WriteLine("Creating Pete")
Dim pete As New Person("Pete", "Pearson",
    "2871 Arc St", "Bugsville ", "CO", "82010")
```

```
' Employees.
Console.WriteLine("Creating Edna")
Dim edna As New Employee() With
{
    .FirstName = "Edna",
    .LastName = "Evers",
    .Street = "200 Beach Blvd",
    .City = "Bugsville",
    .State = "CO",
    .Zip = "82010",
    .EmployeeId = 1002,
    .MailStop = "B-2"
}

Console.WriteLine("Creating Edward")
Dim edward As New Employee("Edward", "Evers",
    "129 Bold Blvd", "Bugsville", "CO", "82010", 1002, "B-2")

' Managers.
Console.WriteLine("Creating Mindy")
Dim mindy As New Manager() With
{
    .DepartmentName = "Research",
    .EmployeeId = 1001,
    .MailStop = "MS-10",
    .FirstName = "Mindy",
    .LastName = "Marvel",
    .Street = "2981 East Westlake Blvd",
    .City = "Bugsville",
    .State = "CO",
    .Zip = "82010"
}

Console.WriteLine("Creating Mike")
Dim mike As New Manager("Mike", "Masco",
    "1298 Elm St", "Bugsville", "CO", "82010",
    1002, "MS-20", "Development")
```

➤ Run the program, close it, and examine the Output window messages to see if they make sense.

1. The following text shows the program's output. You can see which constructors were executed for each object.

```
Creating Paula
Person()
Creating Pete
Person()
Person(parameters)
Creating Edna
Person()
Employee()
```

```
Creating Edward
Person()
Person(parameters)
Employee(parameters)
Creating Mindy
Person()
Employee()
Manager()
Creating Mike
Person()
Person(parameters)
Employee(parameters)
Manager(parameters)
```

 Please select Lesson 26 on the DVD to view the video that accompanies this lesson.

EXERCISES

1. Copy the program you built in Lesson 23, Exercise 3 (or download Lesson 23's version from the book's web site). Change the main program and the ComplexNumber class so they use initializers to prepare ComplexNumber objects.

2. Copy the program you built for Exercise 1. Give the ComplexNumber class a constructor that initializes the new number's real and imaginary parts. Modify the program as needed to use this constructor.

3. Copy the program you built for Lesson 24's Try It (or download the TryIt24 program from the book's web site). Give the BankAccount class a constructor that guarantees that you cannot create an instance with an initial balance under $10. Change the main program so it uses this constructor.

4. Copy the program you built for Exercise 3. Now that the program sets the initial balance via a constructor and updates it via the Credit and Debit methods, it no longer needs to set the balance directly. To make the code safer, make Balance a read-only property.

 You can find solutions to this lesson's exercises in the Lesson26 folder inside the download available on the book's web site at www.wrox.com *or* www .vb-helper.com/24hourvb.html.

27

Fine-Tuning Classes

In Lesson 26 you learned how to build constructors, special methods that execute when an object is created. In this lesson you learn about other special methods you can give a class. In particular, you learn how to overload and override class methods.

OVERLOADING METHODS

Lesson 26 mentioned that you can give a class any number of constructors as long as they have different parameter lists. For example, it's common to give a class a parameterless constructor that takes no parameters, and one or more other constructors that take parameters.

Making multiple methods with the same name but different parameter lists is called *overloading*. Visual Basic uses the parameter list to determine which version to use when you invoke the method.

For example, suppose you're building a course assignment application and you have built `Student`, `Course`, and `Instructor` classes. You could give the `Student` class two versions of the `Enroll` method, one that takes as a parameter the name of the class in which the student should be enrolled and a second that takes a `Course` object as a parameter.

You could give the `Instructor` class similar versions of the `Teach` method to make the instructor teach a class by name or `Course` object.

Finally, you could give the `Course` class different `Report` methods that:

> ➤ Display a report in a dialog if there are no parameters

> ➤ Append a report to the end of a file if the method receives a `FileStream` as a parameter

> ➤ Save the report into a new file if the method receives a `String` (the filename) as a parameter

Making overloaded methods is so easy that there's little else to say. Simply write each version as you normally would write a method. Just remember to give each version of the method a different parameter list.

OVERRIDING METHODS

When one class inherits from another you can add new properties, methods, and events to the new class to give it new features that were not provided by the parent class.

Once in a while it's also useful to replace a method provided by the parent class with a new version. This is called *overriding* the parent's method.

Before you can override a method, you should mark the method in the parent class with the `Overridable` keyword so it allows itself to be overridden. Next, add the keyword `Overrides` to the derived class's version of the method to indicate that it overrides the parent class's version.

> *Overridable methods are also sometimes called* virtual methods, *particularly in other programming languages such as C++ and C#.*

For example, suppose the `Person` class defines the usual assortment of properties: `FirstName`, `LastName`, `Street`, `City`, and so on. Suppose it also provides the following `GetAddress` function that returns the `Person`'s name and address formatted for printing on an envelope:

```
' Return the Person's address.
Public Overridable Function GetAddress() As String
    Return FirstName & " " & LastName & vbCrLf & _
        Street & vbCrLf & City & "    " & State & "    " & Zip
End Function
```

Now suppose you derive the `Employee` class from `Person`. An `Employee`'s address looks just like a `Person`'s except it also includes `MailStop`.

The following code shows how the `Employee` class can override the `GetAddress` function to return an `Employee`-style address:

```
' Return the Employee's address.
Public Overrides Function GetAddress() As String
    Return MyBase.GetAddress() & vbCrLf & MailStop
End Function
```

Notice how the function calls the base class's version of `GetAddress` to reuse that version of the function and avoid duplicated work.

IntelliSense can help you build overridden methods. For example, when you type "Public Overrides" and a space in the `Employee` *class, IntelliSense lists the overridable methods that you might be trying to override. If you select one, IntelliSense fills in a default implementation for the new method. The following code shows the code IntelliSense generated for the* `GetAddress` *function:*

```
Public Overrides Function GetAddress() As String
    Return MyBase.GetAddress()
End Function
```

The most miraculous thing about overriding a method is that the object uses the method even if you invoke it from the base class. For example, suppose you have a `Person` variable pointing to an `Employee` object. Remember that an `Employee` is a kind of `Person`, so a `Person` variable can refer to an `Employee`, as in the following code:

```
Dim bob As New Employee() With
{
    .FirstName = "Bob", .LastName = "Boastful",
    .Street = "22 Breach Blvd", .City = "Bugsville",
    .State = "CO", .Zip = "82789", .MailStop = "B-52"
}
Dim bobAsPerson As Person = bob
```

Now if the code calls `bobAsPerson.GetAddress()`, the result is the `Employee` version of `GetAddress`. The address includes Bob's `MailStop` even though a `Person` object doesn't have a `MailStop`.

You can think of the `Overridable` *keyword as making a slot in the base class for the method. When you override the method, the derived class fills this slot with a new version of the method. Now, even if you call the method from the base class, it uses whatever is in the slot.*

Overriding a class's `ToString` function is particularly useful. All classes inherit a `ToString` method from `System.Object`, the ultimate ancestor of all other classes, but the default implementation of `ToString` isn't always useful. By default, for classes that you defined such as `Person` and `Employee`, `ToString` returns the class's name.

For example, in the ListPeople example program, which is shown in Figure 27-1 and available as part of this lesson's code download, the `Employee` class's `ToString` function returns `ListPeople.Employee`. Though this correctly

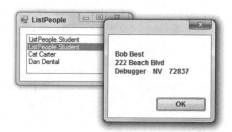

FIGURE 27-1

reports the object's class, it might be nice if it returned something that contained information about the object's properties. In this example, it would be better if it returned the Employee object's first and last names.

The following code shows how you can override the ToString function to return an Employee's first and last name:

```
' Return first and last name.
Public Overrides Function ToString() As String
    Return FirstName & " " & LastName
End Function
```

This makes more sense. Now your program can use an Employee object's ToString method to learn about the object.

Overriding ToString also has a nice side benefit for Windows Forms development. Certain controls and parts of Visual Studio use an object's ToString method to decide what to display. For example, the ListBox and ComboBox controls display lists of items. If those items are not simple strings, the controls use the items' ToString methods to generate output.

If the list is full of Employee objects and you've overridden the Employee class's ToString method, then a ListBox or ComboBox can display the employees' names.

The ListPeople example program demonstrates method overriding. When it starts, the program uses the following code to fill its ListBox with two Student objects and two Employee objects. Both of these classes inherit from Person.

```
' Make some people.
Private Sub Form1_Load() Handles MyBase.Load
    lstPeople.Items.Add(New Student("Ann", "Archer",
        "101 Ash Ave", "Debugger", "NV", "72837"))
    lstPeople.Items.Add(New Student("Bob", "Best",
        "222 Beach Blvd", "Debugger", "NV", "72837"))
    lstPeople.Items.Add(New Employee("Cat", "Carter",
        "300 Cedar Ct", "Debugger", "NV", "72837", "MS-1"))
    lstPeople.Items.Add(New Employee("Dan", "Dental",
        "404 Date Dr", "Debugger", "NV", "72837", "MS-2"))
End Sub
```

The Employee class overrides its ToString method, so you can see the Employees' names in Figure 27-1 instead of their class names. The Student class does not override its ToString method, so Figure 27-1 shows class names for the Student objects.

If you double-click a person in the list, the program executes the following code:

```
' Display the selected Person's address.
Private Sub lstPeople_DoubleClick() Handles lstPeople.DoubleClick
    Dim personClicked As Person = DirectCast(lstPeople.SelectedItem, Person)
    MessageBox.Show(personClicked.GetAddress())
End Sub
```

This code converts the ListBox's selected item into a Person object. The item is actually either a Student or an Employee but both of those inherit from Person (they are kinds of Person), so the program can treat them as Persons.

The program calls the object's GetAddress function and displays the result. If the object is actually a Student, the result is a basic name and address. If the object is actually an Employee, the result is a name and address plus mailstop.

In addition to ListBoxes and ComboBoxes, some parts of Visual Studio use an object's ToString method, too. For example, if you stop an executing program and hover the mouse over an object in the debugger, a tooltip appears that displays the results of the object's ToString function.

TRY IT

In this Try It, you build a simple drawing application. You build a Shape class to represent a drawn shape and then derive the ShapeRectangle and ShapeEllipse classes from that one.

You give the Shape class an overridable Draw method that takes as a parameter a Graphics object and draws the shape on the object. The Shape class's version of Draw simply draws a rectangle with a big X in it.

You make the ShapeRectangle and ShapeEllipse classes override Draw to produce their own shapes.

Finally, you add overloaded versions of Draw that take pen and brush objects as parameters to use when drawing.

 You can download the code and resources for this Try It from the book's web page at www.wrox.com or www.vb-helper.com/24hourvb.html. You can find the programs in the Lesson27 folder.

Lesson Requirements

In this lesson:

➤ Start a new program and create the Shape class.

  ➤ Give the class a property named Bounds of type Rectangle. (Rectangle is a structure with properties X, Y, Width, and Height.)

  ➤ Make a constructor that takes x, y, width, and height parameters and uses them to initialize the Bounds property.

  ➤ Make an overridable Draw method that takes three parameters of type Graphics, Pen, and Brush. Make this method draw a box with an X in it on the Graphics object using the Pen and Brush.

  ➤ Make a second Draw method that takes only a Graphics object as a parameter. Make it invoke the other Draw method, passing it the pen and brush Pens.Red and Brushes.Transparent.

➤ Derive the `ShapeRectangle` class from the `Shape` class.

   ➤ Make a constructor that takes `x`, `y`, `width`, and `height` parameters and invokes the base class's constructor.

   ➤ Override the `Shape` class's version of the `Draw` method that takes four parameters so it draws a rectangle.

   ➤ Override the second `Draw` method so it calls the first, passing it the pen and brush `Pens.Black` and `Brushes.Transparent`.

➤ Repeat the previous steps for the `ShapeEllipse` class.

➤ In the main form, create a `List(Of Shape)`.

➤ In the form's `Load` event handler, create some `ShapeRectangles` and `ShapeEllipses` and add them to the list.

➤ Give the form a `CheckBox` labeled "Colored." In its `CheckedChanged` event handler, invalidate the form to force a redraw.

➤ In the form's `Paint` event handler, redraw the form by looping through the `Shapes` in the list. If the `CheckBox` is checked, invoke the `Shape` objects' `Draw` methods, passing them the pen and brush `Pens.Blue` and `Brushes.LightBlue`. If the `CheckBox` is not checked, invoke the `Draw` methods with no parameters.

Hints

If `gr` is the `Graphics` object, then you can use these methods to draw:

➤ `gr.Clear(Me.BackColor)` — Clears the object with the form's background color

➤ `gr.FillRectangle(`*brush*`, `*rect*`)` — Fills a rectangle defined by *rect* with *brush*

➤ `gr.DrawRectangle(`*pen*`, `*rect*`)` — Outlines a rectangle defined by *rect* with *pen*

➤ `gr.FillEllipse(`*brush*`, `*rect*`)` — Fills an ellipse defined by *rect* with *brush*

➤ `gr.DrawEllipse(`*pen*`, `*rect*`)` — Outlines an ellipse defined by *rect* with *pen*

In the `Paint` event handler, draw on the `Graphics` object provided by the event handler's `e.Graphics` parameter.

Step-by-Step

➤ Start a new program and create the `Shape` class.

   ➤ Give the class a property named `Bounds` of type `Rectangle`. (`Rectangle` is a structure with properties `X`, `Y`, `Width`, and `Height`.)

   1. Use code similar to the following:

   ```
   Public Property Bounds As Rectangle
   ```

   ➤ Make a constructor that takes `x`, `y`, `width`, and `height` parameters and uses them to initialize the `Bounds` property.

1. Use code similar to the following:

```
Public Sub New(ByVal x As Integer, ByVal y As Integer,
 ByVal width As Integer, ByVal height As Integer)
    Bounds = New Rectangle(x, y, width, height)
End Sub
```

➤ Make an overridable `Draw` method that takes three parameters of type `Graphics`, `Pen`, and `Brush`. Make this method draw a box with an X in it on the `Graphics` object using the `Pen` and `Brush`.

1. Use code similar to the following:

```
' Draw a box with an X in it using a pen and brush.
Public Overridable Sub Draw(ByVal gr As Graphics,
 ByVal thePen As Pen, ByVal theBrush As Brush)
    gr.FillRectangle(theBrush, Bounds)
    gr.DrawRectangle(thePen, Bounds)
    gr.DrawLine(thePen, Bounds.Left, Bounds.Top,
        Bounds.Right, Bounds.Bottom)
    gr.DrawLine(thePen, Bounds.Right, Bounds.Top,
        Bounds.Left, Bounds.Bottom)
End Sub
```

➤ Make a second `Draw` method that takes only a `Graphics` object as a parameter. Make it invoke the other `Draw` method, passing it the pen and brush `Pens.Red` and `Brushes.Transparent`.

1. Use code similar to the following:

```
' Draw a box with an X in it.
Public Overridable Sub Draw(ByVal gr As Graphics)
    Draw(gr, Pens.Red, Brushes.Transparent)
End Sub
```

➤ Derive the `ShapeRectangle` class from the `Shape` class.

➤ Make a constructor that takes x, y, `width`, and `height` parameters and invokes the base class's constructor.

1. Use code similar to the following:

```
Public Sub New(ByVal x As Integer, ByVal y As Integer,
 ByVal width As Integer, ByVal height As Integer)
    MyBase.New(x, y, width, height)
End Sub
```

➤ Override the `Shape` class's version of the `Draw` method that takes four parameters so it draws a rectangle.

1. Use code similar to the following:

```
Public Overrides Sub Draw(ByVal gr As Graphics,
 ByVal thePen As Pen, ByVal theBrush As Brush)
    gr.FillRectangle(theBrush, Bounds)
    gr.DrawRectangle(thePen, Bounds)
End Sub
```

➤ Override the second `Draw` method so it calls the first, passing it the pen and brush `Pens.Black` and `Brushes.Transparent`.

1. Use code similar to the following:

```
Public Overrides Sub Draw(ByVal gr As Graphics)
    Draw(gr, Pens.Black, Brushes.Transparent)
End Sub
```

➤ Repeat the previous steps for the `ShapeEllipse` class.

1. The following code shows the `ShapeEllipse` class's code:

```
Public Class ShapeEllipse
    Inherits Shape

    Public Sub New(ByVal x As Integer, ByVal y As Integer,
     ByVal width As Integer, ByVal height As Integer)
        MyBase.new(x, y, width, height)
    End Sub

    Public Overrides Sub Draw(ByVal gr As Graphics,
     ByVal thePen As Pen, ByVal theBrush As Brush)
        gr.FillEllipse(theBrush, Bounds)
        gr.DrawEllipse(thePen, Bounds)
    End Sub

    Public Overrides Sub Draw(ByVal gr As Graphics)
        Draw(gr, Pens.Black, Brushes.Transparent)
    End Sub
End Class
```

➤ In the main form, create a `List(Of Shape)`.

1. Use code similar to the following:

```
' Our list of shapes to draw.
Private Shapes As New List(Of Shape)()
```

➤ In the form's `Load` event handler, create some `ShapeRectangles` and `ShapeEllipses` and add them to the list.

1. You can use code similar to the following, or you can create any `ShapeEllipse` and `ShapeRectangle` objects that you like:

```
' Make some shapes.
Private Sub Form1_Load() Handles MyBase.Load
    Shapes.Add(New ShapeEllipse(50, 50, 200, 200))
    Shapes.Add(New ShapeEllipse(100, 80, 40, 60))
    Shapes.Add(New ShapeEllipse(100, 80, 40, 60))
    Shapes.Add(New ShapeEllipse(120, 100, 20, 30))
    Shapes.Add(New ShapeEllipse(160, 80, 40, 60))
    Shapes.Add(New ShapeEllipse(180, 100, 20, 30))
    Shapes.Add(New ShapeEllipse(135, 130, 30, 50))
    Shapes.Add(New ShapeRectangle(120, 190, 60, 5))
    Shapes.Add(New ShapeRectangle(75, 25, 150, 50))
```

```
        Shapes.Add(New ShapeRectangle(50, 75, 200, 10))
    End Sub
```

➤ Give the form a CheckBox. In its CheckedChanged event handler, invalidate the form to force a redraw.

1. The following code shows this event handler:

```
' Force a redraw.
Private Sub chkColored_CheckedChanged() _
  Handles chkColored.CheckedChanged
    Me.Invalidate()
End Sub
```

➤ In the form's Paint event handler, redraw the form by looping through the Shapes in the list. If the CheckBox is checked, invoke the Shape objects' Draw methods, passing them the pen and brush Pens.Blue and Brushes.LightBlue. If the CheckBox is not checked, invoke the Draw methods with no parameters.

1. Use code similar to the following:

```
' Redraw the objects.
Private Sub Form1_Paint(ByVal sender As Object,
  ByVal e As System.Windows.Forms.PaintEventArgs) Handles Me.Paint
    e.Graphics.Clear(Me.BackColor)

    ' Loop through all of the shapes.
    For Each theShape As Shape In Shapes
        If (chkColored.Checked) Then
            ' Draw with a pen and brush.
            theShape.Draw(e.Graphics, Pens.Blue, Brushes.LightBlue)
        Else
            ' Draw with no pen or brush.
            theShape.Draw(e.Graphics)
        End If
    Next theShape
End Sub
```

Figure 27-2 shows the result for the objects you created.

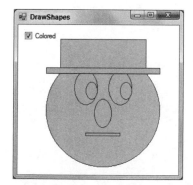

FIGURE 27-2

Please select Lesson 27 on the DVD to view the video that accompanies this lesson.

EXERCISES

1. Copy the complex number program you built in Lesson 26, Exercise 2 (or download Lesson 26's version from the book's web site). Override the class's `ToString` method so it returns the number in a form similar to "2 + 3i." Overload the `ComplexNumber` class's constructor and `AddTo`, `MultiplyBy`, and `SubtractFrom` functions so you can pass them a single `Double` parameter representing a real number with no imaginary part. Modify the form so you can test the new methods.

2. Copy the bank account program you built in Lesson 26, Exercise 4 (or download Lesson 26's version from the book's web site). Derive a new `OverdraftAccount` class from the `Account` class. Give it a constructor that simply invokes the base class's constructor. Override the `Debit` method to allow the account to have a negative balance and charge a $50 fee if any debit leaves the account with a negative balance. Change the main program so the `Account` variable is still declared to be of type `Account` but initialize it as an `OverdraftAccount`. Hints: Don't forget to make the `BankAccount` class's version of `Debit` overridable; and to allow `OverdraftAccount` code to access the `_Balance` backing field, change that field from `Private` to `Protected`.

3. Copy Lesson 24's Turtle program. The `Turtle` class has a `Move` method that moves the turtle a specified distance in the object's current direction. Overload this method by making a second version that takes as parameters the x and y coordinates where the turtle should move. Be sure to raise the `OutOfBounds` event if the point is not on the canvas. Hint: Can you reuse code somehow between the two `Move` methods?

You can find solutions to this lesson's exercises in the Lesson27 folder inside the download available on the book's web site at `www.wrox.com` *or* `www.vb-helper.com/24hourvb.html`.

28

Overloading Operators

In Lesson 27 you learned how to overload a class's methods. Visual Basic also lets you overload operators such as + and * to give them new meanings when working with the structures and classes that you create. For example, you could overload the + operator so the program would know how to add a `Student` object and a `Course` object. Sometimes that enables you to use a more natural syntax when you're working with objects.

In this lesson, you learn how to overload operators so you can use them to manipulate objects.

> *Before you jump into operator overloading, be warned that just because you can overload an operator doesn't mean you should. You should only overload operators in intuitive ways.*
>
> *For example, it makes sense to overload the + operator so you can add two* `ComplexNumber` *objects. It might also make sense to overload + so you can add an item to a purchase order.*
>
> *It probably doesn't make sense to define + between two* `Employee` *objects to return a list of projects that include both employees. You could do that but you probably shouldn't because it would be confusing.*

OVERLOADABLE OPERATORS

In Visual Basic, you can overload unary, binary, and logical operators. Table 28-1 summarizes the operators that you can overload.

TABLE 28-1

TYPE	OPERATORS
Unary	+, -, Not, IsTrue, IsFalse, CType
Binary	+, -, *, /, \, ^, &, Like, Mod, And, Or, Xor, <<, >>
Comparison	=, <>, <, >, <=, >=

The comparison operators come in pairs. For example, if you overload the < operator, then you must also overload the > operator.

The compound assignment operators (+=, -=, *=, /=, \=, &=, ^=, <<=, and >>=) are automatically overloaded when you overload the corresponding binary operator. For example, if you overload *, then Visual Basic automatically overloads *=.

The syntax for overloading operators is easiest to understand by looking at examples. The following sections explain how to overload the different types of operators.

UNARY OPERATORS

The following code shows how you can overload the unary - operator for the ComplexNumber class:

```
Public Shared Operator -(ByVal c1 As ComplexNumber) As ComplexNumber
    Return New ComplexNumber(-c1.Real, -c1.Imaginary)
End Operator
```

The method begins with Public accessibility. The Shared keyword means this operator is shared by all instances of the ComplexNumber class, so you can apply it without using a specific instance of the class. The Operator keyword means the code overloads an operator.

Next comes the operator being overloaded. The parameter list specifies the objects that are involved in the calculation. This example overloads the unary - operator, so it involves only one parameter. That parameter is of type ComplexNumber, so that is the class for which this code defines the operator.

The declaration finishes by declaring the operator's return type.

Note that the overloaded operator must be defined inside the parameter's structure or class. In this case, because the parameter is a ComplexNumber, this code must be in the ComplexNumber class.

The code inside this method simply negates the ComplexNumber's real and imaginary parts and returns a new ComplexNumber.

The following code shows how a program might use this operator:

```
Dim a As New ComplexNumber(1, 2)      '  1 + 2i
Dim b As ComplexNumber = -a           ' -1 - 2i
```

BINARY OPERATORS

Overloading binary operators is similar to overloading unary operators except the operator takes a second parameter. The first parameter is still the object to which the operator is being applied.

For example, the following code overloads the binary – operator to subtract two ComplexNumbers:

```
Public Shared Operator -(ByVal c1 As ComplexNumber,
 ByVal c2 As ComplexNumber) As ComplexNumber
    Return New ComplexNumber(
        c1.Real - c2.Real,
        c1.Imaginary - c2.Imaginary)
End Operator
```

The first parameter indicates the object on the left of the – sign and the second parameter indicates the object on the right.

Note that the overload must be declared inside a class or structure used by one of the parameters. In this case, because both parameters are ComplexNumbers, this code must be in the ComplexNumber class.

While this example subtracts two ComplexNumbers, the parameters do not need to have the same data types. The following code defines the binary – operator for subtracting a Double from a ComplexNumber:

```
Public Shared Operator -(ByVal c1 As ComplexNumber,
 ByVal re As Double) As ComplexNumber
    Return c1 - New ComplexNumber(re)
End Operator
```

Note that this is not the same as subtracting a ComplexNumber from a Double. If you want to handle that situation as well, you need the following separate overload:

```
Public Shared Operator -(ByVal re As Double,
 ByVal c1 As ComplexNumber) As ComplexNumber
    Return New ComplexNumber(re) - c1
End Operator
```

With these overloads, a program could execute the following code:

```
Dim a As New ComplexNumber(2, 3)
Dim b As New ComplexNumber(4, 5)

Dim f As ComplexNumber = a - b          ' ComplexNumber - ComplexNumber
Dim g As ComplexNumber = a - 10         ' ComplexNumber - Double
Dim h As ComplexNumber = 10 - a         ' Double - ComplexNumber
```

 The shift operators << and >> are a little different from the other binary operators because the second parameter must always be an integer.

COMPARISON OPERATORS

The comparison operators are simply binary operators that return a Boolean result. The only oddity to these is that they come in pairs. For example, if you define =, then you must also define <>. The pairs are = and <>, < and >, and <= and >=.

The following code shows how you could overload the < and > operators for the `ComplexNumber` class by comparing the numbers' magnitudes:

```
' Return the number's magnitude.
Public ReadOnly Property Magnitude() As Double
    Get
        Return (Math.Sqrt(Real * Real + Imaginary * Imaginary))
    End Get
End Property

Public Shared Operator <(ByVal c1 As ComplexNumber,
 ByVal c2 As ComplexNumber) As Boolean
    Return (c1.Magnitude < c2.Magnitude)
End Operator

Public Shared Operator >(ByVal c1 As ComplexNumber,
 ByVal c2 As ComplexNumber) As Boolean
    Return (c1.Magnitude > c2.Magnitude)
End Operator
```

CTYPE

The `CType` operator converts a value from one data type to another. You may recall from Lesson 11 that data type conversions can be either *widening* or *narrowing*.

A widening conversion converts a value into a new data type that is guaranteed to be able to hold the value without losing any precision. For example, a `Long` can hold any `Integer` value, so converting from an `Integer` to a `Long` is a widening conversion.

Conversely, not all `Long` values can fit into an `Integer`, so converting from a `Long` to an `Integer` is a narrowing conversion.

To help Visual Basic understand which kind of conversion you are defining, you must provide one of the keywords `Widening` or `Narrowing` when you overload the `CType` operator.

For example, the following code overloads `CType` to convert between the `Double` and `ComplexNumber` data types:

```
' Convert between Double and ComplexNumber.
Public Shared Widening Operator CType(ByVal re As Double) As ComplexNumber
    Return New ComplexNumber(re, 0)
End Operator

Public Shared Narrowing Operator CType(ByVal c1 As ComplexNumber) As Double
    Return c1.Magnitude
End Operator
```

The first overload converts from Double to ComplexNumber and the second converts from ComplexNumber to Double.

Visual Basic will use CType to convert from one type to another if it can to perform other operations that are not directly defined. For example, suppose you define the + operator for two ComplexNumbers and you also define the CType operator to convert from Double to ComplexNumber. In that case, the following code will work even though you haven't defined + for Doubles and ComplexNumbers:

```
Dim a As New ComplexNumber(1, 2)
Dim b As Double = 3
Dim c As ComplexNumber = a + b
```

When it reaches the third line, the program doesn't know how to add the ComplexNumber a and the Double b. However, it does know how to use CType to make a widening conversion to promote b to a ComplexNumber. It does so and adds the ComplexNumbers.

This very convenient feature of CType enables you to skip defining a huge number of operators.

 TRY IT

In this Try It, you extend the ComplexNumber class you built in Lesson 27, Exercise 1. That version of the class included methods such as AddTo and SubtractFrom to perform simple operations. Now you'll replace those cumbersome methods with overloaded +, -, *, and unary - operators.

 You can download the code and resources for this Try It from the book's web page at www.wrox.com *or* www.vb-helper.com/24hourvb.html. *You can find them in the Lesson28 folder of the download.*

Lesson Requirements

In this lesson:

➤ Copy the ComplexNumber program you built for Lesson 27, Exercise 1 (or download Lesson 27's version from the book's web site). Remove the ComplexNumber class's AddTo, MultiplyBy, and SubtractFrom methods.

➤ Give the class new overloaded operators to handle these cases:

  ➤ -ComplexNumber

  ➤ ComplexNumber + ComplexNumber

  ➤ ComplexNumber * ComplexNumber

  ➤ ComplexNumber - ComplexNumber

  ➤ CType between Double and ComplexNumber

➤ Revise the main form's code to use the new operators.

Hints

➤ You can use operators to define other operators. For example, if you define the unary – operator, then the following two operations have the same result:

```
ComplexNumber - ComplexNumber
ComplexNumber + -ComplexNumber
```

Step-by-Step

➤ Copy the ComplexNumber program you built for Lesson 27, Exercise 1 (or download Lesson 27's version from the book's web site). Remove the ComplexNumber class's AddTo, MultiplyBy, and SubtractFrom methods.

1. This is reasonably straightforward.

➤ Give the class new overloaded operators to handle these cases:

   ➤ -ComplexNumber

   ➤ ComplexNumber + ComplexNumber

   ➤ ComplexNumber * ComplexNumber

   ➤ ComplexNumber - ComplexNumber

   ➤ CType between Double and ComplexNumber

1. You can use code similar to the following:

```
' Unary -.
Public Shared Operator -(ByVal c1 As ComplexNumber) As ComplexNumber
    Return New ComplexNumber(-c1.Real, -c1.Imaginary)
End Operator

' Binary +.
Public Shared Operator +(ByVal c1 As ComplexNumber,
 ByVal c2 As ComplexNumber) As ComplexNumber
    Return New ComplexNumber(
        c1.Real + c2.Real,
        c1.Imaginary + c2.Imaginary)
End Operator

' Binary *.
Public Shared Operator *(ByVal c1 As ComplexNumber,
 ByVal c2 As ComplexNumber) As ComplexNumber
    Return New ComplexNumber(
        c1.Real * c2.Real - c1.Imaginary * c2.Imaginary,
        c1.Real * c2.Imaginary + c1.Imaginary * c2.Real)
End Operator

' Binary -.
Public Shared Operator -(ByVal c1 As ComplexNumber,
 ByVal c2 As ComplexNumber) As ComplexNumber
    Return New ComplexNumber(
```

```
                        c1.Real - c2.Real,
                        c1.Imaginary - c2.Imaginary)
            End Operator

            ' Convert between Double and ComplexNumber.
            Public Shared Widening Operator CType(ByVal re As Double) _
             As ComplexNumber
                    Return New ComplexNumber(re, 0)
            End Operator

            Public Shared Narrowing Operator CType(ByVal c1 As ComplexNumber) _
             As Double
                    Return c1.Magnitude
            End Operator

            ' Return the number's magnitude.
            Public ReadOnly Property Magnitude() As Double
                Get
                        Return (Math.Sqrt(Real * Real + Imaginary * Imaginary))
                End Get
            End Property
```

➤ Revise the main form's code to use the new operators.

1. You can use code similar to the following:

```
            ' Perform the calculations.
            Private Sub btnCalculate_Click() Handles btnCalculate.Click
                Dim a As New ComplexNumber(
                    Double.Parse(txtRealA.Text),
                    Double.Parse(txtImaginaryA.Text))
                Dim b As New ComplexNumber(
                    Double.Parse(txtRealB.Text),
                    Double.Parse(txtImaginaryB.Text))

                Dim aPlusB As ComplexNumber = a + b
                txtAplusB.Text = aPlusB.ToString

                Dim aMinusB As ComplexNumber = a - b
                txtAminusB.Text = aMinusB.ToString

                Dim aTimesB As ComplexNumber = a * b
                txtAtimesB.Text = aTimesB.ToString

                Dim minusA As ComplexNumber = -a
                txtMinusA.Text = minusA.ToString
            End Sub

            ' Perform the calculations with a real number.
            Private Sub btnCalculateRealOnly_Click() _
             Handles btnCalculateRealOnly.Click
                Dim a As Double = Double.Parse(txtRealOnly.Text)
                Dim b As New ComplexNumber(
                    Double.Parse(txtRealB.Text),
                    Double.Parse(txtImaginaryB.Text))
```

```
        Dim aPlusB As ComplexNumber = b + a
        txtAplusB.Text = aPlusB.ToString

        Dim aMinusB As ComplexNumber = a - b
        txtAminusB.Text = aMinusB.ToString

        Dim aTimesB As ComplexNumber = a * b
        txtAtimesB.Text = aTimesB.ToString

        Dim minusA As Double = -a
        txtMinusA.Text = minusA.ToString
    End Sub
```

 Please select Lesson 28 on the DVD to view the video that accompanies this lesson.

EXERCISES

1. Copy the complex number program you built in this lesson's Try It and overload the `ComplexNumber` class's / operator to perform division using this equation:

$$\left(\frac{a+bi}{c+di}\right) = \left(\frac{ac+bd}{c^2+d^2}\right) + \left(\frac{bc-ad}{c^2+d^2}\right)i$$

Change the main program to calculate A / B and display the results. Verify these calculations:

$$(10+11i) / (3+2i) = 4 + 1i$$

$$(15+24i) / 3 = 5 + 8i$$

$$4 / (1+1i) = 2 - 2i$$

 You can find solutions to this lesson's exercises in the Lesson28 folder inside the download available on the book's web site at www.wrox.com *or* www.vb-helper.com/24hourvb.html.

29

Using Interfaces

In .NET programming, an *interface* is like a contract. It defines the public properties, methods, and events that a class must provide to satisfy the contract. It doesn't indicate how the class must provide these features, however. That's left up to the class's code. It only defines an interface that the class must show to the rest of the world.

In this lesson, you learn how to implement interfaces that are predefined by .NET namcspaces. You also learn how to define your own interfaces to make your code safer and more efficient.

INTERFACE ADVANTAGES

The following sections discuss two of the most important advantages provided by interfaces: multiple inheritance and code generalization.

Multiple Inheritance

Suppose you define a `Vehicle` class with properties such as `NumberOfPassengers`, `MilesPerGallon`, and `NumberOfCupHolders`. From this class you can derive other classes such as `Car`, `PickupTruck`, and `Bicycle`.

Suppose you also define a `Domicile` class that has properties such as `SquareFeet`, `NumberOfBedrooms`, and `NumberOfBathrooms`. From this class you can derive `Apartment`, `Condo`, and `VacationHome`.

Next you might like to derive the `MotorHome` class from both `Vehicle` and `Domicile` so it has the properties and methods of both parent classes. Unfortunately, you can't do that in Visual Basic. In Visual Basic a class can inherit from only a single parent class.

Though a class can have only one parent, it can implement any number of interfaces. For example, if you turn the `Domicile` class into the `IDomicile` interface, the `MotorHome` class can inherit from `Vehicle` and implement `IDomicile`. The interface doesn't provide the code needed to implement such `IDomicile` features as the `HasAnnoyingNeighbor` property, but at least it defines that property so code that uses a `MotorHome` object knows the property is available.

 To make recognizing interface names easy, you should begin them with `I` as in `IDomicile`, `IComparable`, *and* `IWhatever`.

Defining the property but not implementing it might not seem like a big deal, but it enables your code to treat all `IDomicile` objects in a uniform way. Instead of writing separate functions to work with `Duplex`, `RusticCabin`, and `HouseBoat` objects, you can write a single function that manipulates objects that implement `IDomicile`.

That brings us to the second big advantage provided by interfaces: code generalization.

Code Generalization

Interfaces can make your code more general while still providing type checking. They enable you to treat objects that have common features as if they were of the interface type, rather than their true individual types.

For example, suppose you write the following method that displays an array of strings in a `ListBox`:

```
Private Sub DisplayValues(ByVal items() As String)
    lstItems.Items.Clear()
    For Each item As String In items
        lstItems.Items.Add(item)
    Next item
End Sub
```

This function works reasonably well, but suppose you later decide that you need to display the items in a `List(Of String)` instead of an array. You could write a new version of the function that was nearly identical to this one but that works with a list instead of an array, as shown in the following code:

```
Private Sub DisplayValues(ByVal items As List(Of String))
    lstItems.Items.Clear()
    For Each item As String In items
        lstItems.Items.Add(item)
    Next item
End Sub
```

If you compare these two functions you'll see that they are practically identical, so if you use them you must write, debug, and maintain two pieces of code that do almost exactly the same thing.

This is where interfaces can help.

Look again at the two functions. They differ only in their parameter definitions; the rest of their code is the same. The functions don't care whether the parameters are arrays or lists. All they really care about is that a `For Each` loop can be used to iterate through them.

The predefined `IList(Of ...)` interface requires that a class provide various list-like features such as `Clear`, `Add`, and `RemoveAt` methods. It also requires support for `For Each`. This is a generic interface, so you must provide a type parameter for it to indicate the type of items over which the interface can loop.

Both `String()` and `List(Of String)` implement `IList(Of String)`, so you can combine and generalize the functions by making their list parameter have the type `IList(Of String)` instead of `String()` or `List(Of String)`.

The following code shows the new version of the method. This version can display the items in a `String()`, `List(Of String)`, or any other object that implements `IList(Of String)`:

```
Private Sub DisplayValues(ByVal items As IList(Of String))
    lstItems.Items.Clear()
    For Each item As String In items
        lstItems.Items.Add(item)
    Next item
End Sub
```

IMPLEMENTING INTERFACES

To make a class that implements an interface, add an `Implements` statement after the `Class` statement and any `Inherits` statements. For example, the following code shows the declaration for a `Manager` class that inherits from `Person` and implements `IComparable`:

```
Public Class Manager
    Inherits Person
    Implements IComparable

    ...
End Class
```

The only other thing you need to do is implement the properties, methods, and events defined by the interface. The `IComparable` interface defines a `CompareTo` function that takes an object as a parameter and returns an integer that is less than, equal to, or greater than zero to indicate whether the object should be considered less than, equal to, or greater than the parameter.

For example, the following code shows a `Person` class that defines `FirstName` and `LastName` properties. It implements `IComparable(Of Person)` to order `Person` objects according to their last names first.

```
Public Class Person
    Implements IComparable(Of Person)

    Public Property FirstName As String
    Public Property LastName As String
```

```
' Compare this Person to another Person.
Public Function CompareTo(
 ByVal other As Person) As Integer Implements System.
 IComparable(Of Person).CompareTo
    ' If our last name comes first, we come first.
    If (LastName.CompareTo(other.LastName) < 0) Then Return -1

    ' If our last name comes second, we come second.
    If (LastName.CompareTo(other.LastName) > 0) Then Return 1

    ' If our last names are the same, compare first names.
    Return FirstName.CompareTo(other.FirstName)
End Function
End Class
```

If the current object's LastName alphabetically precedes the other object's LastName, the function returns -1. If the current object's LastName alphabetically follows the other object's LastName, the function returns 1.

If the two objects' LastNames are the same, the function compares their FirstNames and returns the result.

Visual Studio is very helpful in writing methods to implement interfaces. When you type the Implements statement and press [Enter], Visual Studio generates empty properties, methods, and events to implement the interface. All you need to do is fill in their code. For example, if you type Implements IComparable(Of Person) and press [Enter], Visual Studio generates the following code (I added the line break to make the code fit in the book):

```
Public Function CompareTo(ByVal other As Person) As Integer _
 Implements System.IComparable(Of Person).CompareTo

End Function
```

Now you just need to fill in the code.

There are several ways you can learn more about what an interface is for and what it does. First, you can search the online help. Second, you can right-click on the interface's name in the Code Editor and select Go To Definition to see information, as shown in Figure 29-1.

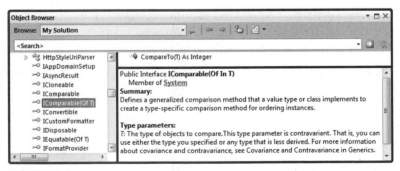

FIGURE 29-1

Finally, you can open the Object Browser (use the View menu's Object Browser command) and search for the interface's name to see a display similar to the one provided by the Go To Definition command (refer to Figure 29-1).

DEFINING INTERFACES

The examples in the preceding sections implement predefined interfaces. This section explains how you can define your own.

Defining an interface is a lot like defining a class with two main differences:

➤ You use the keyword `Interface` instead of `Class` in the declaration.

➤ You don't provide any code for the properties, methods, and events that you declare in the interface.

The following code shows a simple `IDrawable` interface:

```
Public Interface IDrawable
    Property X As Integer
    Property Y As Integer
    Property Background As Brush
    Property Foreground As Pen
    Sub Draw(ByVal gr As Graphics)
End Interface
```

A class that implements `IDrawable` must provide `X`, `Y`, `Background`, and `Foreground` properties, and a `Draw` subroutine.

The declarations for the properties look like they are providing a default implementation for them, but they actually only define the required accessors. A class that implements `IDrawable` must still provide its own implementations, although it can use auto-implemented properties. For example, the following code shows how the `DrawableCircle` class implements its `X` property:

```
Public Property X As Integer Implements IDrawable.X
```

 In this example, you might be better off using true inheritance instead of an interface. If you make a Drawable *class that implements the* X, Y, Background, *and* Foreground *properties, other classes such as* DrawableCircle *could inherit them. In this example an interface makes sense only if the classes already inherit from some other class so they cannot also inherit from* Drawable.

 ## TRY IT

In this Try It, you build the `Vehicle` class and the `IDomicile` interface described earlier in this lesson. You then make a `MotorHome` class that inherits from the first and implements the second. Finally, you create an instance of the derived class.

You can download the code and resources for this Try It from the book's web page at www.wrox.com *or* www.vb-helper.com/24hourvb.html. *You can find them in the Lesson29 folder of the download.*

Lesson Requirements

In this lesson:

➤ Start a new project. Create a `Vehicle` class with the properties `NumberOfPassengers`, `MilesPerGallon`, and `NumberOfCupHolders`. Give it a constructor to make it easy to initialize a new object's properties. Override its `ToString` method so it returns the object's property values separated by newlines.

➤ Make an `IDomicile` interface that defines the properties `SquareFeet`, `NumberOfBedrooms`, and `NumberOfBathrooms`. Also make it define a `ToString` function that returns a string.

➤ Derive the `MotorHome` class from `Vehicle`, making it implement `IDomicile`. Give it a constructor to make it easy to initialize a new object's properties. Override its `ToString` method so it returns the object's property values separated by newlines.

➤ Create an instance of the `MotorHome` class. Then use its `ToString` method to display its properties in a textbox.

Hints

➤ Don't forget to make the `MotorHome` class's constructor invoke the base class's constructor. If you don't remember how, see the section "Invoking Other Constructors" in Lesson 26.

➤ Save a little work by making the `MotorHome` class's `ToString` method call the `Vehicle` class's version.

Step-by-Step

➤ Start a new project. Create a `Vehicle` class with the properties `NumberOfPassengers`, `MilesPerGallon`, and `NumberOfCupHolders`. Give it a constructor to make it easy to initialize a new object's properties. Override its `ToString` method so it returns the object's property values separated by newlines.

1. Use code similar to the following:

```
Public Class Vehicle
    Public Property NumberOfPassengers As Integer
    Public Property MilesPerGallon As Single
    Public Property NumberOfCupHolders As Integer

    Public Sub New(ByVal newNumberOfPassengers As Integer,
     ByVal newMilesPerGallon As Single,
```

```
        ByVal newNumberOfCupHolders As Integer)
            NumberOfPassengers = newNumberOfPassengers
            MilesPerGallon = newMilesPerGallon
            NumberOfCupHolders = newNumberOfCupHolders
        End Sub

        Public Overrides Function ToString() As String
            Return "# Passengers: " & NumberOfPassengers & vbCrLf & _
                "MPG: " & MilesPerGallon & vbCrLf & _
                "# Cupholders: " & NumberOfCupHolders
        End Function
    End Class
```

➤ Make an IDomicile interface that defines the properties SquareFeet, NumberOfBedrooms, and NumberOfBathrooms. Also make it define a ToString function that returns a string.

1. Use code similar to the following:

```
Public Interface IDomicile
    Property SquareFeet As Integer
    Property NumberOfBedrooms As Integer
    Property NumberOfBathrooms As Single

    Function ToString() As String
End Interface
```

➤ Derive the MotorHome class from Vehicle, making it implement IDomicile. Give it a constructor to make it easy to initialize a new object's properties. Override its ToString method so it returns the object's property values separated by newlines.

1. Use code similar to the following:

```
Public Class MotorHome
    Inherits Vehicle
    Implements IDomicile

    Public Property NumberOfBathrooms As Single _
        Implements IDomicile.NumberOfBathrooms
    Public Property NumberOfBedrooms As Integer _
        Implements IDomicile.NumberOfBedrooms
    Public Property SquareFeet As Integer _
        Implements IDomicile.SquareFeet

    Public Sub New(ByVal newNumberOfPassengers As Integer,
     ByVal newMilesPerGallon As Single,
     ByVal newNumberOfCupHolders As Integer,
     ByVal newNumberOfBathrooms As Single,
     ByVal newNumberOfBedrooms As Integer,
     ByVal newSquareFeet As Integer)

        MyBase.New(newNumberOfPassengers, newMilesPerGallon,
            newNumberOfCupHolders)
        NumberOfBathrooms = newNumberOfBathrooms
```

```
                NumberOfBedrooms = newNumberOfBedrooms
                SquareFeet = newSquareFeet
            End Sub

            Public Overrides Function ToString() As String _
              Implements IDomicile.ToString
                Return MyBase.ToString() & vbCrLf &
                    "# Bathrooms: " & NumberOfBathrooms & vbCrLf &
                    "# Bedrooms: " & NumberOfBedrooms & vbCrLf &
                    "Square Feet: " & SquareFeet
            End Function
        End Class
```

➤ Create an instance of the `MotorHome` class. Then use its `ToString` method to display its properties in a textbox.

1. The following code creates an instance of the `MotorHome` class and displays its properties in `resultTextBox`:

```
' Make a MotorHome and display its properties.
Private Sub Form1_Load() Handles MyBase.Load
    ' Make a MotorHome.
    Dim myMotorHome As New MotorHome(6, 8.25, 32, 0.5, 3, 150)

    ' Display its properties.
    txtMotorHome.Text = myMotorHome.ToString()
End Sub
```

 Please select Lesson 29 on the DVD to view the video that accompanies this lesson.

EXERCISES

1. Build a program that defines the `IDrawable` interface described earlier in this lesson. Make the `DrawableCircle` and `DrawableRectangle` classes implement the interface. Hints: Give `DrawableCircle` an additional `Radius` property and give `DrawableRectangle` additional `Width` and `Height` properties. (For bonus points, make a `DrawableStar` class that has a `NumberOfPoints` property and draws a star with that number of points.)

2. An array's `Sort` method can take as a parameter an object that implements the generic `IComparer` interface. Because this interface is generic, you can tell it what kinds of objects the class can compare. For example, `IComparer(Of Car)` means the class can compare `Car` objects.

   Build a `Car` class with the properties `Name`, `MaxSpeed`, `Horsepower`, and `Price`. Override the `ToString` method to display the object's properties formatted with fixed-column widths so the values for different `Cars` in a listbox will line up nicely as shown in Figure 29-2. (The listbox uses the fixed-width font Courier New, so all the letters have the same width.)

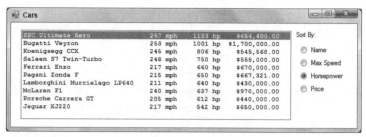

FIGURE 29-2

Build a `CarComparer` class that implements `IComparer(Of Car)`. Give it the following `SortType` enum:

```
' Different kinds of sorts.
Public Enum SortType
    ByName
    ByMaxSpeed
    ByHorsepower
    ByPrice
End Enum
```

Next, give `CarComparer` a `Sort` property that has type `SortType`.

Finally, give the `CarComparer` a `Compare` method to satisfy the `IComparer(Of Car)` interface. Use a `Select Case` statement to make the function return a value that varies according to the `Sort` value. For example, if `Sort` is `ByPrice`, then compare the two `Cars`' prices. Make the function sort the `MaxSpeed`, `Horsepower`, and `Price` values in decreasing order.

3. If you set a `ListView` control's `ListViewItemSorter` property equal to an object that implements the `IComparer` interface, then the `ListView` uses that object to sort its rows. To sort the rows, the control calls the object's `Compare` method, passing it two `ListViewItem` objects. (Unfortunately, the `ListView` control's `ListViewItemSorter` property is a nongeneric `IComparer`, so it works with nonspecific `objects` instead of something more concrete like `ListViewItems`.)

For this exercise, make a program with a `ListView` control similar to the one shown in Figure 29-3. At design time, edit the `ListView`'s `Columns` collection to define the columns. Edit its `Items` collection to define the data and set the control's `View` property to `Details`.

Next, make a `ListViewItemComparer` class that implements `IComparer`. Give it a `ColumnNumber` property that indicates the number of the column in the `ListView` that the object should use when sorting.

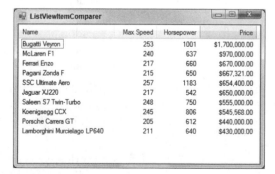

FIGURE 29-3

Finally, give the ListView a ColumnClick event handler. The event handler should create a new ListViewItemComparer object to sort on the clicked column and then set the control's ListViewItemSorter property to that object.

You can find solutions to this lesson's exercises in the Lesson29 folder inside the download available on the book's web site at www.wrox.com *or* www.vb-helper.com/24hourvb.html.

30

Making Generic Classes

The section on collection classes in Lesson 16 explained how to use generic collection classes. For example, the following code defines a list that holds `Employee` objects:

```
Public Employees As New List(Of Employee)
```

This list can hold `Employee` objects only, and when you get an object out of the list, it has the `Employee` type instead of the less specific `Object` type.

Lesson 16 also described the main advantages of generic classes: code reuse and specific type checking. You can use the same generic `List(Of ...)` class to hold a list of `Strings`, `Doubles`, or `Person` objects. By requiring a specific data type, the class prevents you from accidentally adding an `Employee` object to a list of `Order` objects, and when you get an object from the list you know it is an `Order`.

In this lesson, you learn how to build your own generic classes so you can raise code reuse to a whole new level.

 Many other things can be generic. You can probably guess that you can build generic structures because structures are so similar to classes. You can also build generic methods (in either generic or nongeneric classes), interfaces, delegate types, and so on. This lesson focuses on generic classes.

DEFINING GENERIC CLASSES

A generic class declaration looks a lot like a normal class declaration with one or more generic type variables added in parentheses. For example, the following code shows the basic declaration for a generic `TreeNode` class:

```
Public Class TreeNode(Of T)
    ...
End Class
```

The `(Of T)` means the class takes one type parameter, `T`. Within the class's code, the type `T` means whatever type the program used when creating the instance of the class. For example, the following code declares a variable named `rootNode` that is a `TreeNode` that handles strings:

```
Dim rootNode As New TreeNode(Of String)()
```

> *A generic class's type parameter is analogous to a parameter passed into a subroutine or function. In this example, `T` is the name by which the type is known within the class, just as a parameter list gives the name by which a parameter is known within a subroutine.*

If you want the class to use multiple type parameters, separate them with commas. For example, suppose you want to make a `Matcher` class that takes two kinds of objects and matches objects of the two kinds. It might match `Employee` objects with `Job` objects to assign employees to jobs. The following code shows how you might declare the `Matcher` class:

```
Public Class Matcher(Of T1, T2)
    ...
End Class
```

The following code shows how you might create an instance of the class to match `Employees` with `Jobs`:

```
Dim jobAssigner As New Matcher(Of Employee, Job)
```

> *Many developers use `T` for the name of the type in generic classes that take only one type.*
>
> *If the class takes more than one type, you should try to use more descriptive names so it's easy to tell the types apart. For example, the generic `Dictionary` class has two type variables named `TKey` and `TValue` that represent the types of the keys and values that the `Dictionary` will hold.*

Inside the class's code, you can use the types freely. For example, the following code shows more of the `TreeNode` class's code. A `TreeNode` object represents a node in a tree, with an associated piece of data attached to it. The places where the class uses the data type `T` are highlighted in bold.

```
Public Class TreeNode(Of T)
    ' This node's data.
    Public Property Data As T

    ' This node's children.
    Private Children As New List(Of TreeNode(Of T))()

    ' Initializing constructor.
    Public Sub New(ByVal newData As T)
        Data = newData
    End Sub
```

```
      ' Override ToString to display the data.
      Public Overrides Function ToString() As String
          If Data Is Nothing Then Return ""
          Return Data.ToString()
      End Function

      ...
  End Class
```

Notice how the class uses the type T throughout its code. The class starts with a Data property of type T. This is the data (of whatever data type) associated with the node.

Each node also has a list of child nodes that should be other TreeNodes of the same kind as this one. To hold the right kind of objects, the Children variable is a generic List(Of TreeNode(Of T)), meaning it can hold only TreeNode(Of T) objects.

The class's constructor takes a parameter of type T and saves it in the object's Data property.

To make displaying a TreeNode easier, the class overrides its ToString method so it calls the ToString method provided by the Data object. For example, if the object is a TreeNode(Of String), then this simply returns the string's value.

USING GENERIC CONSTRAINTS

The previous example overrides the TreeNode class's ToString method so it calls the Data object's ToString method. Fortunately, all objects inherit a ToString method from the Object ancestor class so you know this is possible, but what if you want to call some other method provided by the object?

For example, suppose you want to create a new instance of type T by using a parameterless constructor. How do you know type T provides a parameterless constructor? What if you want to compare two objects of type T to see which is greater? Is that possible? Or what if you want to compare two type T objects to see if they are the same (an important test for the Dictionary class)? How do you know whether two type T objects are comparable?

You can use *generic constraints* to require that the types used by the program meet certain criteria such as comparability or providing a parameterless constructor.

To use a generic constraint, follow the type with the keyword As and the constraint. Some typical constraints include the following:

➤ A class from which the type must inherit

➤ An interface (or interfaces) that the type must implement

➤ New, to indicate that the type must provide a parameterless constructor

➤ Structure, to indicate that the type must be a value type such as the built-in value types (Integer, Boolean) or a structure

➤ Class, to indicate that the type must be a reference type

You can use multiple constraints surrounded with braces and separated by commas.

For example, the following code defines the generic `Matcher` class, which takes two generic type parameters `T1` and `T2`. (To keep things simple, this code skips important error handling such as checking for null values.)

```
Public Class Matcher(Of T1 As {IComparable(Of T2), New}, T2 As New)
    Private Sub Test()
        Dim object1 As New T1()
        Dim object2 As New T2()
        ...
        If object1.CompareTo(object2) < 0 Then
            ' The object1 is "less than" object2.
            ...
        End If
    End Sub
    ...
End Class
```

The first constraint requires that type parameter `T1` implement the generic `IComparable` interface for the type `T2` so the code can compare `T1` objects to `T2` objects. The next constraint requires that the `T1` type also provide a parameterless constructor. You can see that the code creates a new `T1` object and uses its `CompareTo` method (which is defined by `IComparable`).

The second constraint clause requires that the type `T2` also provide a parameterless constructor. The code needs that because it also creates a new `T2` instance.

> *In general you should use as few constraints as possible because that makes your class usable in as many circumstances as possible. If your code won't need to create new instances of a data type, don't use the* New *constraint. If your code won't need to compare objects, don't use the* IComparable *constraint.*

MAKING GENERIC METHODS

In addition to building generic classes, you can also build generic methods inside either a generic class or a regular nongeneric class.

For example, suppose you want to rearrange the items in a list so the new order alternately picks items from each end of the list. If the list originally contains the numbers 1, 2, 3, 4, 5, 6, then the alternated list contains 1, 6, 2, 5, 3, 4.

The following code shows how a program could declare an `Alternate` function to return an alternated list. Note that you could put this function in any class, generic or not.

```
Public Function Alternate(Of T)(ByVal values As List(Of T)) As List(Of T)
    ' Make a new list to hold the results.
    Dim alternatedItems As New List(Of T)()
    ...
    Return alternatedItems
End Function
```

The `Alternate` function takes a generic type parameter `T`. It takes as a regular parameter a `List` that holds items of type `T` and it returns a new `List` containing items of type `T`.

This snippet creates a new `List(Of T)` to hold the results. (Note that it does not need to require the type `T` to have a default constructor because the code is creating a new `List`, not a new `T`.) The code then builds the new list (not shown here) and returns it.

The following code shows how a program might use this function:

```
Dim names As New List(Of String)(
    {"Ant", "Badger", "Cat", "Dog", "Eagle", "Frog"}
)
Dim alternatedNames As List(Of String) = Alternate(Of String)(names)
```

The first statement defines a `List(Of String)` and initializes it with the some strings.

The second statement calls `Alternate(Of String)` to create an alternated `List(Of String)`. Notice how the code uses `(Of String)` to indicate the data type that `Alternate` will manipulate. (This is actually optional and the program will figure out which version of `Alternate` to use if you omit it. However, this makes the code more explicit and may catch a bug if you try to alternate a list containing something unexpected such as `Person` objects.)

Generic methods can be quite useful for the same reasons that generic classes are. They enable code reuse without the extra hassle of converting values to and from the nonspecific `Object` class. They also perform type checking, so in this example, the program cannot try to alternate a `List(Of Integer)` by calling `Alternate(Of String)`.

 TRY IT

In this Try It, you build a generic `Randomize` function that randomizes an array of objects of any type. To make it easy to add the function to any project, you define the function in a code module.

 You can download the code and resources for this Try It from the book's web page at www.wrox.com *or* www.vb-helper.com/24hourvb.html. *You can find them in the Lesson30 folder of the download.*

Lesson Requirements

In this lesson:

➤ Start a new project and give it a code module named `ArrayFunctions`.

➤ Create a generic `Randomize` function with one generic type parameter `T`. The function should take as a parameter an array of `T` and return an array of `T`.

➤ Make the main program test the function.

Hints

➤ Use the following code for the function's body. Try to figure out the function's declaration yourself before you read the step-by-step instructions that follow.

```
' Make a Random object to use to pick random items.
Dim rand As New Random()

' Make a copy of the array so we don't mess up the original.
Dim randomizedItems() As T = DirectCast(items.Clone(), T())

' For each spot in the array, pick
' a random item to swap into that spot.
For i As Integer = 0 To items.Length - 2
    ' Pick a random item j between i and the last item.
    Dim j As Integer = rand.Next(i, items.Length)

    ' Swap item j into position i.
    Dim temp As T = randomizedItems(i)
    randomizedItems(i) = randomizedItems(j)
    randomizedItems(j) = temp
Next i

' Return the randomized array.
Return randomizedItems
```

Step-by-Step

➤ Start a new project and give it a code module named ArrayFunctions.

1. This is reasonably straightforward.

➤ Create a generic Randomize function with one generic type parameter T. The function should take as a parameter an array of T and return an array of T.

1. The following code shows how you can implement this function:

```
' Randomize the items in an array.
Public Function Randomize(Of T)(ByVal items() As T) As T()
    ' Make a Random object to use to pick random items.
    Dim rand As New Random()

    ' Make a copy of the array so we don't mess up the original.
    Dim randomizedItems() As T = DirectCast(items.Clone(), T())

    ' For each spot in the array, pick
    ' a random item to swap into that spot.
    For i As Integer = 0 To items.Length - 2
        ' Pick a random item j between i and the last item.
        Dim j As Integer = rand.Next(i, items.Length)

        ' Swap item j into position i.
        Dim temp As T = randomizedItems(i)
        randomizedItems(i) = randomizedItems(j)
        randomizedItems(j) = temp
    Next i
```

```
                    ' Return the randomized array.
                    Return randomizedItems
                End Function
```

➤ Make the main program test the function.

1. The program I wrote uses two `TextBoxes`, one to hold the original items and one to display the randomized items. When you click the Randomize button, the following code executes:

```
' Randomize the list and display the results.
Private Sub btnRandomize_Click() Handles btnRandomize.Click
    ' Get the items as an array of strings.
    Dim items() As String = txtItems.Lines

    ' Randomize the array.
    Dim randomizedItems() As String = Randomize(Of String)(items)

    ' Display the result.
    txtRandomized.Lines = randomizedItems
End Sub
```

Notice that the code uses the `TextBox`'s `Lines` property to get the entered values. That property returns the lines in a multiline `TextBox` as an array of strings.

 Please select Lesson 30 on the DVD to view the video that accompanies this lesson.

EXERCISES

1. Finish building the generic `Alternate` function described earlier in this lesson. Add the code needed to make the alternating version of the list. To make using the function easy, add it to the `ArrayFunctions` module you built for the Try It. Make the main program test the method with lists containing odd and even numbers of items.

2. Modify the `TreeNode` class described earlier in this lesson. Give it `X` and `Y` properties and add them to the initializing constructor.

Give the class a `DrawLinks` method that takes as a parameter a `Graphics` object and draws lines between the node and its children. It should then recursively call its children's `DrawLinks` methods to make them draw their links.

Also give the class a `DrawNode` method that takes a `Graphics` object and a `Font` as parameters. It should draw a circle centered at (X, Y) and then draw the node's value inside it. You can use code similar to the following:

```
' Draw the node itself.
Public Sub DrawNode(ByVal gr As Graphics, ByVal theFont As Font)
    ' Recursively draw the children.
    For Each child As TreeNode(Of T) In Children
        ' Draw the child.
```

```
            child.DrawNode(gr, theFont)
        Next child

        ' Draw this node.
        Using string_format As New StringFormat()
            ' Draw a circle.
            gr.FillEllipse(Brushes.White, X - 10, Y - 10, 20, 20)
            gr.DrawEllipse(Pens.Black, X - 10, Y - 10, 20, 20)

            ' Draw the text.
            string_format.Alignment = StringAlignment.Center
            string_format.LineAlignment = StringAlignment.Center
            gr.DrawString(ToString(), theFont, Brushes.Green,
                X, Y, string_format)
        End Using
    End Sub
```

Make the main program build a tree and draw it in its Paint event handler. Figure 30-1 shows an example solution.

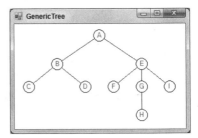

FIGURE 30-1

3. Make a generic PriorityQueue class. The class is basically a list holding generic items, with each item having an associated priority. Give the class a nested ItemData structure similar to the following to hold an item. This structure is defined inside the PriorityQueue class and won't be used outside of the class, so it can be Private. Note that this structure uses the class's generic type parameter T for the data it holds.

```
' A structure to hold items.
Private Structure ItemData
    Public Property ItemPriority As Integer
    Public Property Data As T
End Structure
```

The class should store its ItemData objects in a generic List.

Give the class a read-only public Count property that returns the number of items in the list.

Give the class an AddItem method that takes as parameters a piece of data and a priority. It should make a new ItemData to hold these values and add it to the list.

Finally, give the class a GetItem method that searches the list to find the item with the smallest priority number (priority 1 means top priority), removes that item from the list, and returns the item and its priority via parameters passed by reference. (If there's a tie for lowest priority number, return the first item found with that priority.)

You can find solutions to this lesson's exercises in the Lesson30 folder inside the download available on the book's web site at www.wrox.com *or* www.vb-helper .com/24hourvb.html.

SECTION V
System Interactions

The lessons up to this point have explained how you can do some pretty remarkable things. Using the techniques they demonstrate, you can read inputs entered by the user, perform intricate calculations, easily repeat a sequence of complex commands, and even build your own classes to model complex situations.

All the programs that you've written so far, however, are self-contained: They get input from the user, but otherwise they don't interact with the computer.

The lessons in this section explain some of the ways a program can interact with the system. They explain how to read and write files, explore the file system, print, and use the clipboard to interact with other applications.

▶ **LESSON 31:** Reading and Writing Files

▶ **LESSON 32:** Using File System Classes

▶ **LESSON 33:** Printing

▶ **LESSON 34:** Using the Clipboard

▶ **LESSON 35:** Providing Drag and Drop

There are many other ways a program can interact with the computer. It can interact with hardware through serial ports and special devices, and connect to web sites or other programs over a network. There are even many different ways to interact with the same part of the system — for example, it can manipulate files, read and modify the Windows registry, and save and restore program parameters. The lessons in this section describe some of the ways a program can interact with the operating system in general, but keep in mind that other ways are possible.

31

Reading and Writing Files

Files play an extremely important role on a computer. They hold text, pictures, Microsoft Word documents, spreadsheets, and all sorts of other data. They also hold executable programs, including those that provide the operating system itself.

In this lesson you learn some basic techniques for reading and writing text files. Using some fairly simple techniques, you can use text files to store and retrieve data used by a program.

UNDERSTANDING STREAMS

There are many kinds of files: web pages, video, audio, executable, and many others. At some level, however, files are all the same. They're just a series of bytes stored on a file system somewhere.

Thinking about files at this very low level enables you to treat them uniformly. That is, you can define common classes and methods that you can then use to manipulate any kind of file.

Many programming languages, including Visual Basic, make working with files at a low level easier by defining the concept of a stream. A *stream* is simply an ordered series of bytes.

 Streams can also represent things other than files. For example, a stream could represent data being sent from one program to another, a series of bytes being downloaded from a web site, or the flow of data as it moves through some complex process such as encryption or compression. This lesson focuses on file streams.

Stream objects provide methods for manipulating streams at a low level. For example, the `Stream` class provides `Read` and `Write` methods that move bytes of data between the stream and an array of bytes in your program.

Working with streams at this low level is convenient for some programs, but it makes day-to-day file handling difficult. You probably don't want to read the bytes from a text file and then reassemble them into characters.

The `StreamReader` and `StreamWriter` classes make reading and writing text streams much easier. As you can probably guess from their names, `StreamReader` enables a program to read text from a stream, and `StreamWriter` enables a program to write text into a stream. If that stream happens to represent a file, then you're reading and writing files.

The .NET Framework uses namespaces to categorize the classes it provides so they are easier to find and organize. The `StreamReader` and `StreamWriter` classes are in the `System.IO` namespace, so you can refer to them as `System.IO.StreamReader` and `System.IO.StreamWriter`.

However, to make it easier to use these classes, you can add the following `Imports` directive at the very beginning of a code file:

`Imports System.IO`

After adding that directive, you can refer to these classes without the `System.IO` prefix.

WRITING FILES

The `StreamWriter` class provides several constructors to build a `StreamWriter` associated with different kinds of streams. One of the simplest constructors takes a filename as a parameter. It opens the file for writing and associates the new `StreamWriter` with it.

Before you create a `StreamReader` or `StreamWriter`, however, you should know a bit about the `Dispose` method and the `Using` statement (see the accompanying "Using Using" sidebar).

The following code shows how a program can open the file `Memo.txt` for writing. If the file already exists, it is overwritten.

```
' Write into the file, overwriting it if it exists.
Using memoWriter As New StreamWriter("Memo.txt")
    ' Write into the file.
    '...
End Using
```

If you pass the constructor a filename without a path, such as `Memo.txt`, the program creates the file in its current directory. You can use a fully qualified filename such as `C:\Temp\Memo.txt` to create the file in a particular directory.

USING USING

Some classes, including `StreamReader` and `StreamWriter`, provide a `Dispose` method that you can call to free up resources when you no longer need an object. Calling `Dispose` isn't required but it makes your program more efficient, so you should do it whenever you can.

To make calling `Dispose` easier for classes that implement the `IDisposable` interface (most that have a `Dispose` method implement `IDisposable`), you can use a `Using` statement. The basic syntax of `Using` is

```
Using variableName As New className()
    ...
End Using
```

where `variableName` is the name of the variable that you want to create and dispose and `className()` is code that invokes its constructor. When the program leaves the `Using` block, it automatically calls the variable's `Dispose` method so you can't forget.

Another version of the class's constructor takes a second `Boolean` parameter that indicates whether you want to open the file for appending. If you set this parameter to `True`, the `StreamWriter` opens the existing file and prepares to add text to the end. If the file doesn't exit, the object silently creates a new file and gets ready to append.

The `StreamWriter` class provides a `Write` method to add text to the file. The `WriteLine` method adds text followed by a new line. Both `Write` and `WriteLine` have a bunch of overloaded versions that write various data types into the file: `Boolean`, `Char`, `String`, `Integer`, `Decimal`, and so on. They also provide versions that take a format string and parameters, much as the `String.Format` method does.

The `StreamWriter` provides one other very important method that I want to cover here: `Close`. The `Close` method closes the `StreamWriter` and its associated file. When you use the `Write` and `WriteLine` methods, the `StreamWriter` may actually buffer its output in memory and only write to the file when it has saved up enough data to make writing to the disk efficient. The `Close` method forces the `StreamWriter` to flush its buffer into the file. Until that point, the data may not actually be in the file. If your program crashes or ends without calling `Close`, there's a very good chance that some or all of your text may be lost.

The following code shows how a program could save the contents of a textbox in a file:

```
' Write the file, overwriting it if it exists.
Using memoWriter As New StreamWriter("Memo.txt")
    ' Write the file.
    memoWriter.Write(txtMemo.Text)
    memoWriter.Close()
End Using
```

READING FILES

The `StreamReader` class enables you to easily read text from a file. Like the `StreamWriter` class, `StreamReader` provides a constructor that takes a parameter specifying the name of the file to open. It also implements `IDisposable`, so you should call a `StreamReader`'s `Dispose` method or use it in a `Using` statement.

Note that the constructor throws an exception if the file doesn't exist, so your program should verify that the file is there before you try to open it. One way to do that is to use the `File` class's static `Exists` method. For example, the code `File.Exists("Memo.txt")` returns `True` if the file `Memo.txt` exists in the program's current directory.

The `StreamReader` class provides a `Read` method that enables reading from the file one or more bytes at a time, but usually you'll want to use its `ReadLine` and `ReadToEnd` methods.

As you may be able to guess, `ReadLine` reads the next line from the file and returns it as a string. `ReadToEnd` reads the rest of the file from the current position onward and returns it as a string.

The following code reads the file `Memo.txt` and displays its contents in a textbox:

```
' Read the file.
Using memoReader As New StreamReader("Memo.txt")
    txtMemo.Text = memoReader.ReadToEnd()
    memoReader.Close()
End Using
```

The `StreamReader`'s `EndOfStream` property returns `True` if the reader is at the end of the stream. This is particularly useful when reading a stream of unknown length. For example, the program can enter a `While` loop that uses `ReadLine` to read lines and continue as long as `EndOfStream` is false.

TRY IT

In this Try It, you build the program shown in Figure 31-1. When the program starts, it loads previously saved values into its textboxes. When it stops, the program saves the values that are currently in the textboxes.

FIGURE 31-1

You can download the code and resources for this Try It from the book's web page at www.wrox.com *or* www.vb-helper.com/24hourvb.html. *You can find them in the Lesson31 folder of the download.*

Lesson Requirements

In this lesson:

➤ Start a new project and arrange its form as shown in Figure 31-1.

➤ Give the form a Load event handler that uses a StreamReader to open the file Values.txt and read the file's lines into the form's textboxes.

➤ Give the form a FormClosing event handler that uses a StreamWriter to open the file Values.txt and write the values in the textboxes into the file.

Hints

➤ Use an Imports System.IO directive.

➤ Use the StreamReader and StreamWriter inside Using blocks.

➤ Make sure the file exists before you try to open it.

➤ Use a module-scope constant to hold the file's name so all of the code can share it.

Step-by-Step

➤ Start a new project and arrange its form as shown in Figure 31-1.

1. This is reasonably straightforward.

➤ Give the form a Load event handler that uses a StreamReader to open the file Values.txt and read the file's lines into the form's textboxes.

1. Use code similar to the following:

```
' The file's name.
Private Const FileName As String = "Values.txt"

' Load the saved values.
Private Sub Form1_Load() Handles MyBase.Load
    ' See if the file exists.
    If File.Exists(FileName) Then
        ' Open the file.
        Using valueReader As New StreamReader(FileName)
            txtFirstName.Text = valueReader.ReadLine()
            txtLastName.Text = valueReader.ReadLine()
            txtStreet.Text = valueReader.ReadLine()
            txtCity.Text = valueReader.ReadLine()
            txtState.Text = valueReader.ReadLine()
            txtZip.Text = valueReader.ReadLine()
            valueReader.Close()
        End Using
    End If
End Sub
```

➤ Give the form a `FormClosing` event handler that uses a `StreamWriter` to open the file `Values.txt` and write the values in the textboxes into the file.

1. Use code similar to the following:

```
' Save the current values.
Private Sub Form1_FormClosing() Handles Me.FormClosing
    ' Create the file.
    Using As New StreamWriter(FileName)
        valueWriter.WriteLine(txtFirstName.Text)
        valueWriter.WriteLine(txtLastName.Text)
        valueWriter.WriteLine(txtStreet.Text)
        valueWriter.WriteLine(txtCity.Text)
        valueWriter.WriteLine(txtState.Text)
        valueWriter.WriteLine(txtZip.Text)
        valueWriter.Close()
    End Using
End Sub
```

 Please select Lesson 31 on the DVD to view the video that accompanies this lesson.

EXERCISES

1. Build a Memo program that saves and loads a single memo saved in the file in a multiline textbox. Hint: Should you use `Write` or `WriteLine`? (This is so easy I wouldn't normally use it as an exercise but it's actually useful. You can use it to record notes during the day and easily review them the next day.)

2. Make a program that lets the user select a number N from a `NumericUpDown` control and then generates a file containing a multiplication table showing the products 1×1 through $N \times N$. Use formatting to make the numbers line up in columns.

3. Build a program with a `TextBox`, a `ListBox`, an Add button, and a Save button. When the user enters a value in the `TextBox` and clicks Add, add the value to the `ListBox`. When the user clicks Save, write the values from the `ListBox` into a file and then clear the `ListBox`. When the form loads, make it read the values back into the `ListBox`.

4. Build a simple text editor. Give it a `MenuStrip` with Open and Save commands and a `TextBox`. Use an `OpenFileDialog` and a `SaveFileDialog` to let the user select the file to open and save. (Don't worry about any of the other things a real editor would need to handle, such as locked files and ensuring that the user doesn't close the program with unsaved changes.)

 You can find solutions to this lesson's exercises in the Lesson31 folder inside the download available on the book's web site at www.wrox.com *or* www.vb-helper .com/24hourvb.html.

32

Using File System Classes

The techniques described in Lesson 31 enable you to read and write text files. They also demonstrate techniques that you'll find useful when you deal with streams other than text files.

Those techniques won't enable you to manipulate the file system itself, however. You can read from or write to a file using them, but not rename a file, move a file to a different directory, or delete a file.

This lesson describes file system classes that make these and other common file manipulation operations easy. In this lesson you learn how to manipulate the file system to rename, move, or delete files and directories. You also learn how to read or write a text file's contents all at once, rather than using a StreamReader.

These classes are in the System.IO *namespace, so you can make using them in your code easier by including the following directive:*

```
Imports System.IO
```

THE DRIVEINFO CLASS

The DriveInfo class provides information about the system's drives. Its static GetDrives function returns an array of DriveInfo objects describing all of the system's drives.

Table 32-1 summarizes the `DriveInfo`'s most useful properties.

TABLE 32-1

PROPERTY	PURPOSE
AvailableFreeSpace	The total number of bytes available
DriveFormat	The drive format, as in NTFS or FAT32
DriveType	The drive type, as in Fixed or CDRom
IsReady	True if the drive is ready. A drive must be ready before you can use the AvailableFreeSpace, DriveFormat, TotalSize, or VolumeLabel properties.
Name	The drive's name, as in C:\
RootDirectory	A DirectoryInfo object representing the drive's root directory
TotalFreeSpace	The number of bytes available, taking quotas into account
TotalSize	The drive's total size, in bytes
VolumeLabel	The drive's label

Example program ListDrives (found as part of this lesson's code download and shown in Figure 32-1) uses the following code to describe the system's drives:

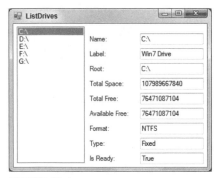

FIGURE 32-1

```
' List the available drives.
Private Sub Form1_Load() Handles MyBase.Load
    lstDrives.DataSource = DriveInfo.GetDrives()
End Sub

' Display information about the selected drive.
Private Sub lstDrives_SelectedIndexChanged() _
 Handles lstDrives.SelectedIndexChanged
```

```
        Dim info As DriveInfo = DirectCast(lstDrives.SelectedItem, DriveInfo)
        txtName.Text = info.Name
        txtRoot.Text = info.RootDirectory.FullName
        txtType.Text = info.DriveType.ToString()
        txtIsReady.Text = info.IsReady.ToString()

        ' See if the drive is ready.
        If (info.IsReady) Then
            ' Display values.
            txtLabel.Text = info.VolumeLabel
            txtTotalSpace.Text = info.TotalSize.ToString()
            txtTotalFree.Text = info.TotalFreeSpace.ToString()
            txtAvailableFree.Text = info.AvailableFreeSpace.ToString()
            txtFormat.Text = info.DriveFormat
        Else
            ' Clear values that are unavailable.
            txtLabel.Clear()
            txtTotalSpace.Clear()
            txtTotalFree.Clear()
            txtAvailableFree.Clear()
            txtFormat.Clear()
        End If
    End Sub
```

THE DIRECTORYINFO CLASS

The DirectoryInfo class provides information about directories. Table 32-2 summarizes useful DirectoryInfo methods for manipulating directories.

TABLE 32-2

METHOD	PURPOSE
Create	Creates a new directory. To use this, make a DirectoryInfo object, passing its constructor the name of the directory to create. Then call the Create method.
CreateSubdirectory	Creates a subdirectory inside this directory
Delete	Deletes the directory. If you pass no parameters to this method, it only deletes the directory if it is empty. Alternatively, you can pass it a Boolean parameter indicating whether you want to delete all of the directory's files and subdirectories.
GetDirectories	Returns the directory's immediate subdirectories. Optionally, you can include a search string to select particular subdirectories.
GetFiles	Returns the directory's files. Optionally, you can include a search string to select particular files.
MoveTo	Moves the directory to a new path

The `DirectoryInfo` class also provides a few useful properties, which are summarized in Table 32-3.

TABLE 32-3

PROPERTY	PURPOSE
Attributes	The directory's attributes, such as `Compressed`, `Hidden`, or `System`
CreationTime	The time at which the directory was created on your computer
Exists	Returns `True` if the directory actually exists
FullName	Gives the directory's fully qualified path
LastAccessTime	The time at which the directory was last accessed
LastWriteTime	The time at which the directory was last written
Name	The directory's name without the path
Parent	A `DirectoryInfo` representing this directory's parent directory
Root	The directory's file system root

Example program UseDirectoryInfo (found in this lesson's code download) uses a `DirectoryInfo` object to display information about directories.

THE DIRECTORY CLASS

The `Directory` class provides shared methods for manipulating directories. For simple tasks these are sometimes easier to use than the comparable `DirectoryInfo` class methods because you don't need to create a `DirectoryInfo` object to use them. Table 32-4 summarizes the `Directory` class's most useful methods.

TABLE 32-4

METHOD	PURPOSE
CreateDirectory	Creates the directory and any missing directories in its path up to the root
Delete	Deletes a directory
Exists	Returns `True` if the directory exists
GetCreationTime	Returns the time at which the file was created on your computer
GetDirectories	Returns a directory's subdirectories
GetDirectoryRoot	Returns the directory's root
GetFiles	Returns a directory's files, optionally looking for files matching a pattern

METHOD	PURPOSE
GetLastAccessTime	Returns a directory's last access time
GetLastWriteTime	Returns a directory's last write time
GetParent	Returns a DirectoryInfo representing a directory's parent directory
Move	Moves a file or directory to a new location
SetCreationTime	Sets a directory's creation time
SetLastAccessTime	Sets a directory's last access time
SetLastWriteTime	Sets a directory's last write time

THE FILEINFO CLASS

The FileInfo class, as you can probably guess at this point, provides information about files. Table 32-5 summarizes useful FileInfo methods for manipulating files.

TABLE 32-5

METHOD	PURPOSE
CopyTo	Copies the file to a new location
Decrypt	Decrypts a file that was encrypted by the Encrypt method
Delete	Deletes the file
Encrypt	Encrypts the file so it can be read only by the account used to encrypt it
MoveTo	Moves the file to a new location

The FileInfo class also provides some useful properties, summarized in Table 32-6.

TABLE 32-6

PROPERTY	PURPOSE
Attributes	The file's attributes, such as Compressed, Hidden, or System
CreationTime	The time at which the file was created on your computer
Directory	A DirectoryInfo object for the directory containing the file
Exists	Returns True if the file actually exists

continues

TABLE 32-6 *(continued)*

PROPERTY	PURPOSE
Extension	Returns the file's extension
FullName	Gives the file's fully qualified path
IsReadOnly	Returns True if the file is marked read-only
LastAccessTime	The time at which the file was last accessed on your computer
LastWriteTime	The time at which the file was last written on your computer
Length	The file's size, in bytes
Name	The file's name without the path

Example program UseFileInfo (found in this lesson's code download) uses a FileInfo object to display information about files.

THE FILE CLASS

The File class provides static methods for manipulating files. For simple tasks these are sometimes easier to use than the comparable FileInfo class methods because you don't need to create a FileInfo object to use them. The AppendAllText, ReadAllLines, ReadAllText, WriteAllLines, and WriteAllText methods are particularly useful for reading and writing text files all at once, although you may still want to use StreamReader and StreamWriter if you need to manipulate files one line at a time. Table 32-7 summarizes the File class's most useful methods.

TABLE 32-7

METHOD	PURPOSE
AppendAllText	Appends a string to the end of a file
Copy	Copies a file to a new file
Create	Creates a file
Decrypt	Decrypts a file that was encrypted by the Encrypt method
Delete	Deletes a file
Encrypt	Encrypts a file so it can be read only by the account used to encrypt it
Exists	Returns True if a file exists
GetAttributes	Returns a file's attributes, such as ReadOnly, System, or Hidden
GetCreationTime	Returns a file's creation time on your computer
GetLastAccessTime	Returns a file's last access time

METHOD	PURPOSE
GetLastWriteTime	Returns a file's last write time
Move	Moves a file to a new location
ReadAllBytes	Returns a file's contents in an array of bytes
ReadAllLines	Returns the lines in a text file as an array of strings
ReadAllText	Returns a text file's contents in a string
SetAttributes	Sets a file's attributes
SetCreationTime	Sets a file's creation time
SetLastAccessTime	Sets a file's last access time
SetLastWriteTime	Sets a file's last write time
WriteAllBytes	Writes a file's contents from an array of bytes
WriteAllLines	Writes a text file's contents from an array of strings
WriteAllText	Writes a text file's contents from a string

THE PATH CLASS

The Path class provides static methods that perform string operations on file paths. For example, you can use the ChangeExtension method to change the extension part of a filename. Note that this doesn't affect the file with that name (if there is one); it just manipulates a string holding a filename.

Table 32-8 summarizes the Path class's most useful methods.

TABLE 32-8

METHOD	PURPOSE
ChangeExtension	Changes a filename's extension
Combine	Combines two path strings, adding a backslash between them if needed
GetDirectoryName	Returns the directory name part of a path
GetExtension	Returns the extension part of a filename
GetFileName	Returns the filename part of a file's path
GetFileNameWithoutExtension	Returns the filename part of a file's path without the extension
GetTempFileName	Returns a name for a temporary file
GetTempPath	Returns the path to the system's temporary folder

TRY IT

In this Try It, you build the program shown in Figure 32-2, which enables the user to search for files matching a pattern containing a target string. Enter a directory at which to start the search, select or enter a file pattern in the Pattern combo box, and enter a target string in the Search For textbox. When you click Search, the program searches for files matching the pattern and containing the target string.

FIGURE 32-2

You can download the code and resources for this Try It from the book's web page at www.wrox.com *or* www.vb-helper.com/24hourvb.html. *You can find them in the Lesson32 folder of the download.*

Lesson Requirements

In this lesson:

➤   Start a new project and arrange its form as shown in Figure 32-2.

➤   Give the combo box the options *.vb, *.txt, *.*, and any other patterns that you think would be useful.

➤   Give the form a Load event handler that places the application's startup path in the Directory textbox (just to have somewhere to start).

➤   Give the Search button a Click event handler that searches for the desired files.

Hints

➤   Use the DirectoryInfo class's GetFiles method to search for files matching the pattern.

➤   Use the File class's ReadAllText method to get the file's contents. Then use string methods to determine whether the text contains the target string.

➤   To ignore case, convert the target string and the files' contents to lowercase.

Step-by-Step

➤   Start a new project and arrange its form as shown in Figure 32-2.

➤   Give the combo box the options *.vb, *.txt, *.*, and any other patterns that you think would be useful.

1.   This is reasonably straightforward.

➤ Give the form a `Load` event handler that places the application's startup path in the Directory textbox (just to have somewhere to start).

1. Use code similar to the following:

```
' Start at the startup directory.
Private Sub Form1_Load() Handles MyBase.Load
    txtDirectory.Text = Application.StartupPath
End Sub
```

➤ Give the Search button a `Click` event handler that searches for the desired files.

1. Use code similar to the following:

```
' Search for files matching the pattern
' and containing the target string.
Private Sub btnSearch_Click() Handles btnSearch.Click
    lstFiles.Items.Clear()

    ' Get the file pattern and target string.
    Dim pattern As String = cboPattern.Text
    Dim target As String = txtTarget.Text.ToLower()

    ' Search for files.
    Dim dirinfo As New DirectoryInfo(txtDirectory.Text)
    For Each info As FileInfo In
        dirinfo.GetFiles(pattern, SearchOption.AllDirectories)

        ' See if we need to look for target text.
        If target.Length > 0 Then
            ' If this file contains the target string,
            ' add it to the list.
            Dim content As String =
                File.ReadAllText(info.FullName).ToLower()
            If (content.Contains(target)) Then _
                lstFiles.Items.Add(info)
        Else
            ' Just add this file to the list.
            lstFiles.Items.Add(info)
        End If
    Next info
End Sub
```

 Please select Lesson 32 on the DVD to view the video that accompanies this lesson.

EXERCISES

1. Copy the Memo program you built in Lesson 31, Exercise 1 (or download Lesson31's version from the book's web site). Modify the program to use the `File` class's `ReadAllText` and `WriteAllText` methods instead of using streams.

2. Write a program that sorts a text file. Hint: Load the file's lines of text into an array and use `Array.Sort` to do the actual sorting. Test the program on the file `Names.txt` included in this lesson's download.

3. Write a program that removes duplicate entries from a text file. Hint: Copy the program you built for Exercise 2. After you sort the array, run through the entries, copying them into a new list. If you see a duplicate entry, skip it and write it to the Immediate window. Test the program on the `Names.txt` file included in this lesson's download.

 You can find solutions to this lesson's exercises in the Lesson32 folder inside the download available on the book's web site at www.wrox.com *or* www.vb-helper .com/24hourvb.html.

33

Printing

Most of the programs described in earlier lessons display output on the computer's screen. Lessons 31 and 32 explain how to save output in files.

This lesson explains a third method for saving output: printing. Using these techniques, you can print text, shapes, images — just about anything you want.

Before you start a printing project, however, be warned that printing in Visual Basic isn't trivial. It's easy enough to display some text or a few lines in a printout, but producing a complex formatted document can be a lot of work.

If you need to produce a nicely formatted resume, graph, or grid of values, you should ask yourself whether there's an easier way than writing a bunch of Visual Basic code. For example, Microsoft Word is great at producing nicely formatted text documents, and Microsoft Excel does a wonderful job of making charts and graphs. You can certainly generate these sorts of printouts using Visual Basic, but it may be a lot faster if you use another tool such as Word or Excel.

BASIC PRINTING

The `PrintDocument` component sits at the center of the printing process. To print, a program creates an instance of this class either at design time or at run time. It adds event handlers to catch the object's events and then lets the object do its thing. As the object generates pieces of the printout, it raises events to let the program supply graphics for it to print.

The `PrintDocument` object raises four key events:

➤ `BeginPrint` — Raised when the object is about to start printing. Here the program can do whatever it must to get ready to print such as opening files, gathering information from a database, or downloading data from a web page.

➤ QueryPageSettings — Raised when the object is about to start printing a page. The program can modify the page's settings. For example, it might adjust the margins so even pages have bigger margins on the left than odd pages or vice versa to allow for a staple in a double-sided document.

➤ PrintPage — Raised when the object needs to generate contents for a page. This is where the program does its drawing. It should set the event handler's e.HasMorePages parameter to False if this is the last page.

➤ EndPrint — Raised after the object has finished printing. The program can perform any necessary cleanup here.

The BeginPrint, QueryPageSettings, and EndPrint event handlers are optional. For simple printouts, you may only need the PrintPage event handler.

The PrintPage event handler gives you a parameter named e of type PrintPageEventArgs. This object contains the HasMorePages parameter that you use to tell the PrintDocument whether this is the last page, a Graphics object that you use to draw the page's contents, a PageBounds property that indicates how big the page is, and a MarginBounds property that specifies the page's margins.

Drawing Shapes

The easiest way to generate a printout using the PrintDocument object is to place the object on a form and give the object a PrintPage event handler to generate the pages. When you're ready to print, simply call the object's Print method to send the printout to the default printer. As it builds the pages, the PrintDocument raises its PrintPage event to find out what to draw.

Once you've done this much, it's practically trivial to add a print preview capability to the program. Add a PrintPreviewDialog object to the form and set its Document property to the PrintDocument object that you already created. To display a print preview, simply call the dialog's ShowDialog method. The dialog uses the associated PrintDocument object to generate the necessary preview and displays the result.

Figure 33-1 shows the PrintShapes example program (available as part of this lesson's code download) displaying a four-page print preview that contains a triangle, rectangle, ellipse, and diamond.

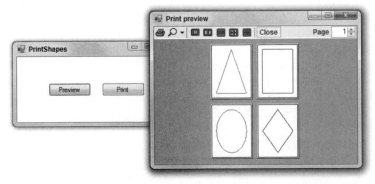

FIGURE 33-1

The following code shows the program's `PrintPage` event handler:

```
' The number of the next page.
Private NextPageNum As Integer = 0

' Print a page.
Private Sub pdocShapes_PrintPage(ByVal sender As System.Object, _
 ByVal e As System.Drawing.Printing.PrintPageEventArgs) _
 Handles pdocShapes.PrintPage
    ' These are used to draw the triangle and diamond.
    Dim xmid As Single =
        CSng((e.MarginBounds.Left + e.MarginBounds.Right) / 2)
    Dim ymid As Single =
        CSng((e.MarginBounds.Top + e.MarginBounds.Bottom) / 2)

    ' See which page this is.
    Select Case NextPageNum
        Case 0 ' Draw a triangle.
            Dim trianglePoints() As PointF =
            {
                New PointF(xmid, e.MarginBounds.Top),
                New PointF(e.MarginBounds.Left, e.MarginBounds.Bottom),
                New PointF(e.MarginBounds.Right, e.MarginBounds.Bottom)
            }
            Using thePen As New Pen(Color.Red, 10)
                e.Graphics.DrawPolygon(thePen, trianglePoints)
            End Using

        Case 1 ' Draw a rectangle.
            Using thePen As New Pen(Color.Blue, 10)
                e.Graphics.DrawRectangle(thePen, e.MarginBounds)
            End Using

        Case 2 ' Draw an ellipse.
            Using thePen As New Pen(Color.Green, 10)
                e.Graphics.DrawEllipse(thePen, e.MarginBounds)
            End Using

        Case 3 ' Draw a diamond.
            Dim diamondPoints() As PointF =
            {
                New PointF(xmid, e.MarginBounds.Top),
                New PointF(e.MarginBounds.Right, ymid),
                New PointF(xmid, e.MarginBounds.Bottom),
                New PointF(e.MarginBounds.Left, ymid)
            }
            Using thePen As New Pen(Color.Black, 10)
                e.Graphics.DrawPolygon(thePen, diamondPoints)
            End Using
    End Select

    NextPageNum += 1
    If (NextPageNum > 3) Then
        ' This is the last page. Start over if we print again.
        e.HasMorePages = False
```

```
        NextPageNum = 0
    Else
        ' We have more pages.
        e.HasMorePages = True
    End If
End Sub
```

The NextPageNum variable stores the number of the next page for the program to print.

The event handler uses a Select Case statement to determine which shape it should draw. Depending on the page number, it uses the e.Graphics object's DrawPolygon, DrawRectangle, or DrawEllipse method to draw different shapes.

The code uses different Pen objects to draw the various shapes. For example, it draws the triangle with a 10-pixel-wide red pen. The Using statements automatically dispose of the Pens' resources when the program is done with them.

After it draws the current page's shape, the program increments NextPageNum. If the new page number is greater than 3, the program has finished drawing all of the pages (there are 4 of them, numbered starting with 0), so it sets e.HasMorePages to False. It also resets NextPageNum to 0 so the program starts over the next time you click one of the buttons.

If the next page number is not greater than 3, then the program has more pages to print, so it sets e.HasMorePages to True.

The following code shows how the program displays print previews and generates printouts:

```
' Display a print preview.
Private Sub btnPreview_Click() Handles btnPreview.Click
    ppdShapes.ShowDialog()
End Sub

' Print to the default printer.
Private Sub btnPrint_Click() Handles btnPrint.Click
    pdocShapes.Print()
End Sub
```

Unfortunately, there isn't room in this lesson to really get into the drawing routines that you use to generate fancier printouts. For a more complete introduction to graphics programming in Visual Basic, see my PDF-format Wrox Blox Visual Basic Graphics Programming *available at* www.wrox.com/WileyCDA/WroxTitle/ Visual-Basic-Graphics-Programming.productCd-0470343486.html.

Drawing Text

The PrintShapes program described in the preceding section demonstrates the basic techniques you need to print. It uses a PrintPage event handler to draw different shapes on four pages of a printout.

You can print text in much the same way you print shapes. The only real difference is that to draw text you use the e.Graphics object's DrawString method instead of one of the other Graphics methods such as DrawPolygon or DrawEllipse.

Example program PrintText (available as part of this lesson's code download) uses the following code to print a series of names on a single page:

```
' Print some text on one page.
Private Sub pdocShapes_PrintPage(ByVal sender As System.Object,
 ByVal e As System.Drawing.Printing.PrintPageEventArgs) _
 Handles pdocText.PrintPage
    ' Make a font to use.
    Using theFont As New Font("Times New Roman", 20)
        ' Get the coordinates for the first line.
        Dim x As Integer = e.MarginBounds.Left
        Dim y As Integer = e.MarginBounds.Top

        ' Print some text.
        Dim names() As String =
        {
            "Arsenal", "Burnley", "Chelsea", "Liverpool",
            "Man City", "Portsmouth", "Tottenham", "Wigan"
        }
        For Each name As String In names
            ' Print the name.
            e.Graphics.DrawString(name, theFont, Brushes.Black, x, y)

            ' Move down for the next line.
            y += 30
        Next name
    End Using

    ' We only have one page.
    e.HasMorePages = False
End Sub
```

The program first creates a large font to use when drawing text. It uses a Using statement to dispose of the font's resources when the program is done with it.

Next the code sets variables x and y to the coordinates where the first name should appear. In this example, the program displays the first line in the upper-left corner of the page's margin bounds.

The program then loops through an array of names. For each name, the program uses the e.Graphics object's DrawString method to draw the name. It then adds 30 to the variable y so the next name is printed farther down the page.

TRY IT

In this Try It, you build a program that prints and displays a preview of the table shown in Figure 33-2. You build an array of Student objects and then loop through them displaying their values as shown in the figure.

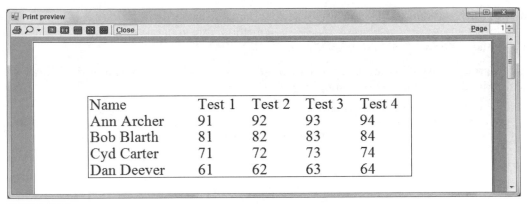

FIGURE 33-2

 You can download the code and resources for this Try It from the book's web page at www.wrox.com *or* www.vb-helper.com/24hourvb.html. *You can find them in the Lesson33 folder of the download.*

Lesson Requirements

In this lesson:

➤ Start a new project and create the program's main form. Add `PrintDocument` and `PrintPreviewDialog` components to do the printing and previewing.

➤ Add appropriate event handlers to the Preview and Print buttons.

➤ Add a `Student` class with `FirstName` and `LastName` properties. Also give it a `TestScores` property that is an array of integers.

➤ Create the `PrintPage` event handler.

➤ Create an array of `Student` objects. Initialize them using array and object initializers.

➤ Loop through the `Student` objects, printing them using code similar to the code used by the PrintText example program described earlier.

➤ Draw a rectangle around the table.

Hints

➤ Don't forget to set the `PrintPreviewDialog`'s `Document` property to the `PrintDocument` component.

➤ This example doesn't do anything fancy with properties so they can be auto-implemented.

➤ It might help to define variables x0, x1, and so on to keep track of where each column should begin.

Step-by-Step

➤ Start a new project and create the program's main form. Add `PrintDocument` and `PrintPreviewDialog` components to do the printing and previewing.

1. This is reasonably straightforward.

➤ Add appropriate event handlers to the Preview and Print buttons.

1. Use code similar to the following:

```
' Display a print preview.
Private Sub btnPreview_Click() Handles btnPreview.Click
    ppdTable.ShowDialog()
End Sub

' Print to the default printer.
Private Sub btnPrint_Click() Handles btnPrint.Click
    pdocTable.Print()
End Sub
```

➤ Add a `Student` class with `FirstName` and `LastName` properties. Also give it a `TestScores` property that is an array of integers.

1. Use code similar to the following:

```
Public Class Student
    Public Property FirstName As String
    Public Property LastName As String
    Public Property TestScores As Integer()
End Class
```

➤ Create the `PrintPage` event handler.

  ➤ Create an array of `Student` objects. Initialize them using array and object initializers.

  ➤ Loop through the Student objects, printing them using code similar to the code used by the PrintText example program described earlier.

  ➤ Draw a rectangle around the table.

1. Use code similar to the following:

```
' Print the table.
Private Sub pdocTable_PrintPage(ByVal sender As System.Object,
ByVal e As System.Drawing.Printing.PrintPageEventArgs) _
Handles pdocTable.PrintPage
    ' Make some data.
    Dim students() As Student =
    {
        New Student() With {.FirstName = "Ann",
            .LastName = "Archer",
            .TestScores = {91, 92, 93, 94}},
        New Student() With {.FirstName = "Bob",
            .LastName = "Blarth",
            .TestScores = {81, 82, 83, 84}},
        New Student() With {.FirstName = "Cyd",
```

```vbnet
                    .LastName = "Carter",
                    .TestScores = {71, 72, 73, 74}},
                New Student() With {.FirstName = "Dan",
                    .LastName = "Deever",
                    .TestScores = {61, 62, 63, 64}}
        }

        ' Get the coordinates for the first row and the columns.
        Dim y As Integer = e.MarginBounds.Top
        Dim x0 As Integer = e.MarginBounds.Left
        Dim x1 As Integer = x0 + 200
        Dim x2 As Integer = x1 + 100
        Dim x3 As Integer = x2 + 100
        Dim x4 As Integer = x3 + 100

        ' Make a font to use.
        Using theFont As New Font("Times New Roman", 20)
            ' Draw column headers.
            e.Graphics.DrawString("Name", theFont, Brushes.Black, x0, y)
            e.Graphics.DrawString("Test 1", theFont, Brushes.Black, x1, y)
            e.Graphics.DrawString("Test 2", theFont, Brushes.Black, x2, y)
            e.Graphics.DrawString("Test 3", theFont, Brushes.Black, x3, y)
            e.Graphics.DrawString("Test 4", theFont, Brushes.Black, x4, y)

            ' Move Y down for the first row.
            y += 30

            ' Loop through the Students displaying their data.
            For Each aStudent As Student In students
                ' Display the Student's values.
                e.Graphics.DrawString(aStudent.FirstName & " " &
                    aStudent.LastName, theFont, Brushes.Black, x0, y)
                e.Graphics.DrawString(aStudent.TestScores(0).ToString(),
                    theFont, Brushes.Black, x1, y)
                e.Graphics.DrawString(aStudent.TestScores(1).ToString(),
                    theFont, Brushes.Black, x2, y)
                e.Graphics.DrawString(aStudent.TestScores(2).ToString(),
                    theFont, Brushes.Black, x3, y)
                e.Graphics.DrawString(aStudent.TestScores(3).ToString(),
                    theFont, Brushes.Black, x4, y)

                ' Move Y down for the next row.
                y += 30
            Next aStudent
        End Using

        ' Draw a box around it all.
        e.Graphics.DrawRectangle(Pens.Black,
            x0, e.MarginBounds.Top,
            x4 - x0 + 100,
            y - e.MarginBounds.Top)

        ' We're only printing one page.
        e.HasMorePages = False
End Sub
```

Please select Lesson 33 on the DVD to view the video that accompanies this lesson.

EXERCISES

1. Copy the program you built in this lesson's Try It and add additional drawing code to produce the result shown in Figure 33-3.

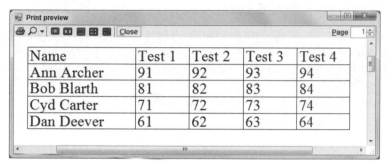

FIGURE 33-3

2. Make a program that prints a bar chart similar to the one shown in Figure 33-4.

3. Copy the program you built for Lesson 21's Try It (or download the version available on the book's web site) and add a File menu with Print Preview and Print commands. Figure 33-5 shows the program displaying a print preview.

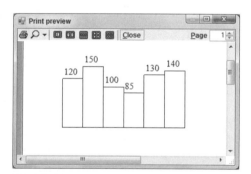

FIGURE 33-4

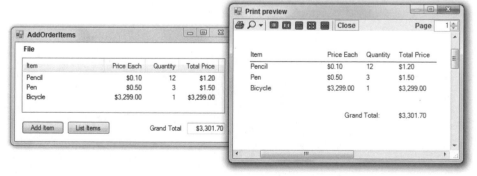

FIGURE 33-5

Hints:

➤ Make a column widths array to hold the columns' widths, and loop through the ListView's Columns collection to set them.

➤ Loop through the Columns collection to draw column headers, using the columns widths array to determine how much room each header needs.

➤ Loop through the ListView's Items collection. For each item, loop through its SubItems collection to print the sub-items, using the columns widths array to determine how much room each sub-item needs.

➤ Finish by displaying the grand total.

 You can find solutions to this lesson's exercises in the Lesson33 folder inside the download available on the book's web site at www.wrox.com *or* www.vb-helper .com/24hourvb.html.

34

Using the Clipboard

Earlier lessons have explained how your program interacts with the user (through controls), the file system, and most recently the printer. This lesson explains how your program can interact with other programs via the clipboard.

In this lesson, you learn how to place text, image, and other data on the clipboard so you can paste it into other applications. You also learn how to receive data pasted into your program from the clipboard.

ADDING DATA TO THE CLIPBOARD

Adding data to the clipboard is fairly easy. The `Clipboard` class provides several static methods to place certain kinds of data on the clipboard. Table 34-1 summarizes those methods.

TABLE 34-1

METHOD	PURPOSE
SetAudio	Copies an audio stream to the clipboard
SetFileDropList	Copies a list of files to the clipboard as if the user had selected them in Windows Explorer and pressed [Ctrl]+C
SetImage	Copies an image to the clipboard
SetText	Copies a string to the clipboard

Example program AddToClipboard, shown in Figure 34-1 and included as part of this lesson's code download, demonstrates these methods. Use the Copy buttons to copy the corresponding content on the left to the clipboard. (When the program starts, it copies the names of the files in its startup directory into the list box. The bottom image represents an audio file.)

FIGURE 34-1

The program uses the following code to copy data to the clipboard:

```
' Copy the text to the clipboard.
' Then manually try pasting into Word, WordPad, etc.
Private Sub btnCopyText_Click() Handles btnCopyText.Click
    Clipboard.SetText(txtData.Text)
    System.Media.SystemSounds.Beep.Play()
End Sub


' Copy the picture to the clipboard.
' Then try pasting into Word, Paint, etc.
Private Sub btnCopyPicture_Click() Handles btnCopyPicture.Click
    Clipboard.SetImage(picData.Image)
    System.Media.SystemSounds.Beep.Play()
End Sub

' Copy the picture to the clipboard.
' Then try pasting into ReadFromClipboard.
Private Sub btnCopyFiles_Click() Handles btnCopyFiles.Click
    ' Make a StringCollection holding the file names.
    Dim files As New StringCollection()
    For Each filename As String In lstFiles.Items
        files.Add(filename)
    Next filename

    ' Save the list to the clipboard.
    Clipboard.SetFileDropList(files)

    System.Media.SystemSounds.Beep.Play()
End Sub

' Copy some audio to the clipboard.
Private Sub btnCopyAudio_Click() Handles btnCopyAudio.Click
    Clipboard.SetAudio(My.Resources.boing)
```

```
    Using player As New SoundPlayer(My.Resources.boing)
        player.Play()
    End Using
End Sub
```

The text and image copying event handlers are straightforward. They simply use the appropriate `Clipboard` method to copy data to the clipboard and then play the system's beep sound.

The file list copying button builds a `StringCollection`, adds the files in the list box to it, and calls the `Clipboard`'s `SetFileDropList`. (You might prefer to use a `List(Of String)` for a list of file names but the `SetFileDropList` method requires a `StringCollection` parameter.)

 The `StringCollection` *class is in the* `System.Collections.Specialized` *namespace, so the program includes an* `Imports` *directive (in code not shown here) to make using the class easier.*

The audio copying button copies an audio resource to the clipboard.

 To add an audio resource to the project at design time:

1. Open the Project menu and select Properties at the bottom.

2. Click the Resources tab.

3. Click the Add Resource drop-down arrow at the top of the page and select Add Existing File.

4. Select the audio file that you want to add to the project and click Open.

The audio copying button calls the `Clipboard`'s `SetAudio` method, passing it the audio resource. Then, instead of playing the system's beep sound, the program creates a `SoundPlayer` associated with the audio resource and calls the player's `Play` method.

 The `SoundPlayer` *class is in the* `System.Media` *namespace, so the program includes an* `Imports` *directive (in code not shown here) to make using the class easier.*

 Programs that accept audio pasted from the clipboard are uncommon. To test this program's ability to copy audio to the clipboard, you can use the ReadFromClipboard *example program described in the following section.*

GETTING DATA FROM THE CLIPBOARD

Getting data from the clipboard is just as easy as putting it there because the Clipboard class provides static methods that return audio streams, file drop lists, images, and text.

Before you try to copy data from the clipboard, however, you should make sure the data you want is present. To do that, the Clipboard class also provides a set of functions that tell you whether data in a given format is available.

For example, the following code checks whether text is available on the clipboard; if so, it copies the text into the textbox named txtData:

```
If Clipboard.ContainsText() Then txtData.Text = Clipboard.GetText()
```

The ReadFromClipboard example program (included in this lesson's code download) uses the following code to paste audio, file drop lists, images, or text from the clipboard:

```
' Paste whatever data is available from the clipboard.
Private Sub btnPaste_Click() Handles btnPaste.Click
    ' Clear previous results.
    txtData.Clear()
    lstFiles.Items.Clear()
    picData.Image = Nothing

    ' Paste the text if available.
    If Clipboard.ContainsText() Then txtData.Text = Clipboard.GetText()

    ' Paste the picture if available.
    If Clipboard.ContainsImage() Then picData.Image = Clipboard.GetImage()

    ' Paste file drop list if available.
    If Clipboard.ContainsFileDropList() Then
        Dim files As StringCollection = Clipboard.GetFileDropList()
        For Each filename As String In files
            lstFiles.Items.Add(filename)
        Next filename
    End If

    ' Paste audio if available.
    If Clipboard.ContainsAudio() Then
        Using player As New SoundPlayer(Clipboard.GetAudioStream())
            player.Play()
        End Using
    End If

    ' Make the form big enough to show the image.
    Me.ClientSize = New Size(Me.ClientSize.Width, picData.Bottom + 8)
End Sub
```

The code starts by clearing its current text, file list, and image. It then copies whatever data is available from the clipboard.

If the program finds audio content is available, it makes a `SoundPlayer` associated with the audio stream provided by the clipboard and plays it.

TRY IT

In this Try It, you create a program that backs up files. The program contains a button and a textbox where you can enter a directory name. When you click the button, the program copies any files in the clipboard's file drop list into the backup directory, adding a numeric version number at the end.

> *You can download the code and resources for this Try It from the book's web page at* www.wrox.com *or* www.vb-helper.com/24hourvb.html. *You can find them in the Lesson34 folder of the download.*

Lesson Requirements

In this lesson:

➤ Start a new project and add a textbox and button.

➤ When the user clicks the button, see if the clipboard contains a file drop list. If it does:

  ➤ Use the value in the textbox to create a `DirectoryInfo` object. Create the directory if necessary.

  ➤ For each file in the drop list, make a `FileInfo` object. Try adding 001, 002, 003, and so on to the file's name and see if there's already a file with that name in the backup directory. When you find a filename that isn't already in use, copy the file using that name.

Hints

➤ Use `Path.Combine` to combine the directory's path and the file's name.

➤ Don't try to copy a file to a new name and catch an error if it fails. Use `File.Exists` to see if the new file exists before you try to copy there.

Step-by-Step

➤ Start a new project and add a textbox and button.

  1. This is straightforward.

➤ When the user clicks the button, see if the clipboard contains a file drop list. If it does:

   ➤ Use the value in the textbox to create a `DirectoryInfo` object. Create the directory if necessary.

   ➤ For each file in the drop list, make a `FileInfo` object. Try adding 001, 002, 003, and so on to the file's name and see if there's already a file with that name in the backup directory. When you find a filename that isn't already in use, copy the file using that name.

1. Use code similar to the following:

```
' Back up any files listed on the clipboard's file drop list.
Private Sub btnBackup_Click() Handles btnBackup.Click
    If Clipboard.ContainsFileDropList() Then
        ' Get the backup directory.
        Dim dirInfo As New DirectoryInfo(txtDirectory.Text)

        ' Create the directory if necessary.
        dirInfo.Create()

        ' Process the files.
        For Each filename As String In Clipboard.GetFileDropList()
            Dim info As New FileInfo(filename)

            ' Add a version number to the end.
            ' Keep trying until we find one that isn't
            ' already there.
            Dim i As Integer = 1
            Do
                ' Compose a file name in the backup directory
                ' with the file's name and the version number.
                Dim newFileName As String =
                    Path.Combine(dirInfo.FullName, info.Name) &
                    "." & i.ToString("000")

                ' See if this file exists.
                If (Not File.Exists(newFileName)) Then
                    ' Copy the file here.
                    info.CopyTo(newFileName)

                    ' Exit the Do loop.
                    Exit Do
                End If
                i += 1
            Loop
        Next filename

        MessageBox.Show("Backed up " &
            Clipboard.GetFileDropList().Count & " files")
    End If
End Sub
```

Please select Lesson 34 on the DVD to view the video that accompanies this lesson.

EXERCISES

1. Copy the ReadFromClipboard application available on the book's web site and modify it so it pastes data when you press [Ctrl]+V.

Hints: Move the code that does the pasting into a new `PasteAvailableData` subroutine. Set the form's `KeyPreview` property to `True`. Then use code similar to the following to determine when the user presses Ctrl+[V]. Notice that the code sets `e.Handled = True` to indicate that the key press can be discarded after the event handler is done with it.

```
' If the user pressed Ctrl+V, paste data from the clipboard.
Private Sub Form1_KeyDown(ByVal sender As Object,
  ByVal e As System.Windows.Forms.KeyEventArgs) Handles Me.KeyDown
    If (e.Control AndAlso e.KeyCode = Keys.V) Then
        PasteAvailableData()
        e.Handled = True
    End If
End Sub
```

2. The clipboard can contain several different kinds of text. Overloaded versions of the `ContainsText` and `GetText` methods take a `TextDataFormat` parameter that indicates the kind of text you want.

Build a program with two `TextBox`es and a `RichTextBox`. When the user clicks a button or presses [Ctrl]+V, see what kind of text is available and paste plain text into one `TextBox`, HTML text into the other, and rich text format (RTF) text into the `RichTextBox`. Test the program by pasting text copied from programs such as Microsoft Word and WordPad.

 You can find solutions to this lesson's exercises in the Lesson34 folder inside the download available on the book's web site at www.wrox.com *or* www.vb-helper .com/24hourvb.html.

35

Providing Drag and Drop

In some ways, drag and drop performs the same task as the clipboard. Both enable one application to give data to another. The difference is that the clipboard saves data for later delivery, whereas drag and drop delivers the data immediately and is done.

In this lesson, you learn how to add drag and drop to your program so it can interact with other applications.

UNDERSTANDING DRAG AND DROP EVENTS

There are two participants in a drag and drop operation: a *drag source* and a *drop target*.

➤ The **drag source** initiates a drag — for example, when you right-click it. It determines what data is in the drag and what kinds of operations are allowed on the drag, such as a copy or move.

➤ The **drop target** is a potential recipient of a drag's data. When the drag moves over it, the target can decide whether it can accept the data in an offered operation such as copy or move.

To handle all of the potential interactions among the drag source, the drop target, and the user, you can use several event handlers. Some of these events occur in the drag source and others occur in the drop target.

Table 35-1 summarizes the key drag source events.

TABLE 35-1

EVENT	PURPOSE
GiveFeedback	The drag has entered a valid drop target. The source can indicate the type of drop allowed. For example, it might allow Copy if the target is a Label and allow Move or Copy if the target is a TextBox.
QueryContinueDrag	The keyboard or mouse button state has changed. For example, the user may have pressed or released the [Ctrl] key. The drag source can determine whether to continue the drag, cancel the drag, or drop the data immediately.

The drop target has more events than the drag source. The drag source merely provides data. The drop target can provide a lot more interaction to tell the user what it can do with the data.

Table 35-2 describes the events received by a drop target when data is dragged over it.

TABLE 35-2

EVENT	PURPOSE
DragEnter	The drag is entering the target. The target can examine the type of data available and set e.Effect to indicate the types of drops it can handle. It can also display some sort of highlight to tell the user that it can accept the data and where it might land.
DragLeave	The drag has left the target. The target should remove any highlighting or other hints that it displayed in DragEnter.
DragOver	The drag is over the target. This event continues to fire a few times per second until the drag leaves. For example, the target could change its appearance to show exactly where the data would land if dropped. It can also check things such as the keyboard state — for example, it might allow a Copy if the [Ctrl] key is pressed, and a Move otherwise.
DragDrop	The user dropped the data on the target, so the target should process it.

STARTING A DRAG

Starting a drag is fairly easy. First create an instance of the DataObject class to indicate the type of data being dragged and to hold the data itself. Then simply call a control's DoDrag method, passing it the DataObject.

The DragSource example program (available in this lesson's code download) uses the following code to start dragging text when you press the right mouse button down over its `lblDrag` control:

```
' Start a drag.
Private Sub lblDrag_MouseDown(ByVal sender As System.Object,
 ByVal e As System.Windows.Forms.MouseEventArgs) Handles lblDrag.MouseDown
    ' If it's not the right mouse button, do nothing.
    If e.Button <> MouseButtons.Right Then Return

    ' Make the data object.
    Dim data As New DataObject(DataFormats.Text, lblDrag.Text)

    ' Start the drag allowing only copy.
    lblDrag.DoDragDrop(data, DragDropEffects.Copy)
End Sub
```

The code first checks whether the right mouse button is pressed, and exits if it is not. It then creates a `DataObject`. It passes the object's constructor the value `DataFormats.Text` to indicate that it will hold text data, and the text that the object should hold.

Finally, the code calls the `Label` control's `DoDrag` method, passing it the `DataObject` and the value `DragDropEffects.Copy` to indicate that the drag allows only the copy operation.

This example doesn't bother with the `GiveFeedback` and `QueryContinueDrag` event handlers, so that's the extent of its participation in the drag.

> *The* `DoDrag` *function returns a* `DragDropEffects` *value that indicates what the drop target did with the data. For example, if the function returns* `DragDropEffects.Move`, *then the user is performing a Move operation, so the drag source should remove the data from its application. For example, a file explorer such as Windows Explorer would remove the file from the source location and move it to the drop location.*

Note that a drag is completely separate from the drop target. If a drop target can accept the data, it is free to do so. That means you don't need to wait until you read about the DropTarget example program described in the next section to test the DragSource program. You can test the program right now by using it to drag text data into Word, WordPad, or any other program that accepts dropped text. (Notepad doesn't know how to accept dropped text.)

CATCHING A DROP

Before a control can accept a drop, you must set its `AllowDrop` property to `True`. If `AllowDrop` is `False`, the control will not allow drops no matter what event handlers you create.

The only other thing a drop target must do is provide `DragEnter` and `DragDrop` event handlers.

The `DragEnter` event handler should examine the data available and set the event handler's `e.Effect` parameter to indicate whether it wants to allow the drop. The drag and drop system automatically changes the mouse cursor to indicate the kind of drop the target allows.

The DropTarget example program (available in this lesson's code download) uses the following `DragEnter` event handler:

```
' A drag entered. See if text is available.
Private Sub lblDrop_DragEnter(ByVal sender As Object,
 ByVal e As System.Windows.Forms.DragEventArgs) Handles lblDrop.DragEnter
    ' Allow text data.
    If e.Data.GetDataPresent(DataFormats.Text) Then
        ' Only allow the Copy operation.
        e.Effect = DragDropEffects.Copy
    End If
End Sub
```

This code checks whether the drag contains text data and, if it does, sets `e.Effect` to allow the Copy operation.

 The `DragEnter` *event handler's* `e.Effect` *parameter has the value* `DragDropEffects.None` *by default, so you don't need to set it if you want to prevent a drop. In the DropTarget example program, if no text is available, the program doesn't allow any kind of drop operation.*

The `DragDrop` event handler should use its `e.Data` parameter to see what data is available and to get it. It should then set `e.Effect` to indicate what operation it performed, such as Copy or Move so the drag source knows what happened to the data.

The DropTarget example program uses the following `DragDrop` event handler:

```
' Accept dropped data.
Private Sub lblDrop_DragDrop(ByVal sender As Object,
 ByVal e As System.Windows.Forms.DragEventArgs) Handles lblDrop.DragDrop
    ' Get the dropped data.
    If e.Data.GetDataPresent(DataFormats.Text) Then
        lblDrop.Text = e.Data.GetData(DataFormats.Text).ToString()

        ' Indicate that we copied.
        e.Effect = DragDropEffects.Copy
    End If
End Sub
```

This code checks for text data. If text is available, the code gets it and displays it in a label. It also sets `e.Effect = DragDropEffects.Copy` to tell the drag source that the target performed a Copy operation.

Note that accepting a drop is completely separate from the drag. If data is available in a format that your program can use, you are free to use it. In this case, that means you don't need to use the DragSource example program described in the previous section to test the DropTarget example program. You can also drag text from Word, WordPad, or any other program that knows how to start dragging text. (Notepad doesn't know how to start a drag.)

TRY IT

In this Try It, you elaborate on the DragSource and DropTarget example programs. You modify DragSource so it allows Copy or Move operations.

You make DropTarget perform Copy or Move operations depending on whether the [Ctrl] key is pressed during the drop. You also provide feedback if the user changes the state of the [Ctrl] key during the drag.

> *You can download the code and resources for this Try It from the book's web page at* www.wrox.com *or* www.vb-helper.com/24hourvb.html. *You can find them in the Lesson35 folder of the download.*

Lesson Requirements

In this lesson:

➤ Copy the DragSource and DropTarget example programs into new directories.

➤ In DragSource, allow Copy and Move operations. Check the result of DoDragDrop and if the operation was a Move, remove the text from the source Label control.

➤ In DropTarget, make the DragEnter event handler allow Copy and Move operations.

➤ In DropTarget, add a DragOver event handler. The value e.KeyState And 8 is nonzero if the [Ctrl] key is pressed. If [Ctrl] is pressed, allow Copy. If [Ctrl] is not pressed, allow Move.

➤ In DropTarget, make the DragDrop event handler check the state of the [Ctrl] key just as DragOver does. If [Ctrl] is pressed, tell the drag source that the operation is a Copy. If [Ctrl] is not pressed, tell the drag source that the operation is a Move.

Hints

➤ To make DragSource allow either Move or Copy operations, use DragDropEffects.Copy Or DragDropEffects.Move.

➤ Similarly to make DropTarget allow either Move or Copy operations, use DragDropEffects.Copy Or DragDropEffects.Move.

➤ Don't use the magic number 8; use a constant instead. What scope do you need to give the constant to enable the DragOver and DragDrop event handlers to see it?

Step-by-Step

➤ Copy the DragSource and DropTarget example programs into new directories.

1. This is straightforward.

➤ In DragSource, allow Copy and Move operations. Check the result of DoDragDrop and if the operation was a Move, remove the text from the source Label control.

1. Pass the DoDragDrop function the parameter DragDropEffects.Copy Or DragDropEffects.Move for the allowed operations.

2. Check the result returned by DoDragDrop. If the result is DragDropEffects.Move, clear the Label control.

3. The code should look something like this:

```
' Start a drag.
Private Sub lblDrag_MouseDown(ByVal sender As System.Object,
  ByVal e As System.Windows.Forms.MouseEventArgs) _
  Handles lblDrag.MouseDown
    ' If it's not the right mouse button, do nothing.
    If e.Button <> MouseButtons.Right Then Return

    ' Make the data object.
    Dim data As New DataObject(DataFormats.Text, lblDrag.Text)

    ' Start the drag allowing only copy.
    If lblDrag.DoDragDrop(data, DragDropEffects.Copy Or
        DragDropEffects.Move) = DragDropEffects.Move _
    Then
        ' It's a move. Remove the data from here.
        lblDrag.Text = ""
    End If
End Sub
```

➤ In DropTarget, make the DragEnter event handler allow Copy and Move operations.

1. In the DragEnter event handler, if text data is available, set e.Effect = DragDropEffects.Copy Or DragDropEffects.Move to allow both Copy and Move operations. The code should look something like this:

```
' A drag entered. See if text is available.
Private Sub lblDrop_DragEnter(ByVal sender As Object,
  ByVal e As System.Windows.Forms.DragEventArgs) _
  Handles lblDrop.DragEnter
    ' Allow text data.
    If e.Data.GetDataPresent(DataFormats.Text) Then
        ' Only allow the Copy operation.
        e.Effect = DragDropEffects.Copy Or DragDropEffects.Move
    End If
End Sub
```

➤ In DropTarget, add a `DragOver` event handler. The value `e.KeyState And 8` is nonzero if the [Ctrl] key is pressed. If [Ctrl] is pressed, allow Copy. If [Ctrl] is not pressed, allow Move.

1. Add the `DragOver` event handler. If [Ctrl] is pressed, set `e.Effect = DragDropEffects.Copy`. If [Ctrl] is not pressed, set `e.Effect = DragDropEffects.Move`.

```
' The numeric code for Ctrl.
Private Const KeyCtrl As Integer = 8

' Provide feedback. Allow Copy if Ctrl is pressed.
' Otherwise allow Move.
Private Sub lblDrop_DragOver(ByVal sender As Object, _
 ByVal e As System.Windows.Forms.DragEventArgs) _
 Handles lblDrop.DragOver
    ' See if the Ctrl key is pressed.
    If (e.KeyState And KeyCtrl) <> 0 Then
        ' The Ctrl key is pressed. Allow Copy.
        e.Effect = DragDropEffects.Copy
    Else
        ' The Ctrl key is not pressed. Allow Move.
        e.Effect = DragDropEffects.Move
    End If
End Sub
```

➤ In DropTarget, make the `DragDrop` event handler check the state of the [Ctrl] key just as `DragOver` does. If [Ctrl] is pressed, tell the drag source that the operation is a Copy. If [Ctrl] is not pressed, tell the drag source that the operation is a Move.

1. Display the data as before.

2. Determine whether Ctrl is pressed. If [Ctrl] is pressed, set `e.Effect = DragDropEffects.Copy`. If [Ctrl] is not pressed, set `e.Effect = DragDropEffects.Move`.

```
' Accept dropped data.
Private Sub lblDrop_DragDrop(ByVal sender As Object, _
 ByVal e As System.Windows.Forms.DragEventArgs) _
 Handles lblDrop.DragDrop
    ' Get the dropped data.
    If e.Data.GetDataPresent(DataFormats.Text) Then
        lblDrop.Text = e.Data.GetData(DataFormats.Text).ToString()

        ' See if the Ctrl key is pressed.
        If (e.KeyState And KeyCtrl) <> 0 Then
            ' The Ctrl key is pressed. We did a Copy.
            e.Effect = DragDropEffects.Copy
        Else
            ' The Ctrl key is not pressed. We did a Move.
            e.Effect = DragDropEffects.Move
        End If
    End If
End Sub
```

Please select Lesson 35 on the DVD to view the video that accompanies this lesson.

EXERCISES

1.   Copy this lesson's Try It (both the DragSource and DropTarget programs). Modify the DropTarget program in these ways:

➤   Add a `ListBox` named `lstFormats`. In the program's `DragEnter` event handler, loop through the string array returned by `e.Data.GetFormats` and list the available formats in the `ListBox`.

➤   In the `DragEnter` event handler, allow the Copy operation for the `Text` and `FileDrop` types of data.

➤   Add a `DragLeave` event handler that clears `formatsListBox`.

➤   In the `DragDrop` event handler, display text in a `TextBox` as before. If the dropped data is a `FileDrop`, it is an array of strings. Loop through the array and display the dropped filenames in a `ListBox` named `lstFiles`. Test this feature by dragging files from Windows Explorer onto the program.

2.   Copy the program you built for the Try It in Lesson 34 (or download Lesson 34's version from the book's web site). Add the capability to accept a dropped file list instead of only getting a file list from the clipboard.

Hint: Don't forget to set the `AllowDrop` property to `True`.

Hint: It would be nice to move the code that backs up the files into a new `BackupFiles` function so you could call it for a file list taken from the clipboard or from drag and drop. Unfortunately, the clipboard's file list is a `StringCollection`, but drag and drop's file list is an array of strings. Because they have different data types, you cannot make `BackupFiles` handle them both easily.

To solve this problem, make `BackupFiles` take a `filenames` parameter of the nongeneric interface type `IList`. The clipboard data implements this interface, so you can simply pass it to `BackupFiles`. To pass the drag and drop data to `BackupFiles`, convert the file list to an array of strings, which also implements `IList`.

 You can find solutions to this lesson's exercises in the Lesson35 folder inside the download available on the book's web site at www.wrox.com *or* www.vb-helper .com/24hourvb.html.

SECTION VI
Specialized Topics

The lessons so far have dealt with general programming topics. For example, every desktop application needs to use controls, and most also need to use variables, classes, and files.

The lessons in this section explain more specialized topics. Although they describe ideas and techniques that you won't need for every program you write, you will still find them useful under many circumstances.

▶ **LESSON 36:** Using the My Namespace

▶ **LESSON 37:** Localizing Programs

▶ **LESSON 38:** Manipulating Data with LINQ to Objects

▶ **LESSON 39:** Manipulating Databases with the Entity Framework

36

Using the My Namespace

The .NET Framework is huge, containing thousands of classes that provide all sorts of useful features. To make finding things easier, the Framework is arranged in hierarchical groups called *namespaces*. For example, the System.Drawing namespace contains classes such as Pen, Brush, and Graphics that deal with drawing.

The My namespace is slightly different. It provides shortcuts to make performing common tasks easier. You can achieve many of the same results by using tools in other parts of the .NET Framework. My just gives you another, often easier way to find and use those tools.

In this lesson, you learn about the My namespace. After learning what tools it provides, you get to practice using some of the most useful of them.

MY SUB-NAMESPACES

The My namespace only contains tools for performing common tasks but the list of common tasks is big enough that finding what you need could be difficult. To make finding things within the My namespace easier, it is divided into the sub-namespaces summarized in Table 36-1.

TABLE 36-1

SUB-NAMESPACE	PROVIDES TOOLS TO WORK WITH:
Application	The current application
Computer	The computer's software and hardware
Forms	Default instances of the application's forms
Resources	Application resources such as pictures or sound files
Settings	Program settings

continues

TABLE 36-1 *(continued)*

SUB-NAMESPACE	PROVIDES TOOLS TO WORK WITH:
User	The user
WebServices	Any Web Services used by the application (Web Services are fairly advanced, so they are not covered in this book.)

The following sections provide brief overviews of the most useful of these sub-namespaces. Some of these sub-namespaces contain a lot more tools than you're likely to need any time soon, so these sections cover the most useful tools they provide.

My.Application

The My.Application namespace provides information about the current application. It includes such things as the program's current directory, culture, and splash screen.

Table 36-2 summarizes the most useful My.Application tools.

TABLE 36-2

ITEM	PURPOSE
CommandLineArgs	Returns a collection containing the application's command-line arguments
CurrentCulture	Returns information about the program's culture
DoEvents	Makes the program process any pending events in the Windows event queue. This is useful for making the user interface continue to work while the program is performing a long series of tasks.
GetEnvironmentVariable	Returns the value of an environment variable. (You can also just use the Environ function.)
Info	Returns information about the application's assembly name, copyright, version, and so forth. To set most of these values at design time, open the Project menu, select Properties, go to the Application tab, and click the Assembly Information button.
Log	Returns an object that you can use to write to the application's log file
MainForm	Gets or sets the program's main form
OpenForms	Returns a collection holding references to the program's open forms
ShutDown	This event occurs when the application is shutting down. It occurs after all forms' FormClosing and FormClosed events are finished.
Startup	This event occurs when the application is starting, before it creates any forms.

My.Computer

The My.Computer namespace enables you to interact with the computer's hardware and system software. Its Name property returns the computer's name.

Table 36-3 summarizes the most useful of the My.Computer tools.

TABLE 36-3

ITEM	PURPOSE
Audio	This object provides access to the computer's audio system. Its most useful methods are Play, which plays an audio file or stream, and PlaySystemSound, which plays a system sound.
Clipboard	Provides extra tools for manipulating the clipboard, described in Lesson 34
Clock	Returns the system's time in GMT, local time, or ticks (milliseconds) since the system started
FileSystem	Provides methods to manipulate the file system, much like the classes in the System.IO namespace do. It includes methods to create, read, write, rename, and delete files and directories. The FindInFiles method returns a collection of files that contain a particular string.
Info	Returns information about the computer, such as available memory and the operating system version
Keyboard	Indicates whether special keys such as [Alt] and [Caps Lock] are down
Mouse	Indicates whether the mouse's buttons are swapped and whether the mouse has a scroll wheel
Network	Provides a few simple properties for working with the network. The IsAvailable property tells you whether the network is available.
Ports	Enables you to manipulate the computer's serial ports
Registry	Enables you to manipulate the system registry
Screen	Provides information about the computer's screen(s)

My.Forms

The My.Forms namespace holds default instances of each of the form types defined by the application. Normally, you should use New to create new form instances and use those instead of the default instances because it's less confusing.

My.Resources

The My.Resources namespace provides access to the application's resources. You can define resources at design time by opening the Project menu, selecting Properties, and clicking the Resources tab.

After you create a resource, using it is easy. For example, if you create an image resource named StatusOk, then the following code displays that image in the PictureBox named picStatus:

```
picStatus.Image = My.Resources.StatusOk
```

My.Settings

The My.Settings namespace provides access to the application's settings. These are values that the program can change and that are saved between program runs.

For example, if you define the Top, Left, Width, and Height integer settings, then the following code saves and restores a form's size and position when it closes and loads:

```
Private Sub Form1_FormClosing() Handles Me.FormClosing
    My.Settings.Left = Me.Left
    My.Settings.Top = Me.Top
    My.Settings.Width = Me.Width
    My.Settings.Height = Me.Height
End Sub

Private Sub Form1_Load() Handles MyBase.Load
    Me.SetBounds(
        My.Settings.Left,
        My.Settings.Top,
        My.Settings.Width,
        My.Settings.Height)
End Sub
```

My.User

The My.User namespace gives information about the current user. Its most commonly used property is Name, which returns the user's name in the format domain\name.

TRY IT

In this Try It, you build the program shown in Figure 36-1 to display the computer's current network status. To build the program, you use the My.Resources and My.Computer.Network namespaces.

FIGURE 36-1

You can download the code and resources for this Try It from the book's web page at www.wrox.com *or* www.vb-helper.com/24hourvb.html. *You can find them in the Lesson36 folder of the download.*

Lesson Requirements

In this lesson:

➤ Build the program shown in Figure 36-1.

➤ Give the program resources named Happy and Sad.

➤ Write a CheckNetworkStatus subroutine to check the network's availability and display the appropriate text and image.

➤ Write an event handler to catch the My.Network.NetworkAvailabilityChanged event.

➤ In the form's Load event handler, register the event handler and call CheckNetworkStatus.

Hints

➤ The event handler should look something like this:

```
Private Sub NetworkChanged(ByVal sender As System.Object,
  ByVal e As Microsoft.VisualBasic.Devices.NetworkAvailableEventArgs)
    ...
End Sub
```

Step-by-Step

➤ Build the program shown in Figure 36-1.

   1. This is straightforward.

➤ Give the program resources named Happy and Sad.

   1. Make some images to show whether the network is available.

   2. Open the Project menu, select the Properties item, and click the Resources tab.

   3. On the Add Resources drop-down at the top of the page, click the drop-down arrow and select Add Existing File.

   4. Browse to the image files you created, select them, and click OK. (If they are in the same directory, you can select both at the same time.)

➤ Write a CheckNetworkStatus subroutine to check the network's availability and display the appropriate text and image.

   1. Use My.Computer.Network.IsAvailable to see if the network is available.

2.   Use `My.Resources` to get the resources you created.

3.   The code should look similar to the following:

```
' Indicate whether the network is available.
Private Sub CheckNetworkStatus()
    ' See if the network is available.
    If My.Computer.Network.IsAvailable Then
        ' The network is available.
        lblStatus.Text = "Up!"
        lblStatus.ForeColor = Color.Green
        picStatus.Image = My.Resources.Happy
    Else
        ' The network is not available.
        lblStatus.Text = "Down"
        lblStatus.ForeColor = Color.Red
        picStatus.Image = My.Resources.Sad
    End If
End Sub
```

➤   Write an event handler to catch the `My.Network.NetworkAvailabilityChanged` event.

1.   Use code similar to the following:

```
' Handle the My.Computer.Network.NetworkAvailabilityChanged event.
Private Sub NetworkChanged(ByVal sender As System.Object,
  ByVal e As Microsoft.VisualBasic.Devices.NetworkAvailableEventArgs)
    CheckNetworkStatus()
End Sub
```

➤   In the form's Load event handler, register the event handler and call `CheckNetworkStatus`.

Use code similar to the following:

```
' Install an event handler to catch
' My.Computer.Network.NetworkAvailabilityChanged.
Private Sub Form1_Load() Handles MyBase.Load
    ' Check the network status now.
    CheckNetworkStatus()

    ' Register an event handler so we can detect changes
    ' in network availability.
    AddHandler _
        My.Computer.Network.NetworkAvailabilityChanged,
        AddressOf NetworkChanged
End Sub
```

 Please select Lesson 36 on the DVD to view the video that accompanies this lesson.

EXERCISES

1. Make a program with three buttons labeled Fore Color, Back Color, and Font. When the user clicks a button, display an appropriate dialog from which the user can select a new foreground color, background color, or font, and apply the result to the form. Save the new values in program settings. In the form's Load event handler, load the saved values from the settings.

2. Write a program with buttons that call My.Computer.Audio.PlaySystemSound to play each of the system sounds.

3. The value My.Computer.Screen.WorkingArea is a Rectangle that indicates the location of the primary screen's desktop, not including taskbars, docked windows, and docked tool-bars. Write a program that displays a main form and four other forms of type CornerForm. Place each CornerForm so it is one of the working area's corners. Hint: Set CornerForm's StartPosition property to Manual at design time. Then use the working area to calculate where to position the forms.

 You can find solutions to this lesson's exercises in the Lesson36 folder inside the download available on the book's web site at www.wrox.com *or* www.vb-helper .com/24hourvb.html.

37

Localizing Programs

Many programmers write applications that are used only in their countries. It's easy enough to find plenty of customers for a small application without looking for long-distance customers.

However, the world has grown smaller in the past few decades, and it's common for software to spread far beyond its country of origin. Customers can download your software over the web and pay for it using online payment systems in a matter of minutes. Web applications that run in a browser are even more likely to be used by people all over the world.

With such a potentially enormous market, it makes sense in some cases to make programs accessible to people in different countries, particularly since Visual Basic and Visual Studio make it relatively easy.

In this lesson, you learn how to make a program accessible to customers in other countries with different cultures. You learn how to make multiple interfaces for a program so users can work in their own languages. You also learn how to work with values such as currency and dates that have different formats in different locales.

Localization is a huge topic so there isn't room to cover everything there is to know about it here. In particular, you should always get a native of a particular locale to help in localizing your application whenever possible. Unless you are extremely well-versed in a locale's language, customs, and idioms, it's very easy to make mistakes.

Note that I am not fluent in all of the locales that this lesson uses. I used the Babel Fish automatic translation tool at `babelfish.yahoo.com` *to make the simple translations shown here, but these are for demonstration purposes. You can use Babel Fish or a similar tool for practice and for this lesson's exercises, but you should get human help before releasing a program to users.*

UNDERSTANDING LOCALIZATION

A computer's *locale* is a setting that defines the user's language, country, and cultural settings, which determine such things as how dates and monetary values are formatted.

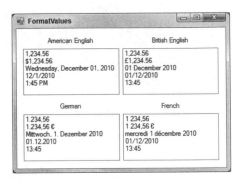

FIGURE 37-1

For example, the FormatValues example program shown in Figure 37-1 (and available in this lesson's code download) displays the same values in American, British, German, and French locales.

If you look closely at Figure 37-1, you can see that the same values produce very different results in the different locales. For example, the currency value 1234.56 is displayed variously as follows:

➤ $1,234.56

➤ £1,234.56

➤ 1.234,56€

➤ 1 234,56€

Not only do these results use different currency symbols, but they even use different decimal and thousands separators.

Globalization is the process of building an application that can be used by users from different cultures.

Localization is the process of customizing a globalized application for a specific culture.

Localizing an application involves two main steps: building a localized user interface and processing locale-specific values.

BUILDING LOCALIZED INTERFACES

At first this may seem like a daunting task. How do you build completely separate interfaces for multiple locales? Fortunately this is one thing that Visual Basic and Visual Studio do really well.

To build a globalized program, start by creating the form as usual. Add controls and set their properties as you would like them to appear by default.

After you've defined the program's default appearance, you can localize it for a particular locale. First set its Localizable property to True. Then select a new locale from the drop-down list provided by the form's Language property. Now modify the form to handle the new locale. You can change control properties such as the text they display. You can also move controls around and change their size, which is particularly important because the same text may take up a different amount of room in different languages.

At run time, the program automatically checks the computer's locale settings and picks the language that is closest. Note that many languages have several sublocales. For example, English includes the varieties used in India, Ireland, New Zealand, and more than a dozen other locales.

There's also a locale listed simply as "English." If the user's computer is set up for one of the English locales that the program doesn't support explicitly, the program falls back to the generic English locale. If the program can't support that locale either, it uses the default locale that you used when you initially created the form.

The LocalizedWeekdays example program (available in this lesson's code download) is localized for English (the form's default) and German. Figure 37-2 shows the form's English interface and Figure 37-3 shows its German interface.

FIGURE 37-2

Having the program check the computer's locale automatically at run time is convenient for the user but it makes testing different locales tricky.

One way to force the program to pick a particular locale so you can test it is to select the locale in code. You must do this before the form is initialized because after that point the form's text and other properties are already filled in and setting the locale won't reload the form.

FIGURE 37-3

To add code to select a locale before the controls are loaded, you need to give the form a new constructor. If you type Public Sub New() and press [Enter], Visual Studio creates the following default constructor for a form:

```
Public Sub New()

    ' This call is required by the designer.
    InitializeComponent()

    ' Add any initialization after the InitializeComponent() call.

End Sub
```

Now you can add code to this constructor *before* the call to InitializeComponent. The following code block shows all the code used by the LocalizedWeekdays program:

```
Public Class Form1
    Public Sub New()
        ' English.
        'My.Application.ChangeCulture("en-US")
        'My.Application.ChangeUICulture("en-US")
```

```
        ' German.
        My.Application.ChangeCulture("de-DE")
        My.Application.ChangeUICulture("de-DE")

        ' This call is required by the designer.
        InitializeComponent()

        ' Add any initialization after the InitializeComponent() call.

    End Sub
End Class
```

The code uses the `My.Application.ChangeCulture` method to change the culture the program uses for string manipulation and formatting when processing dates, currency, numbers, and other values in the code. It then uses `My.Application.ChangeUICulture` to change the culture the program uses to retrieve localized resources to build the form's user interface elements.

 For a list of more than 100 culture values that you can use in code, such as en-US and de-DE, see `msdn.microsoft.com/library/ee825488(CS.20).aspx`.

The code contains statements that set the program's locale to English or German. Comment out the one that you don't want to use for a given test.

After you finish testing a form's localized version, be sure to remove the code that selects the culture so the program can use the system's settings. Otherwise, you might end up with some very confused users.

 One trick some developers use is to give all labels and other controls nonsensical text such as Pig Latin initially. Then when you run the program it's obvious if you fail to localize a control.

Of course then you also need to localize the program for every locale that you want to support including your home locale, and if someone uses the program in an unexpected locale, they will see Pig Latin.

PROCESSING LOCALE-SPECIFIC VALUES

Within a Visual Basic program, variables are stored in American English formats. To avoid confusion, Microsoft decided to pick one locale for code values and stick with it. For example, if you're a German programmer your code still says `For Each customer As Person in Customers` and not `Für Jeden Kunde Als Person In Kunden` (or whatever it would work out to be).

When you move data in and out of the program, however, you need to be aware of the computer's locale. For example, suppose the program uses the following code to display an order's due date:

```
txtDueDate.Text = dueDate.ToString("MM/dd/yy")
```

If the date is October 31, 2011, this produces the result "10/31/11," which makes sense in the United States but should be "31/10/11" in France and "31.10.11" in Germany.

The problem is that the program uses a custom date format that is hard-coded to use an American-style date format. To produce a format appropriate for the user's system, you should use predefined date, time, and other formats whenever possible. The following code uses the standard short date format:

```
dueDateTextBox.Text = dueDate.ToString("d")
```

This produces "10/31/2011" on an American system and "31/10/2011" on a French system.

You can run into the same problem if you assume the user will enter values in a particular format. For example, suppose you want to get the whole number part of the value 1,234.56 entered by the user. If you assume the decimal separator is a period and just use whatever comes before it as the integer part, then you'll get the answer 1 when a German user enters "1.234,56"; and the program will crash when a French user enters the value "1 234.56."

To avoid this problem, use locale-aware functions such as the numeric classes' Parse methods to read values entered by the user. In this example, a good solution is to use Single.Parse to read the value and then truncate the numeric result as shown in the following code, rather than try to truncate the value while it's still in its string form:

```
Dim value As Integer = Int(Single.Parse(txtValue.Text))
```

For a list of standard numeric formats, see msdn.microsoft.com/library/ dwhawy9k(VS.100).aspx.

For a list of standard date and time formats, see msdn.microsoft.com/library/ az4se3k1(VS.100).aspx.

For more information on parsing strings, see msdn.microsoft.com/library/ b4w53z0y(VS.100).aspx.

Previous lessons have shown how to use Parse *methods to parse currency values. For example, the following statement parses a currency value entered by the user:*

```
value = Decimal.Parse(txtValue.Text, NumberStyles.Any);
```

This isn't completely foolproof. If the user has a German system but types a value in a French format, the program will fail (use TryParse *or* Try Catch *to prevent a crash), but it seems reasonable to ask a German user to enter German values.*

The LocalizedParsing example program shown in Figure 37-4 (and available in this lesson's code download) parses currency values displayed in labels in different languages, doubles the parsed decimal values, and displays the results. For each language, it selects the appropriate culture so it can parse and display the correct formats.

FIGURE 37-4

TRY IT

In this Try It, you write the program shown in Figures 37-5 and 37-6, which lets you select foreground and background colors in American English and Mexican Spanish.

FIGURE 37-5

FIGURE 37-6

You can download the code and resources for this Try It from the book's web page at www.wrox.com *or* www.vb-helper.com/24hourvb.html. *You can find them in the Lesson37 folder of the download.*

Lesson Requirements

In this lesson:

➤ Build the default interface in English.

➤ Add code to handle the RadioButtons' Click events.

➤ Localize the application for Mexican Spanish.

➤ Add code to test the form for either locale.

Hints

➤ There's no need to build a separate event handler for each RadioButton. Use one event handler for all the foreground buttons, and one event handler for all the background buttons.

➤ These event handlers must then figure out which button was clicked, but they cannot use the buttons' text because that will vary according to which locale is selected. They could use the buttons' names because they don't change, but it's even easier to store the corresponding colors' names in their `Tag` properties and then use the `Color` class's `FromName` method to get the appropriate `Color`.

Step-by-Step

➤ Build the default interface in English.

1. Build a form that looks like the one shown in Figure 37-5.

2. Store the color names (red, green, blue, and so forth) in the radio buttons' `Tag` properties.

➤ Add code to handle the `RadioButtons`' `Click` events.

1. Write an event handler similar to the following. The code converts the `sender` object into a `RadioButton` and uses its `Tag` property to get the appropriate color. It then applies that color to the form and the two `GroupBoxes`. (The `RadioButtons` inherit the colors from the form, but the `GroupBoxes` do not.)

```
' Set the foreground color.
Private Sub Foreground_Click(ByVal sender As Object,
 ByVal e As EventArgs)
    ' Get the sender as a RadioButton.
    Dim rad As RadioButton = DirectCast(sender, RadioButton)

    ' Use the color.
    Dim clr As Color = Color.FromName(rad.Tag.ToString())
    Me.ForeColor = clr
    fgGroupBox.ForeColor = clr
    bgGroupBox.ForeColor = clr
End Sub
```

2. Connect the foreground `RadioButtons` to this event handler.

3. Repeat these steps for the background `RadioButtons`.

➤ Localize the application for Mexican Spanish.

1. Set the form's `Localizable` property to `True`. Click the Language property, click the drop-down arrow to the right, and select "Spanish (Mexico)."

2. Change the form's and controls' `Text` properties so they have the values shown in Figure 37-6.

➤ Add code to test the form for either locale.

1. Use code similar to the following in the form's constructor:

```
' Select a locale for testing.
Public Sub New()
    ' English.
    'My.Application.ChangeCulture("en-US")
    'My.Application.ChangeUICulture("en-US")
```

```
' Spanish.
My.Application.ChangeCulture("es-MX")
My.Application.ChangeUICulture("es-MX")

' This call is required by the designer.
InitializeComponent()

' Add any initialization after the InitializeComponent() call.

End Sub
```

 Please select Lesson 37 on the DVD to view the video that accompanies this lesson.

EXERCISES

1. Copy this lesson's Try It and add support for Italian (it-IT), as shown in Figure 37-7. Don't forget to add code to test it.

2. When a program reads data from a file, it must use the correct locale. Download the files `Dutch.txt`, `German.txt`, and `English.txt` from the book's web site and make a program that can read them. The program should let the user select a file, check the filename to see

FIGURE 37-7

   which locale it should use, and select the correct locale. It should read and parse the values into appropriate data types and then display the values again in a `DataGridView` control.

   Hint: Use the locale name nl-NL for Dutch.

   Hint: The values within a line in the file are separated by tabs, so use `File.ReadAllLines` to get the lines, and `Split` to break each line into fields.

   The following text shows the values in the file `Dutch.txt`:

```
Potlood     € 0,10        12    € 1,20
Blocnote    € 1,10        10    € 11,00
Laptop      € 1.239,99    1     € 1.239,99
```

3. Copy the program you built for Exercise 2 and modify it so it calculates the total values instead of reading them from the files. Edit the text files to change the quantity values and remove the total values.

 You can find solutions to this lesson's exercises in the Lesson37 folder inside the download available on the book's web site at www.wrox.com *or* www.vb-helper.com/24hourvb.html.

38

Manipulating Data with LINQ to Objects

Visual Basic provides many tools for storing data. You can store data in individual variables, arrays, and collections. Generic collection classes even let you store data in a strongly typed way — so, for example, you know that a List(Of Student) contains only Student objects and nothing else.

However, those storage methods by themselves don't give you an easy way to manipulate their contents. For example, suppose you have a List(Of Student) and you want to find the entry for the student with the highest average test score; or you want to find all students who are missing a test score; or you want to sort the students by midterm scores in ascending order.

None of these operations is very difficult. You can loop through the list looking for the items you want. Sorting is a little trickier depending on how you want to sort the items, but in any case you can accomplish all of these operations with a dozen or two lines of code.

Language-Integrated Query (LINQ) provides another method for manipulating these sorts of data collections. Instead of just giving you a way to search collections, however, LINQ enables a program to access data stored in databases, arrays, collections, or files in basically the same way.

LINQ provides four basic technologies that give you access to data stored in various places:

- ➤ **LINQ to SQL** — Data stored in SQL Server databases
- ➤ **LINQ to Dataset** — Data stored in other databases
- ➤ **LINQ to XML** — Data stored in XML (Extensible Markup Language) files
- ➤ **LINQ to Objects** — Data stored in collections, lists, arrays, strings, files, and so forth

In this lesson you learn how to use LINQ to Objects. You learn how to extract data from lists, collections, and arrays, and how to process the results.

The other forms of LINQ are even more specialized than the topics that I want to cover in this part of the book, so I won't discuss them here. After you learn about LINQ to Objects, you will be able to learn about the others on your own. Microsoft's "Language-Integrated Query (LINQ)" page at msdn.microsoft.com/library/bb397926.aspx *is a good starting point for learning more about LINQ.*

LINQ BASICS

Using LINQ to process data takes three steps:

1. Create a data source.

2. Build a query to select data from the data source.

3. Execute the query and process the result.

You might expect the third step to be two separate steps, "Execute the query" and "Process the result." In practice, however, LINQ doesn't actually execute the query until it must — when the program tries to access the results. This is called *deferred execution*.

The EvenNumbers example program (which is available for download on the book's web site) uses these steps in the following code that displays the even numbers between 0 and 99:

```
' 1. Create the data source.
Dim numbers(0 To 100) As Integer
For i As Integer = 0 To 100
    numbers(i) = i
Next i

' 2. Build a query to select data from the data source.
Dim evenQuery =
    From num As Integer In numbers
    Where (num Mod 2 = 0)
    Select num

' 3. Execute the query and process the result.
For Each num As Integer In evenQuery
    lstEvenNumbers.Items.Add(num)
Next num
```

First, the program creates the data source: an array containing the numbers 0 through 100. In this example the data source is quite simple, but in other programs it could be much more complex. Instead of an array of numbers, it could be a list of Customer objects, or an array of Order objects that contain lists of OrderItem objects.

Second, the program builds a query to select the even numbers from the list. I explain queries in more detail later, but the following list describes the key pieces of this query:

➤ Dim — This declares the variable that represents the query. Notice that this code doesn't include an As keyword and a data type. In this example, the result will be an

IEnumerable(Of Integer), but in general the results of LINQ queries can have some very strange data types. Rather than try to figure out what a query will return, most developers omit the LINQ query's data type and let Visual Basic figure out what the data type is.

Visual Basic can figure out the query's data type if Option Infer *is* On, *which it is by default. Unfortunately, if* Option Infer *is* On, *then code such as the following is also allowed.*

```
Dim x = 10
```

In this case, Visual Basic sees that you are assigning the value 10 to the variable x *so it infers that* x *must be an* Integer. *That's fine if you want* x *to be an* Integer *but what if you want it to be a* Short, Long, *or* Double? *In that case, you must explicitly give the variable a data type.*

To avoid possible confusion, I use inferred data types only for LINQ queries and in fact turn Option Infer Off *in files that don't need it.*

➤ evenQuery — This is the name the code is giving to the query. You can think of it as a variable that represents the result LINQ will later produce.

➤ From num As Integer In numbers — This means the query will select data from the numbers array. It will use the Integer variable num to range over the values in the array. Because num ranges over the values, it is called the query's *range variable.* (If you omit As Integer, the compiler will implicitly figure out its data type based on what's in the array.)

➤ Where (num Mod 2 = 0) — This is the query's *where clause.* It determines which items are selected from the array. This example selects the even numbers where num mod 2 is 0.

➤ Select num — This tells the query to return whatever is in the range variable num for the values that are selected. Often, you will want to return the value of the range variable, but you could return something else such as 2 * num or a new object created with a constructor that takes num as a parameter.

In its third step, the code loops through the result produced by the query, adding each selected value to a ListBox.

The following sections provide more detailed descriptions of some of the key pieces of a LINQ query: where clauses, order by clauses, and select clauses.

WHERE CLAUSES

Probably the most common reason to use LINQ is to filter the data with a *where clause.* The where clause can include normal Boolean expressions that use AndAlso, OrElse, Or, >, and other Boolean and comparison operators. It can use the range variable and any properties or methods that it provides (if it's an object). It can even perform calculations and invoke functions.

The where clause is optional. If you omit it, the query selects all of the items in its range.

For example, the PrimeNumbers example program (which is available for download on the book's web site) uses the following query. It is similar to the earlier one that selects even numbers, except this one's where clause uses the `IsPrime` function to select only prime numbers. (How the `IsPrime` function works isn't important to this discussion, so it isn't shown here. Download the example program to see how it works.)

```
Dim evenQuery =
    From num As Integer In numbers
    Where IsPrime(num)
    Select num
```

The FindCustomers example program shown in Figure 38-1 (and available in this lesson's code download on the web site) demonstrates several where clauses.

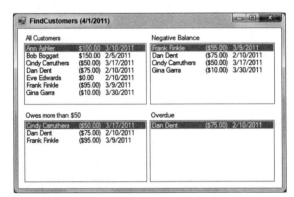

FIGURE 38-1

The following code shows the `Customer` class used by the FindCustomers program. It includes some auto-implemented properties and an overridden `ToString` method that displays the `Customer`'s values.

```
Public Class Customer
    Public Property FirstName As String
    Public Property LastName As String
    Public Property Balance As Decimal
    Public Property DueDate As Date

    Public Overrides Function ToString() As String
        Return FirstName & " " & LastName & vbTab &
            Balance.ToString("C") & vbTab & DueDate.ToString("d")
    End Function
End Class
```

The following code shows how the FindCustomers program displays the same customer data selected with different where clauses:

```
Dim billDate As Date = #4/1/2011#
'Dim billDate As Date = DateTime.Today

Me.Text = "FindCustomers (" & billDate.ToString("d") & ")"

' Make the customers.
Dim customers() As Customer =
{
    New Customer() With {.FirstName = "Ann", .LastName = "Ashler",
        .Balance = 100, .DueDate = #3/10/2011#},
    New Customer() With {.FirstName = "Bob", .LastName = "Boggart",
        .Balance = 150, .DueDate = #2/5/2011#},
    New Customer() With {.FirstName = "Cindy", .LastName = "Carruthers",
        .Balance = -50, .DueDate = #3/17/2011#},
    New Customer() With {.FirstName = "Dan", .LastName = "Dent",
        .Balance = -75, .DueDate = #2/10/2011#},
    New Customer() With {.FirstName = "Eve", .LastName = "Edwards",
        .Balance = 0, .DueDate = #2/10/2011#},
    New Customer() With {.FirstName = "Frank", .LastName = "Finkle",
        .Balance = -95, .DueDate = #3/9/2011#},
    New Customer() With {.FirstName = "Gina", .LastName = "Garra",
        .Balance = -10, .DueDate = #3/30/2011#}
}

' Display all customers.
lstAll.DataSource = customers

' Display customers with negative balances.
Dim negativeQuery =
    From cust As Customer In customers
    Where (cust.Balance < 0)
    Select cust
' Place before the Select clause:
'    Order By cust.Balance Ascending, cust.FirstName
lstNegativeBalance.DataSource = negativeQuery.ToArray()

' Display customers who owe at least $50.
Dim owes50Query =
    From cust As Customer In customers
    Where (cust.Balance <= -50)
    Select cust
lstOwes50.DataSource = owes50Query.ToArray()

' Display customers who owe at least $50
' and are overdue at least 30 days.
Dim overdueQuery =
    From cust As Customer In customers
    Where (cust.Balance <= -50) AndAlso
            (billDate.Subtract(cust.DueDate).TotalDays > 30)
    Select cust
lstOverdue.DataSource = overdueQuery.ToArray()
```

The program starts by creating a `DateTime` named `billDate` and setting it equal to April 1, 2011. In a real application you would probably use the current date (commented out), but this program uses a specific date so it works well with the sample data no matter when you run it. The program displays the date in its title bar (so you can compare it to the `Customers`' due dates) and creates an array of `Customer` objects.

Next, the code sets the `lstAll` control's `DataSource` property to the array so that `ListBox` displays all the `Customer` objects. The `Customer` class's overridden `ToString` method makes it display each `Customer`'s name, balance, and due date.

The program then executes the following LINQ query:

```
' Display customers with negative balances.
Dim negativeQuery =
    From cust As Customer In customers
    Where (cust.Balance < 0)
    Select cust
lstNegativeBalance.DataSource = negativeQuery.ToArray()
```

This query's where clause selects `Customers` with `Balance` properties less than 0. The query returns an `IEnumerable`, but a `ListBox`'s `DataSource` property requires an `IList` or `IListSource` so the program calls the result's `ToArray` method to convert it into an array that the `DataSource` property can handle.

After displaying this result, the program executes two other LINQ queries and displays their results similarly. The first query selects `Customers` who owe at least $50. The final query selects `Customers` who owe at least $50 and who have a `DueDate` older than 30 days.

ORDER BY CLAUSES

Often the result of a query is easier to read if you sort the selected values. You can do this by inserting an *order by clause* between the where clause and the select clause.

The order by clause begins with the keywords `Order By` followed by one or more values separated by commas that determine how the results are ordered.

Optionally, you can follow a value by the keyword `Ascending` (the default) or `Descending` to specify whether the results are ordered in ascending (1-2-3 or A-B-C) or descending (3-2-1 or C-B-A) order.

For example, the following query selects `Customers` with negative balances and orders them such that the smallest (most negative) values come first:

```
Dim negativeQuery =
    From cust As Customer In customers
    Where (cust.Balance < 0)
    Order By cust.Balance Ascending
    Select cust
```

The following version orders the results first by balance; then, if two customers have the same balance, by last name:

```
Dim negativeQuery =
    From cust As Customer In customers
    Where (cust.Balance < 0)
    Order By cust.Balance Ascending, cust.FirstName
    Select cust
```

SELECT CLAUSES

The select clause determines what data is pulled from the data source and stored in the result. All of the previous examples select the data over which they are ranging. For example, the FindCustomers example program ranges over an array of Customer objects and selects certain Customer objects.

Instead of selecting the objects in the query's range, a program can select only some properties of those objects, a result calculated from those properties, or even completely new objects. Selecting a new kind of data from the existing data is called *projecting* or *transforming* the data.

The FindStudents example program shown in Figure 38-2 (and available in this lesson's code download on the web site) uses the following simple Student class:

```
Public Class Student
    Public Property FirstName As String
    Public Property LastName As String
    Public Property TestScores As List(Of Integer)
End Class
```

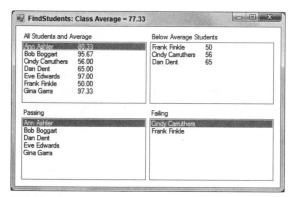

FIGURE 38-2

The program uses the following query to select all of the students' names and test averages ordered by name:

```
' Select all students and their test averages ordered by name.
Dim allStudents =
    From stu As Student In students
```

```
        Order By stu.LastName, stu.FirstName
        Select stu.FirstName & " " & stu.LastName & vbTab &
            stu.TestScores.Average().ToString("0.00")
    lstAll.DataSource = allStudents.ToArray()
```

This query's select statement does not select the range variable `stu`. Instead it selects a string that holds the student's first and last names and the student's test score average. (Notice how the code calls the `TestScore` list's `Average` method to get the average of the student's test scores.) The result of the query contains `Strings` instead of `Students`.

The program next uses the following code to list the students who have averages of at least 60, giving them passing grades:

```
    ' Select passing students ordered by name.
    Dim passingStudents =
        From stu As Student In students
        Order By stu.LastName, stu.FirstName
        Where (stu.TestScores.Average() >= 60)
        Select stu.FirstName & " " & stu.LastName
    lstPassing.DataSource = passingStudents.ToArray()
```

This code again selects a string instead of a `Student` object. The code that selects failing students is similar, so it isn't shown here.

The program uses the following code to select students with averages below the class average:

```
    ' Select all scores and compute a class average.
    Dim allAverages =
        From stu As Student In students
        Order By stu.LastName, stu.FirstName
        Select stu.TestScores.Average()
    Dim classAverage As Double = allAverages.Average()

    ' Display the average.
    Me.Text = "FindStudents: Class Average = " & classAverage.ToString("0.00")

    ' Select students with average below the class average ordered by average.
    Dim belowAverageStudents =
        From stu As Student In students
        Order By stu.TestScores.Average()
        Where stu.TestScores.Average() < classAverage
        Select New With
        {
            .Name = stu.FirstName & " " & stu.LastName,
            .Average = stu.TestScores.Average()
        }
    For Each info In belowAverageStudents
        Debug.WriteLine(TypeName(info))
        lstBelowAverage.Items.Add(info.Name & vbTab & info.Average.ToString("0.00"))
    Next info
```

This snippet starts by selecting all of the students' test score averages to get a list of `Doubles`. The program calls that list's `Average` function to get the class average.

Next, the code queries the student data again, this time selecting students with averages below the class average.

This query demonstrates a new kind of select clause that creates a list of objects. The new objects have two properties, Name and Average, that are given values by the select clause.

The data type of these new objects is created automatically and isn't given an explicit name in the code, so it is known as an *anonymous type.*

After creating the query, the code loops through its results, using each object's Name and Average property to display the selected students in a ListBox. Notice that the code doesn't give an explicit data type to the looping variable info, so it doesn't need to figure out what data type it really has.

> *Objects with anonymous data types actually have a true data type, just not one that you want to have to figure out. For example, you can add the following statement inside the previous code's* For Each *loop to see what data type the objects actually have:*
>
> ```
> Debug.WriteLine(TypeName(info))
> ```
>
> *If you look in the Immediate window, you'll see that these objects have the following ungainly data type:*
>
> ```
> VB$AnonymousType_0(Of String,Double)
> ```
>
> *Though you can sort of see what's going on here (note that the object contains a string and a double), you probably wouldn't want to type this mess into your code even if you could. In this case, using an inferred type makes the code a lot easier to read.*

LINQ provides plenty of other features that won't fit in this lesson. It lets you:

➤ Group results to produce output lists that contain other lists

➤ Get only a certain number of results or get results while a certain condition is true

➤ Skip a certain number of results or skip results while a certain condition is true

➤ Join objects selected from multiple data sources

➤ Use aggregate functions such as Average (which you've already seen), Count, Min, Max, and Sum

TRY IT

In Lesson 32's Try It, you built a program that used the DirectoryInfo class's GetFiles method to search for files matching a pattern and containing a target string. For example, the program could search the directory hierarchy starting at C:\VBProjects to find files with the .vb extension and containing the string "DirectoryInfo."

In this Try It, you modify that program to perform the same search with LINQ. Instead of writing code to loop through the files returned by `GetFiles` and examining each one, you make LINQ examine the files for you.

 You can download the code and resources for this Try It from the book's web page at www.wrox.com *or* www.vb-helper.com/24hourvb.html. *You can find them in the Lesson38 folder of the download.*

Lesson Requirements

In this lesson:

➤ Copy the program you built for Lesson 32's Try It (or download Lesson 32's version from the book's web site) and modify the code to use LINQ to search for files.

Hints

➤ Use the `DirectoryInfo` object's `GetFiles` method in the query's from clause.

➤ In the query's where clause, use the `File` class's `ReadAllText` method to get the file's contents. Convert it to lowercase and use `Contains` to see if the file holds the target string.

➤ To display the files, convert the query into an array and then set the `ListBox`'s `DataSource` property equal to the result.

➤ You cannot clear a `ListBox` while it has a `DataSource`, so set `DataSource = Nothing` before you clear the list. (Otherwise, the program will crash if you perform more than one search.)

Step-by-Step

➤ Copy the program you built for Lesson 32's Try It (or download Lesson 32's version from the book's web site) and modify the code to use LINQ to search for files.

   1. Copying the program is reasonably straightforward.

   2. To use LINQ to search for files, modify the Search button's `Click` event handler so it looks like the following.

```
' Search for files matching the pattern
' and containing the target string.
Private Sub btnSearch_Click() Handles btnSearch.Click
    lstFiles.DataSource = Nothing
    lstFiles.Items.Clear()

    ' Get the file pattern and target string.
    Dim pattern As String = cboPattern.Text
    Dim target As String = txtTarget.Text.ToLower()
```

```
        ' Search for files.
        Dim dirinfo As New DirectoryInfo(txtDirectory.Text)
        Dim fileQuery =
            From info As FileInfo
            In dirinfo.GetFiles(pattern, SearchOption.AllDirectories)
            Where File.ReadAllText(info.FullName).
                ToLower().Contains(target)
            Select info.FullName

        ' Display the result.
        lstFiles.DataSource = fileQuery.ToArray()
    End Sub
```

 Please select Lesson 38 on the DVD to view the video that accompanies this lesson.

EXERCISES

1. Build a program that lists the names of the files in a directory together with their sizes, ordered with the biggest files first.

2. Copy the program you built for Exercise 1 and modify it so it searches for files in the directory hierarchy starting at the specified directory.

3. Use LINQ to make a program that lists the perfect squares between 0 and 999.

 You can find solutions to this lesson's exercises in the Lesson38 folder inside the download available on the book's web site at www.wrox.com *or* www.vb-helper .com/24hourvb.html.

39

Manipulating Databases with the Entity Framework

I have seen estimates claiming that 80% or more of all Visual Basic applications involve a database. I've even seen one estimate that claims 95% of all Visual Basic applications involve a database at some point. Whatever the true number is, it's clear that a large fraction of Visual Basic programs use databases.

There are some good reasons for this. Databases provide a lot of useful features for storing, manipulating, updating, and retrieving data. A well-designed database can store huge amounts of data and still find a particular record quickly.

With such a strong emphasis on databases, it's small wonder that Microsoft spends a lot of time and effort providing tools to manipulate databases, and over the years Microsoft has developed many such tools. The latest of these is the ADO.NET Entity Framework.

In this lesson, you learn the basics of using the Entity Framework. You learn how to use it to map data in a database to objects in a program. You also learn how to build a simple program that uses the objects created by the Entity Framework to manipulate the data in the database.

ENTITY FRAMEWORK FEATURES

Although a detailed discussion of the Entity Framework is beyond the scope of this book, this section explains its general concepts and key features.

In brief, the Entity Framework is an *object-relational mapper* (abbreviated *ORM*, *O/RM*, or *O/R mapper*), a tool that maps between pieces of data in a relational database and objects in a program. That mapping enables you to program using objects such as Person, Customer, and Order without worrying about how those objects are stored in the database; and the ORM automatically loads and saves data as needed.

For example, suppose an Order object defines an OrderedBy property that refers to the Customer who placed an order. When the program fetches an Order object from the database, the ORM automatically loads the `OrderedBy` property without the program needing to know how that happens.

Some of the more important features provided by the Entity Framework include the following:

➤ **Generating classes from a database** — The Entity Framework can automatically generate classes to hold the data contained in some or all of a database's tables. It can even give classes properties that link tables together.

➤ **Generating classes from a model** — After you design an entity data model, the designer automatically generates classes to hold the data in the model.

➤ **Model-first development** — You can build a data model first and then use the Entity Framework to build an empty database for it.

➤ **Lazy loading** — If an `Order` object has a collection of `OrderItems`, the Entity Framework `Order` class can defer loading the `OrderItems` until they are actually needed.

USING THE ENTITY FRAMEWORK: A BASIC APPROACH

Following is one basic approach to using the Entity Framework:

1. Build a SQL Server database containing the data.

2. Use the Entity Framework to make a data model and generate classes.

3. Use the Entity Framework classes to manipulate data.

Rather than explain these steps in excruciating detail that won't make much sense to you until you actually try it yourself, the following sections walk you through these steps so you can see how they work. Basically, they form an extra-detailed walk-through similar to a Try It's Step-by-Step instructions.

To follow along you'll need the following:

➤ Microsoft Visual Studio 2010 (which you should have if you're reading this book)

➤ The .NET Framework 4 (which you should also have if you're reading this book)

➤ Microsoft SQL Server 2005 or later, with Database Services or Microsoft SQL Server 2005 Express Edition or later

If you don't meet these requirements — in particular, if you don't have SQL Server installed — you can skim the rest of this lesson but you won't be able to work through the Try It or Exercises.

You may also want to install SQL Server Management Studio for use in building and manipulating databases. You can download SQL Server Management Studio Express from Microsoft's web site.

Building a SQL Server Database

If you haven't installed SQL Server, you might want to do so now. The Visual Studio installation software comes with SQL Server (at least the versions I've seen) or you can download the free SQL

Server Express edition at www.microsoft.com/express/Database. You should probably download the management tools, too. You will find SQL Server Management Studio Express particularly useful for building databases.

> *If you need information about SQL Server and how to use it, there are many good books available, such as Robert Vieira's* Beginning Microsoft SQL Server 2008 Programming *(Wrox, 2009) and* Professional Microsoft SQL Server 2008 Programming *(Wrox, 2009).*
>
> *You might also be interested in my book* Beginning Database Design Solutions *(Wrox, 2008), which explains how to design a database that is robust and flexible.*

Assuming you have SQL Server installed, you need to create the database that your program will manipulate. To do that:

FIGURE 39-1

1. Start Microsoft SQL Server Management Studio Express.

2. When the program starts, it asks you to connect to the server that you will use. Enter the appropriate information and click Connect. Figure 39-1 shows the connect dialog that appears when I open my SQL Server Express server named Gothmog.

3. After you connect to the server, the Object Explorer should display the server's objects as shown in Figure 39-2. In this figure you can see the OrdersDatabase and its Customer, OrderItem, and PurchaseOrder tables.

You can use SQL Server Management Studio to build the database interactively. See the program's help for details.

Alternatively, you can execute a SQL script that contains commands to build the database for you. The file MakeOrdersDatabase.sql, which is available in this lesson's download, builds a database called OrdersDatabase that contains Customer, PurchaseOrder, and OrderItem tables.

FIGURE 39-2

To run the script, download it from the book's web site. In SQL Server Management Studio, open the File menu, select Open, and pick File; or click [Ctrl]+O. Browse to the script and click Open. After you load the script, execute it by opening the Query menu and selecting Execute, or by pressing [F5].

The following code shows the parts of the script that create the database and its tables:

```
-- Create and use the OrdersDatabase.
CREATE DATABASE OrdersDatabase;
GO
USE OrdersDatabase;

-- Create the Customer table.
CREATE TABLE Customer
(
    CustomerId      int             PRIMARY KEY,
    FirstName       nvarchar(50)    NOT NULL,
    LastName        nvarchar(50)    NOT NULL,
)

-- Create the PurchaseOrder table.
CREATE TABLE PurchaseOrder
(
    OrderId         int             PRIMARY KEY,
    OrderDate       datetime        NOT NULL,
    CustomerId      int             NOT NULL
        FOREIGN KEY REFERENCES Customer (CustomerId),
)

-- Create the OrderItem table.
CREATE TABLE OrderItem
(
    OrderId         int             NOT NULL
        FOREIGN KEY REFERENCES PurchaseOrder (OrderId),
    ItemNumber      int             NOT NULL,
    ItemDescription nvarchar(50)    NOT NULL,
    Quantity        int             NOT NULL,
    CONSTRAINT PK_OrderItem PRIMARY KEY (OrderId, ItemNumber)
)
```

You don't need to understand every detail of this script. You should be able to get the gist of it even if you're unfamiliar with the Transact-SQL database language that it uses.

The CREATE DATABASE statement creates the OrdersDatabase inside the server.

The CREATE TABLE Customer statement creates the Customer table and gives it the fields CustomerId, FirstName, and LastName. CustomerId is an integer, and the table's primary key. FirstName and LastName are strings with lengths up to 50. The NOT NULL clause means all records must have these values filled in. (Primary keys must also always have values.)

The CREATE TABLE PurchaseOrder statement similarly creates the PurchaseOrder table. The only new concept used by this statement is the FOREIGN KEY clause, which indicates that this table's CustomerId field references the Customer table's CustomerId field. That means any record in the PurchaseOrder table must have a CustomerId value that is already present in the Customer table. The idea is that a PurchaseOrder record's CustomerId indicates the ID of the customer who placed the order.

Finally, the CREATE TABLE OrderItem statement creates the OrderItem table. Its FOREIGN KEY clause requires that its OrderId field match a value in the PurchaseOrder table. The idea here is that an OrderItem record's OrderId value indicates which PurchaseOrder includes the OrderItem.

This last CREATE TABLE statement also uses a PRIMARY KEY clause to indicate that the table's primary key includes the combination of OrderId and ItemNumber. Each order may contain several items, and their ItemNumber values indicate the order in which they should appear in the purchase order.

You'll see a graphic representation of this database design in the next section.

 This script tries to create the database without checking whether you already have a database named OrdersDatabase, so if one already exists it fails without damaging your existing database.

In addition to creating the OrdersDatabase and its Customer, PurchaseOrder, and OrderItem tables, the script inserts records in the tables to give your programs some data to manipulate. That code is long and not very interesting so it isn't shown here.

Making the Data Model and Classes

To make the data model, start a new Visual Basic Windows Forms project. Then open the Project menu and select Add New Item. On the Add New Item dialog, shown in Figure 39-3, pick the Data category on the left and select ADO.NET Entity Data Model. Enter a name for the model (such as OrdersModel.edmx) and click Add to launch the Entity Data Model Wizard.

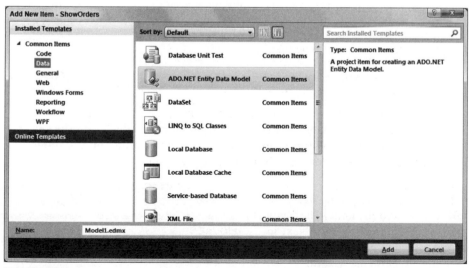

FIGURE 39-3

The wizard's first page, which is shown in Figure 39-4, lets you decide whether you want to generate a model from a database or create an empty model. An empty model is useful if you want to build the model from scratch and then use Entity Framework tools to build a database from it.

For this example, pick "Generate from database" and click Next to display the Choose Your Data Connection page shown in Figure 39-5. If you have previously defined database connections (which you probably haven't at this point), you can select one from the drop-down list.

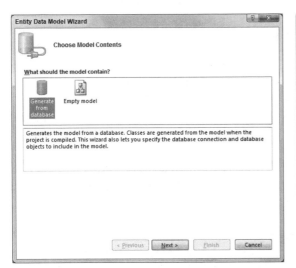

FIGURE 39-4

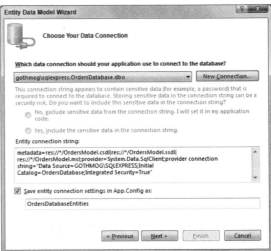

FIGURE 39-5

If you have no previously defined connections, click New Connection to display the Choose Data Source dialog shown in Figure 39-6. Select the type of data source that you want to use and click Continue. In Figure 39-6, I selected a database server, but the documentation says that Visual Studio Express Edition can select only database files, not servers, so you might need to make a different selection.

When you click Continue, the Connection Properties dialog shown in Figure 39-7 appears. Fill in the server name and database name. Note that you must append \SQLEXPRESS to the server name if you are using SQL Server Express Edition. If you don't, you'll get a confusing error message saying, "The server was not found or was not accessible."

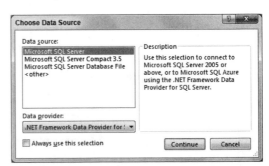

FIGURE 39-6

When you finish entering the server and database names, click OK to return to the Entity Data Model Wizard page shown in Figure 39-5. Click Next to see the page shown in Figure 39-8. Select all of the tables and click Finish to close the wizard.

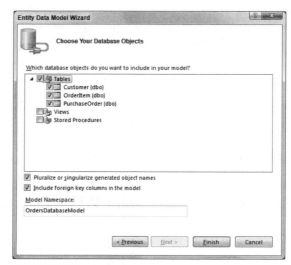

FIGURE 39-7   FIGURE 39-8

At this point the wizard builds the data model and displays it graphically, as shown in Figure 39-9. In addition to building a pretty picture of the model, the wizard builds classes to represent the data. If you look closely at this figure, you can learn about those classes and how they are related.

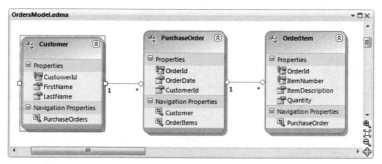

FIGURE 39-9

 If you close the data model editor shown in Figure 39-9, you can reopen it by double-clicking on the .edmx *file in Solution Explorer.*

Each class is represented by a box that lists the properties built by the wizard to correspond to the database table's fields. At the bottom of each class is a list of navigation properties that your program can use to link one class to others. For example, the Customer class's PurchaseOrders property is a collection of PurchaseOrder objects.

If you click on a property in the model, the Properties window displays information about that property such as its name, whether it is nullable (allows null or missing values), and its data type.

The links connecting the classes shown in Figure 39-9 indicate the relationships among the classes. The numbers at either end of a link indicate the numbers of objects from the corresponding classes that are involved in the link.

For example, the link between the Customer and PurchaseOrder classes in Figure 39-9 has a 1 at the Customer end and a * at the PurchaseOrder end. That means one Customer object corresponds to any number of PurchaseOrder objects. Similarly, one PurchaseOrder object corresponds to any number of OrderItem objects.

If you click a link, the Properties window provides information about the link such as the names of the fields in the two tables it connects and their multiplicities.

USING THE ENTITY FRAMEWORK CLASSES

The model displayed in Figure 39-9 shows the main classes that represent database tables: Customer, PurchaseOrder, and OrderItem. There's one more key class that the Entity Data Model Wizard creates to represent the database as a whole: OrdersDatabaseEntities. This class is named after the database (OrdersDatabase) with the word "Entities" added to the end.

To use the classes, create a new instance of the OrdersDatabaseEntities class.

Because the entities object provides a context for manipulating the data, programmers often add "Context" to the name of that class's instance. For example, the following code creates an instance of the OrdersDatabaseEntities *class named* OrderContext:

```
' Create the database context.
Private OrderContext As New OrdersDatabaseEntities()
```

After you create the entities object, you can use its properties to access objects representing the data in the database. In this example, the OrdersDatabaseEntities object's Customers, PurchaseOrders, and OrderItems collections let you manipulate the data.

Note that you can use LINQ as described in Lesson 38 to filter and arrange the data. For example, you could use a LINQ query to select Customer objects with certain FirstName and LastName values and then display the results in a list.

There are two final steps you can take to make the program more useful:

1. Call the context object's SaveChanges method to save any changes that you have made to the data. For example, if you add, modify, or delete data objects, calling SaveChanges will copy those changes to the database.

2. When the program is done with the database, it should call the context object's `Dispose` method to free its resources.

Microsoft's "Getting Started (Entity Framework)" page at `http://msdn.microsoft.com/en-us/library/bb386876` is a good starting point for learning more about the Entity Framework.

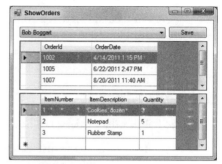

TRY IT

In this Try It, you add code to the OrdersDatabase example described so far in this lesson. You build the program shown in Figure 39-10 to display the orders placed by a customer and the items contained in each order.

FIGURE 39-10

 You can download the code and resources for this Try It from the book's web page at www.wrox.com or www.vb-helper.com/24hourvb.html. You can find them in the Lesson39 folder of the download.

Lesson Requirements

In this lesson:

➤ Build the OrdersDatabase described in this lesson.

➤ Build the user interface shown in Figure 39-10. The two large controls displaying order and order item data are `DataGridView` controls.

➤ Make a `CustomerWithName` class to hold a `Customer` object and its full name. Override its `String` method so the `ComboBox` at the top in Figure 39-10 can display the customer's full name.

➤ When the program starts, create the data context object. Use LINQ to select the `Customer` objects and make `CustomerWithName` objects from them. Display them in the `ComboBox`.

➤ When the user selects a customer, display the customer's orders in the first `DataGridView`.

➤ When the user selects an order from the first `DataGridView`, display its order items in the second `DataGridView`.

➤ Make the Save button save the data.

Hints

➤ You can make a `DataGridView` display a collection of data by setting its `DataSource` property to the collection. It will figure out what rows and columns to display.

➤ Watch out for customers with no orders or orders with no items.

➤ To display `CustomerWithName` objects in the `ComboBox`, set the control's `DataSource` property to an array of `CustomerWithName` objects. Then set its `DisplayMember` property to `FullName`, the name of the property that you want the control to display.

➤ Hide `DataGridView` columns that are used only for navigation so the user doesn't see them, as in the following code:

```
dgvCustomerOrders.Columns("CustomerId").Visible = False
```

Step-by-Step

➤ Build the OrdersDatabase described in this lesson.

   1. Follow the instructions earlier in this lesson to build the SQL Server database. Download and use the `MakeOrdersDatabase.sql` script if you like.

➤ Build the user interface shown in Figure 39-10. The two large controls displaying order and order item data are `DataGridView` controls.

   1. This is reasonably straightforward. Make the `ComboBox`, `Button`, and two `DataGridView` controls as shown in Figure 39-10.

➤ Make a `CustomerWithName` class to hold a `Customer` object and its full name. Override its `String` method so the `ComboBox` at the top in Figure 39-10 can display the customer's full name.

   1. Use code similar to the following:

```
Public Class CustomerWithName
    Public Customer As Customer
    Public FullName As String
    Public Overrides Function ToString() As String
        Return FullName
    End Function
End Class
```

➤ When the program starts, create the data context object. Use LINQ to select the `Customer` objects and make `CustomerWithName` objects from them. Display them in the `ComboBox`.

   1. Use code similar to the following:

```
' The database context.
Private OrderContext As OrdersDatabaseEntities

' Load the data.
Private Sub Form1_Load() Handles MyBase.Load
    ' Load the data.
    OrderContext = New OrdersDatabaseEntities()

    ' Select the Customers.
    Dim customersQuery =
        From cust As Customer In OrderContext.Customers
        Order By cust.FirstName, cust.LastName
        Select New CustomerWithName With
        {
```

```
            .Customer = cust,
            .FullName = cust.FirstName & " " & cust.LastName
        }

    ' Bind the Customers to the cboCustomer ComboBox.
    cboCustomers.DisplayMember = "FullName"
    cboCustomers.DataSource = customersQuery.ToArray()
End Sub
```

➤ When the user selects a customer, display the customer's orders in the first `DataGridView`.

   1. Give the `ComboBox` a `SelectedIndexChanged` event handler similar to the following:

```
' Display this customer's orders.
Private Sub cboCustomers_SelectedIndexChanged() _
 Handles cboCustomers.SelectedIndexChanged
    If cboCustomers.SelectedItem Is Nothing Then Exit Sub

    ' Get the selected Customer.
    Dim custWithName As CustomerWithName =
        DirectCast(cboCustomers.SelectedItem, CustomerWithName)
    Dim cust As Customer = custWithName.Customer

    ' Display this customer's orders.
    dgvCustomerOrders.DataSource = cust.PurchaseOrders

    ' Hide navigation properties.
    dgvCustomerOrders.Columns("CustomerId").Visible = False
    dgvCustomerOrders.Columns("Customer").Visible = False
    dgvCustomerOrders.Columns("OrderItems").Visible = False

    ' Size the columns.
    dgvOrderItems.AutoResizeColumns()

    ' Select the first order (if there is one).
    If dgvCustomerOrders.Rows.Count > 0 Then
        dgvCustomerOrders.Rows(0).Selected = True
    End If
End Sub
```

➤ When the user selects an order from the first `DataGridView`, display its order items in the second `DataGridView`.

   1. Give the `ComboBox` a `SelectedIndexChanged` event handler similar to the following:

```
' Display this order's items.
Private Sub dgvCustomerOrders_SelectionChanged() _
 Handles dgvCustomerOrders.SelectionChanged
    If dgvCustomerOrders.SelectedRows.Count = 0 Then Exit Sub

    ' Display the selected purchase order's items.
    Dim po As PurchaseOrder = DirectCast(
        dgvCustomerOrders.SelectedRows(0).DataBoundItem,
        PurchaseOrder)
```

```
        ' Display this order's items.
        If po Is Nothing Then
            ' There are no items to display.
            dgvOrderItems.DataSource = Nothing
        Else
            ' Display this order's items.
            dgvOrderItems.DataSource = po.OrderItems

            ' Hide navigation properties.
            dgvOrderItems.Columns("PurchaseOrder").Visible = False
            dgvOrderItems.Columns("OrderId").Visible = False

            ' Size the columns.
            dgvOrderItems.AutoResizeColumns()
        End If
    End Sub
```

➤ Make the Save button save the data.

1. Use code similar to the following:

```
' Save changes to the data.
Private Sub btnSave_Click() Handles btnSave.Click
    Try
        OrderContext.SaveChanges()
        MessageBox.Show("Changes Saved", "Changes Saved",
            MessageBoxButtons.OK, MessageBoxIcon.Information)
    Catch ex As Exception
        Dim msg As String = ex.Message
        If ex.InnerException IsNot Nothing Then
            msg &= vbCrLf & vbCrLf & "***** Inner Exception *****" &
                vbCrLf & ex.InnerException.Message
        End If
        MessageBox.Show(msg)
    End Try
End Sub
```

 Please select Lesson 39 on the DVD to view the video that accompanies this lesson.

EXERCISES

1. The Try It uses the `CustomerWithName` class to enable its `ComboBox` to display customer first and last names while also storing a reference to the corresponding `Customer` object. This is somewhat awkward and makes the program convert back to a `Customer` object when the user selects a new `CustomerWithName` object.

A more elegant solution is to override the `ToString` method in the `Customer` class so you can display `Customer` objects directly in the `ComboBox`. Because the `Customer` class is automatically generated, you don't really want to mess with its code. However, you can add new methods to the class by using the `Partial` keyword. That keyword tells Visual Basic that you are defining a class, but part of the class is defined elsewhere.

The following code adds the necessary `ToString` override to the `Customer` class:

```
Partial Public Class Customer
    Public Overrides Function ToString() As String
        Return FirstName & " " & LastName
    End Function
End Class
```

Copy the solution you built for the Try It and add this code. Delete the `CustomerWithName` class and modify the program to work directly with `Customer` objects.

2. Copy the program you built for Exercise 1 and add a New Customer button. When the user clicks the button, display a dialog in which the user can enter first name, last name, and customer ID values. If the user clicks OK, create a new `Customer` object and add it to the context object's `Customers` collection by calling its `AddObject` method. Then call the context object's `SaveChanges` method.

Hint: To show the new customer, move the code that uses LINQ to build the customer list into a new subroutine and call it after you add the new customer.

3. Build a program similar to the one you built for Exercise 1 to display student test scores. The Student table should have fields `FirstName`, `LastName`, and `StudentId`. The TestScore table should have fields `StudentId`, `TestNumber`, and `Score`. You can download the `MakeTestScoresDatabase.sql` script from the book's web page to make building the database easier.

The program should display the students' names in a `ComboBox`. When the user selects a student, it should display that student's scores in a `DataGridView`.

4. Copy the program you built for Exercise 3 and add two `RadioButtons` to the form. Label them All Students and Failing Students. Move the code that loads the `ComboBox` into a `DisplayStudents` subroutine and make it check the `RadioButtons` to see what LINQ query to use in selecting the students.

Give the `Student` class a new `Average` function that uses LINQ to return the student's test score average. When the Failing Students `RadioButton` is checked, make the `DisplayStudents` subroutine use the following LINQ query:

```
Dim failingStudentsQuery =
    From stu As Student In ScoresContext.Students.ToArray()
    Order By stu.FirstName, stu.LastName
    Where stu.Average() < 60
    Select stu
```

You can find solutions to this lesson's exercises in the Lesson39 folder inside the download available on the book's web site at www.wrox.com *or* www.vb-helper.com/24hourvb.html.

Glossary

This appendix provides a glossary of key terms that you may encounter while studying Visual Basic programs.

accelerator   Underlined character, usually in a menu item, that activates that menu item when the user presses [Alt] plus the letter.

AcceptButton   Form property that determines the button triggered when the user presses [Enter].

accessibility   Determines which code is allowed to access subroutines, fields, properties, methods, and other class members. This can be Public, Private, Protected, Friend, or Protected Friend.

accessor   The Get and Set methods that allow a class to save and return a property's value.

Anchor   Property that enables a control to attach its left, right, top, and bottom edges to those of its container.

anonymous type   A data type that is automatically created by LINQ and never given a name for your code to use.

API   Application Programming Interface. A library of methods, classes, and other programming tools.

array   A group of values stored together in a single variable and accessed by index.

assembly   The smallest independent unit of compiled code. Typically, this is a Dynamic Link Library (DLL) or executable program.

assertion   A statement that the code claims is true. If the statement is false, the program stops running so you can decide whether a bug occurred.

backing field   A private field used to store the value of a property. The property's accessors get and set the backing field's value.

bit   A single binary digit. A bit can hold the value 0 or 1.

breakpoint   A marked piece of code that stops execution when running in the IDE.

bug   A programming error that makes a program fail to produce the correct result. A bug may make the program crash, produce an incorrect result, or perform the wrong action.

by reference   When you pass a parameter to a procedure by reference, Visual Basic passes the location of the value's memory into the procedure. If the procedure modifies the parameter, the value is changed in the calling code as well. Use the ByRef keyword to pass a value by reference.

by value   When you pass a parameter by value, Visual Basic makes a copy of the value and passes the copy to the procedure. Changes that the procedure makes to the value do not affect the value in the calling code. Use the ByVal keyword to pass a value by value.

byte   Eight bits. When considered as an unsigned integer, a byte can hold values between 0 and 255. When considered as a signed integer, a byte can hold values between -127 and 128.

CAD   See *computer aided design.*

camel casing   A naming convention whereby multiple words are strung together with the first letter of each word except the first capitalized, as in firstName or numberOfEmployees.

CancelButton   Form property that determines the button triggered when the user presses [Esc].

catch   When an exception occurs, a program can *catch* the exception to take control and perform some remedial action (or just tell the user that something's wrong). When an object raises an event, the program can *catch* the event and take action.

class   Defines a data type with properties, methods, events, and other code encapsulated in a package. After you define a class, you can make as many instances of that class as you like. Very similar to a structure except classes are reference types, whereas structures are value types.

code module   A code file that is not associated with any form or other class.

comment   Text within the program that is not executed by the program. Use comments to make the code easier to understand.

component   A programming entity similar to a control except it has only code and doesn't have a visible appearance on the screen. You still place it on a form at design time, however, and the program's code can interact with it. Some components such as ErrorProvider and ToolTip may display visible effects on the screen.

Component Tray   The area below the form where components sit at design time.

compound assignment operators   Operators such as += and &= that combine a variable's current value with a new value.

computer aided design (CAD)   A program that helps the user design something, often something graphical such as an architectural drawing or an electronic circuit. Many CAD systems do more than just draw. For example, they may produce lists of materials, validate electronic circuits, or calculate physical properties of the system designed.

concatenate   To join two strings together.

conditional operator   The `AndAlso` and `OrElse` operators, which evaluate their second operands only if necessary.

constant   Similar to a variable, but you must assign it a value when you declare it and you cannot change the value later. You can use constants to make your code easier to read.

constructor   A method that executes when an object is created.

control   A programming entity that combines a visible appearance on the screen with code that defines its appearance and behavior.

Coordinated Universal Time (UTC)   Basically, Greenwich Mean Time (GMT), the time at the Royal Observatory in Greenwich, London. (See `en.wikipedia.org/wiki/Coordinated_Universal_Time` for details and history.)

data type   A particular kind of data such as `Integer`, `String`, `Date`, or `TextBox`. All variables must have a data type.

default constructor   The parameterless constructor that is created by default when you create a class.

deferred execution   When a program delays performing some task until a later time. LINQ uses deferred execution when it delays performing a query until the results of the query are actually needed.

derive   To make one class inherit from another.

design time   The stage of development when you are editing a program in Visual Studio. During this time, you use the Form Designer, Code Editor, Properties window, and other IDE features to build the program. Contrast this with *run time*.

DialogResult   The result returned by a dialog to tell the calling code which button was clicked. Also a `Button` property that determines the `DialogResult` the button sets for the form.

Dock   Property that enables a control to fill the left, right, top, bottom, or remaining area of its container.

dominant control   When you select a group of controls in the Form Designer, one is marked as the dominant control. Arranging tools use this control to determine how the controls are displayed. For example, the Format ⇨ Align ⇨ Left tool aligns the selected controls' left edges to the dominant control's left edge.

drag source   An object that initiates a drag-and-drop operation.

drop target   An object that is a candidate to receive data dropped in a drag-and-drop operation.

edit-and-continue   A debugger feature that enables you to modify a stopped program's code and continue running without stopping and restarting the program.

empty constructor   A parameterless constructor.

encapsulation   Detail hiding. A class hides its internal details so the rest of the program doesn't need to understand how they work, just how to use them.

enumerated type   See *enumeration*.

enumeration   A data type that can take one of a list of specific values.

Euclid's algorithm   Also called the Euclidean algorithm. An efficient algorithm for finding the greatest common divisor (GCD) of two numbers.

event   An object *raises* an event to tell the program that something interesting has occurred. The program can *catch* the event to take action.

event handler   An event handler *catches* an event and takes appropriate action.

exception   Object that represents some kind of error such as an attempt to divide by zero or an attempt to parse a string that has an invalid format.

factorial   The factorial of a number N is written N! and equals 1 * 2 * 3 * ... * N.

Fibonacci number   The Nth Fibonacci number Fib(N) is defined recursively by Fib(0) = 0, Fib(1) = 1, and Fib(N) = Fib(N − 1) + Fib(N − 2).

field   A variable defined in a class or structure that's not inside any method so it is visible throughout the class or structure.

function   A packaged set of code that other pieces of code can invoke and that returns a result value. See *procedure*.

GDI   Graphics Device Interface. A library of methods for rendering graphics in Windows used by Windows Forms controls.

GDI+   The .NET version of GDI.

generic class   A class that takes as a parameter one or more data types that it uses to work more closely with those data types. See Lesson 30 for information about generic classes.

generic constraint   A constraint on the types passed to a generic class, such as requiring the type to have a parameterless constructor or requiring that it implement the `IComparable` interface.

gigabyte (GB)   1,024 megabytes.

globalization   The process of building an application for users from different cultures.

greatest common divisor (GCD)   The largest integer that evenly divides two other integers.

IDE   See *integrated development environment*.

index   A value that selects an item from a group. For example, in an array, the index is an integer between 0 and one less than the number of elements in the array used to identify a specific item in the array.

instance   An instance of a class is an object of the class's type. Different instances of the same class have the same properties, methods, and events but they may have different property values.

integrated development environment (IDE)   An environment for building, testing, and debugging programs, such as Visual Studio.

interface Defines public properties, methods, and events that a class must provide to satisfy the interface.

kilobyte (KB) 1,024 bytes.

LINQ Language Integrated Query. A set of extensions provided by the .NET Framework that allows Visual Basic code to query and select data from data sources such as arrays and lists.

locale A setting that defines the user's language, country, and cultural settings, which determine such things as how dates and monetary values are formatted and parsed.

localization The process of customizing a globalized application for a specific culture.

lower bound An array's smallest index (always 0 in Visual Basic).

machine language A low-level language that gives instructions directly to the computer's central processing unit to perform tasks on the machine's hardware. Machine language is much harder for humans to read and understand than a higher-level programming language such as Visual Basic.

magic number A value hard-coded into a program that is difficult to remember. To make code clearer, use constants such as `taxRate` instead of magic numbers such as `0.09D`.

megabyte (MB) 1,024 kilobytes.

method A procedure implemented by a class. See *procedure*.

method scope A variable that is declared inside a method and not inside any other code block has method scope. It is visible to all of the following code within that method.

modal When a program displays a modal form, the user cannot interact with any other part of the application until closing that form. Dialogs are generally modal. A form's `ShowDialog` method displays the form modally.

modeless When a program displays a modeless form, the user can interact with other parts of the application while the modeless form is still visible. A form's `Show` method displays a modeless form.

Me A special object reference that means "the object that is currently executing this code."

My A namespace containing properties and methods shortcuts that make it easier to access commonly needed tools.

namespace A classification of classes with a common purpose. Use `Imports` directives at the top of a code file to tell Visual Basic which namespaces to search for classes that the code uses.

narrowing conversion A conversion from a "wide" data type such as `Single` to a "narrower" data type such as `Integer`. Some precision may be lost in a narrowing conversion.

nibble Half a byte (4 bits).

NumberStyles.Any Passed as a second parameter to `Decimal.Parse`, this allows that method to correctly interpret values formatted as currency.

object-relational mapper (ORM) A tool that maps between pieces of data in a relational database and objects in a program.

operator overloading   Defining a new meaning for an operator such as + or * when working with arguments of specific data types.

order by clause   A clause in a LINQ query that orders the returned data.

ORM   See *object-relational mapper*.

overloading   Giving a class more than one method with the same name but different parameter lists.

overriding   Replacing a parent class method with a new version.

parameterless constructor   A constructor that takes no parameters.

parse   To try to find structure and meaning in text.

Pascal casing   A naming convention whereby multiple words are strung together with the first letter of each word capitalized, as in `TextBox` and `ProgressBar`.

pixel   A single point on the screen or in an image. The word pixel comes from "picture element."

polymorphism   The ability to treat an object as if it were an instance of an ancestor class. For example, if `Employee` inherits from `Person`, then a method that takes a `Person` as a parameter can also take an `Employee` as a parameter.

precedence   The order in which operators are applied in an equation.

precision specifier   Part of a formatting string passed to `String.Format` that affects the way a formatting character works. For example, the 10 in the format D10 formats an integer value with digits only (no thousands separators), padded on the left with zeros if necessary so it is 10 digits long.

procedure   A packaged set of code that other pieces of code can invoke. Types of procedures include subroutines, functions, methods, and property procedures.

programming language   A language used by developers to build programs. Contrast this with machine language, which is at a much lower level intended for use by the computer.

projecting LINQ query   A LINQ query that uses a select clause to return data other than the values over which the query ranges.

property procedure   A `Get` or `Set` procedure used to implement a property for a class. See *procedure*.

queue   A list that lets you add items at the front and remove them from the back. Also called a *FIFO list* or *FIFO*. (FIFO stands for *first-in-first-out*.)

raise   An object *raises* an event to tell the program that something interesting occurred.

range variable   The variable that a LINQ query uses to range over the data in the data source.

recursion   The process of a method calling itself.

recursive method   A method that calls itself.

refactoring   Restructuring a program to make it more reliable, easier to read, or easier to maintain without changing its outward behavior.

reference type   A data type such as a class reference that refers to an item instead of holding the item itself. Variables referring to class instances are reference variables. Contrast this with a *value type*.

relatively prime   Two numbers are relatively prime if their greatest common divisor is 1.

run time   The time when the program is running. Contrast this with *design time*.

scope   A variable's scope is the code that can "see" or access the variable.

select clause   A clause in a LINQ query that determines what data is returned for the selected data.

shared method   A method that is provided by the class itself, rather than an instance of the class. You invoke it as in `ClassName.MethodName()`.

short-circuit operator   See *conditional operator*.

shortcut   Key combination such as [Ctrl]+S or [Ctrl]+N that immediately activates a menu command.

side effects   Consequences that last after a method has finished. Side effects make code harder to understand and debug, so you should try to avoid writing methods with non-obvious side effects.

splitter   An area that you can click and drag to adjust the sizes of the areas on either side of the splitter.

stack   A list that lets you add items at the top and remove them from the bottom. Also called a *LIFO list* or *LIFO*. (LIFO stands for *last-in-first-out*.)

stream   An ordered series of bytes, sometimes representing a file.

strong type checking   Requiring values to have specific data types such as `Person` or `String` instead of more general types such as `Object`.

structure   Defines a data type with properties, methods, events, and other code encapsulated in a package. After you define a structure, you can make as many instances of that structure as you like. Very similar to a class except classes are reference types, whereas structures are value types.

sub procedure   See *subroutine*.

subroutine   A packaged set of code that other pieces of code can invoke that does not return a value. See *procedure*.

terabyte (TB)   1,024 gigabytes.

throw   A program *throws* an exception to indicate that something bad has happened that it cannot handle. Other code higher up in the call stack can *catch* the exception and take action.

transforming LINQ query   See *projecting LINQ query*.

upper bound   An array's largest index. Because Visual Basic arrays start with lower bound 0, the upper bound (for one-dimensional arrays) is one less than the array's length.

value type   A data type that holds its data, not a reference to it. Primitive data types such as `Integer` and `Single`, as well as structures, are value types. Contrast this with a *reference type*.

variable   A named piece of memory that can hold a piece of data.

Visual Basic   A general-purpose, high-level programming language. It is one of the programming languages that can run in the powerful Visual Studio integrated development environment (IDE).

Visual Studio   A development environment for building programs in several programming languages, including Visual C#, Visual Basic, Visual C++, and F#. Home page: `msdn.microsoft.com/vstudio`.

where clause   A clause in a LINQ query that filters the data to return only selected items.

widening conversion   A conversion from a "thin" data type such as `Integer` to a "wider" data type such as `Single`. No precision is lost in a widening conversion.

B

Control Summary

This appendix summarizes the purposes of the most common Windows Forms controls. The intent of this appendix is to let you know what kinds of controls are available, not to provide an exhaustive reference.

For additional details on how to use a control, see the online documentation. The web page describing a control is named after the control, including its namespace. For example, the web page describing the ComboBox class is msdn.microsoft.com/library/system.windows .forms.combobox.aspx.

Unless otherwise noted, all the controls listed here are in the System.Windows.Forms namespace (which you need to know to enter the correct URL).

CONTROL	PURPOSE
BackgroundWorker	Executes a background task on a separate thread. Events provide notification of progress and completion (System.ComponentModel namespace).
Button	A button.
CheckBox	A checkbox.
CheckedListBox	A list of items with checkboxes that let the user easily select one or more items without needing the Click/[Shift]+Click/[Ctrl]+Click techniques used by the regular ListBox control.
ColorDialog	A dialog that lets the user select a color.
ComboBox	A combo box.
ContextMenuStrip	A context menu. Assign this object to another control's ContextMenu property and the menu automatically appears when the user right-clicks the control.

continues

Continued

CONTROL	PURPOSE
DataGridView	Displays a grid of data, possibly bound to a data source.
DateTimePicker	Allows the user to select a date and a time.
DomainUpDown	Displays a spin box (up-down control) that lets the user scroll through a list of predefined options.
ErrorProvider	Displays an error indicator for other controls.
EventLog	Allows a program to interact with system event logs (System.Diagnostics namespace).
FileSystemWatcher	Raises events when a directory or file changes so you can keep track of it (although I've had mixed success with this control) (System.IO namespace).
FlowLayoutPanel	A panel that dynamically arranges its contents in either rows or columns.
FolderBrowserDialog	A dialog that lets the user select a folder (directory).
FontDialog	A dialog that lets the user select a font.
Form	Displays a window on the desktop.
GroupBox	Groups controls inside an outline and displays a header for the group.
HelpProvider	Provides a tooltip or online help for other controls.
HScrollBar	A horizontal scrollbar.
ImageList	Stores a list of images for use by other controls.
Label	Displays non-editable text in a single font.
LinkLabel	Displays a label that contains a hyperlink. When the user clicks the hyperlink, the control raises an event so the program can take action.
ListBox	Displays a list of items.
ListView	Displays a group of items in one of four different views: LargeIcon, SmallIcon, Details, and Tile.
MaskedTextBox	Similar to a TextBox except it displays an input mask to prompt the user and restrict entry. For example, a telephone mask might look like (___)-___-____.
MenuStrip	A form's main menu.
MessageQueue	Provides tools for creating and interacting with message queues (System.Messaging namespace).

CONTROL	PURPOSE
MonthCalendar	Allows the user to select a date or date range from a calendar.
NotifyIcon	Displays an icon in the notification area or system tray (usually on the right end of the taskbar). Can provide a context menu, and the program can use the icon to indicate status to the user.
NumericUpDown	Displays a spin box (up-down control) that lets the user pick a numeric value.
OpenFileDialog	A dialog that lets the user select a file for opening. Can require that the file actually exists.
PageSetupDialog	A dialog that allows the user to define printer page settings, such as margins and printout orientation.
Panel	A simple container that holds other controls. Set `AutoScroll = True` to make the `Panel` automatically display scrollbars if needed. (This is its coolest feature!)
PerformanceCounter	Provides access to Windows NT performance counters (`System.Diagnostics` namespace).
PictureBox	Displays an image. The `SizeMode` property determines how the image is sized and can take the values `Normal` (clip the image if it doesn't fit), `StretchImage` (make the image fit the `PictureBox` even if that distorts it), `AutoSize` (size the `PictureBox` to fit the image), `CenterImage` (center the image, clipping it if it is too big), and `Zoom` (make the image as large as possible without distorting it).
PrintDialog	A dialog that allows the user to select a printer, set printer properties, and pick the pages to print.
PrintDocument	Represents a printed document. Catch the `PrintPage` event to generate output.
PrintPreviewControl	Displays a preview of a `PrintDocument` in a control.
PrintPreviewDialog	Displays a preview of a `PrintDocument` in a dialog.
Process	Lets a program control processes running on the system. You can use the `Start` method to run the default application for a file.
ProgressBar	Indicates the progress of some task to the user.
PropertyGrid	Displays an object's properties at run time and lets the user edit them, much like the Properties window lets you change a control's properties at design time.
RadioButton	A radio button.

continues

Continued

CONTROL	PURPOSE
RichTextBox	Lets the user edit text. Can display multiple fonts, images, bulleted and numbered lists, and other formats.
SaveFileDialog	A dialog that lets the user select a file for saving. Can prompt the user to overwrite the file if it already exists.
SerialPort	Allows a program to control serial ports (System.IO.Ports namespace).
ServiceController	Allows a program to control Windows services (System.ServiceProcess namespace).
SplitContainer	Displays two Panels separated by a Splitter to let the user easily resize the panels.
StatusStrip	A status bar, usually displayed at the bottom of a form.
TabControl	Displays a series of tabs holding groups of controls.
TableLayoutPanel	A panel that arranges its contents in rows and columns.
TextBox	Lets the user edit text in a single font.
Timer	A component that raises a Tick event at regular repeating intervals.
ToolStrip	A toolbar.
ToolStripContainer	A container that can hold ToolStrips. The user can drag the ToolStrips to new positions within the ToolStripContainer.
ToolTip	Displays a tooltip for other controls when the mouse hovers over them.
TrackBar	Displays a trackbar that lets the user select a numeric value. It behaves much like a scrollbar does but with a different appearance.
TreeView	Displays a hierarchical set of items, much like the left panel in Windows Explorer normally does (if you haven't customized its appearance).
VScrollBar	A vertical scrollbar.
WebBrowser	A web browser control. You can use this to control a browser inside your application. For example, your program can go to specific sites, examine URLs and cancel navigation for some URLs, examine the links and images on a web page, and so on.

What's on the DVD?

This appendix provides you with information on the contents of the DVD that accompanies this book. For the latest and greatest information, please refer to the ReadMe file located at the root of the DVD. Here is what you will find in this appendix:

➤ System Requirements

➤ Using the DVD

➤ What's on the DVD

➤ Troubleshooting

SYSTEM REQUIREMENTS

Most reasonably up-to-date computers with a DVD drive should be able to play the screencasts that are included on the DVD. You may also find an Internet connection helpful for searching Microsoft's online help and for downloading updates to this book. Finally, the system requirements for running Visual Studio are much greater than those for simply running a DVD.

If your computer doesn't meet the following requirements, then you may have some problems using Visual Studio:

➤ PC running Windows XP, Windows Vista, Windows 7, or later

➤ A processor running at 1.6GHz or faster

➤ An Internet connection

➤ At least 1GB of RAM

➤ At least 3GB of available hard disk space

➤ A DVD-ROM drive

You may be able to run Visual Studio using a slower processor or with less memory, but things may be slow. I highly recommend more memory, 2GB or even more if possible. (I do fairly well with an Intel Core 2 system running Windows 7 at 1.83 GHz with 2GB of memory and a 500GB hard drive.)

USING THE DVD

To access the content from the DVD, follow these steps:

1. Insert the DVD into your computer's DVD-ROM drive. The license agreement appears.

 *The interface won't launch if you have autorun disabled. In that case, click Start ▷ Run (for Windows 7, click Start ▷ All Programs ▷ Accessories ▷ Run). In the dialog box that appears, type **D:\Start.exe**. (Replace D with the proper letter if your DVD drive uses a different letter. If you don't know the letter, check how your DVD drive is listed under My Computer.) Click OK.*

2. Read through the license agreement, and then click the Accept button if you want to use the DVD.

The DVD interface appears. Simply select the lesson number for the video you want to view.

WHAT'S ON THE DVD

Each of this book's lessons contains one or more Try It sections that enables you to practice the concepts covered by that lesson. The Try It includes a high-level overview, requirements, and step-by-step instructions explaining how to build the example program.

This DVD contains video screencasts showing my computer screen as I work through key pieces of the Try Its from each lesson. In the audio I explain what I'm doing step-by-step so you can see how the techniques described in the lesson translate into actions performed in Visual Studio.

I don't always show how to build every last piece of a Try It's program. For example, if the requirements ask you to build 10 controls and set their properties, I may only do the first few and let you do the rest so you don't need waste time watching me do the same thing again and again.

I recommend using the following steps when reading a lesson:

1. Read the lesson's text.

2. Read the Try It's overview, requirements, and hints.

3. Try to write a program that satisfies the requirements.

4. Read the step-by-step instructions. If the program you wrote doesn't satisfy all the requirements, use these instructions to improve it. Also look for places where my solution differs from yours. In programming there's always more than one way to solve a problem, and it's good to know about several different approaches.

5. Watch the screencast to see how I handle the key issues.

Sometimes a screencast mentions useful techniques and shortcuts that didn't fit in the book, so you may want to watch the screencast even if you feel completely confident about your solution.

After finishing with the Try It section, I recommend that you work through the exercises or at least skim them and figure out how you would solve them.

You can also download all of the book's examples, solutions to the Try Its, and solutions to the exercises at the book's web sites.

Finally, if you're stuck and don't know what to do next, e-mail me at `RodStephens@vb-helper.com`, and I'll try to point you in the right direction.

TROUBLESHOOTING

If you have difficulty installing or using any of the materials on the companion DVD, try the following solutions:

➤ **Reboot if necessary.** As with many troubleshooting situations, it may make sense to reboot your machine to reset any faults in your environment.

➤ **Turn off any anti-virus software that you may have running.** Installers sometimes mimic virus activity and can make your computer incorrectly believe that it is being infected by a virus. (Be sure to turn the anti-virus software back on later.)

➤ **Close all running programs.** The more programs you're running, the less memory is available to other programs. Installers also typically update files and programs; if you keep other programs running, installation may not work properly.

➤ **Reference the ReadMe.** Please refer to the ReadMe file located at the root of the DVD for the latest product information at the time of publication.

CUSTOMER CARE

If you have trouble with the DVD, please call the Wiley Product Technical Support phone number at (800) 762-2974. Outside the United States, call 1(317) 572-3994. You can also contact Wiley Product Technical Support at `http://support.wiley.com`. John Wiley & Sons will provide technical support only for installation and other general quality control items. For technical support on the applications themselves, consult the program's vendor or author.

To place additional orders or to request information about other Wiley products, please call (877) 762-2974.

INDEX